Praise for Harville Hendrix and Helen Hunt's

Giving the Love that Heals

The remarkable parenting guide seen on national bestseller lists including *The Wall Street Journal* • *The Washington Post* • *USA Today*

"*Giving the Love that Heals* . . . may help explain exactly why your children 'push your buttons' some of the time, and—more important—what you can do about it. . . . Hendrix and Hunt give plenty of sound advice about how to begin looking backward, and within, to gain the kind of self-knowledge that will stand you in good stead during the parenting years." **—*New York Newsday***

"Not the typical child-rearing facts book. . . . [A] thought-provoking work."

—*Library Journal*

"Harville Hendrix and his wife, Helen Hunt, have cowritten a remarkable new book on parenting. . . .The authors suggest that early experiences with parents may lead to unresolved issues that later surface in one's own parenting. . . . The book is filled with arresting ideas and practical guidelines. It will be a wonderful value to many readers, and I recommend it to all parents."

—Jerry M. Lewis, M.D., senior research psychiatrist, Timberlawn Research Foundation (Dallas)

"*Giving the Love that Heals* exposes the jugular vein feeding disrupted families—our tendency to replay our childhood relations with our parents with both our children and spouse."

—Don Browning, The Divinity School, The University of Chicago

Also by Harville Hendrix, Ph.D., and Helen Hunt

The Couples Companion:
Meditations and Exercises for Getting the Love You Want

The Personal Companion:
Meditations and Exercises for Keeping the Love You Find

Giving the Love that Heals:
A Guide for Parents

Also by Harville Hendrix, Ph.D.

Getting the Love You Want:
A Guide for Couples

Keeping the Love You Find:
A Personal Guide

The Parenting Companion

Meditations and Exercises for *Giving the Love That Heals*

Harville Hendrix, Ph.D., and Helen Hunt, M.A., M.L.A.

ILLUSTRATIONS BY CAROL RILEY

POCKET BOOKS
New York London Toronto Sydney Tokyo Singapore

An *Original* Publication of POCKET BOOKS

POCKET BOOKS, a division of Simon & Schuster Inc.
1230 Avenue of the Americas, New York, NY 10020

ISBN: 0-671-86885-3

First Pocket Books trade paperback printing April 1999

10 9 8 7 6 5 4 3 2 1

POCKET and colophon are registered trademarks of Simon & Schuster Inc.

Book design by Lili Schwartz
Cover design by Jim Lebbad

Printed in the U.S.A.

RRDH/✕

To all the parents who asked for this book,
and to their children

Special Appreciation for Jean Coppock Staeheli

We want to express our deep appreciation to Jean Coppock Staeheli for her success in translating the text of *Giving the Love that Heals: A Guide for Parents* into a daily meditation for parents. Using her keen intelligence, her deep insight into what we were trying to accomplish, her superior writing skills, and her own compassionate heart and life experience, she has helped us provide parents with a practical tool that will guide them each day into the process of becoming conscious parents.

Contents

INTRODUCTION

We invite you to start using this daybook of meditations on this very day, no matter where you find yourself in the yearly cycle. You do not need to wait until January 1 to get the guidance and support that will help make parenting a happier and more successful experience. Any day can be the beginning of your year of conscious parenting.

Every day we learn more about parenting, the greatest of human adventures. We have six children in our blended family, two of them still young enough to live at home with us. Altogether they have given us thirty years of education in how to be parents, and we are happy to say that we are still learning from them. In fact, in all of our life experiences our children have been our greatest teachers. Without them how would we have developed whatever constancy and optimism we have? And how would we have known about the healing power of love?

We might not have known that the parent-child connection, when forged early, can withstand the stresses that time and chance inevitably impose. We would not have experienced the deepening of our own capacity for conscious action in the face of occasional provocation, boredom, and exhaustion.

We wish we had been able to pick up this book and read it day by day thirty years ago when the first child in our family made his appearance. We would have found courage, support, and understanding in its pages. But we console ourselves by realizing that writing it now has perhaps done us and others as much good as reading it then would have done.

There are particular aspects of our parenting featured in the book that we have found to be successful. With our two younger children, we have discovered the potential for joy and closeness that is offered in the bedtime ritual. For years, we have made it a point to spend at least fifteen minutes every night settling each of our children into bed.

After writing *Giving the Love that Heals*, which was published in 1997, we wanted to do something practical that would support parents as they go about the real-world job of parenting their children. No job is so important. No job is so difficult. And for many it is done under difficult conditions with very little support. Parents face real challenges. For all of us there are work responsibilities and love relationships and personal issues from the past and social concerns—and then there are children.

This daybook of meditations was written to provide the support that every parent needs. It is a companion book to *Giving the Love that Heals*. We have woven the observations, experiences, and theories of that book into this book. We believe we've done the weaving in such a way that the central concepts will be *easy for you to use and understand in your own life*. You will be able to see how the theory of symbiosis, for example, relates to your feelings about your own kids. You will be able to observe your conversations with your children with more insight than you used to. Gradually, you will find yourself becoming more thoughtful and less reactive with every passing month.

A central theme in these pages is our gentle but consistent urging that you learn to take care of yourself. You are a precious, one-of-a-kind, irreplaceable resource for your children. They will never find anyone else to fill your shoes. They need and want you to bring your best self into your relationship with them.

We are not talking about your *perfect* self. The concept of your best self includes your recognition of the sacredness of your children, your tireless efforts to maintain connection with them, and your commitment to doing the personal work on yourself that is yours to do.

It goes without saying that parenting is about making mistakes as well as about loving. Our assumption and our experience has been that parenting is a process that is made up of baby steps and baby *mis*steps. But if you are focusing your thoughts on the importance of staying alert and noticing the cause-and-effect connections that crisscross the parent-child relationship, then you will learn as you go. You will know more next year than you know now and even more the year after that.

As we said in the beginning, you can pick up this book today and start reading the entry for today's date. You don't have to begin the book on January 1. The book is designed to be read a little at a time, so by the time you've read the 366 entries, you will be able to transform yourself into a wise and more effective parent (or at least, you will have come closer than you are now).

Each month in this book unfolds a particular theme or focus. This has helped us organize our thoughts, and we believe it will help you remember the major concepts of the book.

One last note: Our work here is based on Imago Relationship Theory as we have developed it over many years. Although this theoretical backdrop is not presented here in a comprehensive way, we do use and explain its terminology throughout. Whenever we refer to a concept or idea that is part of Imago Relationship Theory, we have underlined it. You will find an explanation of underlined terms at the end of the book in the Glossary. You do not have to have read *Giving the Love that Heals* or *Getting the*

Love You Want in order to enjoy this book and benefit from it, but it would be helpful to do so. Although this companion book can stand on its own, there is no doubt that reading *Giving the Love that Heals* would enlarge your understanding and enrich your parenting experience.

We wish you as much pleasure in reading the book as we have had in writing it. It has helped us take a few more steps toward conscious parenting, and we are excited that you will now be joining us. So, open to today's page, and let the journey continue. . . .

Harville Hendrix and Helen Hunt
June 1998

January

INTRODUCTION TO THE MONTH OF JANUARY

Connection is a wonderful theme for our first month of the year. As we begin this new part of our parenting journey, we welcome the opportunity to become aware of all the ways we participate in the life around us. We rejoice at the threads of love and caring that weave our experience together with the people we love. Whatever the new year brings, we know that we and our children will create this newest part of the tapestry together.

January 1 CONNECTION

My dear brothers and sisters, we are already one. But we imagine that we are not. What we have to recover is our original unity.[1]

—THOMAS MERTON

We begin this first day of the year with a first truth: We share more in common with each other than not. We are connected in many seen and unseen ways, and when we feel these connections, our actions in the world are more loving and more patient than they would be otherwise.

A recovery of our sense of oneness can begin with an expansion of conscious awareness and a change of pronouns. We can stop operating so often from the "me" and the "I" and the "mine" and grow toward the "us" and "ours." As we establish kinship with others, we get closer to the truth of life as it really is. We come to know that we are brothers and sisters under the skin despite our occasional sense of being separate. We are united by our common human potential. And we are united to other living things on the planet through the simple recognition that we share life and the elements of life in common.

As our awareness of connection grows, so does our sense of interdependence. We are not so quick to separate ourselves from what we see as "different." Contemporary science has encouraged us in this view by explaining how interconnected systems in nature actually work, even when we can't observe the mechanism. And we've been able to borrow some of their vocabulary. Since the 1930s we've used the term "ecosystem" to talk about the way a community of organisms interacts with its environment. Recently, we have added to our understanding of ecosystems by recognizing that interactions are really acts of creation. We interact with our environment and, in so doing, help to create it. We interact with each other and help create ourselves and each other in the process.

The ecosystem of family life is very special and very powerful. If the family we create is positive, its influence reaches deep into the life of the community and beyond—sometimes to the nation and the world. If the family we create is negative, it too influences the larger ecosystem of our life together on this planet. And what we create will be influenced by how well we understand the connections we have to our own parents and grandparents and how well we understand the connections we have to our spouse and our children. Whether we think of it this way or not, we live in the ecosystems of our families. We are formed by them and we form them.

One way to increase your awareness of connection is to purposely bring it to your conscious awareness. You can do this by finding a few moments today to sit quietly and relax your body and follow your breathing. Say these words to yourself slowly and with feeling: "I am part of the life around me. The life around me is part of me." Sit with these words and whatever feelings or thoughts they arouse in you for as long as you can.

As you live your life today, identify one person outside your family who you feel is very different from you. This person can be someone you have seen on the street or have talked to in the store or spoken to on the phone. Or it can be someone you know fairly well and often encounter at meetings or other activities. Take a moment to experience this person, and then find one thing that connects the two of you. It can be as simple as sharing the same gender or as subtle as sharing the same facial expression or emotion. Let yourself feel the reality of the connection between you. Perception affects behavior. Enjoy noticing the difference that an expanded sense of connection makes in your life.

January 2 COLLECTING YOUR THOUGHTS

You may be writing, and the fullness of your heart will come to your hand also.[2]

—MOTHER TERESA

As you open the pages of this book you are beginning a new chapter in your life. You are allowing yourself to spend some time each day reflecting on your relationships with yourself, your domestic partner (if you have one), and your children. Instead of rushing through your days, propelling yourself from one person and task to another, you are giving yourself permission to slow down. You will be amazed at what happens. You don't have to go a lot slower to reap great rewards. Just a little will make a big difference.

Slowing down will help you see more clearly what is happening around you. You will be able to connect with your own feelings and integrate your experiences more fully. Your enjoyment of your family will deepen as you observe, record, and appreciate yourself in relation to the people around you. And you will become a better problem solver when your family life requires it.

When you take more time with your life, you honor your life. An important way to express the value you put on your own experience and your personal relationships is to record your thoughts and feelings in a journal. Getting to know yourself in this way is the most exciting adventure you can undertake. Through personal writing, you not only provide yourself with valuable information, but you discover meaning in your life that might otherwise have escaped your notice.

You might want to buy a notebook and a pen so you can begin the process of keeping a parenting journal or simply noting where you and your child are, what you are thinking, and how you are doing. This is not a requirement, but many people find it helpful when they undertake a program of personal change. If you do decide to make a written record of your thoughts, you can give yourself the pleasure of buying equipment that is just right for you.

Take your time to choose a pen that feels comfortable and writes fast. And spend some time in a stationery store or bookstore so you can choose a notebook that feels right and fits your needs. Don't choose something that feels too "nice" or too formal, because it will make it difficult for you to be free and unself-conscious about your writing. You don't want to feel pressured to produce; you want to be free to play, experiment, try things on, daydream, and vent. In this way, you discover who you are. The personal exploration you are beginning will be for your eyes only, a record of your journey and of yourself as a work in progress. As Natalie Goldberg says, "Think about your notebook. It is important. This is your equipment, like hammer and nails to a carpenter. (Feel fortunate—for very little money you are in business!)."[3]

The new year has begun, and you have started the process that will lead you into more conscious parenting and more enjoyment of your children.

January 3 RITUALS OF CARING AND DISCOVERY

Writing can be a road map into the invisible geography of your feelings, enabling you to chart their hairpin turns or see unexpected sideroads.[4]

—GABRIELE LUSSER RICO

Whether you intend to keep a parenting journal or not, there will be times during the next twelve months when it makes sense for you to write about your thoughts and feelings as they evolve in connection with these meditations. Through the act of writing, you demonstrate to yourself that you and your children are worthy subjects of your careful and loving attention. You matter and they matter, and the writing helps you see how both of you matter together.

There is no doubt that the best way to establish a new behavior is to do it every day, preferably at the same time and in the same place. When you make it a regular part of your life, connected to your other daily activities, your energy flows into and out of the writing easily and naturally.

We also know that the writing doesn't have to be sustained, and it doesn't have to be elaborate to serve the purpose. You don't have to be a "good writer." You are keeping a record for yourself as a way of helping yourself clarify your own thoughts and experiences. You are finding out what's inside you and becoming more aware of what's inside your spouse and your children. For some of you, writing will become a ritual, an activity that you repeat that carries meaning for you.

In addition to writing, there is another ritual we would like to suggest to you now. This one occurs at bedtime and involves each parent spending some minutes with each child in close conversation before the child goes to sleep. We have found this to be a most illuminating and bonding experience. Our children have the chance to speak with us about intimate and heartfelt matters, and we have a chance to respond with full, loving attention. This is a time for the gentle exploration of feelings and affirmations of love and esteem. In this setting children feel safe and relaxed and can more easily discover how they feel about an issue or a problem and express it openly.

Both writing and bedtime sharing can help you learn more about yourself and your children and lead to discoveries that will help you become a more conscious parent. Rituals of caring bind you to each other as you begin this journey of discovery.

January 4 CONNECTION WITH YOURSELF

A teacher visited me during this difficult time, and I remember her saying to me, "When you have made good friends with yourself, your situation will be more friendly too."[5]

—PEMA CHÖDRÖN

The next time you are in a difficult situation, make the effort to become a good friend to yourself. You'll notice that Pema Chödrön doesn't suggest making an effort to become better organized or more controlling or more communicative. She suggests that you turn your attention to yourself in the spirit of gentle inquiry and concern, the way an interested friend might. Among other things, this means that you drop the mask, let go of the defenses and the self-delusions, and stop trying to manipulate the situation you are in. You will soon find out what you don't need to hold on to and what is indestructible and central in you.

But there is something you need to do first. Before you can befriend yourself, you have to know who you are. You have to be in tune with yourself enough to know what you think and how you feel and what you want. For most of us this kind of self-focus was easier before we had children. After all, one of the sacred duties of adolescence is self-discovery. If you listen to teenagers talk, you can hear how often events in the external world become excuses for self-investigation and self-revelation. Even the first years of marriage seem emotionally self-indulgent compared to the parenting years.

As parents we can become so busy responding to the needs and desires of others that we break the connection we have to our own inner lives. For some of us this connection is so weak it's hard to reestablish after the children are grown. Twenty years later we have to learn who we are all over again.

It's so much better for us and for our children when we are able to act from the knowledge of who we are. At the same time we can help them find out who they are. The more self-aware we are, the better parents we will be. When we live authentically, from our center, we are more likely to interact with our children in ways that preserve their innate wholeness and promote their development. When we lose contact with our deepest selves, our reactions are always unconscious, often inadequate, and sometimes harmful.

Reestablishing connection with yourself is easier than you might think. Start by sitting quietly for just sixty seconds every day. Find a time and a place when you are not likely to be interrupted and simply quiet your body and your mind. And then see what happens. Notice your feelings and your thoughts, without trying to hold on to them or change them into something else. Notice and accept them. Feel what you feel. Worry what you worry. Think what you think. Isn't it interesting how these things come and go?

Starting today, you can also practice a mental exercise for increasing self-awareness by finding two or three opportunities to ask yourself how you feel in response to some experience in your life. Ask yourself *why* you feel that way. School starts again after the winter vacation and you feel anxious. Why? The snow crunches when you step on it and you feel flooded with happiness. Why? Why do you feel like listening to sixties rock music instead of Bach? You have the opportunity to get to know yourself better than any other person on earth. This is one of the deepest and richest of human experiences.

January 5 BECOMING AN EXAMPLE

Even before a boy or girl is born, his or her parents are already giving expression to their values in a way that will matter for their son or daughter.[6]

—ROBERT COLES

All parents have values, but some are more aware of them than others. Some parents could sit down right now and write them all down—one, two, three. And others would struggle for quite a while to give voice to the guiding principles they can intuit but may have trouble stating. Being able to articulate your values is important for you, and talking to your children about values is important. It's clarifying for a child when a parent can give a name to the moral lesson she wants her child to learn.

But children learn more by watching what their parents do than by listening to what they say. A mother who says one thing and does another is creating moral confusion for her children. What does a child learn when his mother talks about honesty but doesn't return the extra ten-dollar bill the clerk accidentally gave her as change, or when she talks about being "nice" but curses the driver in front of her?

A recent significant poll of American adults[7] found that their number one national concern today is children. But the concern isn't about their health, safety, or economic well-being—it's about their lack of moral education. Americans are deeply troubled by the lack of character and values exhibited by today's young people. More than sixty-one percent think that youngsters' failure to learn such values as honesty, respect, and responsibility is a very serious problem.

It has always been the primary right and responsibility of parents to teach children values. The question for parents is, "What values are my children learning from me through my word and deed?" Such a question causes us to look more closely at our own behavior. One way to get a sense of what our values are and how closely we are living up to them is to imagine that a camera has been recording all of our public moments during the last week. If we were to watch the footage, what would our values demonstrate to us and our children? Would we be able to discern the guiding principles of our lives from this sample of our actions?

It will be helpful to you to write a list of the values you want your life to express. These moral principles are an important part of the legacy you want to leave to your children. For right now, don't worry about how well you are living up to these values. It's important just to identify them for yourself. Throughout the year we will be reviewing and editing this list. Today, just sow the seed and record your thoughts.

Also be on the lookout for behavior in your child that expresses one of her values. Look for an opportunity to acknowledge and praise this value-centered behavior. You might say something like, "I know it was hard for you to tell me that you took Jamie's toy when we left his house. I'm glad you told me the truth. Honesty is important."

January 6 CELEBRATION

> Make sure that every family member has a vital role to play in the traditions your family already has. People generally take the most pleasure in activities they are really involved in.[8]
>
> —JO ROBINSON AND JEAN COPPOCK STAEHELI

January is a month when many of us are recovering from the overabundance of the Thanksgiving and Christmas holiday season. We are happy that we have navigated the big dinners, the presents, and the family reunion—and now we are tired. This residual exhaustion, combined with cold and dark winter weather, makes us feel like we need a break. Yet we may still yearn for more light and more laughter and for the return of the spirit of celebration.

As conscious parents we must always be alive to the possibilities of celebration, even in the "slow" month of January. There may be a birthday in your family, and you already know something about how to celebrate birthdays. There are birthdays of famous, inspirational people like Benjamin Franklin (January 17) or Martin Luther King (January 15). There are also religious holidays such as Epiphany (January 6), which is the traditional date of the coming of the Wise Men to the baby Jesus and is the traditional date for the celebration of Christmas in the Orthodox tradition. In a country as rich with traditions as ours, you can find some event to celebrate with your children that will turn a drab day into a special one. You can also choose a day to celebrate an aspect of your own ethnic heritage—a special meal or ritual that helps your children understand their history and their identity.

It is unfortunate that we don't have more opportunities to celebrate in this society, especially to celebrate in ways that are meaningful and noncommercial. But you can create your own traditions with your children by using what you already have. You have a family history. You have knowledge about events and people in our nation's history. You have family anniversaries. You have the current preferences and interests of your children All it takes to create a family celebration is the desire to make a particular moment meaningful by intentionally focusing your attention on it. Have fun with it, and make it memorable by finding a way to involve everyone in the family. True celebration is about participation and about connection—connection to each other, to family traditions, and to the wider culture. Sometimes the smallest excuse to celebrate is a good opportunity to reestablish central family values and traditions.

Think about how celebrations work in your family. Is everyone included? Do you have fun? Is there a role for children? Does the celebration end up being a connecting experience? Do gifts, television, alcohol, or food play the dominant role, or is there a broader sense of belonging together that is central? Afterward, do you feel drained and grateful that the celebration is over, or will you all want to do the same thing again when the time comes next year?

January 7 BEGIN TO FIND OUT WHO YOUR FAMILY IS

The greatest gift we give each other is the quality of our attention.[9]

—RICHARD MOSS

You are part of the family you have created. You are a parent, and you have a child or children. You may also have a partner or spouse who lives with you, and you may have that person's children also living with you, or you may share your children with a parent who is not living with you. Families are like flowers: they bloom in many different shapes and colors.

Whether your family is traditional or not, you have helped create this vital, living tapestry of life. It will grow and flourish as you give it your care and attention. Find the time today to sit quietly for a few moments and call to mind each member of your family. Start with yourself. In your mind place yourself in the center of your loving attention and stay there for a moment. Then hold in that center the next family member, and regard that person with your loving attention. And so on, for the whole of your family.

Each person in your family is connected to every other, but not *bound* to every other. Each person is a thread in the tapestry, free to be unique and held in place by the caring attention of the others. Celebrate the connections among you. *Then celebrate the differences among you!*

Today, observe in what ways each of you is connected to the others. There are many ways: through dependence, caring, humor, obligation, love, shared history. And perhaps sometimes through anger, bad habits, or neediness. And then observe the ways in which you are different from the other members of your family: gender, age, temperament, preference, experience.

Most of us reach first for words to express the essence of our relationships with the people we love. We describe how we feel. But it can also be illuminating to express your family connections through diagrams, drawings, pictures, or maps. If you are so inclined, you can do the drawing yourself, or you can look for images in magazines and newspapers that you instinctively respond to. You may gravitate toward perfect photos of loving families, or you may be attracted to pictures that show more division and conflict.

Visual representations help you register a different kind of emotional "truth" about your family than words do. They are revealing in a different way. If what you reveal is painful, that's okay. The reason you are reading this book is to get to know yourself and your family better so you can make the changes that will make your life together more satisfying. Simply give your family your full attention today, and be interested in what you find. Learn to look in the spirit of acceptance.

January 8 BEGIN TO SEE WHO YOUR CHILD IS

They were beautiful in the way that babies are, and they were funny-looking, in that way no one admits babies can sometimes be.[10]

—NICK KELSH AND ANNA QUINDLEN

In our overwhelming love for our children, it's sometimes hard to see them as they are. It's as though our vision were distorted—sometimes by romance and fantasy and sometimes by fear and our own bad memories. Only occasionally are we able to squint our eyes just right and see them as they are, miniature Winston Churchills or not.

Because it's so easy to confuse our sons and daughters with

our own parents or our spouses or ourselves or even with the fantasy children of our imagination, it is doubly important to make an effort to see them as they are. Each child is unique and, at the same time, each child shares much in common with all other children. Parents must hold both of these truths in their hearts at once.

Today, begin the effort to see your children with unclouded vision. Who are they? What do they do? What do they say? Begin with the simplest observations. Observe what you can about each of them throughout the day, as though they were strangers to you. How do they talk? How do they make connections with other people? How do they look? What are their moods? What do they do when they have a few unstructured moments? How do they express frustration? At the end of the day record the most significant of your observations.

Connecting to reality—observing and recording what is really there—is a habit you can develop. Practice allows you to cultivate a realistic perspective with fewer self-deceptions and distortions. Don't assume you know your children already; don't let your own preformed ideas keep you from seeing what is there. Each of your children reveals himself or herself to you every day. Allow yourself to be present for the unfolding.

January 9 GROWING WITH YOUR CHILD

Structures emerge but only as temporary solutions that facilitate rather than interfere.[11]
—MARGARET WHEATLEY

One of the miracles of having children is experiencing the deliciousness of their uniqueness. If you have more than one child, you will be in no doubt about the capacity of nature to produce variations on a theme. At the same time it is important to begin educating yourself about what all normal children share in common. All children—unless there are serious developmental problems—go through well-described and well-understood stages of growth. It is worth reading a complete description of this process in *Giving the Love that Heals.* But at this point, we will present as a convenient reminder a summary of each stage, including the child's primary impulse or goal during that stage and the most important thing a parent can do to support the developmental impulse.

As you read through this summary, pinpoint where your children are in this evolutionary cycle. Then spend a few moments thinking about each of your children and how you can tell they are trying to achieve their developmental goal. How do your children let you know where they are in this cycle? If your child is a toddler, for example, is she into everything? Can you see that this is the way she is programmed to learn about her world and her place in it? Ask yourself how you are helping her realize this inborn impulse toward growth and maturity, even when it is bothersome and frustrating for you.

Attachment Stage,
birth through eighteen months:

Your child's most important impulse is to remain attached to you, the parents.
The most important thing you can do is remain reliably warm and reliably available.

Exploration Stage,
eighteen months through three years:

Her most important impulse is to become a distinct self through interaction with the outside world, while still remaining attached to you.
The most important thing you can do is support her curiosity while providing consistent warmth and positive interest.

Identity Stage,
three through four years:

Her most important impulse is to explore the world for the purpose of identifying the ways she is different from you.
The most important thing you can do is validate and mirror back whatever identity your child is trying on at the moment.

Competence Stage,
four through seven years:

Her most important impulse is to discover her power in relation to other people and objects in her world.
The most important thing you can do is continue to be available and warm, provide praise for her efforts to master skills, and celebrate her new achievements.

Concern Stage,
seven through twelve years:

Her most important impulse is to shift her interest from herself to the outside world and the world of her peers.

The most important thing you can do is communicate consistently in a way that offers flexible support and a sense of balance between peer approval and personal autonomy.

Intimacy Stage,
twelve to eighteen years:

Her most important impulse is to explore the sexual impulse at the same time she is keeping same sex friends and building competence in the world.
The most important thing you can do is nurture emotional intimacy within the family.

You and your children will benefit when you see and appreciate their distinct qualities and when you are knowledgeable and responsive to the stages that all children go through.

January 10 FAMILY TIES

Too little attention has been paid to the links between "traditional" and "nontraditional" families, the fluidity of those categories, and the many transitions people make in their lives, as they or their relatives move through several different types of families and households.[12]

—STEPHANIE COONTZ

The world is filled with connections, seen and unseen. One of the easiest kinds of connections to see is how grandparents are linked to parents and how they are linked to children who, in turn, are linked to grandchildren. As you trace through this line of descendants, it's possible to deviate from the main trunk and follow along the shoots and branches leading to numerous aunts, uncles, and cousins. All are connected by genes and by affection, or, if not affection, at least by affiliation.

When someone asks you about your family, do you think first of your immediate family, or do you cast a wider net to include the members of your extended family? One family we know used to make the distinction by referring to their "four family" of father, mother, and two children, as opposed to their "big" family.

"Family" is both a definition and an idea. Any anthropologist can tell you accurately who your family is, and it's equally true that you might give the anthropologist a different response, based on feelings and familiarity rather than lineage. Both ways would be right. "Family" is an emotional idea that gets to the heart of who we are and how we see ourselves.

If you are lucky enough to have a recorded family tree, you can include your children in a conversation about who their forebears are and where they came from. You can look at the family tree together to help them get a sense of the full and rich history that is their legacy. Each person is part of the tapestry of your children's lives. Your children carry physical traces and emotional imprints from all of these people. That is an amazing thing. Allow yourself to feel the wonder of what it is to be connected by birth and marriage to others who know you and care about you and your children.

January 11 A DECLARATION OF INTENTION

Mostly I want to be kind.
And nobody, of course, is kind,
or mean,
for a simple reason.[13]

—MARY OLIVER

Our goal is to help you become a more conscious parent by helping you gain a greater understanding of the reasons behind your actions and the actions of others. As you become more aware, you will learn how to interpret your experiences, your needs, and your motivations. And you will become more aware of your children as they really are, their experiences, their needs, and their motivations.

A first step is simply to *declare your intention* of becoming a more <u>conscious parent</u>. After that, you can begin to cultivate the habit of observing, without prejudice, how you are and how your children are. A declaration of intention helps, because it focuses your attention when you are operating with full awareness and when you are operating on automatic pilot. When people start paying attention, they are often startled to realize how much of what they do is unconscious. You may also not realize how much of your parenting is unexamined and reactive rather than consciously responsive to the here and now.

We love our children absolutely, and our bonding with them ensures their survival. But as they grow older, we often have trouble distinguishing their needs and desires from ours. Without realizing it, we can get confused and start treating them as extensions of ourselves. This is the essence of unconscious parenting. In order to turn this situation around and become focused on what is best for our children, we must come to terms with an essential truth: *We are not our children, and they are not us.*

As you work to become more aware of the ways you are an unconscious parent, it can be helpful to know what to look for. Below are the most common patterns of unconscious parenting. In contrast to the essential truth of individuation just stated, an unconscious parent believes:

1. His children are an extension of himself and thus privy to all he thinks and feels.
2. *His* reality is the only true reality, thus confusing parental authority and responsibility with god-like authority.
3. He is responding to the child's behavior when he is usually responding to something that happened to himself in the past.
4. All children are alike and remain alike over time. He is unaware that children develop in stages.

Do you recognize yourself in these patterns? It would be surprising if you didn't. All parents are unconscious some of the time, to some degree. The question isn't, Are you an unconscious parent? The question is, *When* are you an unconscious parent and in what way?

Observe yourself today with an eye toward your own unconscious patterns. See if you can catch yourself reacting toward your children in ways that do not recognize and honor their individual uniqueness. When you do catch yourself, you will know that you are on the right track. Becoming a better parent starts with your intention to become one and to develop a reality-based appraisal of what you need to change.

January 12 EXPERIENCING THE UNCONSCIOUS

Intimacy and diversity are at the heart of our universe.[14]

—RICHARD MOSS

It is so easy to see your children as extensions of yourself. You may assume, without thinking about it, that your daughter should share your taste in clothes and music, that you and your son will agree on which interests he pursues after school, and that both of them will grow up to have the same ambitions and goals that you have. When your ready-made assumptions overwhelm your ability to see your kids for who they really are, we say in Imago Relationship Theory that you have a *symbiotic relationship* with your children. All forms of unconscious parenting come from symbiosis. Symbiosis is present when a parent acts as though his child necessarily feels and thinks as he himself does, with no recognition or respect for the otherness of the child.

You will be able to tell if your relationships are symbiotic by how you feel and by what you say. If you are deeply invested in your child's decision to try out for the school play—when she gets the lead, *you* feel like the star—then it's time to slow down and take a good look at what you are doing.

Here's one way to tell if you need to back off a little. Let's assume that your son has a decision to make about whether to take flute lessons or go to soccer practice. You played a musical instrument when you were his age and are a committed classical music lover. Would it really be okay with you if he decided to play soccer instead of taking lessons? Stating your preference and feeling disappointed when he makes another choice is okay. Trying to strong-arm him or make him feel guilty or feeling defeated is a sign you do not recognize that he is a person separate from you.

Today, listen to what you say to your children. Listen for phrases that sound as though you know what your child thinks, feels, or wants. And look for phrases that label or judge: "I know you . . ." (fill in the blank: "are happy, want to go to bed now, get mad when I . . ., don't want a second helping. . ."). "Of course, you will want to . . ." (fill in the blank: "go to law school, start exercising, invite Jamie to your party, thank your teacher . . .").

All of us are symbiotic part of the time. But as conscious parents who celebrate both the intimacy and diversity we share with our children, we must make a conscious effort to support our children's inner drive to wholeness rather than try to make them over in our own image. Once again, take a few moments during your quiet time today and contemplate the ways that each of your children is different from you. Decide to celebrate the difference.

January 13 INTENTIONAL DIALOGUE: MIRRORING

Thou art thy mother's glass.[15] —WILLIAM SHAKESPEARE

As parents we connect with our children in all kinds of ways every day, but the most important and the most revealing is through the words we use. How we talk and how we listen is often as important as what we say. There are ways to communicate that nurture the growth of our children and our relationship with them. And there are ways to do it that cut them down and poison our relationship with them.

In our work we teach people, through the use of intentional dialogue, how to talk to each other in ways that enhance their mutual understanding. The three processes of intentional dialogue are not hard to understand, although it takes conscious effort and lots of practice to use them consistently, especially when the conversation is distressing or intense.

The primary idea is that no matter what you say to your children, even if you need to be critical or stern, you want to convey the message: *You are okay. You have my permission to be who you are and to express who you are.* This message can be conveyed no matter how angry, disappointed, or worried you are.

The first of the three processes is *mirroring*. You are doing this when you accurately reflect back (express) the content of what your child has told you. It shows that you are listening with a minimum of distortion. The second is validating, and you do it by letting your child know that what she is saying makes sense, that her feelings are valid, regardless of whether you agree with them or not. The third is empathizing, and this happens when you let yourself feel what your child is feeling. When you empathize, you transcend your separateness and experience a genuine meeting of minds and hearts.

Today, you can start making intentional dialogue the cornerstone of your relationship with your children by mirroring. Repeating your child's words back to her is one form of mirroring. But the most common form is paraphrasing. When you paraphrase, you state in your own words exactly—no more and no less—what you think she is saying.

As you become sensitized to the communication between you and your kids, you will find many opportunities to mirror. In very young children who are too young to talk with you, you mirror by reflecting back to them the sounds and gestures they make to you. Your baby smiles, you smile; she looks intently, you look intently. But in older children, mirroring might go something like this:

Parent: Can you tell me what is on your mind? I want to understand what is going on with you.
Child: I feel that [sends the message].
Parent: Let me make sure I've got that right. You feel that [mirrors back the message].

As you can see, mirroring is particularly effective when there is emotional content in the conversation.

Sometime toward the end of this day you might want to record your mirroring experience with your child. What effect did it have on him and therefore on the rest of your conversation? How would it have been different if you hadn't mirrored him? It's a powerful experience to both understand and be understood. This evening, as you spend some private time with each of your children at bedtime, you can be aware of mirroring his or her thoughts as you come to understand even more about the unique and wonderful gifts your children offer you.

January 14

INTENTIONAL DIALOGUE: VALIDATING AND EMPATHIZING

But the language of empathy does not come naturally to us. It's not part of our "mother tongue."[16] —ADELE FABER AND ELAINE MAZLISH

As we have seen, letting your children know that you are listening, that you hear them, and that you understand what they are saying is the most basic and important step you can take to improve your communication and honor them as people. But there are additional steps that a conscious parent can take.

After you mirror your child and you check to make sure that you have understood, look for an opportunity to validate your child by *validating* what he is saying. Remember that your underlying goal in all communication with your children is to convey the message that they are okay and that they have permission from you to be who they are. When you validate, you are sending that message clearly. You are setting aside your own frame of reference and relinquishing your place at the center of the universe as the embodiment of all truth. You are acknowledging another's point of view. Your words send the message that what your child is saying makes sense (given her age, experience, *etc.*).

Examples of validating phrases are: "I can see why you would feel that way." "That makes sense to me." "I don't think you're out of line to feel that way." "That sounds logical."

The third step you can take transcends the boundaries between you and your child. By empathizing, you understand the feelings of another person while he or she is expressing a point of view or telling a story. There are two levels of empathy. On the first level, you reflect and imagine the feelings your child is expressing. On a deeper level you experience emotionally—or actually feel—what your child is feeling. Such empathic experiences are healing and transforming, independent of what is being communicated.

Examples of empathizing phrases are: "I can feel your sadness [or whatever]." "When you tell me about it, I feel angry on your behalf." "You are feeling afraid, aren't you?" "That hurts, doesn't it?" It's hard to read these sentences without putting in the body language. We let our children know that we are feeling along with them through words but also through gestures, tone of voice, and facial expressions.

Spend a few moments today re-creating for yourself experiences you have had when someone validated you and when someone empathized with your deepest feelings. Do you remember what you were expressing? Can you say what it meant to you to have another person respond to you that way? Allow yourself to experience again how it felt in your body when the person you were talking to let you know that your feelings were valid and that he or she was feeling along with you. Now resolve to give those gifts more often to your children by practicing the three processes of intentional dialogue: mirroring, validating, and empathizing.

January 15 IMAGO: MAKING CHOICES

If you want to know what your wife will be like in thirty years, look at her mother.
—FOLK WISDOM

Through this daybook and your other reading, you are engaged in the process of becoming a more conscious parent. You want to interact with your children less often in a mindless and automatic way and more often in a way that is consistent, self-aware, and intentional. As you make the effort to become more conscious, you can become aware of the patterns that influence and even regulate your behavior and your attitudes in the different roles you play in your family as a spouse, a parent, and a child yourself. It's true that some of these patterns are unique to you, but many of the most powerful patterns are general and apply to everyone. Until you've learned about them, you are probably unaware that to some extent the choices you make and the way to react to life's experiences are the result of psychological patterns that hold true for everyone.

Imago Relationship Theory studies and describes these patterns. The primary one explains how we choose our marriage partners. What happens is this: Each person stores in his brain an inner picture of all the traits, interactions, and experiences he had with his parents. This inner picture is called the "imago." Even though he is not aware of the imago, it is powerful. The imago functions to connect the person with a partner who in many ways replicates the character structure of his parents. In this way, the person has the chance to try to work out old conflicts, heal wounds, and take care of unfinished business left over from childhood.

If your chosen mate shares traits with one (or both) of the parents you had trouble with when you were growing up, you can see where this leads. After the honeymoon period is over, conflicts, difficulties, and disappointments will inevitably arise. It also means that you have a second chance to heal these old wounds by entering into a healing relationship with your spouse when difficulties begin to surface.

This is an occasion when you might want to do some writing, making sure that your written thoughts will remain for your eyes only. You can start by listing those qualities or traits you attribute to your spouse that you think of as positive and those you find annoying, disturbing, or disappointing. Beside each positive and negative trait, indicate whether it is also present in your mother or father. Then take some time to reflect on whatever insights emerge. Keep in mind that you may have reacted strongly to a negative trait in one of your parents by choosing somebody who represents the polar opposite. The significance of this is that you understand that your experience with your parents has in some important way determined your choice of life partner.

January 16 VOICES FROM THE PAST

Nothing has a stronger influence psychologically on their environment and especially on their children than the unlived life of the parent.[17]

—CARL JUNG

We are beginning to get a sense of how important our unconscious is as a reservoir of past experience and as a source of present thoughts and feelings. We know that children unconsciously internalize the experiences they have with their parents—the emotional maturity or immaturity of the parent, as well as their parents' moral characters. This inner picture will influence their choice of marriage partners, and it will also influence what kind of parents they become.

Because of the power of internalized experiences and images in the unconscious, *the single most important predictor of how you will parent is how you were parented as a child.* Your parents' actions and inactions have formed the person you are today, even if you can't remember them all. It's as if we all had "parenting prints" in our brains, as unique as the fingerprints on our fingers. Although we can't see them, we come to know our own prints by observing how we interact with our own children.

Our parenting imagos are so much a part of us that our actions and reactions may have the feel of unassailable truth. We hold to our ideas with strong conviction—certain behaviors and attitudes just feel "right," and others feel "foreign." If we never examine them or seek to understand why we do what we do and what effect our actions have on our children, we are parenting unconsciously. If we were lucky and blessed with wonderful parents, most of our unconscious reactions may be good for us and good for our children. But most people don't want to repeat the parenting they got; they want to do better. This means they will have to make an effort to become conscious of how their own parenting has been influenced by their experiences as children.

Visualization is a powerful way to absorb new ideas and learn new ways of looking at things. Today, allow yourself time for a short visualization that will help you feel the flow of influence from your parents through you and on to your children. Choose a time when you won't be interrupted. Close your eyes, become aware of your breathing, and let go of the tension in your body. Let yourself see a stream of water flowing gently through a rocky streambed. The water moves uninterrupted for a few feet until it flows over a few rocks. There it changes its pattern some and then continues until it is disturbed again by another group of small rocks until it flows down and out of sight. You can think of the water as your inheritance from your parents flowing over you and on to your children, eventually flowing on to and over their children. To change the flow, you will need to wade in and move things around, creating dams here and opening the flow wider there.

This visualization is a metaphor for the power every parent has to preserve some parts of her inheritance and eliminate or modify others. You get to choose.

January 17 LISTENING TO YOUR MOST DIFFICULT MOMENTS

There are no perfect parents . . . just as there are no perfect children.[18]

—FRED ROGERS

Parenting is the most demanding and the most important job there is. The responsibility we undertake to nurture, guide, and set limits for another human life is usually not something we fully understand when our babies are born. We don't realize how much growing *we* will have to do to ensure that they grow up mentally, physically, and emotionally healthy.

When things are going well, we feel blessed beyond measure, grateful and happy to experience such transcendent love. But when things are not going well, we may feel an equal measure of despondency. At such difficult or jarring times it helps to know that things pass; nothing will last forever. And it helps to develop some understanding of why and how the bumpy times happen in the first place.

In the effort to understand it's helpful to start with yourself. The perspective of Imago Relationship Theory is that there are reasons to explain what kind of problem you are having with your child now. . . . And why? . . . And why now? These reasons are linked to the problems your parents had parenting you at the same age, around the same issues. Whether they intended it or not, there were clumsy or hurtful interactions. They may have ignored you or criticized you or smothered you with unwanted attention or undercut your efforts to be independent, or perhaps they didn't allow you to express anger.

At the places where your own growth and wholeness were damaged, you responded by scarring over the wound. These scars protected you from further pain, but at the cost of distorting your natural self into something that was not natural to you. You developed defensive behaviors that showed that you were denying some parts of your natural self and exaggerating others in an effort to gain the approval of your parents and keep yourself safe.

Your scarred over wounds impair your ability to respond as a conscious parent to your own child. *You will have trouble parenting your child at exactly those places where your parents had trouble parenting you.* Your own wounds interfere because your own unmet needs keep getting confused with your child's needs. If, for example, you have trouble praising your child, you can be sure that the difficulty has more to do with the praise you needed but didn't get from your parents than it does with your child. If you have trouble saying "no" to your child, look no farther than your own history to discover why a lack of appropriate limits caused you such pain.

Learning how to trace your parenting difficulties back to your own childhood is one of the most important conscious-parenting skills you can develop. Today, you can learn more about your own history by writing or thinking about a recent episode with your child that you felt did not go well, or a time when you had a negative reaction that seemed overly intense and out of proportion to something your child did. What happened? How did you react? How did your child react to your reaction then?

Assume for a moment that the problem is *your* problem and not your child's problem. Assume that the problem arose from a wound that you sustained while you were a child. Do you have any sense or intuition about what that wound might be, or what could have happened to cause you pain in this spot? Take time to relive the problem you had with your child, feel the pain it caused you, think back to a time when you were the same age as your child and in a similar situation, and let yourself see if a particular episode or event forms itself in your memory.

By making a note of the times when you overreact and feel out of control, you are identifying a "growth point" for yourself. You are discovering a place where you need to do further healing work on yourself in order to help your child develop well through this particular stage of development.

January 18 WORKING WITH A PARTNER

Grow old along with me!
The best is yet to be.[19]
—ROBERT BROWNING

As we begin our journey with a life partner, we envision the joys of growing old together. We imagine ourselves sharing the adventure of romance, parenthood, and the contentment that comes from having surmounted life's obstacles. Unfortunately, as the years pass, the grind of daily existence often wears away that vision until it is abandoned altogether.

Parenthood is one of the greatest tests of our original vision. All too often difficulties arise that cause us to focus on the differences between us and our parenting partners. The differences that attracted us and that we hoped would help us complete our fragmented selves become so great that the connection between us grows weaker. It is sad but true that our children often magnify the differences between us.

It is important to remember from time to time that the connection between parenting partners is what the partnership is founded upon. We are co-equals in this parenting partnership. Neither of us represents the whole. We must find ways to communicate to our children the whole of our connection together.

Let's examine the covenant we made and continue to make together as parenting partners: Our marriage was not a commercial contract. In some sense, it was a sacred commitment. Even when we want to go our separate ways, we are obligated to maintain our unity as parents. We respect each other. When we have conflict, we agree to work out the conflict in conjunction with each other, as adults. We take responsibility for our own healing and growth. We do not rely on our children to help us complete our healing work. We look to our partner to become our surrogate parent in order to help us with this work, and we expect to help our partner do the same.

Today take time to think about the things that connect you to your partner, not the property you have or want to have in common, not the career goals you have for yourselves, but the values you share together. What values do you want your child to receive as a legacy from your life together with your partner? You may want to write these shared values in your journal. Think about discussing them with your partner.

In addition, allow yourself to spend some time constructing in your thoughts the covenant you shared with your partner when you began your journey together. What elements have been added to it now that you are raising a child together?

January 19 CONNECTED IN COMMUNICATION

We have followed too much the devices and desires of our own hearts.[20]

—THE BOOK OF COMMON PRAYER

One of the truths we have discovered about why we choose our partners—for love, marriage, and for raising children—is that the very nature of the choice contains within it the seeds of conflict. A life partner is even more likely to arouse feelings of conflict than other people in our lives, because we have chosen partners who can re-create for us the battlefields of our childhoods. In making the choice, we have gravitated toward partners we hope will resolve those battles in our favor. They embody the traits we have learned to reject, devalue, or ignore in ourselves, traits that have been lost to us as positive forces in our lives by our childhood wounds.

But there are many ways we can keep our intimate partnerships from deteriorating into permanent battlegrounds. The dance of courtship doesn't need to become a power struggle forever. Whether we realize it or not, our conflicts present us with opportunities to restore connection and grow together as partners and parents.

Today you can begin to work toward turning areas of conflict with your partner into a bond between you. Begin by recalling a time recently when something your partner said or did caused your hackles to rise. You may or may not have reacted visibly, but you felt a strong negative response, whether you struck back or not.

What feelings did the incident arouse in you? Take a moment, to acknowledge the validity of those feelings. Now, for the moment, try to become your partner. What was he or she thinking and feeling? Explain, as best you can, the purpose behind his or her actions. Given what you know about your partner, imagine your partner's feelings. Take a moment to acknowledge the validity of those feelings. Can you imagine a dialogue in which you both calmly discuss the situation? In this dialogue, you would mirror your feelings to each other. And then you would acknowledge to each other their validity.

Let yourself construct an internal dialogue in which each of you responds to the same situation in a way that protects the other's point of view. This sounds so simple, perhaps because you are controlling both sides of the conversation, and there is no threat here. This internal dialogue will help you see how real dialogue works to restore, enhance, and cement the connection between you.

January 20 OTHER ADULTS AS PARTNERS

You, the same person, are difficult, obliging, charming, unpleasant. I can live neither with you nor without you.[21] —MARTIAL

In our contemporary world there are very few families that fit the "traditional" model of the family. For parents who are single or in the process of combining families, partnership can be problematic. And even if you are part of a "traditional family," it is often necessary to form partnerships with other adults who, for greater or lesser periods of time, can supply you with the kind of committed, adult relationships that can help you gain perspective on your parenting journey.

Who are the people you can turn to when you want and need help from adults outside your family? Certainly they can be friends, as well as lovers and acquaintances. They are people you can trust and who trust you. Their interest is in your well-being and the well-being of your children. They are people whom you have known for some time, with whom you have a history of sharing, whom you allow to see you and accept you for the most part as you really are. They are people who are willing to take the time to listen to you and whom you in turn can listen to with confidence, knowing that they are not trying to manipulate you or use you.

But because you have not committed to these friends as life partners, you cannot expect them to share all of your trials and be completely disinterested observers. You have to choose those areas of your parenting where their time and attention will be most valuable to you.

What if you were to approach a friend with a particular request for a dialogue about your problem? Could you help your friend mirror back to you your understanding of the problem, validate your understanding and give his or her own point of view, and then help you decide on a course of action? Would you and your friend agree to hold each other accountable for working through the problem through this course of action?

Consider who among your friends would be a suitable parenting partner. Would you be willing to share a serious concern with this friend? Do you think your friend would consent to work with you on this concern—your finances, your relationship to your child, a part of your life where you are unable to move forward?

January 21 LEARNING FROM OTHERS

Adapt yourself to the things among which your lot has been cast and to the men among whom you have your portion; love them, and do it truly and sincerely.[22]

—MARCUS AURELIUS

As adults we are connected not only to the world of our immediate families but to the universe from which we spring. Yet how isolated we often feel, how disconnected, as though our own particular problems are uniquely ours to experience and solve. And, of course, perceiving others as separate from ourselves only leads us down a path to further isolation.

Sometimes it is difficult if not impossible to feel our connection to others, particularly when they give us feedback about ourselves or how we parent that we don't want to hear. We are often resistant to other people's opinions about how we are doing. We are averse to hearing about parts of our lives, ways we behave, or problems we may be seen to have that are painful. We screen out through oversensitivity the information that touches us most.

And it is important to be cautious. After all, not everyone you hear from has your best interests at heart. And often those who say they do may be working through their own problems at your expense. They may be responding to you based on their own experiences, motives, and agendas. They may not be able to really relate to your situation independent of theirs. At least that is what you might tell yourself.

Given that some feedback will not be helpful to you, you still need to develop more openness to the observations of others whom you trust. You may not want to accept everything that other people tell you, but you do need to learn how to listen. The people who are closest to you have perceptions you can use. You will need to learn to deal with these perceptions as though they are not threatening. Partners, friends, grandparents, teachers, your child's friends, all offer you feedback that can be helpful if you can learn to step back from the areas of your life where you are most fearful and accept their contributions. Although not all information is useful, very little of it is a serious threat, except to your preconceptions. And sometimes these need to be shaken up.

Think about at least two separate situations where you reacted defensively to information you didn't want to hear. Did someone criticize the way you talked with your child, your work habits, your alcohol consumption, your lack of concern over your finances, or something else? How could you reframe those criticisms so that you could learn from them? How could you reframe your response so that you'd be more able to learn something from them?

January 22 FEEDBACK AND ADVICE

Yesterday he came to me
I shouted "Go away"
Grace danced toward me
I shut my door.[23]

—RUMI

Feedback from other adults rarely comes without advice, whether we have asked for it or not. We may feel that this advice is not only more than we were looking for but dead wrong. Yet we are tempted to act on it, because we accept either the person or the advice as authoritative. Perhaps it comes from our own parents, our child's grandparents. After all, they have more experience than we do, and what they are telling us may be drawn from time-honored tradition. How can we pit our own inexperience against that?

It is especially easy for us to replace our own judgment with that of others when we are not on secure ground ourselves. Sometimes we will listen to another adult's assessment in place of our own understanding of our child or our life circumstances. It is as though, instead of filtering the information, we remove all our filters and let it come through without comment, despite our awareness that something doesn't seem quite right.

Another person's concerns or comments aren't proof that a problem exists or that its solution is obvious. The information that your child is disruptive or uncooperative in school, for example, may very well be a clue that there is an underlying problem in the classroom, and not that there is an underlying problem with your child. Unacceptable behavior can originate from many sources. Since you don't always know the value of the feedback or information you are getting, you would do well to develop the habit of hearing them without fear and defensiveness. Later, you can gain a deeper understanding of problems and solutions through investigation and the exercise of your thought and judgment.

Today, let yourself recall a conversation with another adult—a partner, a friend, or a teacher, for example—during which you received some feedback and advice about your child or your parenting that you found difficult to understand. Did you pay attention to the information contained in the feedback? Did you accept the other adult's judgment about the nature of problem? Did you accept the advice as a solution to the problem? Did you feel immediately compelled to either defend your child or "fix" the problem? In making a judgment about the information and advice, were you responding to your own fears, or were you focusing your attention on your child's real-life situation and need?

How do you practice listening to others? Consider what you might do differently to accept new information about yourself or about how you parent. You don't have to act on new information, just listen.

January 23 THE WHEAT FROM THE CHAFF

Let the wise also hear and gain in learning,
and the discerning acquire skill. . . .[24]

—PROVERBS 1:5

Like many of our most common sayings, "separating the wheat from the chaff" can be best understood in the context of our long agricultural folk tradition. When we harvest wheat, we want the wheat and we don't want the chaff. So, too, when we receive feedback about our parenting or about our child, we want the useful information, and we need to discard, or at least separate out, those portions of the feedback that are not helpful. In this case, the "wheat" is the part of the feedback that belongs to a truer understanding of the child. The "chaff" consists of the part that belongs to us and our own fears and the part that belongs to those who gave us the feedback and *their* own fears. If someone tells you that your child is "spoiled" or "rebellious" or "slow," or that you are "too strict" or "not strict enough," how can you make some conscious decisions about whether or how to proceed?

Think about some "negative" feedback you have recently received or would be afraid to receive about your child. What part of the information were you afraid of receiving? When you consider who your child is, do you see the information as a part of her? Does it in some sense belong to her, or does it belong to you?

In order to be able to answer these questions, you need to focus your attention for a few moments on your child. What does she enjoy? How does she express herself when she is happy? What things make her unhappy? What things interest her? What bores her? What fears does she have? What activities does she excel at? Since you understand that children express themselves differently at different stages, consider the age of your child and what you know about other children of that age.

Now consider the source of the information. What is the nature of your relationship to the person who provided the information? Do you feel that there is a judgment attached to the information? If so, is your child being judged, or are you afraid that it is you yourself who is being judged?

Today, take time to reflect on how others experience your child and your interactions with her or him. As you think about who your child is, ask yourself, What part of these experiences of others might be valid? Given what you know about your own fears and insecurities, what part of them do you want your child to "own," and what part of them do you want yourself to own? Can you tell what the wheat is?

January 24 CONNECTED THROUGH THE YEARS

Our birth is but a sleep and a forgetting:
The soul that rises with us, our life's star,
Hath had elsewhere its setting,
And cometh from afar.[25]

—WILLIAM WORDSWORTH

There is no greater obvious connection between you and your child than the one that exists in the first few months after birth. The child is totally dependent on you for his well-being, nourishment, safety, and a sense of belonging to a gentle, benign world. Even as your child grows, and the connection with you isn't so obvious, it is important for you to know that it will always be there. Even a rebellious teenager who wants to be anywhere but in your presence still has a need to remain attached.

Understanding that a child develops through well-established stages of growth is essential to your maintaining your mutual connection. The older the child grows the more he will explore, establish his separate identity, and develop competence. Finally he will learn a sense of concern for others, his friends, and become a partner in an intimate relationship. Throughout this journey toward adulthood, he will still need to be connected to you. The nature of the connection will change, and you, as a mature adult, must find ways to adapt to the kind of connection he needs as he grows.

This is not an easy task. But it is made easier when you understand that the growth of a child implies continuous change along a well-determined path. You needn't be surprised as he changes. You needn't feel that your connection is threatened, even though you must be the one to guard it and keep it alive and healthy.

During the quiet of a few restful moments, take the time to imagine your child as he is right now. What is he like? Now think of him at birth and let yourself remember how he has gradually changed, both physically and emotionally, until you can see him as he is now, at his present age. When you do this "time lapse" exercise, you are also tracing the history of your connection to him. Let yourself imagine, as you probably already have, how this child will change as he becomes an adult. Now you are not working from what you know, so focus on the essence your child carries into the future as you imagine him moving away from the present. Can you feel your connection?

January 25 ATTACHMENT

It is necessary for us to form in happiness ties of confidence and attachment that are both sweet and strong in order that their rupture may cause us the heart-rending but so valuable agony which is called unhappiness.[26]

—MARCEL PROUST

Our ties of confidence and attachment with our children are given to us with their birth. These ties can never really be broken, although they can be severely tested and even ruptured. The journey we embark on with our children at their birth is ongoing and lasts as long as either we or they are alive. In order to take the journey together and avoid the unhappiness of rupture, we must learn to remain flexible as our children grow. We have to see who they are as part of a continuum, even when their behavior makes them temporarily unrecognizable to us. We must acknowledge and honor that continuum by focusing on our mutual connection throughout all the inevitable changes. Along with Proust, we may agree that the unhappiness of rupture can be an inspiration for growth and therefore a "valuable agony," but it is one we want to minimize.

From birth to about eighteen months a child is completely dependent on his adult caregivers. The attachment/connection at this stage is obvious. It is intensely physical and involves holding the child, through most of her waking hours and many while she sleeps. Carrying your child around as you move around the house, go shopping, or feed and change her is the norm. This is as it should be. Establishment of this loving, physical bond is the single most important act of parenting at this age of attachment. A child cannot get too much of it.

But at about eighteen months the child will begin her first moves away from her parents. This is the age of exploration. Maintaining the connection not only involves holding and physical attachment, but it also expands to include the idea that parents must learn to lovingly "let go." The child will be exploring the world, seeing what she can discover about her immediate environment. She doesn't want to go too far, but she wants to be free to go on her own. Your role at this stage is to maintain your connection by letting her explore. At the same time, you continue to be available physically and emotionally whenever she wants to come back and assure herself that you are still there. Sometimes this age of exploration is difficult for both parents and child. That's why it's sometimes called the "terrible twos." That's when maintaining the connection can be difficult.

Have you had the experience of seeing your child move from one stage to another? What were the clues that the pattern of your relationship with your child was changing? Was it gradual, or can you remember an event that signaled the change? As you realized that your child had become somehow different, and not always in pleasant ways, how did you respond? If your responses to the long-term changes in your child were not what you might have wished, how would you like to have done it differently? If you were able to go with the flow and adapt pretty well, what skills did you learn that will make it easier as your child continues to grow and evolve in the future? Times of change present opportunities for growth, both for you and your child. There is nothing to fear except loss of connection.

January 26 LETTING GO

. . . self-hood begins with walking away,
And love is proved in the letting go.[27]

—CECIL DAY LEWIS

Letting go within connection means paying attention and being available while not controlling your child's behavior. This is particularly true when your child is trying on new identities, which he begins to do around the age of three. At this time, he will start to find out the difference between who he is as a person and who his parents are. He needs to establish a separate identity. This is the age of pretending. Sometimes he is a cowboy, sometimes a fireman or a doctor or a space ranger. He may try on many roles, and the key to maintaining the connection during this stage is your acceptance of, approval of, and involvement in these identities.

It's easy to be too busy to pay attention to your child's playacting. And sometimes you can become disturbed by a role he is simply trying on for size. But there is no need to attempt to prevent him from continuing in the role. Neither ignoring him nor overreacting to him maintains the connection. You can relax. He is not going to be wearing those ridiculous clothes forever. He is not setting the course of his life in a permanent way. He doesn't need to hear about the impracticalities of becoming a circus clown.

But he does need to feel validated. This is an opportunity to mirror back to him the role he is playing and to validate him in it: "You certainly are a very scary monster." "I like firemen, because they help people in trouble." "You are a very brave bullfighter." All of these are affirmations of your child's experimentation with his identity. They allow your child to try out a role and at the same time feel that you approve of him and take him seriously.

At a later stage your child will strive, for his own sake, to become competent at the things he does. Right now, he just needs you to pay attention to him and accept him.

Today, ask yourself how your child experiments with new roles. Do you stop to notice, and do you give him the space to experiment? Are you overly concerned with your child's performance? Try to think of this affirmation: What I want for my child is the freedom to explore and experiment, to learn who he is, as long as he is not in danger or endangering others. When he asks me to take part, my role is to be a cheerleader and to enter into the game with him. This keeps us connected.

January 27 BECOMING CONSCIOUS

Our knowledge of self must be clear—of the good in us as well as the bad. Each one of us has plenty of good as well as plenty of bad inside.[28]

—MOTHER TERESA

While it is true that we are all products of our own parenting, and we have all experienced some wounding as a result, it is equally true that we each have the responsibility to move past what we have been given. A conscious parent knows that gaining maturity means taking responsibility for what we have learned rather than casting blame for what we have been taught. With maturity comes a requirement to own our actions.

As parents we need to pay attention to ourselves and how we interact with our children and with our partners, so that we can short-circuit our own automatic reactions. These are the unthinking things we do that arise from deep within us, and which unconsciously pass our wounds along to others. When we are able to stop these automatic reactions and take time to respond from our conscious understanding, we are well on the way to becoming conscious parents.

What are your growth points, areas where you will need to concentrate and withhold your reactions? You will recognize these growth points whenever you find yourself in an emotional interaction with your child where you either suddenly react with fear or anger or are able to repress your reaction only with great difficulty.

Obviously, we are often called upon to intervene immediately in our children's activities, and sometimes anger and fear are justifiable. They can be useful emotions. But they can also signal our own growth points, areas where as conscious parents we need to engage in self-examination and perhaps healing in order to safeguard our children in future.

Think about a recent incident where you were unable to control a negative response to something your child said or did. Did your reaction trigger a conflict? Did you see the incident as a part of an ongoing pattern? When you reacted, were you operating from anger or fear? How did you justify the anger or fear to yourself? What did your child really need from you at that point? Sometimes growth points are easier to see in others than in ourselves. If you are in a marriage relationship, can you think of a time when you observed a growth point in your partner? What do you think this says about personal healing work that your partner may need to do?

January 28 BECOMING CONSCIOUS II

Men are disturbed not by things, but by the views which they take of things.[29]

—EPICTETUS

What can we do when we find our emotions suddenly going out of control as we react unconsciously to something our children are saying or doing? At such times, we know we are in danger of creating a rupture of connection with our children, and we need to find another course of action.

The first thing we can do is slow down, pause, and realize that we need to take some time out. Next we can remember that the primary tool we have to work with is <u>intentional dialogue</u>. Intentional dialogue helps us do two things: step back from our emotions and consider the needs of the child. When we are engaging in dialogue, we are able to concentrate on what our child is saying and feeling. We are able to practice <u>mirroring</u> our child's experience back to her, <u>validating</u> it, and <u>empathizing</u> with it. When we can put ourselves in her place by truly listening to what she has to say, and when we can hear her feelings and validate her point of view, we gain a new perspective on our monopoly on truth. This doesn't mean that we are always wrong, but it does mean that our view of how things really are is sometimes skewed by our particular fears and distorted by those parts of ourselves we have rejected or of which we are unaware. What we need at times like this is a new perspective.

Intentional dialogue enables us to learn from our children rather than impose our own "system" on them. It is not enough for us to be "right" by justifying our own prejudices. We need to arrive at a shared point of view.

Today, allow yourself to take the time to revisit a recent difficult interaction you have had with your child. After you have thought about it and sought further understanding in your own mind about why you overreacted, find an opportunity to engage your child in dialogue about this matter. As a conscious parent, you will want to learn how to tell your child that you are sorry when you have reacted unconsciously. After the apology, you can initiate an intentional dialogue that will allow you to heal the breach in your relationship and more fully understand each other's point of view. This takes practice. Intentional dialogue may be difficult at first, but setting the stage carefully so that both you and your child have the time and the inclination to talk will help.

It's all right to admit to your child that you sometimes overreact, and that when you do, you would like to back up and take some time to hear how she is thinking and feeling. When she gives you the opportunity, listen, mirror her words back, and validate her point of view. Be conscious of wanting to understand her, instead of pressing the rightness of your own actions.

January 29 GOALS OF CONSCIOUSNESS

Rage (and scheme) against the dying of the light of childhood's fascination.[30]

—STEPHEN JAY GOULD

In all our interactions with our children, we have learned that the primary goal is to allow each child to develop into a person who is fully alive to the world: *Every child has the need to survive, to feel alive and express his aliveness, and to experience connection to others and to that which is greater than himself.* As parents, the way we interact to provide safety, support, and structure to our children at each stage of their development determines how successful we are at achieving this goal.

Throughout your child's development, he needs to feel safe,

not only physically but also emotionally. The home you provide is an island of safety, a place where he can retreat when he needs comfort, and a safe haven where he can try out the identities and competencies he needs to develop in order to succeed in the wider world. Does your child feel safe and secure at home and in your presence?

Structure is not stricture; that is, structure does not mean creating arbitrary bonds that keep your child under control. But it does mean helping your child work within limits that he understands and that make sense to him. These limits include rules that keep him and others out of danger, and they include models of moral and ethical behavior that he can use in his dealings with others. Does your child understand the boundaries you have set for him, and do those boundaries make sense to both of you?

Conscious parents also recognize that providing support for a child means keeping abreast of his changing needs, his efforts to gain competence in various skills, his development of friendships as he enters the world outside his home, and his growth into adolescence and intimacy. At each developmental stage, the kind of support that you need to provide is a little different. As you continue to explore conscious parenting throughout the year, you will gain a greater understanding of how to support your growing child as he matures.

The primary thing to remember is that you want to be giving your child what *he* needs rather than what you need or are most comfortable with. You can begin to get a sense of how well you are meeting your child's needs by asking yourself, "Does my child feel I am providing support when he requests it or needs it?" Do you think he feels free to express himself, knowing that you are accepting rather than judging him?

Think about who your child is as a growing person right now. What are some ways that you can provide him safety, support, and structure? You might find it useful to write these things down in your journal. As you learn more about who your child is over time, it may be interesting and helpful to review, at a later date or at moments of crisis, what you have written.

January 30 RITUALS

Goodnight light
And the red balloon.[31]
—MARGARET WISE BROWN

Most people think of rituals as ceremonies performed on religious or public occasions, but ritual can be as simple, in fact, as a handshake greeting or a good-bye wave. The primary purpose of ritual is to establish connection between people or to establish spiritual connection to God or to build community connection.

Early on in their relationship lovers begin to establish ritual words and actions that they use to stay connected to each other or to reestablish connection, especially when they are afraid of emotional separation. Anyone with a small child has probably developed a bedtime ritual. As we mentioned earlier in the month, we have found time alone with each child just before sleep to be a primary way of maintaining connection. To our surprise this ritual is lasting into the teenage years as our children look forward to our special time together. Although parents often think the primary purpose of such a ritual is to get the child off to bed at long last, a successful bedtime ritual really assures both parents and children that everything is safe, everyone is loved, and everyone is truly connected, even though they are now separated by sleep.

The soothing nature of ritual is obvious. Rituals let us know that no matter how buffeted we are by the world, there is a place inside where we can rely on our connection. This is why children always respond eagerly to ritual. "We always do it this way at our house," is an important rationale that both parents and children use for eating the same kind of food on a particular holiday, for example, or for going back to the same Christmas tree lot every year, or for starting meals with a blessing. These rituals remind us that our lives have meaning and continuity.

There are also rituals that parents and children create together that help them feel loved and connected to each other. Reading aloud together, having weekly special meals, turning off the TV one night a week and playing games, participating in sports, going fishing, sharing a hobby—all of these activities assure parents and children that they are connected through mutual values and experiences.

It is also true that sometimes rituals can lose their magic. Your ten-year-old son no longer wants you to read him a bedtime story. Your entire family loses interest in the Saturday night games of Pictionary that used to be so much fun. Rituals should grow and change as your family grows and changes, but there will never come a time when you no longer need them at all. Your need for ritual will last as long as your need for connection.

What rituals do you enjoy in your life? What rituals make your child feel safe, supported, and loved? Which rituals have outgrown their usefulness and need to be put aside in place of others that provide connection?

January 31 FAITH AND CONNECTION

In this faith there are truths preached that surpass every human intellect. . . .[32]

—SAINT THOMAS AQUINAS

Most of us have a sense of what we mean by faith. Certainly, when we speak of faith we mean to include the confidence we have in others and the trust we have in the future. In addition, our understanding of faith also involves a sense of the spiritual connection we have with nature and with what many of us call God. In a profound sense we are expressing our intuitive understanding that we are connected to the universe in many and wondrous ways.

Over and over again we have experienced the importance of a faith tradition in the successful rearing of children. Such traditions provide the context for maintaining the holy nature of the bond between parents and children and also the holy nature of our connection with the larger world. Through our faith traditions we come to realize that our lives have meaning and that everything we do matters.

Take a few moments today to reflect on the faith you have in your children. You have faith in them, even though you know that sometimes they will disappoint you, as you will disappoint them. You also know that throughout the long history of your lives together you will continue to believe in them and in the strength of your connection to them. Your faith in them transcends your daily experience. And because you have faith in them, your words and actions show them that you do. You learn to act and speak out of your love for them and your faith in them as valuable human beings.

As you become more and more <u>conscious</u> in your actions and speech together, your faith is a sustaining element. It will keep your internal compass pointing north. It will enable you to correct your course when you seem to lose your way. It allows you to forgive both yourself and your children and to start over again. It allows you to be the role model of consciousness that your children are always looking for.

Notes

1. Thomas Merton, *The Asian Journal of Thomas Merton* (New York: New Directions 1973).

2. Mother Teresa, *Jesus: The Word to be Spoken* (Ann Arbor, MI: Servant Books, USA, 1986).

3. Natalie Goldberg, *Writing Down the Bones* (Boston, Shambhala Publications, 1986).

4. Gabriele Lusser Rico, *Pain and Possibility: Writing Your Way Through Personal Crisis* (Los Angeles: Jeremy P. Tarcher, 1991).

5. Pema Chödrön, *When Things Fall Apart: Heart Advice for Difficult Times* (Boston and London: Shambhala Publications, 1997).

6. Robert Coles, *The Moral Intelligence of Children* (New York, Random House, 1997).

7. Steve Farkas and Jean Johnson, *Kids These Days: What Americans Really Think About the Next Generation* (Public Agenda, 1997).

8. Jo Robinson and Jean Coppock Staeheli, *Unplug the Christmas Machine* (New York: William Morrow, 1982).

9. Richard Moss, *The Second Miracle: Intimacy, Spirituality, and Conscious Relationships* (Berkeley: Celestial Arts, 1995).

10. Nick Kelsh and Anna Quindlen, *Naked Babies* (New York: Penguin Group, 1996).

11. Margaret Wheatley, *Leadership and the New Science* (San Francisco: Berrett-Koehler Publishers, 1992).

12. Stephanie Coontz, *The Way We Really Are: Coming to Terms With America's Changing Families* (New York: HarperCollins, 1997).

13. Mary Oliver, "Dogfish," in *New and Selected Poems* (Boston: Beacon Press, 1992).

14. Richard Moss, *The Second Miracle: Intimacy, Spirituality, and Conscious Relationships* (Berkeley: Celestial Arts, 1995).

15. William Shakespeare, "Sonnet III, in *The Complete Illustrated Shakespeare,* ed. Howard Staunton (New York: Gallery Books, 1989).

16. Adele Faber and Elaine Mazlish, *How to Talk So Kids Will Listen and Listen So Kids Will Talk* (New York: Avon Books, 1980).

17. Julia Cameron, *The Artist's Way: A Spiritual Path to Higher Creativity* (New York: Jeremy P. Tarcher/Perigree, 1992).

18. Fred Rogers, *You Are Special* (New York: Penguin Books, 1994).

19. Robert Browning, "Rabbi Ben Esra," in *Browning, Poetical Works, 1833–1864,* ed. Ian Jack (Oxford: Oxford University Press, 1970).

20. *The Book of Common Prayer*, According to the use of the Episcopal Church (New York: The Church Hymnal Corporation, 1979).

21. *Difficilis, facilis, iucundus, acerbus es idem: nec tecum posum vivere nec sine te*. Martial (Valerius Martialis, A.D. c.40–c.104), *Epigrams* (XII, 46), in Gavin Betts, *Latin* (Chicago: NTC Publishing Group, 1992).

22. Marcus Aurelius, Meditation No. 39, *Marcus Aurelius and His Times*, trans. George Long (Roslyn, NY: Walter J. Black, 1945).

23. Rumi, *Speaking Flame,* re-created by Andrew Harvey (New York: Meeramma Publications, 1989).

24. *The New Oxford Annotated Bible* (New York: Oxford University Press, 1994).

25. William Wordsworth, "Ode on Intimations of Immortality from Recollections of Early Childhood," in Lynn Altenbernd and Leslie L. Lewis, *Introduction to Literature: Poems*, second ed. (New York: Macmillan, 1969).

26. Marcel Proust, *The Past Recaptured*, trans. Andreas Mayor (New York: Vintage, 1971).

27. C. Day Lewis, "Walking Away," in *The Complete Poems of C. Day Lewis* (London: Sinclair-Stevenson, 1992).

28. Mother Teresa, *Jesus: The Word to Be Spoken* (Ann Arbor, MI: Servant Books, 1986).

29. Epictetus, *The Enchiridion*, trans. Thomas W. Higginson (New York: Liberal Arts Press, 1948).

30. Stephen Jay Gould, "Drink Deep or Taste Not the Pierian Spring," *Natural History* (Sept., 1997).

31. Margaret Wise Brown, *Goodnight Moon* (New York: Harper & Row, 1947).

32. Herman Shapiro, ed., *Medieval Philosophy, Selected Readings from Augustine to Buridan* (New York: Modern Library, 1964).

February

INTRODUCTION TO THE MONTH OF FEBRUARY

This month we are exploring the theme of patterns. Patterns allow us to perceive the world as beautiful and as meaningful. They comfort us with their power to make our lives coherent and predictable. Some patterns are easy to see, while some are less obvious; but when we become aware of them, we are rewarded with a rich source of information we can use to make our lives even happier and more fulfilling.

February 1 FEELING THE MEANING

The striving to find a meaning in one's life is the primary motivational force in man.[1]

—VIKTOR E. FRANKL

As human beings we all strive to make sense of our lives. We look for ways to decipher the hidden code of our experience. When for some reason we can't make meaningful connections, we become overwhelmed, convinced that life's events are frighteningly random. Platitudes about "the meaning of life" don't help much because what we need is to discover the meaning of life for *us* as individuals.

What allows us to discover meaning is our capacity to become aware of patterns. Our brain is continuously registering, evaluating, and sorting data from the outside. On the simplest level that's how we know what to do next—whether to slow down or go faster, whether to reach out to help someone or hightail it out of there. We have to work a little harder to see patterns in human behavior, because the information we are sorting is often very complex. It requires that we see the common denominators in different events over a long period of time. The intuitive connections that are necessary to find meaning come from our ability to see consistencies and designs in our own personalities and the personalities of the people around us.

How do we make these intuitive connections? To a great extent we rely on our feelings. Our feelings form the basis of our "emotional intelligence." If we didn't have emotional intelligence and had only rational intelligence, we wouldn't be very smart. Our lives would be incoherent. Our feelings let us know when we are on the right track, when we are in danger, and when something doesn't quite fit. Without them we wouldn't know what to make of the things that happen to us.

Given how central our feelings are to our experience of being alive and how essential they are to our discernment, it's surprising how often and how intensely we try not to feel. Perhaps it's not so surprising when we stop to consider how many of our feelings are painful or at least uncomfortable. Just as we are driven to seek meaning in our lives, so, too, we are driven to avoid pain. Trying to avoid pain by ignoring or denying how we feel sometimes has the useful purpose of delaying a realization or an action that we're not yet ready for. But sooner or later our feelings confront us. If we can learn to make friends with them sooner, we'll harness their potential for informing our understanding and enriching our experience.

Here is one way to think about it: The more connected you are to your feelings, the more intelligent you are about what's happening and the more likely you are to detect the meaning in your life. Let yourself begin this month with this realization, and keep it in the forefront of your awareness. Remember to be open and receptive to the subtle shifts of feeling that connect you to the events and people in your life. Become more sensitive to your nuances of feeling, and then ask yourself what these nuances add to your understanding. How do they contribute to your recognition of the meaning that your unique and wonderful life has for you?

February 2 LETTING THE FEELINGS THROUGH

In essence, we never operate with a "full deck," but rather with only a small portion of the system live and on the spot at any one time.[2]

—ROBERT ORNSTEIN AND DAVID SOBEL

Unless we make an effort to do otherwise, we can live great stretches of time on "automatic pilot." It's a great advantage to us not to have to think hard about everything we do. Who wants to re-create the minute steps we mastered when we began driving a car? But there are minutes and hours every day when it is to our advantage to come alive, to wake up, and to assume that we do not know the drill. The possibility of learning something new is real and present at such times. So is the possibility of change. We can't change when we are asleep to life, stuck in the repetition of mindless patterns that may have worked once but are now old, cold, and worn out.

It is especially important to be awake and alive when you are with your children. They are growing and changing every day. They are dynamic, and the energy systems they create are dynamic. As a parent, your values may remain relatively stable, but your implementation of those values must be flexible and receptive in order to keep up with them.

Right now is a good time to practice being receptive to what is happening between you and your children. As we discussed yesterday, tracking your feelings will help you become more emotionally literate and therefore more intelligent about your own experience. For several reasons it's a good idea to start with feelings that really get your attention. If these feelings happen to be negative, so much the better. You can use your own overly intense negative reactions to find out more about what makes you tick. Begin by asking yourself to be more specific about the negative feelings you have in certain interactions with your children. For example, you may feel an overwhelming "no," voiced or not, when your teenage daughter tells you she wants to take the bus downtown after school. You may feel the same way when your youngest child refuses to eat his peas. And your reaction to your ten-year-old telling you he wants to run for class president may also be "oh, no!" Each of these situations is different. And it's likely that what you are feeling in each case is also different.

See if you can refine your own understanding of what you really feel the next time you react in a negative way. In the examples above you might be afraid that your daughter is moving away from your tight circle of safety; you might be angry that your toddler is not bowing to your authority; or you might be worrying that your fifth-grader is going to be rejected by his classmates.

It's interesting, isn't it, how often our "noes" are related to our fears. In order not to establish symbiotic relationships with our children, it's a good idea to learn as much about ourselves as we can. When we know what we are afraid of, we can assess whether our fears have anything to do with our children.

Today, spend a few moments recalling an instance when you responded negatively to one of your children. What happened? What do you remember feeling at the time? Now that you are paying more attention to shades and nuances, what do you think you were actually feeling? You will be able to go even deeper if you can figure out why you felt as you did at that moment. Did this encounter remind you of something that may have happened to you in the past? Does it feel like something else? Allowing yourself to ask questions like these and giving yourself the time to think about them will help you become more sensitive to the people you love. And it opens the possibility of change.

A prayer for today: *As I move into my time of quiet today, may I still my heart and mind enough to accept the wisdom that is already within me. May I allow my wisdom to teach me more about my thoughts and my actions so that I can be a better parent to my children.*

February 3 WHAT DO YOU SEE?

The bonds that unite us with those we love are invisible bonds. They become visible only indirectly, only by what we do as a result of them.[3]

—HENRI J. M. NOUWEN

All of us have inherited memories, emotions, and values from the past. Along with our measure of love and happiness, we arrive at the present moment laden with emotional baggage that can be burdensome. Whether we want to or not, we carry that baggage with us into our relationship with our children. Fortunately, we live in a time where advances in psychological studies have given us the language and concepts that can help us understand the connection between what happened then and what is happening now.

Over the years, our study of couples and families has convinced us that much of who we are as adults and parents, both consciously and unconsciously, has been inherited from our own parents. We carry with us an internalized picture of our observations and interactions with our parents that we call the "imago." Our <u>imago</u> influences our choices, our motivations, and our thoughts as we love and guide our own children. It is the source of many of the <u>unconscious</u> patterns of behavior that distinguish our own parenting style.

It is fairly easy to see how early experiences that were memorable and important continue to influence us now. Think of the death of a parent or sibling, for example, or a major change in economic circumstances. Early experiences with alcoholism and divorce often have profound implications on our development. But what is harder to see is that small, unremembered events have an impact on us as well: repeated outbursts of anger, lack of concern when we wanted attention, nagging over schoolwork, fear over who we were and what we were doing at a particular stage of our lives. These experiences become part of who we are, whether we consciously remember them or not.

Some of these negative reactions from our parents created feelings within us that caused us to devalue particular traits in ourselves or others. Some of them allowed us to lose portions of ourselves or reject aspects of ourselves that we were afraid weren't acceptable. These patterns of negative reactions created wounds that continue to affect each of us today. <u>Wounding</u> is an inevitable result of human imperfection. It is important to acknowledge, but it doesn't need to stop us from becoming whole, healthy people and parents.

As you move through your day today, carry these thoughts with you. Let yourself be aware of those things that cause anger, fear, or regret in you. These feelings are neither good nor bad; they just *are*. As you experience these emotions, begin to connect them to events in your past. For example, consider how both of your parents might have reacted to the thought or situation that has upset you. Would they have expressed intense emotion? Would they have withdrawn? How were your mother or father different in this regard? What patterns do you see that might help you understand yourself better? Such questions help you gain insight into aspects of yourself that might have been murky to you until now.

February 4 STORIES

> Wintertime is storytelling time for the Navajo, and the right place to tell the old stories is in the hogan. When the ground is frozen, families gather to hear the old legends.[4]
>
> —JEAN GUARD MONROE AND RAY A. WILLIAMSON

Many times the truths we experience in our lives are best expressed as stories. As children we hear stories that scare us, encourage us, and make us laugh. Always, they teach us something about problems and how people overcome them or are beaten by them. The beauty of our family stories is that they reduce the complexity of life to the essential details, allowing us to see clearly the threads of action and emotion that run through events that are often unmanageable and overwhelming in real life. And when we tell stories to our own children, we are passing along the wisdom that we and our parents and grandparents have put into them.

Sometimes we tell stories on a smaller scale. We create vignettes for ourselves that justify our behavior and excuse our weaknesses. We repeat these dressed-up rationalizations over and over to explain our prejudices and demonstrate values. Over time they become more elaborate as we add dramatic lead-ins and punchy endings, until without realizing it, our characters act within plots filled with private symbols of our unconscious fears and desires.

Whether our stories are public family accounts of triumph and despair, or private scenes we replay only for ourselves, they can be illuminating. They let us see with clarity what we really think about the way life is.

In this spirit of discovery, let yourself now create a story about your parents, as you experienced them in childhood. Imagine a situation in which your mother or father, or perhaps both, face obstacles they must try to overcome. They may have to deal with death or illness or some other kind of loss. What do they reveal about themselves as they struggle to face their difficulties? Do they approach these challenges with bluster or confidence or resignation or fear?

To gain further insight, now put them in a scene of great, good fortune. Perhaps they have won the lottery or attained a long-desired professional goal. Are they happy? How do they interpret their good fortune, and how does it affect their future choices? Spend time thinking about how your parents look, what they are wearing, where the action is taking place, other people who may be present. What sources of energy do the characters draw on as they deal with the hand they've been dealt?

When we recount the stories of our lives, or when we let our imaginations create new stories, we find ourselves making all kinds of connections we might miss in real life. Do you see patterns or connections in your stories that surprise you?

February 5 THE SHAPE OF THE JUG

How long will you make love with the shape of the jug? Leave aside the jug's shape: Go seek water![5]
—RUMI

You are familiar with the form of your family's stories. You know the plots: how your mother saved her sewing machine from the flood, how your father spent his last dime helping a homeless veteran after World War II. Some families tell stories about courage in overcoming difficulties, others tell stories about being cheated and victimized. Many of us come from immigrant roots, and our stories are about finding a place in an enormous new country.

But more important than the plots are the patterns that run through these stories and illuminate their truths, even though some of our favorites leave out these underlying dynamics of cause and effect. They don't tell us why Aunt Marie never spoke to her sister again, or why crazy Don was never invited to Thanksgiving dinner. Either the storyteller doesn't know or doesn't want *us* to know or doesn't think to look for reasons.

Because of this you may listen to these stories in your family and hear something different from what the teller intended. Your mom may tell you about the unreasonable demands of her family when she was young, intending to solicit your sympathy. But you may hear her complaints as evidence of her selfishness. Or your parents may tell you about themselves as teenagers and not make the psychological connections that you, with your greater sophistication, think are obvious.

Stories are like onions. Everyone can see what's on the outside. But peel down a layer beneath the obvious facts of the plot and ask yourself, *Why did this happen this way*? Peel a little deeper beneath the personal motivation and you find links to the social context of the time. You hear funny stories about how your family moved from place to place every year. You speculate that your father was restless and found it difficult to settle down. You then realize he must have had trouble holding a job. You wonder if maybe he drank. That would explain your mother's unhappiness.

Today, let yourself remember one story your parents told you about themselves or the early years of their marriage. After you have fleshed it out in your in memory, see if you can peel the layers of the story to get to the heart of it. What does this story mean? When you have a sense of its meaning, let yourself sit with this insight for a few minutes, holding it within you as a gift from your parents to you.

February 6 CONTEMPORARIES

To change personality means to learn new patterns of attention.[6]

— MIHALY CSIKSZENTMIHALYI

Every so often it's a good idea to shake ourselves up, to loosen our attachment to the preconceived notions we're so fond of. If you have brothers or sisters, you know what valuable services they can perform in this regard. All you have to do is tell a good story about when you were kids, and right in the middle, you're interrupted with, "That's not the way it happened at all!"

The upside of this kind of disruption is that your siblings can often recapture a truth that you cannot see. They add a new twist to the world you remember, not only because they filter experiences differently, but because their actual experience really was different from yours. Even aside from the obvious differences of gender and birth order, each child elicits something different from each parent. In a real sense each child grows up in a slightly different family.

An only child may not have these advantages of multiple perspectives. But even the only child had occasion to observe her parents interacting with other people's children from time to time. Some of these interactions may have been surprises. "Who are these people?" she may have asked herself.

It can be fun, as well as instructive, to swap stories with a brother, sister, cousin, or even a close childhood friend. You will certainly find things you agree on. Yes, your father really was stingy. But you might be surprised to hear that your sister found him affectionate, and your cousin found him funny, while you always thought he was a stick-in-the-mud.

It's not unusual for siblings to have quite opposite experiences in some ways. Perhaps the dominant parent for you was your workaholic, autocratic father, while for your brother, your quiet, subdominant mother was the primary influence. Or perhaps, you share common memories but reacted to them in radically different ways.

As you think about your childhood, retain an open and receptive frame of mind. Question your long-held, well entrenched versions of reality. Ask other people for their insights and observations. There's not much value in reconfirming old prejudices, but there can be tremendous value in being able to spot them.

February 7 THE CHILD YOU REMEMBER

I cannot paint what then I was.[7] —WILLIAM WORDSWORTH

Of all of your childhood memories, the most pivotal are the ones that help you know who you were as a child. Through the years you have undoubtedly give this some thought. But now that you are a parent, your answer to the question, "Who was I?" takes on more significance. It lies at the heart of who you are now as a parent.

Your children, even if they can't quite imagine you being little, are probably interested in what you have to say about yourself when you were young. They love to hear stories about your trials and tribulations, especially if they are funny. And especially if the story starts out with you being klutzy or forgetful or slightly incompetent in some way—and ends up with you winning in the end. Our children never get tired of hearing about our "most embarrassing moments." You know the kind of story that has your skirt tucked up in your underclothes or that features you tripping onstage after forgetting the lines of your speech. Somehow they can identify with that version of you.

But besides amusing your children, you are, of course, passing on important information to them in these stories. You let them know important aspects of your experience: what worried you, what your longings were, how you tried but didn't always succeed. Whether you are aware of it or not, you are not only trying to enrich your child's life when you share these memories, you are trying to keep her from harm. You want her to know more and to do better than you did.

Today, during the quiet moments you have to yourself, recall a poignant or deeply affecting memory of yourself as a youngster. It can be either happy or sad. Let yourself feel what you were like then in that situation. Can you put yourself back into that scene as that child? No matter how powerful or grown-up you are now, you are in significant ways the same person as the child you were then. Is this a memory can you see yourself sharing with your own children?

A different kind of exercise, but equally useful is to make a list of what you like best about yourself as a child. Be patient if the list is a short one. Really spend some time scrolling through your memories with the intention of calling forth every positive quality you can. Now, write another list of things you don't like about yourself as a child. As you review the negative list, do so with the perspective that uncomfortable, disruptive, and obnoxious traits in children are often perfectly normal signs of developmental growth. Are any of your early negative traits still with you in ways that you consider detrimental? Are you still impatient and short-tempered or ungenerous?

As you think more deeply about yourself as a child, do so with the awareness that part of the reason for your retrospective investigation is to gain further understanding of your own child's needs and feelings. What insights surface for you in this regard? They are gifts from your past that you will want to safeguard for your child's future.

February 8 REMEMBERING HEROES

The hero, therefore, is the man or woman who has been able to battle past his personal and local historical limitations to the generally valid, normally human forms.[8]

—JOSEPH CAMPBELL

Because the birthdays of Abraham Lincoln (February 12) and George Washington (February 22) occur during this month, on Presidents' Day our thoughts turn toward people in public office and what we can learn about the way they have lived their lives. Despite their faults, we find ourselves drawn to the best of them as leaders who accomplished a great deal at great personal cost. Some of them have become our heroes.

This is a good day to think about heroes. You can begin by asking yourself who your heroes are. Who are the people you admire for knowing how to live a life of service and integrity, embodying, at least in part, the human qualities you aspire to? Some of them may be the cultural and religious heroes we are all familiar with. But in addition, you may think of personal heroes who, in their quiet and unsung lives, exhibited the values you admire: a grandmother who set you an example of unqualified love and endurance; a teacher who, perhaps alone of all the teachers you had, embodied creative learning and dedication to knowledge; a friend who set an example of steadfast devotion when you were not at your best; a priest, minister, or rabbi who helped form your moral and ethical framework from personal example.

Over the years, we have learned that heroes are not perfect. We can no longer view any of our presidents as *perfect* examples of the well-lived life. Even Lincoln, we have learned, had his dark moments; even George Washington owned and used slaves to sustain his wealth. Yet both men are heroes, because they possessed extraordinary qualities among their imperfections.

We can use our heroes to understand more completely the qualities we want to demonstrate as parents. We admire our heroes' steadiness of purpose in overcoming tremendous obstacles under less than perfect circumstances. We admire them as people even when they were not successful in worldly terms. We can see that they were motivated to act for the greater good, rather than propelled by petty self-interest. They offer blueprints of the characteristics we admire and want to enlist in the service of our own lives.

Having heroes isn't being naïve about people; it's being optimistic about the future of the human race. Today, think about someone you consider to be a personal hero. In what ways is this person a role model for you? In what ways is your hero like you? Did she successfully face the same kinds of problems you face? Was he someone with personal resources you admire? How can you demonstrate the heroism that you admire in your daily life? Being a hero begins with being a hero in small things.

February 9 RECOVERING

There is no delusion more damaging than to get the idea in your head that you understand the functioning of your own brain.[9]

—LEWIS THOMAS

All of us must bow, on occasion, to the mystery of our own lives. No matter how enlightened we think we are about our own functioning, we do well to realize that while self-understanding is a continuous process of vital importance we never completely achieve it. There are still parts of us that are opaque. We can live most of our lives and never be aware that parts of our central self have fragmented into different parts that are lost to consciousness. We don't necessarily make the connection between the wounds we've suffered and the effect they have on the way we think, feel, and act in the present.

How does it happen that so much of personal consequence escapes our notice? To understand, we have to know something about the way our brains evolved. The oldest and most primitive parts of our brain help us perform our prime directive: stay alive, do what you can to protect yourself from outside threats. The "old brain" is not rational. It can't distinguish between past and present; it doesn't take into account different contexts. Its job is to sense danger and help us respond defensively.

The "new brain," or cerebral cortex, is a later development that helps us make finer distinctions, allowing us to mediate the primitive directives of the old brain. It enables us to know that *this* situation, which feels a lot like one in the past, is really different and therefore not as threatening. We don't need to respond to this comment or this behavior as though our life were in danger.

We unknowingly split off various parts of ourselves when our old brain signals to us that we are under attack. Whenever something we've done or said is either punished or disapproved of, we tend to respond by trying to eliminate that part of ourselves. You can see how this might happen. Approval from powerful adults is a matter of life and death for an infant. We are born needing to please as a matter of survival. To the old brain, approval is life; disapproval is death. As our parents react negatively to certain traits, we learn to disguise them, to "lose" them, or to reject them in ourselves and others.

We may disguise, lose, disown, or reject certain parts of ourselves, but on some level they are still there. We have pushed them out of awareness, but they are still with us in some form or other. They show themselves in those moments when we react spontaneously and reflexively to certain situations that trigger an unconscious signal of danger. At such times, we don't understand *ourselves* why we react the way we do, so instantaneous and automatic is our reaction.

It takes time and effort to uncover fragmented parts of yourself. You have to be willing to observe yourself and ask questions about what you find. You can start by asking some simple questions. Which of your characteristics do you approve of most strongly? Which characteristics do you disapprove of most strongly? Can you relate these positive and negative traits to ones in you see your parents?

There are many ways to ask these basic questions. To deepen your understanding, you could pose the question in this way: When you think of something you would very much like to do in the future (learn a language, play better tennis, become a calligrapher, travel abroad) which of your personal qualities and skills do you think would aid you in such a new enterprise, and which of the necessary qualities and skills do you think you lack? Every so often we will call your attention to the search for a deeper level of self-understanding by helping you recover parts of your fragmented self.

February 10 ECHOES

> Next to the hunger to experience a thing, men have perhaps no stronger hunger than to forget.[10]
>
> —HERMANN HESSE

Do you ever surprise yourself by sounding just like your mother, or your father? You may have taken an oath never to say to a child of your own, "You don't need me. . . . You can do it by yourself," or "Why can't you just listen!" But sooner or later, as you wrangle with your daughter over her math assignment, these very words slipped out of your mouth. You know you said them, but it feels like they were spoken by someone else. You marvel at the power that some early words and phrases still have over you. Not that the power is all bad. Like many parents you probably find yourself comforted and sustained when you say just the "right" thing automatically, as though the inspiration came from somewhere else.

Such experiences remind us that there is more going on inside us at any given moment than we know. As you continue your effort to know yourself better, let's see if you can shed a little light on the dark corners by identifying any verbal patterns that were typical of your parents. Because some of these verbal patterns may have been irritating to you, or even destructive, it is a good idea to remind yourself of what you already know: your parents came to the task of parenting already wounded, with some degree of incomprehension about their own thoughts and behaviors. You can't blame them for their failures, just as you can't blame yourself. But you can know that they were responsible for how they handled their legacy of wounding, just as you are responsible for how you now handle yours.

When you call to mind certain specific situations, you may jog your memory of routine or predictable things they might have said and done. For example, when you misbehaved in some minor way, what would your mother have done? How about your father? When your misbehavior was more serious, how did your parents respond? Recall a serious conflict with each of your parents. Did you feel that your behavior was under attack, or that you yourself were somehow imperiled? Which of your traits were questioned? Take a moment to relate these patterns of reaction to who you are today. Do you see those traits in yourself still? What connections do you see?

February 11 SYMBIOSIS

I am he as you are he as you are me and we are all together.[11]

—JOHN LENNON AND PAUL McCARTNEY

When we interact with people as if they think and act the same way we do, we call this symbiosis. We treat them as though they are extensions of ourselves, with the same needs, experiences, and reactions. We get upset when they show their independence by veering off into their own thoughts. Somehow, they've been disloyal. They are being obstinate, contradictory, aggressive, rebellious, stupid, ignorant, or any of a thousand other negative things! The truth is so obvious!

Of course, symbiosis is not a rational state of being, even though we can muster a thousand rationalizations to justify our shortsightedness. And in the beginning it serves a real purpose. It is natural to bond so completely with your infant that you think his safety is your safety; his danger is yours. Perhaps you remember feeling this way with your children when they were young. Your identification with them was so complete that you felt like they lived in every cell of your body. Your bonding ensured their survival. But it becomes dysfunctional after the first few months if it isn't tempered with an appreciation for the unique identity that each child is born with and has the right to explore and express.

When we don't encourage our children to differentiate from us, symbiosis acts like a virus that infects them with the same patterns of prejudices, phobias, and defense mechanisms that hinder and inhibit us. It takes effort and self-discipline to stop a symbiotic pattern once it is established. But over time and with consistent use of intentional dialogue we can change it and reestablish a connection that is strong but flexible.

Today, give yourself the pleasure of celebrating the wonderful uniqueness of your children. Bring to mind something about each of your them—a quirk, a quality, a skill, an opinion, an interest, an idiosyncrasy—that distinguishes your child from you and from the other members of your family. When you have a few moments alone, call up this mark of uniqueness in each of your children and savor it. Smile when you think of them. The essence of life is unity within diversity, and recent polls show that very few people would clone themselves if it were possible to do so. What more graphic experience can we have of this truth than the individuality of our own children?

February 12 TWO PARENTING STYLES

So creation is built upon opposites.[12] —RUMI

In our view, there are two principal parenting styles: minimizing and maximizing. Although most parents are not *extreme* manifestations of one style over the other, every parent can be said to have more of the characteristics of a minimizer or more of the characteristics of a maximizer. Every child, also, is influenced by this combination of parental styles and grows up to be more one way than the other when he or she becomes a parent.

A minimizer tends to develop strong boundaries behind which to hide. This style is created during childhood as the child interacts with a parent (often the one with whom he has the most difficulty) who is emotionally and often physically unavailable to meet his needs. Repeatedly throughout childhood he approached his parent with a need, only to have that parent fail to respond or push him away. Eventually the child handles the pain of these rejections by withdrawing. He learned not to express himself and not to expect any guidance. A child who has learned to squelch his sensitivity to himself can easily become insensitive to the needs of others, thus replicating the style of the parent who was the source of his pain in the first place.

As a parent the minimizer is preoccupied with his own life and has little time for his children. He seems cold and incapable of empathy. He leaves child care to others whenever possible. He has trouble sharing feelings and becoming intimate. His children often fear him and learn early on not to bother him.

A maximizer, on the other hand, has very few boundaries and no firm sense of self. When the maximizer was a child, the parent with whom she had the most difficulty was sometimes available and sometimes not. This parent sometimes smothered the child as a way of vicariously meeting his own needs. He continually expressed fears and warnings and gave unasked for advice. Most of the time this parent seemed overly present to the child, but when the going got rough, the child felt pushed away.

As a parent the maximizer has a hard time separating her own thoughts, desires, and opinions from those of the people around her. When frustrated, the maximizer will often explode with rage and then collapse with remorse. Her child grows up without being able to clearly separate from her in order to become an independent adult.

Married couples tend to be paired, with one minimizer matched to one maximizer. One parent will unconsciously respond to his or her children most often in a minimizing style; the other will unconsciously respond most often in a maximizing style.

Although these concepts may be new to you, do you have a sense of which style most often described your father and which style most often described your mother? Since people are complex and categories must be fluid to have any validity, you may be able to say that most of the time this parent had this style and your other parent had the opposite. But it might also be obvious to you that they both crossed over from time to time. Because their styles influenced yours, it's important to pick the strands apart as much as you can and see what you can discover about the formation of the parenting style that you now demonstrate most often with your own children.

February 13 MAXIMIZING AND MINIMIZING

And, through observing her own mind at work over time, she found it was the quality of her awareness rather than the content of her experience that brought contentment and happiness.[13]

—MARLENE A. SCHIWY

It is easier to characterize the behavior of other people than it is to characterize your own. Sometimes we know too much about ourselves and get bogged down with internal discrepancies and paradoxes that are fascinating, but difficult to define. This is especially true when we are dealing with our own patterns of unconscious reactions. It's hard to see our conscious reactions, much less our unconscious ones. Often the only way we can begin to make headway is by noting the reactions that other people have to our behavior. There are times when it's a good idea for that other person to be a professional, but most often it's possible to make better use of the daily interaction we have with the people we live with. We find it easier to see ourselves through the eyes of other people than to look directly into a mirror.

Yesterday, you began to think about which of your parents was a maximizer and which was a minimizer. This is a beginning. Today, we suggest that you let yourself explore your thoughts about the parenting style of your current or former spouse.

Can you predict, for example, whether your spouse would more likely become overly involved in your child's science project and its outcome or ignore it completely? Is your spouse more likely to cry in front of your children or not show emotion? Is your spouse more likely to intrude into your child's relationships with friends or not show any interest at all? These are extreme contrasts that we offer for the purpose of helping you begin your thinking. They may present clues about whether your spouse tends to maximize or minimize. When you have a sense about which it is, further clarity can be achieved when you realize that you will most likely have the opposite style.

Through observing thousands of couples, we have learned that whichever style one spouse has, the other will tend to have the opposite. Each of you chose the other in the first place because of opposing traits. And couples tend to polarize in their responses over time.

Take a few moments to see whether recent interactions between your spouse and your child offer fresh evidence of minimizing or maximizing. What can you observe about how your spouse handled a difficult interaction and about your response to that handling? If your spouse exploded, did you want to hide? Did you wish you could be spared the whole scene? Did you resent the interruption and intrusion? Did you feel your emotions explode inward as you shut down? These reactions describe your spouse as a maximizer and you as a minimizer.

On the other hand, if your partner shied away from the confrontation with your child and withdrew, did you feel like exploding? Maybe you wanted to butt in and take charge of the situation. You wanted your opinions to be asked for and for your emotional needs to be taken into consideration. Did you pursue your partner or child, demanding that they pay attention to you? Did you feel like yelling and screaming? These reactions describe your partner as a minimizer and you as a maximizer.

If you're having trouble sorting all this out, think of a similar situation where another adult, a close friend or relative, was present. If you trust this person to have your best interests at heart, ask him or her to talk about how you were perceived. Encourage other trusted adults to share their observations with you. You don't need to be afraid to know how someone else sees you. At this point in your parenting journey, you are an investigator, and all information is useful.

February 14 BE MY VALENTINE

Tomorrow is St. Valentine's Day,
All in the morning betime,
And I a maid at your window,
To be your Valentine.[14]
—WILLIAM SHAKESPEARE

Perhaps you greet Valentine's Day with joy and loving expectations. After all, you know what it is like to be in love. If you are a parent of an elementary-school-age child, you've probably already spent time helping them make valentines for their classmates. You've been sharing in their happiness as they anticipate giving and receiving these tokens of affection. As for yourself, you may have plans that include intimate dinners, candy, and flowers.

And yet . . . maybe, as in the case of Ophelia in the quote above, your celebration of this day has a touch of irony about it, even bitterness. You may feel manipulated by yet one more commercial holiday, especially if the sentiments being expressed don't feel real to you at the moment. Do you feel like you are being asked to give and receive a mechanical, programmed kind of love on this day? Perhaps all the fanfare has become an occasion to mourn what you don't have, rather than to celebrate what you do have.

It can be helpful to remember that regardless of how you feel, today is a day you can *choose* to celebrate. It is a day given to love. No matter what condition your own love life is in, you have the opportunity to make this day your own, separate from the commercial requirements. As a parent, you have ready access to its deepest meaning. You know what love is. You know something about the kind of love that replenishes itself in giving. Every day, you get back what you give your children.

As you go about your business today, choose to let the love in your life be a blessing to you. Let yourself have some quiet moments to hold your children and anyone else close to you in your loving thoughts. Give thanks for the blessings these people bring into your life. And then let them know how you feel.

A prayer for today: *I enter into a moment of prayerful solitude today to give thanks with my whole being for the love that is in my life. May I have the eyes to see and the heart to feel the many ways the people around me care for me, esteem me, and love me.*

February 15 TRAUMA

I belong to a Clan of One-Breasted Women. My mother, my grandmothers, and six aunts have all had mastectomies.[15]

—TERRY TEMPEST WILLIAMS

All families experience trauma of some kind. In some families, their trauma is a large part of their identity. Everyone who has a family knows that being a member means sharing the pain. The problems may belong primarily to one member, but they reverberate in the lives of all. And they don't have to be big, tragic problems to have an effect. Sometimes, the chronic, low-level difficulties are more insidious than the acute crises. Problems don't have to be dramatic or life-threatening to influence the way a family functions.

Terry Tempest Williams writes movingly about family trauma in her book *Refuge: An Unnatural History of Family and Place*. In her book she chronicles a crucial year in which her mother's last, fatal illness coincides with the natural destruction of the habitat of the Great Salt Lake. In the midst of this devastating loss, she finds patterns of meaning that connect her family's history with the history of their natural surroundings.

Not all of us are so skilled at making such connections, but all of us can benefit from the attempt. For example, you can ask yourself what story your family tells about the dangers it has faced. What strands of meaning are spun from the chaotic events of your past? Knowing that times of trouble leave their mark on us, whether we see it or not, ask yourself what scars you and others carry from the hardships you've endured. Have any of the wounds become places of renewed strength? Injuries don't have to turn into weaknesses; they can become opportunities for new growth.

In your quiet time today, hold each member of your family up to the light of love and understanding. Experience each person with empathy. If there is something that needs to be forgiven, ask yourself if you are ready to forgive. If you are not, allow yourself to heal in your own way, at your own pace, in the knowledge that you will be able to encompass the difficult events of your life within your compassionate understanding.

February 16 GOOD TIMES

Time let me hail and climb
Golden in the heydays of his eyes.[16]
—DYLAN THOMAS

"Ah, nostalgia," goes an old joke, "it ain't what it used to be!" Sometimes we like to kick back and reminisce with our children about our youth and the good times we had with our families. Generally, children love to hear stories about how it was in the "olden" times of their parents. On occasion, however, we notice their eyes glaze over and we can hear them thinking, "Oh, no! Here it comes. Another lesson from the old one."

Whether you get this reaction or not depends, to some extent, on the kinds of stories you tell. After the first or second telling, stories about how hard it was when you were a kid seem to lose their magic. When your child shares something important with you and you react by telling a moralistic story about yourself, you run the risk of weakening the connection between you instead of strengthening it. She knows that you aren't really empathizing with her; you're manipulating her. You don't really understand her feelings; you are too busy explaining your own.

The next time your child comes to you with an incident or event that is important to her, respond in the spirit of <u>intentional dialogue</u>. Encourage her to say more about what happened and how she was feeling. When she says she was mad, ask her if she wants to say more about that. Mirror her feelings and thoughts, without filtering them through your own judgment. "So when your teacher got mad at you in class, you thought that maybe you'd leave school right then." Let her know that you could see why she might react like that. And then <u>empathize</u> with her feelings of rejection. "It's hard to stay in a place where you don't feel you are wanted."

This doesn't mean there is no place for stories about yourself. Think of them in the context of creating a connection for your child with the warm and loving memories of your past. You might want to wait until she is in a quiet, happy, or contented mood—maybe during a bedtime ritual. Remember that the purpose is to connect, not create sympathy for yourself. As you set the mood and the describe the place and the time, fill your heart with love for your child. You want her to be able to recapture your feelings. Don't tell her what she ought to think about the story. She will fill in the blanks for herself.

February 17 RENEWAL

The pursuit of a goal brings order in awareness because a person must concentrate attention on the task at hand and momentarily forget everything else.[17]

—MIHALY CSIKSZENTMIHALYI

As a parent, you have so many things to care about. You care about your children, first of all, and your romantic partner, if you have one, and your health and your work and all the other thousand details that help make your life and the life of your family, as healthy and comfortable as possible. And sometimes in the midst of all this attentive caring, you get tired. For just a little while you want to rest, to be "off duty," to be pampered and taken care of.

Times of rest and safety are essential for parents. You are fortunate if you have a friend or partner who will draw a bath for you, or give you a back rub, or serve you breakfast in bed, or let you sleep an extra hour or two. And you are even more fortunate if you know how to give yourself permission to enjoy these downtimes. You take seriously the realization that you have more to give when you're not running on empty.

But in addition to resting, it's important to find ways to reenergize yourself through activities and experiences that actively engage your interest and that require your participation through focused attention. We have talked to parents who found renewal through mountain climbing and snow camping—activities that make some people want to crawl under the covers and never come out. Other people find relief from the responsibilities of parenting by digging in the dirt, canvassing fabric stores for just the right piece of fabric, writing poetry, or taking piano lessons.

What these activities have in common is that they are *not* parenting. In addition, they are self-motivated, actively engaging, and potentially creative. Equally important, you can tell when you're done, and you know when you've done it well. Sometimes that's hard to tell with parenting. There are very few moments with your kids when you can stop, assess what you've done, and call it finished.

Allow yourself to have some fun today thinking about those activities and experiences you would like to participate in someday. Don't just consider things you've actually done. Create a wish list of things you'd like to do if you were magically relieved of all responsibilities and somehow found yourself in good health, with ample time, and enough money. One parent we know made this list: grow herbs for Indian cooking, make "memory" books with hand-made paper for each grandchild, borrow a camper and spend one month in the wilderness, learn to scull on the river, and take music lessons again. What would be on your list?

February 18 YOURSELF APART FROM BEING A PARENT

Textures, places, and personalities are important on the soul path, which feels more like an initiation into the multiplicity of life than a single-minded assault upon enlightenment.[18]

—THOMAS MOORE

One of the most effective ways to help yourself climb out of a blue mood or resolve a personal or interpersonal conflict is to ask yourself, "What helps?" Sometimes, of course, this is not the most appropriate question, and you need to ask, "What's wrong?" But much of the time we are not facing serious problems, and we would do well to remember how helpful it can be to focus on solutions, to turn toward what lightens our moods and do what we can to rebuild our sense of optimism.

We can expand this idea a little by asking ourselves: "What do I like?" "What makes me happy?" "What do I want more of in my life?" In fact, these are good questions to ask yourself right now, in the middle of these long, dark February days. While you are tending all the other important connections in your life—to your children, your spouse, your friends, your business associates, your other family members, your community responsibilities—you can devote a little attention to the personal connection to your own pleasure.

Throughout this day make note of the things that have helped you feel alive, gave you hope, or filled you with gratitude. You can think of this as your Aliveness Inventory. The longer you keep it, the more valuable it will be to you. It will become a record of your blessings. It will help you see that happiness does not depend so much on extraordinary moments of good fortune, as it does on ordinary moments that give pleasure and meaning to your life as you go about your daily round.

Some of the things that make you happy may be connected to nature: the sun that makes the winter light, the snow that makes everything new, the birds that sing in the cold air, the stars that shine through the night sky. Some of them may be sensual: the fire that warms your feet, the hot water that bathes you after a long day, the tea that restores your spirit, the winter stew that makes your house smell like home. And some of them will undoubtedly be interpersonal: the beautiful faces of your children, your friend's voice on the telephone, your coworker's smile, your lover's words.

As you enjoy this day, approach your experience with this question of happiness and pleasure in mind. Promise yourself that you will notice the small moments and give thanks for them. Even the briefest moments count—a puppy seen from a bus window, a glimpse of unexpected color; the smell of coffee on the street—these are great gifts. And they will favor us more often when we have eyes to see them.

February 19

PATTERNS OF CRITICISM BETWEEN YOU AND YOUR PARTNER

The way to dissolve our resistance to life is to meet it face to face.[19]

—PEMA CHÖDRÖN

If there is another parent in your children's life, you are undoubtedly aware that the two of you form a complex parenting system. You are cocreating the parenting environment your children are growing up in, whatever your relationship. Your parenting partner may be right beside you physically and emotionally, or your parenting partner may be more distant, either through lack of involvement or because the two of you do not share the same household. But whether you are close or far apart, both of you influence your children and each other as you facilitate and respond to the changes that move your children through the gates of childhood.

Although you know that your partner comes to the table with his or her own point of view, it is tempting to believe that your way of looking at the world is the right one. Most people have trouble accepting the limited nature of their own perceptions and tend to see differences as a source of conflict.

If you can become receptive to your partner's perceptions, the differences between you can become sources of further insight and knowledge. Perhaps the richest vein of new information, and one that is hardest to accept, is your partner's criticism of your parenting and your criticism of your partner. In order to find the treasure of information that is hidden in criticism, here are four principles to keep in mind:

Principle 1: Most of your partner's criticisms of you have some basis in fact. If you assume this is true and keep an open mind, you will be able to learn something about yourself from the criticism. You can ask yourself: "How does this criticism make me feel?" "What do I think about these comments?" "What deeper feelings might underlie these thoughts and feelings?" "Did I ever have these thoughts and feelings when I was a child?"

Principle 2: Many of your repetitious, emotional criticisms of your partner are disguised statements of your own unmet needs. You can ask yourself: "In what way is my criticism of my spouse also true of me?" "What do my comments say about me?"

Principle 3: Some of your repetitive, emotional criticism of your partner may be an accurate description of a disowned part of yourself. You can ask yourself: "Is this criticism an expression of an undeveloped or repressed area of my own psyche?" "Am I resentful because I wish I could be more like that?"

Principle 4: Some of your criticisms of your partner may help you identify your own lost self: "What does my criticism say of my partner, or say about what I want or don't want for myself?"

During the next few days listen carefully to your interactions with your parenting partner. If you hear criticism coming from either of you, refer back to the principles above and try to understand better what is happening. Proceed on the assumption that there is something you can learn from the negative remarks that you and your partner make to each other about your parenting. The repetitive, emotional criticism you recall is a message to you. There is something here you need to attend to before you can evaluate whether the criticism has implications for your parenting.

February 20 DIALOGUE BETWEEN PARENTING PARTNERS

If you want to marry me, here's what you'll have to do:
you must learn how to make a perfect chicken-dumpling stew.[20]

—SHEL SILVERSTEIN

Each person in a marriage comes with a separate list of requirements, desires, and requests. Somehow you and your spouse must weave your separate strands into one bigger one that will be able to withstand the stresses and strains of family life. In addition you have the added task of dealing with each other's psychological wounds. These are the parts of you that have been hurt through unintentional or uncaring interactions in the past. These wounds now become part of the environment in which you conduct your marriage and raise your children. If the two of you want to become conscious parents, you must create a relationship that fosters the healing of each other's childhood wounds. Even if you are at the very beginning of this process and still trying to learn how to do it, your children will benefit from your efforts. They get to see you making the effort to understand and accept each other. Whatever success you have stops your legacy of pain from being handed down to your children.

Language is the medium through which most of your healing work is done. You learn to use words to build connection. When you talk to each other in ways that are understanding and accepting, you strengthen connection. When you talk to each other in ways that are diminishing and judgmental, you break connection.

There are many ways of talking that break connection. You can discount what your partner is saying: "I heard you, but I didn't take you seriously." You can judge your partner: "You are . . . [inadequate, ignorant, selfish, shortsighted, insensitive] for feeling that way." You can "educate" them: "I think what you're trying to say is . . ." You can threaten them: "If you're going to . . . [say, feel, do] that, then I'm going to . . ." You can ignore them: "Yeah, that's nice. Now, as I was saying . . ." You can analyze them: "The reason you feel that way is . . ." These are all common ways of invalidating our partner's thoughts and feelings while trying to replace them with our own.

You build connections through conversations that are conducted *in the spirit of* dialogue, or that actually use the techniques of intentional dialogue. As you remember, this three-step process allows you and your partner to express thoughts and feelings without fear of misinterpretation or judgment. Both of you know that you have been heard, validated, and understood on a deep level. This is the best tool we have for building healthy bonds between parents. When parents are good partners for each other (even if the partnership is limited and does not occur within marriage), they are better parents for their children.

Find at least one occasion today to practice intentional dialogue with your partner. Look for an opportunity to mirror, validate, or empathize with something your partner is telling you. If you get a chance, you may want to initiate a more formal dialogue about an issue that is emotionally intense. Since we have been talking about the opportunities that exist within criticism, perhaps it would make sense to choose such a recent instance now for further dialogue.

To review the steps of the dialogue process, see the Glossary in the back of the book. Since the two of you may be new to this kind of interaction, you might want to let your partner know that you would like to have an intentional dialogue for the purpose of reaching greater mutual understanding of the issues you want to talk about, and for the purpose of practicing the technique itself. Remember that your overall goal is to learn how to be healing agents for each other for your own sake and the sake of your children.

After you have completed the dialogue, perhaps later in the day, think about how it went. Were you able to do what you wanted to do? Were there ways you could have done it better? How did the two of you benefit from the process? Remember, the more you practice, the more familiar it will become. And the more you practice with your parenting partner, the more at ease the two of you will be in handling the problems that arise with your children.

February 21

HELPING YOUR CHILD TO FEEL ALIVE AND EXPRESS ALIVENESS

Bliss was it in that dawn to be alive, / But to be young was very heaven.[21]

—WILLIAM WORDSWORTH

Do you remember times when you were young and you felt this way? Dancing, running, singing, painting, laughing, crying with abandon? We have all had such moments—living totally in the moment, free to be part of what was happening right then. Even when these times weren't ecstatic, we felt alive to what we were doing and free to express ourselves through the activity we were engaged in.

Although no one can make these moments happen for anyone else, you can create an environment for your children that coaxes these moments to life. And you can be there, ready to celebrate your children's happiness when they lay such experiences at your doorstep.

Take a few minutes during this day to think of each of your children in turn. Call to mind the last time you saw each of them participating in an activity or experience that was alive and joyful.

What were they doing? How did they express their sense of aliveness? Did they share the experience with you? If they did, what was your reaction? What impact did your reaction have on them?

There are things you can do to encourage your children's creative exploration of their world. Besides engaging in creative activities yourself, you can make sure there are art materials, music, books, cooking utensils, and games in your home. And you can encourage your children to explore these activities by participating along with them, giving them permission to get dirty and make a mess from time to time.

You can also leave some holes in your schedule. An overscheduled child has less opportunity to explore than one who has some free time. And a child who is overtired is less likely to have the energy for spontaneous self-expression than one who is rested.

Perhaps the most important thing you can do is be consistently and warmly receptive to your child's discoveries. Your three-year-old bursts into the living room with a worm in her hand. Your eight-year-old proudly draws the scariest ghost ever. Your twelve-year-old gets all his hair shaved off and loves it. Your fifteen-year-old finds a sixties' tie-dyed skirt in the thrift shop that sends her into raptures. Your rational evaluation of each of these achievements doesn't much matter. What matters is that you feel the joy and the delight right along with your children and that you mirror their exuberance. "Look at that beautiful worm!" "That is a very scary ghost!" "You cut your hair and you like it!" "You finally found the perfect skirt to go with your cotton sweater!"

When your children share their high spirits with you, they are giving you the gift of their real selves. Hold their gifts tenderly and give thanks.

February 22 YOUR PARTNER'S FAMILY

Yet everything that touches us, you and me,
takes us together as a bow's stroke does. . . .[22]

—RAINER MARIA RILKE

The wheel of the seasons has recently turned past Christmas and New Year, the time when many of us reunite with loved ones for family reunions. Like many other people, you may have had the opportunity to spend time with your own family and also with your partner's family. You had the chance to sit down to a meal or a visit and experience once again the peculiarities you find endearing and the idiosyncrasies that drive you crazy.

What can your partner's family teach you about becoming a more conscious parent? Certainly you can see, in living color, some mistakes you don't want to make. When Aunt Bessie pats your sixth-grade son on the head and tells everybody what a cute little fellow he is, you remind yourself not to do that. You feel invaded on your son's behalf and promise yourself not to make intrusive remarks, even if they are well-intentioned.

You may also get a chance to see behavior that your admire. Grandpa Jim, down on the floor on all fours playing with Legos, reminds you to let yourself be drawn in by your children instead of imposing your own order and interests on them.

But the most valuable observations you can make about your parenting partner's family may come from what they can tell you about your partner. The more you know about your partner as a person, the more you will understand about his or her parenting. You may rejoice when you see loving interaction within your partner's family, because you can see where your partner gets his or her generous nature. Conversely, you may also be able to observe where some of the fear and anger come from when you watch your in-laws bicker with each other. You know that as painful as these moments are, they help you understand your partner's personality.

Ask yourself, today, what you know about the wounds your partner sustained in childhood. Do you know which places are tender or undeveloped? Do you know when your partner feels afraid or inadequate? Can you understand, from what you know about your partner's family, how this wounding might have happened?

In your quiet time today, focus on your partner and the places where he or she has been hurt. Maybe your partner was neglected or discounted or abused when young. As you hold your partner lovingly in your mind, surround him or her with gentle, caring thoughts and resolve to be as sensitive as you can to opportunities to help your partner heal from these earlier encounters. Know that when you love others in this way, you are sending powerful energy to yourself for your own healing.

February 23 ALL WORK IS WORK ON YOURSELF

The moments of crisis and decision—when we become fully aware—are junctures of growth, points of initiation.[23]

—GABRIELE LUSSER RICO

You know that feeling you get when you've reached the flash point with your kids. You feel like you're going to fly apart. Your rational, caring, adult self evaporates, and something more primitive takes over. If you've had a lot of practice (or you're in an exceptionally good mood), you may keep your reactions to yourself. But if you let your evil spirits escape and you open your mouth, you may say something you wish hadn't.

Some parents feel this way a lot—not just several times over the course of eighteen years, but several times a day. And sometimes these feelings of outrage are justified. Who can try your patience more than your child? If you are tired and worried, as parents are much of the time, you may feel like a bomb, going off regularly at timed intervals.

What's important is whether your reactions fall into a pattern. Do your kids make you crazy all the time, or are there certain times, certain subjects, or certain behaviors that can be counted on to set you off? The answer is worth knowing. Patterns of strong reactions on your part offer you an opportunity to learn something, when you make the effort to read beneath the lines.

One way to begin to see if there is a pattern is to make a mental note of such moments, perhaps even writing them down over the course of a few days, indicating what happened and what you did about it. After a few days, ask yourself some basic questions: What is my child doing that sets me off? How do I feel? What thoughts come to mind when my child acts this way? What deeper feelings might underlie these thoughts and feelings? Do these thoughts and feelings bring back any strong memories from my earlier life?

Let's suppose that a parent gets triggered when her children "talk back" to her. After thinking about it, she may realize that she felt the same way when her brother and sister taunted her when she was little or when her mother prevented her from speaking her mind. She feels hurt and vulnerable all over again. Realizing the connection is going to help her. She now understands that she reacts as she does because of *her* experience and *her* fears. The root cause of the problem lies within herself. Once she sees this, she can take steps to change her reaction to her kid's mouthing off. With a cooler head, she can figure out if she needs to do something to change her children's behavior.

As you carry this idea with you today, let your thoughts come back to your part in the daily dramas with your children. While we have a serious responsibility to educate and guide our children as they grow, in the end, if we don't like the way we are feeling, the only thing we can change is ourselves.

February 24 THE BEST PRESENT OF ALL

Loving parents spend <u>time</u> with their children.[24] —M. SCOTT PECK

Often it seems that time is the very thing we can't spend with our children, because we don't have enough of it. As tight as our budget is, we may feel as if we have more money than time. We don't doubt that Scott Peck is right when he reminds us of how important it is to simply *be* with our children, but *when* is the question. We know that everybody—basketball players, neuroscientists, artists, business owners—gets the same amount of time, but (we think to ourselves) these high-achieving people either must not have children at home or must have live-in help.

The fact is that the number of hours parents, especially mothers, have available to spend nurturing home and family has dramatically declined throughout this century. More mothers are working outside the home and must scramble for extra time in the early morning, evening, or on weekends in order to do the home and family work that must be done. Arlie Hochschild wrote in her book *The Second Shift,* "As masses of women have moved into the economy, families have been hit by a 'speed-up' in work and family life. There is no more time in the day than there was when wives stayed home, but there is twice as much to get done. It is mainly women who absorb this 'speed-up.'"[25]

Understanding the reality of the time crunch and appreciating the difficulties involved is important, but that still leaves parents with the challenge of how to give their children what they need most from them: their time and attention. Every conscious parent wrestles with this issue sooner or later.

If you were to set yourself a goal of finding an extra fifteen minutes a day for each of your children, where would you find it? What would have to change? Allow yourself to spend a few moments now thinking about this question, keeping in mind that you would want your children to know that they are the center of your attention during these extra child-minutes. You want to be able to see, hear, and sense your child fully; you don't want to be paying superficial attention while thinking about what to make for dinner, or worrying about why your biggest client didn't call you back during the day.

Some parents find that they can successfully center on their children at the same time that they are doing routine household tasks. Grocery shopping, meal preparation, combing the dog, watering indoor plants, and other household chores can be undemanding enough to allow attention for children. They find that it works well to include their children in as many errands and tasks as they can, with the understanding that being with their children is what really matters to them. Getting the work done is secondary.

Other parents find it easier and best for their children if they simply drop everything and become totally absorbed for a few minutes in what their child is doing and saying. They find that it works to return home at the end of the day, prepare snacks, and spend uninterrupted time with each of their children *before* starting household chores. They come to terms with the fact that their own agenda sometimes suffers.

You might find it helpful to think about your options for spending a little more time each day with your children than you do now. Every child needs time alone with each parent, but sometimes this extra time can be spent with all your children together, doing something all of you enjoy. Today, think about where this time could come from, and plan what you would like to do to make it happen.

February 25 DREAMING TIME

I can remember when I started cleaning fish. This stands out because it was the kind of ritual that makes a boy into a boy.[26]

—JAMES P. CARSE

Do you remember the long, lazy days of summer when you woke up in the morning and knew that you had nothing before you but glorious free time? No school, no chores, no lessons. You knew you were free to follow your own interests out the door, into the neighborhood, and out into the fields beyond your friends' houses.

Admittedly, life was different then. Your mother was home, you may not have had a television, there was no car, and everybody in the neighborhood knew everybody else. Time seemed to have a different quality back then. It went by more slowly, and there was more of it.

For many people, these are some of their happiest memories. They luxuriate in remembering stretches of unstructured time when they were open to the world, and free to explore at their own pace without being pushed along by adult schedules. If you, too, can remember afternoons of kickball with friends or rapt exploring along forest paths or listening to music alone in your room, you probably wish the same for your own children.

Today, during your quiet time alone, give yourself the pleasure of remembering some of these times when you were young. Ask yourself how you think these experiences contributed to your growth and to your happiness. How do you think children benefit by being free to participate in activities that are intrinsically interesting to them, without outside interference?

Do your children have such opportunities to dawdle and daydream? Would you like to see them have more of this kind of unstructured time, without the distraction of television or the demands of other people? How do you think you could set the stage for such dreaming time?

February 26 REMEMBERING

Personal stories stay in our memories because they engage our emotions.[27]

—JENNIFER JAMES

Three days ago we talked about keeping track of those moments when you have intense negative reactions to something your children say or do. You may have experienced one or two of these moments since then. Because this is such an important part of your becoming a conscious parent, let's take the time now to look more closely at what your experience has been.

If you can recall an instance of intense reaction, sit quietly for a moment and think about what happened. Once you have a good idea of what your child did to upset you and you remember how you reacted, ask yourself some additional questions. On what other occasions have you felt this way with your child? Can you specifically remember what happened those other times? What are the similarities between those moments in the past and the one that happened most recently?

In order to learn all you can about yourself and your hidden personal feelings, probe a little more and see if this pattern of intense reaction is like anything you have experienced in the past. For example, do you remember either of your parents reacting to *you* the way you reacted to your child? Does your child's irritating behavior feel like something either of your parents did when you were a child? Allow yourself enough time to answer these questions completely. The connections you make between how you feel *now* and how you felt *then* will be productive for you.

In your quiet time today let yourself remember a time when you were a child and you behaved in a way that was similar to your own child's negative behavior. Let yourself reexperience the details of this past moment. How old were you? Can you remember where you were? . . . what you were wearing? . . . the time of day? Now, do you remember anyone else in the picture? How about your mother or father? How did they interact with you, and how did this make you feel?

This kind of exercise will help you develop more sensitivity to your own child and more insight into your own reactions. If such memories are painful, let yourself feel the tender love that you as an adult can now have for the child you once were.

February 27 HELPING YOUR CHILD BE SAFE

The only way you can change is if you feel safe, and you can't feel safe if you feel criticized.[28]

—JOHN GOTTMAN

All of us need some measure of acceptance and safety in order to function at our best. Think of how you feel when the people around you are interested and encouraging in contrast to how you feel when you are surrounded by people who are critical and hostile. There is a big difference, and you can feel it in every part of your body.

Providing safety is one of the three primary goals of conscious parenting. The other two, which we will discuss tomorrow and the next day, are providing support and providing structure. Feeling safe comes from knowing that you will not be harmed physically or emotionally. You are in a setting that will allow you to go on about your business without fear of attack. You are free from fear, and even more than that, your sense of well-being is promoted by the neutral or perhaps even positive atmosphere that surrounds you.

Emotional safety is one of the overriding goals of conscious parenting. Everything a conscious parent does could be said to promote the child's sense of feeling safe. The child knows that the parent has his best interests at heart, that the parent will not cross important boundaries, and that the parent will not let his own needs get in the way of meeting his child's needs.

But underlying even this paramount concern for emotional safety is concern for the child's physical safety. To survive and stay alive is the primary drive of every living thing. And many parents report that they feel it strongest on behalf of their children. When a father holds and protects his baby, he not only *keeps* her safe, but he lets her *know* that she is safe.

As children grow, requirements for physical safety change, but the goal of safety does not change. No matter how old a child is, if he is sure that his parents will be there for him—no matter what form that takes—he will grow to be curious, confident, and adventuresome. A child whose needs for safety are met unevenly by parents who may either smother or neglect will be afraid. He won't try much and he won't trust much.

As you think about the many ways you help your children feel safe every day, think also about yourself. None of us ever outgrows our need for physical and emotional safety. Can you remember a time recently when you have felt especially safe?

What allowed you to feel that way? Perhaps you were in the company of someone who made you feel protected from outside interference. Perhaps you needed comfort and reassurance and you got it. Or perhaps you were alone and you were able to create an island of safety for yourself. What can you learn from your own experiences that will help you provide refuge for your children? Successful adults often talk about the importance of feeling that their families are sanctuaries from the pressures of the outside world. Is there more you can do to help your children live from that same sense of security?

February 28 SUPPORTING YOUR CHILD

We cannot do great things in this world; we can only do small things with great love.[29]

—MOTHER TERESA

Beyond providing physical and emotional safety, an essential part of your responsibility as a conscious parent is to provide support. Above all else this means separating the needs of your child from your own. It means breaking patterns of symbiotic behavior that may have taken root in your relationship with your child. And it means remembering that your child, no matter what his age, is in the process of becoming a separate, emotionally whole person who is learning to relate to you and the world around him as a unique individual. Of course you continue to nurture your connection to your child. But this connection is nourished, not by controlling his development, but by allowing it.

When we talk about supporting your child, we are really discussing the subject on two different levels. One level has to do with accepting and dealing with your child at the specific age and stage of development he is experiencing now. Children need different kinds of support from parents as they evolve through the stages of growth. We will be discussing these needs throughout the year in this book, and we also recommend that you read the relevant chapters of *Giving the Love that Heals*. The second level, and the one we will discuss now, is the kind of general support you can provide your child at *all* ages and stages of development.

First and foremost, you want to honor your child's innate need to express himself, to have his own opinions and feel that his point of view is being heard and respected. A primary way to do this is to encourage dialogue and diversity of opinion in the service of mutual understanding. As well as mirroring, you are conscious of your intention to validate and empathize with your child, even when you don't entirely agree with him. Although the specific ways you do this change over time, you keep in the forefront of your mind the goal of fostering his self-expression when he is small as well as when he is almost grown.

Supporting your child means being consistently available with your attention whenever he needs you. In a busy world this is not always easy to do, but no matter how distracted or uninterested you are at any given moment, you respond with interest and encouragement when he approaches you. This doesn't mean that you pursue him when he needs to explore ideas, behaviors, and friends on his own. If you set up appropriate boundaries with your child, you don't have to be afraid of his independence. You know that you will be able to maintain your connection with him by supporting his forays into the world rather than by controlling them.

A final, universal way of providing support at any age is to create opportunities for your child to express the joy of being alive. We are talking about having fun! It's best, of course, when you're both having it. Let your child see that it's all right to be silly. He can see you as a caring, vulnerable adult who isn't afraid of expressing your native curiosity, enthusiasm, and sense of humor.

Spend some time today thinking about the ways you encourage your children. Are you strengthening the connection between you by being available and interested? Do you also honor and validate their independent impulses? If you were to think of one way you could encourage something your children are doing at this point in their lives, what would it be?

February 29 SETTING LIMITS

Parents have children before they are ready, give them presents instead of guidance and attention, and fail to provide necessary discipline.[30]

—PUBLIC AGENDA

There are vast numbers of Americans who believe that parents are not providing enough discipline for their children. They look around and see a lot of children entering adulthood without the skills or the moral character to help them become successful, contributing members of the society.

Whether you feel the same way or not, you undoubtedly agree that good parents must provide structure for their children. In our view one of the primary responsibilities of conscious parenting is to provide clear boundaries and reasonable limits that reinforce a child's sense of safety and support. Setting limits lets a child know she is loved and cared about, and makes possible an environment where she can develop both the discipline and the creativity that form a healthy balance in a satisfying, productive life.

As a conscious parent, you will want to involve your children in discussions about limits. You can explain why you feel that any particular rule or expectation is in the child's interests and then listen as your child shares his views and feelings. Mutual discussions don't weaken your authority, but they do make it more likely that you will be able to set limits that your children will understand and want to follow.

Another way your children learn about limits is by being around you as you model appropriate personal boundaries for yourself and for them. One of the most important things children learn from their parents is where they end and other people begin. In all your words and deeds you want to show your children how to respect everyone's right to personal space, to privacy, and to the integrity of personal identity. Except in extreme circumstances, you don't read your daughter's diary, snoop in your son's bedroom, intrude into conversations that don't include you, interject your opinions into other people's discussions, or assume that your child's life is yours to manipulate.

In other words, setting appropriate limits is a balancing act. You don't want to be too lax, nor do you want to be rigid. If you are too lax, your children don't grow up with the core values and skills they need to be successful. If you are too restrictive, your children don't feel empowered to reach their full potential as the unique human beings they were born to be.

There are general guidelines for setting appropriate limits at each stage of your child's life, but you will want to adapt them to the unique personality of your particular child. Listen to your child, observe her, get to know her. Then you will be better able to walk the line between limits and freedom.

It's helpful to pause every so often and take stock of how well you are providing structure for your children. Can you see that your children operate from a clear set of values? Do these values help them become better people? Are they able sometimes to be self-regulating and self-disciplined? Are they cooperative when you work out together what needs to happen to keep them safe and supported?

Notes

1. Viktor E. Frankl, *Man's Search for Meaning* (New York: Washington Square Press, 1959).

2. Robert Ornstein and David Sobel, *The Healing Brain* (New York: Simon and Schuster, 1987).

3. Henri J. M. Nouwen, *The Genesee Diary* (New York: Doubleday, 1989).

4. Jean Guard Monroe and Ray A. Williamson, *They Dance in the Sky* (New York: Houghton Mifflin Company, 1987).

5. William C. Chittick, ed. *The Sufi Path of Love: The Spiritual Teachings of Rumi* (New York: State University of New York Press, 1983).

6. Mihaly Csikszentmihalyi, *Creativity* (New York: HarperCollins, 1966).

7. William Wordsworth, "Tintern Abbey," in *Introduction to Literature: Poems*, second ed., eds. Lynn Altenbernd and Leslie L. Lewis (New York: Macmillan, 1969).

8. Joseph Campbell, *The Hero With a Thousand Faces* (Princeton, NJ: Princeton University Press, 1968).

9. Lewis Thomas, *Late Night Thoughts on Listening to Mahler's Ninth Symphony* (New York, Viking Press, 1983).

10. Hermann Hesse, *The Journey to the East*, trans. Hilda Rosner, (New York: Farrar Straus & Giroux, 1969).

11. John Lennon and Paul McCartney, "I Am the Walrus," *The Beatles, 1967–1970* [Sound Recording], Apple Records SKBO 3404, 1973.

12. William C. Chittick, ed., *The Sufi Path of Love: The Spiritual Teachings of Rumi* (New York: State University of New York Press, 1983).

13. Marlene A. Schiwy, *A Voice of Her Own: Women and the Journal-Writing Journey* (New York: Simon and Schuster, 1996).

14. William Shakespeare, *Hamlet*, Act 4, Scene 5, in *The Complete Illustrated Shakespeare*, ed. Howard Staunton (New York: Gallery Books, 1989).

15. Terry Tempest Williams, *Refuge: An Unnatural History of Family and Place* (New York: Vintage, 1991).

16. Dylan Thomas, "Fern Hill," in *Modern Poetry*, ed. Maynard Mack, Leonard Dean, and William Frost, vol. 7, 2nd ed. (Englewood Cliffs, NJ: Prentice-Hall, 1963).

17. Mihaly Csikszentmihalyi, *Flow: The Psychology of Optimal Experience* (New York: HarperPerennial, 1991).

18. Thomas Moore, *Care of the Soul* (New York: HarperCollins, 1992).

19. Pema Chödrön, *When Things Fall Apart* (Boston and London: Shambala Publications, 1997).

20. Shel Silverstein, "My Rules," in *Where the Sidewalk Ends* (New York: Harper & Row, 1974).

21. William Wordsworth, "The Prelude," in *Wordsworth Selected Poetry*, ed. Mark Van Doren (New York: Modern Library, 1950), book XI.

22. Rainer Maria Rilke, "Love Song," in *Translations From the Poetry of Rainer Maria Rilke*, trans. M. D. Herter Norton (New York: W.W. Norton, 1938).

23. Gabriele Lusser Rico, *Pain and Possibility: Writing Your Way Through Personal Crisis* (Los Angeles: Jeremy P. Tarcher, 1991).

24. M. Scott Peck, *The Road Less Traveled: A New Psychology of Love, Traditional Values, and Spiritual Growth* (New York: Simon & Schuster, 1978).

25. Arlie Hochschild, *The Second Shift* (New York: Viking, 1989).

26. James P. Carse, *Breakfast at the Victory: The Mysticism of Ordinary Experience* (San Francisco: HarperSanFrancisco, 1994).

27. Jennifer James, *Thinking in the Future Tense* (New York: Simon & Schuster, 1996).

28. John Gottman, *Why Marriages Succeed or Fail* (New York: Simon & Schuster, 1994).

29. Mother Teresa, *Jesus: The Word to Be Spoken* (Ann Arbor, MI: Servant Books, 1986).

30. *Kids These Days: What Americans Really Think About the Next Generation.* (Public Agenda, 1997).

March

INTRODUCTION TO THE MONTH OF MARCH

We are like the earth, with fires and storms and gentle pools existing beneath our surface. Every so often this secret energy erupts into our lives, and we become aware that there is more to us than we know. This month we are doing what we can to coax these hidden sources of behavior into the light. We will help you focus on becoming more aware of why you think and feel and do what you do, and why you might want to change.

March 1 THE LIGHT OF CONSCIOUS AWARENESS

A dunce once searched for a fire with a
lighted lantern.
Had he known what fire was,
He could have cooked his rice much sooner.[1]

—ZEN SAYING

In our exploration of what it means to become conscious parents, we always come back to a central focus. *Do what you can to maintain and strengthen the connection between you and your children.* It takes some experience to realize that the connection between you can be maintained, even when you are angry or in conflict. Disagreements and disappointments don't automatically have to lead to permanent estrangement. You can be upset with your child and still let him know that he lives within the circle of your love.

Sadly, it does happen sometimes that parents and children "disown" each other. The breakdown is so complete that the damage almost can't be repaired. We grieve for parents and children when this happens. Most often, however, our unthinking or insensitive treatment of our children results in small ruptures that can be repaired if we recognize them and take responsibility for fixing them. These ruptures are like water leaks. Every so often the best-maintained pipes spring a leak. We can tell when this happens, because there is water seeping out onto the floor. When we see it, we pull ourselves together and call the plumber. But if we find the pipes bursting every week, we figure we better take more drastic steps, perhaps replacing them rather than trying to repair them.

Today and tomorrow we're going to take a look at some common ways that parents unconsciously—without thinking about it—cause small ruptures in the relationship with their children. These are not big sins; they are common, everyday sorts of offenses. As you read through our two examples today, see if they sound familiar to you.

You assume you know what your child wants, likes, thinks, or feels. "You're not very athletic. I knew you wouldn't want to go hiking Saturday." "Come on. . . . You don't believe that." "I told the waiter you didn't want any dessert because I know you're too full." Sometimes your unconscious assumptions aren't expressed in words directly but are incorporated into your thinking and show themselves through your actions. You may not bother to ask your son if he wants a birthday party, because you "know" he is shy. You may not check with your daughter first before signing her up for ballet lessons, because you just "know" she'll be a great dancer.

You override your child's wishes in favor of yours without discussion or understanding. "Forget it. You're not going!" "There is no point talking about it. I already made the decision." "I don't care what you want. We are not getting you that for Christmas. Period!" To all of these, we can hear the child asking, silently, "Can't we even talk about it?' It doesn't occur to you that you can stick to your original decision, which may very well be the best one. But you can *still* involve him in a discussion in which he finds out what's in your head, and you find out what's in his.

As you consider these ideas today, vow to sharpen your hearing. Begin to listen for words that sound like the ones we've just talked about. When you hear them, make note of them in your journal. They may be painful to write down, but you need to let yourself hear them before you can change them. They need to move from the shadows into the full light of conscious awareness.

March 2 I HAVEN'T BEEN PERFECT

How is it he knows about me, . . .
That I have not been
a perfect husband and father.[2]
—LOUIS SIMPSON

Even the most conscious parent has moments of unconsciousness, times when in the space of a few seconds we say things we regret. We don't stop to think before we speak. We forget entirely the primary goal of conscious parenting: to maintain connection by supporting the unique aliveness of each child. A minute, an hour, or a day later we realize the unintentional message we have sent.

You may be able to realize your mistakes sooner and correct them or prevent them altogether if you familiarize yourself with some of the more common forms that unconscious parenting can take. Let's continue our quick survey of common parental reactions that can disrupt connection.

You label your child. "You're such a timewaster." "You're so disorganized." "You're so lazy." "You're such a pushover." "You're so competitive." Laid out like this, these examples seem obvious and also endless. But labeling can be harder to detect when it is embedded in more subtle and complex communication. For example, "I washed your baseball uniform because I was afraid you wouldn't get to it." Now this could be a kind and thoughtful act on the part of the parent, or it could be part of a larger assumption that the child is lazy and irresponsible. Another example would be if a teenage boy knocks unexpectedly at your door, and you assume that he is calling on your pretty, outgoing daughter rather than on your quiet, studious one.

You make decisions for your child. "I went ahead and ordered that university catalogue for you." "I knew you wouldn't want to accept Mrs. Shaw's baby-sitting job, so I turned it down for you." "I told the coach you'd be happy to play second base instead of first." "I told your tuba teacher you'd rather play the third march, so that's what you'll be playing in your recital."

Ask yourself how you participate in these common mistakes. You can prepare yourself to recognize and circumvent any tendencies you may have in this direction by spending a few quiet moments meditating on this subject. When you find the time alone, let yourself release the tension in your body. Then become aware of the regular rhythm of your breathing, and hold in your mind these words: "I'm so happy that my child is her own unique self. I want to know who she is. I will clear my mind of preconceptions about her and allow her the room she needs to express herself."

March 3 EVERYTHING HAS A REASON

Everywhere you rest your eyes, invisible stories blossom.[3]

—LEAH HAGER COHEN

A couple we know told us a story about the consequences of an <u>unconscious</u> remark the father made to his teenage daughter some years ago. It shows what effect such thoughtless comments can have without the parent intending it. Our friends had given their daughter permission to drive the car into the city on a Saturday night so she could see a movie with a friend. Her father remembered telling her to put gas in the car before she left their small town. Somehow, she forgot.

Sure enough, the girls get to the edge of town and run out of gas. It's dark, and it's the middle of November. They wander up and down the unlit, rainy streets looking for a gas station or a phone booth. Finally, they find a phone, but the daughter won't call her dad. She is still remembering his parting words, which went something like this: "I don't know if I should let you go out. Remember, last week, you couldn't find your keys. You'd forget your head if it wasn't screwed on."

Naturally, she was reluctant to phone home and tell him what had happened. The girls tried to call a couple of friends but got no answer. Eventually, they saw a couple in the next block who, it turned out, were able to help. Now, the dad may have been right about his daughter's level of responsibility. But the way he expressed his concerns kept her from asking for his help when it was important to get it.

You may be able to remember a time when an abrupt or thoughtless comment from one of your parents made you reluctant to share something with them after that. Perhaps your mother was impatient when she tried to teach you to sew, and you got the idea that you didn't have what it takes to work with your hands. Maybe your father let you know that your poetry wasn't the greatest, and you never wrote again. We know a professional writer who at one point stopped writing for several years because of her father's reaction to something she asked him to critique.

If you can see how these negative reactions once affected your developing sense of your abilities and your worth, you may be able to recognize and stop your impulse to do the same with your own children. Parents do not have to be perfect. Not all unconscious interaction is permanently damaging to children, and there is no such thing as perfection. But why not have the courage to change the things we can?

Make this a day when you become aware of how you are expressing negative feelings to your children. We all feel like saying negative things to our children sometimes. But conscious parents don't say, "You'd lose your head if it wasn't screwed on!" Can you think of a time recently when you wanted to react to your children in one of the unconscious ways we've been reviewing these last three days? What did you say? Were you pleased with yourself, or do you wish, in hindsight, you had done something different? For the next week, focus on reframing any criticism, reservations, or limits you may want to express to your children. Use positive terms that will strengthen your connection to each other and enhance their self-esteem. Carry these thoughts into your conversation with your child as you talk quietly together before bedtime.

March 4 ACCEPTING DISAGREEMENTS

But every married person knows that "conflict-free marriage" is an oxymoron.[4] —JUDITH WALLERSTEIN AND SANDRA BLAKESLEE

We recently conducted an informal poll of people we know. We asked friends and acquaintances if they could recall the last time they and their partner had a disagreement about parenting. We asked them to repeat, as accurately as they could, the words their partner used to signal their dissension. Here's a sample of what people told us:

> "That sounds codependent to me. You're just being codependent when you praise her intention instead of waiting to see if she does it first."
>
> "What! You've got to be kidding. Why did you tell him that??"
>
> "Despite what your Dad says, you absolutely cannot go."
>
> "You did?" (said slowly, with raised eyebrows and disdainful smile)
>
> "You cannot say things like that. That doesn't show any sensitivity to her at all. She'll get the feeling that you don't listen."
>
> "We've gotta talk. I don't like what you just did at all."

In addition, there were one or two people who could remember serious discussions of differences where they ended up agreeing on how they were going to handle similar situations in the future.

Parents often react to each other in the heat of the moment by saying something that signals disagreement—shouts of protest and grimacing body language included. Once they realize they disagree, it's a good idea for one person to say something like, "Sounds like we better talk about this." Then they set up an appointment for later, after they have both had a chance to think about what's happened. Intentional dialogue is a very effective method for understanding each other's point of view and reaching a decision about how to proceed. The couples we talked to agreed that trying to resolve differences on the spot is harder.

How do you let your partner know that you don't like the way she handled a particular parenting situation? Do you think you would be more effective if you used what family therapists call a soft start-up? This is where you approach your partner in a positive or neutral way that lets her know that you seek a dialogue that will help both of you understand each other.

As you spend a few moments today in quiet reflection, center your thoughts on the reality that both you and your partner want the best for your children, that both of you are doing the best you can. You want to create a climate of love and acceptance that allows both of you to grow closer to each other and to your children.

March 5 A BETTER JOB OF TAKING CARE OF PARENTS

There is no more time in the day than there was when wives stayed home, but there is twice as much to get done.[5] —ARLIE HOCHSCHILD

If we want to do a good job of taking care of children, we must do a better job of taking care of parents. When parents are asked about the one thing they wish they had to make their lives easier, they often say they want more time. Some people, mothers especially, say they would use their extra time to get more done. They would clean the hall closet, or weed the yard, or make homemade wrapping paper. But most parents admit they feel selfish. They would use the time for themselves.

Let's have some fun today by playing with this idea of having extra time. Imagine that a magic lamp appears on your kitchen table. You rub it, and a genie appears. He graciously grants you the gift of *four* wishes (hardworking parents get one more than usual).

His first gift is the gift of an extra hour. How do you spend it?

His second gift is the gift of an extra half-day. How do you spend it?

His third gift is the gift of an extra day. How do you spend it?

His fourth gift is the gift of an extra week. How do you spend it?

Now, since we are having fun and playing with fantasy, let's say that Einstein was wrong, and you are not bound by the laws of the universe as we know them. You can instantly transport yourself anywhere you want to be for the allotted time, with anyone else you want, with no money restrictions, and with your heart and soul free from worries of any kind.

What can you learn about yourself and your deepest desires from this fantasy exercise? Specifically, what can you do now, in the real world where the laws of space-time really do apply, to help yourself rest and have fun?

Your flights of fancy may have taken you to Hawaii with Denzel Washington or Julia Roberts, but you may conclude that a real-world treat would be to read a mystery or a romance novel. If you can't spend a week doing underwater archeology off the shores of Turkey, maybe you can join an association devoted to underwater archeology. Even though you might not be able to go skiing in Vermont, you might be able to hike through the woods where you live. And you can always get serious about getting more sleep, which is the number-one desire of most parents anyway.

March 6 THE PERSON YOU PRESENT TO THE WORLD

> ELY: Your grace, we think, should soonest know his mind.
> BUCKINGHAM: Who? I, my lord? we know each other's faces;
> But for our hearts, he knows no more of mine,
> Than I of yours; nor I no more of his, than you of mine.[6]
>
> —WILLIAM SHAKESPEARE, RICHARD III

In the next few days we will be helping you explore your fragmented self, those parts of you which, through the conditioning of your old brain, are still with you, although you may not recognize some of them. We call these fragmented aspects of you the presentational self, the lost self, the disowned self, and the denied self. They are the parts of your character that you disguise, fail to recognize, disapprove of, or reject. They still operate in you, however, and are what speaks out most unexpectedly when you are interacting unconsciously with others, especially when you are responding strongly—and unconsciously—to your children.

Today let's look at the presentational self. Sometimes this is called the false self, because it is the part of you that you create for public consumption rather than the self you know internally. It may or may not be false, but it is, at any rate, an incomplete picture of who you are. You may be working hard to seem confident, dominant, loving, compassionate, rational, rebellious, creative, or well-educated in certain areas. What you know about yourself, however, is that a full picture includes a much more complicated nature, a good deal of which contradicts the image you present to the world.

Your real nature is not necessarily or even primarily negative. But all of us learn to disguise aspects of ourselves that we feel are less than acceptable and might needlessly complicate our relationships. Our sexuality, for example, is generally a private matter, one which we share only in part and only with those who are carefully selected. To do anything else, we feel, may be dangerous. Sometimes it is essential to disguise our fear and trepidation when applying for a job or entering an important meeting or social situation. And there are many other times when a clever presentation enhances our position.

But some portions of the presentational self are a legacy of the person we created to please our parents. Our old brain saw disapproval as a serious threat to survival, and so it helped us create a presentational self that did not generate this disapproval.

Problems arise when the person we know to be our truest, inner self is terribly out of sync with our presentation. Then, we function with less than full authenticity. In its most extreme form this lack of congruity can lead to serious neurosis. We trap ourselves into commitments based on the way we want to *seem* to be, rather than the way we really are. And as parents we are in danger of symbiotically forcing our children into creating presentational selves that are similar to the one that gives *us* so much trouble.

In your time of reflection today think about any disparity you might be aware of between the person you feel you really are, and the person you (sometimes or almost always) pretend to be. When you were a child, do you think your parents needed you to do be a certain kind of person in order to please them? Was this different from who you felt yourself to be? Now that you are an adult, do you feel that the inner and outer parts of you are in sync with each other? Do you act in the world from inner conviction? As a parent, are you aware of pressuring, influencing, or coercing your children to be different than they are? Could you be asking your children to reassure you about who they are, rather than encouraging them to become themselves?

March 7 WHAT'S MISSING IN ME?

An infant who has just learned to hold his head up has a frank and forthright way of gazing about him in bewilderment. . . . In a couple of years, what he will have learned instead is how to fake it.[7]

—ANNIE DILLARD

We have spent time looking at the person you present to the world and how all of us learn to be, in some sense inauthentic. Much of the time we are aware of these inner and outer discrepancies. We know that we are really not as confident as we pretend to be, or as optimistic, or as cheerful. But what about those aspects of yourself which are missing from you, areas that seem invisible both to you and to others? These parts comprise the lost self. They are traits, qualities, or functions that you never developed, and that are not expressed directly. They are aspects of human functioning—thinking, feeling, moving your body, and using your senses—that were ignored or discouraged at an early age and therefore "successfully" suppressed.

Again, the lost self is formed as a defense against the disapproval you experienced in childhood, usually from a parent or parents. Sometimes it wasn't disapproval, but the fact that your parents completely ignored these aspects of your functioning. It is easy to see how this can happen. Certain thoughts or feelings were clearly "out of the question," so you learned unconsciously to ignore them. Perhaps it was your natural desire to feel compassion; perhaps it was your need to question authority or to be curious about a wide variety of human behaviors and beliefs. Maybe it was your sense of being able to perform physical tasks like running, jumping, or moving your body freely. Maybe it was your innate sensuality, your ability to experience and enjoy the full range of sensory adventures available to you.

By no means is most of your functioning missing, of course. But there are gaps, things you "can't" do or don't think, feel, or sense. Certain abilities—physical, mental, or emotional—are not beyond your capability so much as they don't feel like options at all.

Awareness and observation can help you learn about natural parts of you that may have been lost. Observe your spouse, partner, or a close friend. Does this person exhibit skills, abilities, or thought patterns that would never occur to you and that you nonetheless envy or admire and wish you could possess? Ask yourself why, if these are desirable traits or traits that in your opinion would make your life richer, you feel cut off from them.

Now take a good look at your children. Can you tell whether they function in narrow, constricted ways that might indicate there are parts of themselves they are out of touch with? How do their lost selves and the lost self of your spouse complement or contrast with your own? Be aware of looking for new opportunities to reinforce freedom of thought, movement, emotional response, and sensuality in your children. Perhaps some of these missing components will resurface in them and in you.

March 8 THAT'S JUST NOT ME!

Fathers and mothers have lost the idea that the highest aspiration they might have for their children is for them to be wise . . .[8]

—ALLAN BLOOM

There is another part of your fragmented self, which you may have trouble recognizing. We call this the disowned self. It is interesting that your disowned self is hard for you to see, but not so hard for others to see. Not all traits of the disowned self are negative. Other people may see them as positive, but they are unacceptable to you, and therefore disowned by you. What you consider to be "out of control," for example, others may see as free expression. What you consider to be unmanly vulnerability, others may see as positive sensitivity. Your fear that someone would "accuse" you of having these traits caused you to lie to yourself about their existence within you.

"I'm simply not like that," you may say to yourself—and mean it. But you may be getting different feedback from others—a spouse or a close friend, or even your children. You may be sending signals to others about your ambition, your need to dominate situations, your need to control, or your poor self-image, and you may be completely unaware that you are sending these signals at all. Or other people may see you as far more self-assured, optimistic, fully engaged in life, and competent than you see yourself. The disowned self is a part of you that sends mixed messages.

In your meditation today, think about the kinds of feedback you receive from the people closest to you: your spouse, lover, close friends, and especially your children. Is there information there about how they see you that doesn't square with the way you see yourself? Remember that it is sometimes just as difficult to accept positive information about yourself as it is to accept negative information. It all depends on how you are used to thinking about yourself, what is familiar to you, and your ideas about what is acceptable. Can you think of five traits that your family would say are part of you that you have some reluctance to own? If you can, write them down and spend a minute or so pondering each one. Is there a way to connect with this part of you? Reconnecting parts of you that have been cut off takes time, but this would be a start. Whether the trait is positive or negative or neither, it is part of who you are, a portion of the self you were born with. Can you learn to love it as such?

March 9 THAT'S UNACCEPTABLE!

It doesn't matter who my father was; it matters who I remember he was.[9]

—ANNE SEXTON

As we have examined the various aspects of the fragmented self over the last few days, you may have noticed a common thread: Each kind of fragment is the result of the childhood internalization of a defense against disapproval. The disapproval is always seen by a child's old brain as a threat to survival, and the defense is always an attempt to distance the child from behaviors that call forth the disapproval.

This is also true of the last aspect of the fragmented self, the denied self. In this case the child learns to deny traits in herself. This denial is a rationalization for the existence of traits that the child recognizes internally but that she doesn't approve of.

In a family that feels strongly that anger or any manifestation of anger is unacceptable, for example, a child may repress and reconstruct her own angry responses so that anger, which is in many cases a useful and necessary emotion, simply cannot be acknowledged. "I am not angry. I am . . . [concerned, disappointed in you, feel a strong sense of injustice]," a parent might say. This teaches the child that anger is not acceptable. She has no way of knowing that anger that is repressed in the moment can erupt in other inappropriate ways—in unrelated situations, for example—or that it can become directed inwardly against herself. This is especially true when the child is not allowed to express anger against a parent.

"You're so . . . [emotional, irrational, unfeeling, grouchy in the morning, competitive, bossy, impossible to deal with, unpredictable]," says the parent. "I am not!" shouts the child, either out loud or to herself. She understands that these traits that she thinks she might exhibit are unacceptable, so she denies she has them or, what is more likely, creates a "positive" countervailing trait that gets her off the hook. She might learn that her natural drive toward competition at the age of six, for example, must be replaced by a need to keep people happy. "Competition is bad. It creates hard feelings; it's not ladylike." The child's competitive nature then translates itself either into an avoidance of competition altogether or into indirect and perhaps less honest forms of competition.

Make a list of all the traits in yourself that you dislike, fear, or wish you could exchange for something better. Then make a similar list of all the traits you admire in yourself. As you compare these two lists do you see how traits you dislike are similar to or connected with traits in yourself that you like? For example, if you wrote down "bossy " on your dislike list, you might see how it was related to "decisive" on your like list. Or "lazy" might be related to the more positive "laid back." As you look at the traits you dislike, can you see how someone else might see some of them as positive. Do you fear that some of the traits you dislike in yourself might also be part of your child's personality? Why do you fear this?

March 10 THE GREAT WALL

Something there is that doesn't love a wall . . .[10] —ROBERT FROST

All of us are familiar with the Great Wall of China, the greatest construction project ever undertaken by humankind. It was a defensive strategy designed by the Chinese to keep barbarian hordes of Mongols from attacking the northern borders of the empire. And to some extent it was successful, despite its horrendous cost to build and maintain. But in the end, the Great Wall was of little use against the armies of Genghis Khan.

In the end building and maintaining a Great Wall is an expensive and ineffective strategy. Ultimately, it is breached. On the other hand, a good example of a low maintenance, healthy geographical boundary is the border between the United States and Canada. It is a useful line of demarcation, safeguarding the integrity of each country, but it does not create confrontation. People, ideas, and trade flourish across it and on both sides.

Building *emotional* walls is a strategy that some people use unconsciously to protect themselves from other people and from ideas that are in some way threatening. Emotional walls are a fortress against the human interactions all of us require to enjoy full, healthy interaction. At the same time they are expensive in terms of spent energy, and lost richness and opportunity for growth. We miss a lot if our major stance in the world is to protect and defend what we have. And in the end these walls don't work to protect us from serious hurt.

Consider someone who is difficult to reach emotionally. We have already characterized this kind of person as a minimizer, someone who creates strong barriers against the world. The minimizer is emotionally remote and difficult to know. His world is a private place where he can retreat behind routine and structure, rote ways of behaving, or societal norms that follow rules, regardless of their immediate applicability. His remoteness, however, masks a fear of injury. He's doing what he's learned to do to protect his personal safety, but it is hard on his marriage partner and his children.

The minimizer tends to shut down opportunities for what he needs the most—validating and empathy. As a parent he is far more likely to walk away from or ignore his child than to see her for who she is and respond to her need. When the going gets tough, the minimizer withdraws. His child soon learns not to count on him and to leave him alone. This isolates them both from each other still more.

Perhaps you see this kind of minimizing strategy at work in yourself. Or maybe in your partner, your father, or your mother. Personal examples are not hard to find. And loosening the barriers is not easy. But using intentional dialogue to establish a pattern of nonthreatening communication is a start.

Think of a recent instance in which you or your partner or a close friend withdrew rather than talking a problem through. Plan to initiate a dialogue with that other person, even if it only takes place in your imagination. In your mind, or in actuality, make sure you are both at ease. Practice mirroring each other, validating each other, and empathizing with each other. Dialogue helps build healthy boundaries instead of walls, thus facilitating free communication from both sides.

March 11 WHO AM I, AND IS THAT OKAY?

It's frightening to think that you mark your children merely by being yourself.[11]
—SIMONE DE BEAUVOIR

The very nature of the connections we have *requires* us to develop boundaries for ourselves. It's a paradox: In order to mesh together successfully we have to define ourselves clearly to others so that we all know where we stand. We have to make these boundaries not forbidding, but consistent. And the ability to do this consciously requires us to act from a sense of who we are and from a knowledge of the values and principles at the core of our being.

Problems arise when a person presents himself first one way and then another, in an inconsistent way. This can happen when someone acts from an unconscious defensive strategy that derives from an incomplete sense of boundaries. We call such a person a maximizer.

Because a maximizing strategy arises from a need to please rather than from a strong sense of self, the person who relies on it will seem to others to be emotionally inconsistent. Sometimes a maximizer will concede far more than she wants to simply to keep a lid on a difficult situation; at other times she will react resentfully when asked to concede in a similar situation. Sometimes the people closest to her are included in her sphere of loving interaction, and sometimes they are banished to the outer darkness.

The ideas and opinions of others take automatic precedence over her own. And this is not because these ideas and opinions have more value than hers, but because she unconsciously feels that it is better to concede than to displease. She does not know where she stands, and so she will stand in a number of different places, depending on her current frame of mind. In other words, the boundaries move, usually in unpredictable ways.

And the maximizer also has trouble determining where other people's boundaries are. As a parent she will blur the boundaries between herself and her child, acting symbiotically. In some situations she will simply not let her child alone, pursuing him with her concerns, while at other times she will act out her resentment by staging an emotional scene to express her own need. Her child learns that the best way to deal with a maximizing parent is to attempt to please her at any personal cost. He will also learn that his own identity is indistinct and that he has no right to personal boundaries of his own. He will expect his parent to be "in his face."

As you look about you, do you see yourself or your marriage partner using a maximizing style? Can you see either your father or your mother in that role? Can you think of a recent encounter with your partner in which you or he/she felt strongly one way but acted resentfully to keep the peace by conceding? Plan to engage your partner, either actually or in your imagination, in an intentional dialogue to discuss this encounter. By mirroring each other, validating, and doing your best to empathize, discuss how this concession made you both feel and how you might have found common ground instead.

Maximizers desperately need personal time and space, yet they will never ask for it. If you are a maximizer, make a conscious promise to respect your own need for time alone and personal space, and at the same time respect your partner's similar needs. If your partner is a maximizer, create time and space for him/her whether you receive a request to do so or not.

March 12 LOVE IS NEVER HAVING TO SAY YOU'RE SORRY

It is no bad thing that children should occasionally, and politely, put parents in their proper place.[12]

—COLETTE

If you remember *Love Story,* a romantic movie from the early seventies, you'll remember its one famous line, "Love is never having to say you're sorry." At the time, we weren't sure what it meant. But it appears to suggest that if you truly love another person, you will never do or say anything for which you will have to apologize.

While this may be a comforting sentiment—especially if you see yourself as the person who will never be wronged, as opposed to the person who will have to be perfect to keep from wronging—it is exactly the opposite from the way we see it. We would modify the line this way: "Love is *learning* to say you're sorry."

Saying you're sorry must come naturally to some people, but they are few and far between. Most of us have to learn how to do it. We have to hear the lines spoken by someone else many times before we feel comfortable saying them ourselves. Many of us have to be on the receiving end in order to know how good it feels and how healing it is. And then we can be on the giving end.

Children who live with parents who know how to apologize are fortunate indeed. They learn their lines early and grace all their relationships with the gift of healing. They are able to reflect back on an interaction, see their own imperfections, admit them to the other person, and work out a mutual understanding.

If saying you're sorry is already one of your relationship skills, that's worth celebrating. Let yourself be happy that you are giving this gift to your children and your parenting partner. Be happy that you are giving it to yourself. When you admit your faults to other people, you are admitting them to yourself. When you apologize, you are apologizing to yourself. It's a short step from there to forgiving yourself.

If saying you're sorry is hard for you and you rarely if ever do it, then you can look forward to the opportunity to focus on this subject today and for the next few days. Think about the last time you can remember apologizing to someone for something you did. If your memory involves one of your children, that's good. If it doesn't, then a spouse, friend, coworker, or other family member will do. What was your offense and what you did you say to make it right? Now take a few minutes to recall a time when someone apologized to you. What did this person apologize for, and how was it done? How did it make you feel? Let yourself enter into that frame of mind again.

You may find that you can't remember apologizing or being apologized to. This is a clear indication that you have an important skill to learn. Tomorrow and the next day we will be offering you some suggestions for what you can say to your children in certain situations. People often find it easier to come up with their own apologies after they have heard someone else do it first.

March 13 SAYING YOU'RE SORRY

Many people have an almost mystical belief that someday, somehow, there will be a magic moment that will be absolutely perfect for change.[13]

—JAMES PROCHASKA

Today, let's focus on a kind of conversation that can be difficult for some parents: admitting you've made a mistake. Once you learn how to talk with your children in this way, it isn't difficult. But if these words are not common currency in your family, saying them can feel difficult.

First, let's consider how you can go to your son or daughter and admit that you didn't handle a situation as well as you might have. Here are two examples that are intentionally respectful of you and of your child.

Example 1: "When I thought about how I responded when you said/did . . . , I realized that I overreacted. I'm not entirely sure why that happened, but I want to think about it some more and see if I can learn what my overreaction says about me. I want you to know that I am aware of this. The next time a situation like this comes up, I will do the best I can to talk with you about it in a more productive way."

Example 2: "I want to apologize to you for the way I responded [or what I said] a while ago. I wasn't at my best. I think you may have scared me a little when you said/did. . . . What I wished I had done was [asked you more about it, waited a little and then told you what I thought, listened better, asked you what you thought instead of telling you what I thought, been less judgmental]. Next time I intend to do that. But for right now, I'd like to hear how you're feeling about what happened and what I said."

If your child is young, you will want to keep it simple: "I'm sorry I yelled at you. Tell me again what happened." "I want to tell you I'm sorry for [getting mad, not letting you talk, walking away]. That wasn't a nice thing to do. Can we try again? Do you want to tell me what you have to tell me, and I'll be quiet and listen?"

Each of these examples follows the same general pattern: "I'm sorry. I made a mistake. I realize that wasn't a good thing to do. Let's revisit the issue so I can try again." At the next opportunity, let yourself try out one of these responses. It may be that you will find the time you spend with your child before bed to be exactly right for saying you're sorry. With practice, you will be able to find your own words and make them your own. When your children are parents themselves, they will be able to tell their children they're sorry.

March 14 SAYING "NO" WITH LOVE

I am careful not to diminish self-worth."[14] —HAIM GINOTT

In our household, we try to say yes to our children as often as possible. But sometimes we simply must say no. It's not that it's hard to say that one little word. It escapes our lips rather easily in fact. But explaining *why* we have to say it takes a little more practice. Here is one possible "script" for explaining why you are about to frustrate your child's deepest desires:

> "I want to be honest with you about how I'm feeling about your request to do . . . . Frankly, it scares me. It's possible that part of my fear is coming from my own past experience and has nothing to do with you. That's a possibility I'm willing to look at. But I want you to know that I believe there is reason to be careful in this situation. If I gave my permission, you might [hurt yourself, get lost, not be able to control your friends, miss school, not get your homework done, be too tired to enjoy your day]. I want us to look at these possibilities together, so you can really understand why I'm turning you down."

Again, younger children need it shorter. "I want to tell you why I'm saying no. The reason is that I'm afraid that [whatever it is]. I want you to be [safe, rested, full, able to see your grandparents]. Okay?"

No matter how you say it, you are sending the message that you are turning down the request, and that you have a reasonable reason for doing so, one that you are willing to explain and discuss. Only you can then decide what constitutes discussion and what has degenerated into pleading, whining, cajoling, or threatening, either on your part or your child's.

You can see from these examples that it is possible to be open to discussion and still be firm. Sometimes it happens that your child says something to make you change your mind or modify your refusal. When these opportunities come up, they are wonderful, because you get a chance to demonstrate your flexibility and your receptivity to new information.

Can you remember the last time you said no to your child? In that conversation did you also explain your point of view and ask for your child's thoughts and feelings? This may be quite comfortable for you, or it may be foreign. If this is not part of your parenting repertoire, this is a good time to make it so.

A prayer for today: *I draw upon my spiritual strength as I contemplate what it means to be a whole person, with all the beauty and imperfection that go into being human. I rest in the knowledge that my mistakes and misjudgments are parts of me that form the whole. And that I am no less loving or lovable because of them.*

March 15 WORKING TOGETHER

Compassion and connection are most efficiently promoted by giving people a chance to experience the life circumstances of others.[15]

—ALFIE KOHN

Some parenting mistakes are made in tandem. One parent doesn't do something unconscious while the other one is innocent or absent. Rather, they act together as "partners in crime." Most often, their "crime" is in their polarization around a situation or an issue so that one of them is unconscious in a minimizing way and one of them is unconscious in a maximizing way.

Let's give an example. Suppose your fourteen-year-old promised to be home by six for dinner. You wanted to eat earlier, because you have a meeting at seven, but to preserve your vow to eat as many family meals together as possible you accommodate him. The problem is that he doesn't get home until six-thirty. When you ask him why, he doesn't seem to have a reasonable explanation.

In this scenario you become a maximizer. You go ballistic: "You never, ever do what you say you are going to do! You have no consideration for anyone but yourself! You're just like my father, selfish and irresponsible!" You get the picture. Your spouse, on the other hand, goes to the opposite extreme: "Do we have to talk about this now? Do I need to go somewhere where I can eat in peace? I don't need all this hassle." You also get this picture.

It's not that one of these reactions is worse than the other. Neither one is helpful. Now just for fun, let's imagine how two conscious parents would handle this situation. You: "Jeffrey, you have come home late. Later we can talk about why, but right now we are in the middle of dinner. When you weren't here by six-ten, we decided to go ahead and eat because, as you know, I have a meeting tonight at seven." Your spouse: "From now on, if you know you are going to be more than fifteen minutes late, we will expect you to call. Why don't you go on up to your room and start your homework? When we have finished dinner, you can come down and make yourself a sandwich. I'll leave some leftovers in the refrigerator for you."

In order for two parents to work this well together in moments of stress and tension, they need to be talking regularly about their children, and they need to talk often about the parenting issues and problems (and joys!) that arise.

During your quiet time today, take a few moments to breathe deeply and let go of the tension in your body. Center your thoughts on an image of a circle of love that includes you, your parenting partner, and your children. Within this circle, you can feel the warmth of positive energy that binds all of you together and keeps you safe. One or the other of you may get disturbed or out of kilter, but the circle of love keeps you safely within each other's orbit.

March 16 TOO MUCH OF A GOOD THING?

Remember that we deal with alcohol—cunning, baffling, powerful! Without help it is too much for us.[16] —ALCOHOLICS ANONYMOUS

You undoubtedly know someone, perhaps a friend or someone in your extended or maybe even your immediate family, who is addicted to alcohol or some other drug or behavior that causes personal and societal dysfunction. It is not too much to claim that every family in America today has been, is being, or will be touched by addiction.

As parents we are all aware that not only addiction but even occasional heavy use of alcohol creates questions and problems for our children. So many occasions in our society, including many of its most cherished traditions, encourage use and enjoyment of alcohol for adults. For some young people use of alcohol is a rite of passage from adolescence into adulthood. And short of our living within a completely abstaining community with no history of use, alcohol will probably present us with difficult situations and choices. Children have always been exposed to adults who overindulge, and now more than ever they are experiencing other children who make a habit of drug and alcohol use.

It's a scary scene, and we are not going to do more than touch on it here. Fortunately, we also live in a time and place where the magnitude of the problem has created numerous private and professional resources to deal with addiction. Unfortunately, the problem of addiction is not dealt with quickly.

We know that use of alcohol, like the use of any other mind-altering drug, is likely to set up situations where people act in unconscious ways. They may say things, think things, and do things that they would be unlikely to say, think, or do under normal circumstances. This does not mean that anyone who uses alcohol is an addict. But it does mean that excessive use of alcohol, and certainly other drugs, is risky behavior. It's risky because a person who is under the influence of even a moderate amount is likely to be at the mercy of unconscious fear, anger, and inappropriate emotion.

If you remember a particular instance when your child asked you something like, "What's wrong with Grandpa?" or "How come Aunt Jane drinks so much?" think about how you treated the question. Did you feel threatened by your child's question? Did you attempt to disguise what you knew to be a serious problem, both from your child and from yourself? As a conscious parent you owe it to your children to be honest with them about your own family's use of or abstention from alcohol or drugs, especially when they are exposed to the effects of drinking.

So, as difficult as it may be, it is worth thinking ahead of time about how you want to talk with your child about mind-altering drugs like alcohol. If such a question or problem arises, use intentional dialogue in a safe, calm setting, perhaps during your before-sleep time together, to structure your conversation. Remember that your task is not to sweep the problem under the rug but to deal seriously and lovingly with your child and her need to know something important. And remember that your own behavior is a model for your child as she deals with her developing attitudes about this aspect of social and personal life.

March 17 SAINT PATRICK'S DAY

I am of Ireland
And of the holy land
of Ireland.
Good sir, pray I thee,
For of saint charity,
Come and dance with me
in Ireland.[17]

—ANONYMOUS, 14TH CENTURY

In many parts of the country winter is now beginning to come to an end. At last! And in still other parts, spring is well on the way. Today is a day when many Americans of Irish ancestry celebrate—sometimes *too* well, it's true. This is the feast day of Saint Patrick, the saint who came as a missionary to Ireland in the fifth century to convert the Irish and, according to one myth, to drive out the snakes. In Ireland itself this is a religious feast day, but in this country it is a good occasion to celebrate an Irish heritage.

Not everyone can relate to this ancient saint, of course. And not everyone in America is of Irish descent. But it is the kind of day that all traditions celebrate: German, Chinese, Italian, African, Korean, Indian, Pakistani, Scandinavian, Vietnamese, English, Greek, Native American, Latino, Caribbean, French, Middle Eastern, Polish, Jewish, Yankee, Southern, Russian, and all of the other traditions that make up the New World. This is a day to remember your roots and share that connection with your children. If you are of Irish descent, you probably have already thought about whether and how you celebrate this day.

And if you don't celebrate Saint Patrick's Day, perhaps there are other days that you can use to acquaint your children with the rich tradition of their ancestors. Do you have a story of olden times, an old country, an old tradition that you can share with your children? Today would be a good time to look at an encyclopedia or a calendar and pick a time to plan for this celebration. What customs can you recreate in your home? What food can you prepare that would give you an exotic sense of an ancient homeland? This is a gift you can give your children and yourself.

March 18 PASSING ALONG MY OWN FEARS

Your responsibility as a parent is not as great as you might imagine. You need not supply the world with the next conqueror of disease or major motion-picture star.[18]
—FRAN LEBOWITZ

Parenthood is not only a time of challenge and commitment, it is just as much a time of hope and fear. Your child is growing and changing before your eyes, and you feel both elated by the possibilities and occasionally gripped by concern that his behavior is signaling something a little less reassuring. Maybe you see signs in him of things you are unhappy with in yourself or in your marriage partner.

For example, you may be unhappy with your ability to fit into social situations, and so you watch for signs that your child is shy or under stress when he interacts with other children. In your family musical ability was highly valued, so you not only watch for opportunities for your child to listen to and appreciate good music, but you may push them. Anger was always present and out of control in your childhood, so you are distressed to see your child express so much anger and in such strong ways. You have a strong sense of values, and suddenly you see your child violate one of them.

You are also sensitive to the negative traits of your marriage partner, or you were in the past. Your partner is (or was) so different from you, and now you see the same traits being expressed in your child. This makes you afraid, and so you observe even more closely. You may convince yourself that your child is going the *wrong* way.

So let's pause for a reassuring reminder, at the same time that we encourage you to keep observing. Your fears don't necessarily pertain to your child. He is not you; he is himself and no one else. Your life and his life are separate. He is becoming an independent, although fully connected, human being. And to assume that your greatest fears are being realized in him is a symptom of symbiosis, and a function of your inability to see him as a separate person. All of us need to be reminded that we are not fully responsible for anyone's behavior but our own. It's important to be sensitive to our children, but it's counterproductive to "paint the devil on the wall," that is, to forecast failure.

It is true that your child will exhibit unconscious patterns of behavior, just as you do. He is just as human as you are. And, as we have emphasized before, his unconscious patterns result from his defensive response to fear of disapproval, maybe fear of *your* disapproval. When you see him as an extension of yourself, you plant the seeds of the same prejudices and fears in him. Your fear of problems can become a self-fulfilling prophecy.

A few days ago (March 9) we asked you to make two lists, one that described traits you liked in yourself, and one that described those traits in yourself you were unhappy with. If you made up such a set of lists, refer to them now. Now, make two lists for your partner. Which traits do you like most about your partner and which do you dislike most about your partner?

Now, think about who your child is. Write down those traits that you are happiest about. Now write down those you are most fearful of. Do you see any correspondence among the traits that you ascribe to the three of you? Are there things that bother you about yourself that you also see in your spouse or child? Do you share some positive attributes? The traits that worry you in your child—are they actually part of him, or are they really coming from your fears for him? Do you see how some of the traits you think of as negative can also serve you and your child well in slightly different circumstances? Completing this exercise will sharpen your ability to see your family as they really are. You will start making connections that will increase your understanding of who you are as individuals and how you shape and influence each other in your interactions.

March 19 WHEN MY CHILD IS UNDER PRESSURE

Even a minor event in the life of a child is an event of that child's world and thus a world event.[19] —GASTON BACHELARD

You have probably already spent a great deal of time assessing where your child fits in and how she will grow into a fully functional adult. If you are like a lot of parents, from the time of her birth you may have been looking for patterns of behavior that would indicate where she might experience success, or where she might experience problems. There are some obvious things to look for.

First, since you already know something about unconscious behavior and how it arises, see if you can spot unconscious behavior in your child. How does she react when you and she are at odds or when her environment is stressful? Second, observe how she interacts with other children. Is she happy in the company of a large group of friends and acquaintances? Is she more comfortable with one or two close friends? Or, is she often solitary, preferring to spend time by herself? And last, think of a time recently when she was having difficulty. Does she tend to withdraw, or does she explode?

Let's focus on this last point. You already know something about personal boundaries. Does your child often build walls around herself for emotional protection? Or does she have trouble understanding where her own boundaries end and those of others begin? In other words, does she have a tendency to protect herself by closing down in difficult interpersonal encounters, or does she usually seem to give in to the pressure of others' opinions even when it makes her uncomfortable? Most likely, she does something in between, rather than reacting in extremes.

You might already recognize that we are asking you to observe what strategy, minimizing or maximizing, your child tends to use in moments of interpersonal stress. Please understand that by observing your child's tendencies, you are not building a neat little box with a label on it to put her in. Children are in a fluid state, and except in unusual circumstances, they can move back and forth along the spectrum. We speak here in black and white only to help you distinguish, in broad terms, between minimizing and maximizing.

Like every other human being she will react with unconscious behaviors when she feels threatened with disapproval and the loss of personal freedom of expression. It is helpful to you, as the parent, to see what form these reactions take. It is also useful to be aware of the kinds of pressures your child is facing at this point in her life. Ask yourself how you are helping her to resolve her unconscious fears and behaviors by providing safety, support, and structure for her at this stage in her development. At the same time, ask yourself how you might be reinforcing her tendencies to act unconsciously out of fear, insecurity, and the desire to protect herself. When you are fearful for her, are you really being fearful for yourself?

March 20 THE ISSUE OF CONTROL

Discipline is a symbol of caring to a child. He needs guidance. If there is love, there is no such thing as being too tough with a child.[20]

—BETTE DAVIS

We must disagree in part with Ms. Davis. Recently, when Harville was a guest on a nationally syndicated talk show, a point of discussion was raised by a woman who, from long habit and as a result of her own upbringing, believed strongly in spanking her daughter when she "misbehaved." Undoubtedly, as Harville agreed, spanking can be an effective way to stop a behavior in its tracks. It establishes the control of a parent and the subdominance of a child. However, and this is the point Harville was making, spanking leaves behind a residue of humiliation and a memory of violence that can have grave effects.

Trying to control a child's behavior through verbal or physical violence, even if it is not done in anger, is a form of unconscious parenting. When you express yourself in this way, it ruptures your connection to your child. There really are no exceptions. Even when you wait until you are cool and still punish a child physically, the injury is the same. You are operating from a script that you have inherited from a long line of unconscious societal and family parenting. You are operating automatically rather than being present in the here and now. You are not dealing in a loving and listening way with your child and the current situation.

Let's look at control as a way of parenting. Obviously, you are interested in teaching your child the difference between acceptable and unacceptable ways of behaving. But teaching is not controlling. When you are trying to control another person's behavior, you are acting out of your own need rather than from the need of the other person. Except in moments when your child is in real danger, the person you need to change when you are tempted to exercise control over your child is yourself. The goal of teaching moral and ethical behavior is served only by mutual understanding and the reinforcing of connection. And you can do this only when you and your child are connected by love and two-way communication.

Think about some recent experience during which you confronted your child's misbehavior. First, examine the situation. Was he really misbehaving, or was he merely being himself, acting in accordance with his age and level of development? Was his misbehavior in fact actually a symptom of something else that annoyed you or caused fear to rise in you?

Sometimes, of course, patterns of unconscious behavior are already well established in your child, and your child may need your guidance. In that case, your task is to try to interrupt the problem at its source. Perhaps the source is your consistent annoyance or fear. Did the way you dealt with this situation satisfy your child's need or your own? Think about who your child really is and what she really needed from you during this encounter. What could you do to modify your response the next time a similar situation occurs?

Try to envision how you could revisit this situation with your child and reestablish your connection to her. Using the methods of intentional dialogue—mirroring, validating, and empathizing—you might want to say honestly and openly, "You know when you did . . . , and I responded by . . . ? Well, I don't think I should have acted without hearing you out. I'm sorry. Let's discuss how you were feeling and what we can do about this."

March 21 THE UPWARD SPIRAL

The Child is the father of the Man.[21] —WILLIAM WORDSWORTH

The first day of spring. What a good time to think about growth! We have discussed briefly the stages of growth that every child goes through on the way to adulthood, and now we will explore some aspects of these stages in depth. As a parent, you know that you need to allow for and support this development of your child, and you need to know what this means in practical terms.

As your child moves from babyhood into greater and greater self-awareness and an independent relation to his environment, he deals successively with impulses that preoccupy him. First, he is totally dependent and attached to you, his parent. Then he has an impulse to

explore his world while still remaining attached. His impulse to establish his own identity follows and then gives way to his need to become competent in as many areas as he can.

These are the primary stages, and throughout his life he will repeat these impulses in later, more complex, contexts. It's like an upward spiral. As he moves through his life having mastered these impulses (or not having mastered them so well), he will revisit them again and again. If he has mastered an impulse well, he will use the knowledge and experience he gained to serve him in succeeding stages and life experiences. If he has not fully dealt with one of these fundamental impulses, he will encounter problems whenever he meets the same impulse later in life.

Beginning about the age of seven your child has the need to make friends and relate to them. We call this the stage of concern. He will use his mastery of the first four stages (attachment, exploration, identity, and competence) to master his relationships with peers. Finally, again using his earlier skills, he will begin to relate to an intimate other, usually of the opposite sex, and to develop the range of sexual and intimacy skills that will serve him as a complete adult. This begins to occur at about the age of thirteen and extends through puberty and adolescence.

In thinking about who your child is now, and knowing his age, you can probably tell which impulse your child is currently feeling the need to express. How can you tell? How can you tell that you are supporting his impulse? When you think about the road he has already traveled, can you remember how he demonstrated his need to express previous developmental impulses? Was there one that seemed easy for you to support, and was there one that was more difficult? Every parent finds some stages easier and more congenial than others.

In your quiet time today, think about yourself as a child. Do you remember a stage that was more difficult for you than the others? How did your parents support you or not support you in dealing with this impulse? Is this the same stage that has been difficult for you as a parent? Most parents will have trouble supporting the same development impulse in their own children that their parents had trouble supporting in them. This is what we mean by a legacy of wounding. This legacy exists in an unconscious parenting environment. When parents become conscious they can eliminate the legacy and establish new patterns of healthy connection that their children will pass on instead. A legacy of wounding is then replaced with a legacy of positive connection.

March 22 ATTACHMENT

The pressures of being a parent are equal to any pressure on earth. To be a conscious parent, and really look to that little being's mental and physical health, is a responsibility which most of us, including me, avoid most of the time because it's too hard.[22] —JOHN LENNON

Remember the first few days after the birth of your first child? It was a time filled with wonder and confusion, but also a time when the awesome nature of your responsibility hit you full force. This child was completely dependent on you! And what's more, this dependency would last you both throughout your life together.

During this first stage of attachment, you feel the romance of early infancy. And, while this romance never really disappears, it is soon tempered by the daily necessity of constant care and feeding. You may have felt overwhelmed, but you soldiered on by being ever ready to give feedings in the dead of night, soothe cries of distress, change diapers, and observe minute changes in mood and behavior.

All parents sometimes feel exhausted by the incessant demands of their new baby. It's helpful to know that you cannot go wrong by being totally warm and available. The constant attention is just what she needs. There is no chance that you will "spoil" her with too much holding or interaction.

Children who don't receive the holding and cuddling and loving they need at this stage can experience problems later whenever the attachment impulse reoccurs. We don't mean to scare you. You aren't going to damage your child through momentary thoughtlessness. But an unconscious pattern of response over time can do damage. The patterns to watch for in yourself, even at this age, are patterns of minimizing and maximizing in their more extreme form.

A parent who minimizes, that is, withdraws from his infant consistently and avoids contact with her, leaves her care to others or to no one, and allows her to feel isolated and abandoned, runs the risk of an avoidant, locked-in child who will have trouble making emotional connections. A parent who maximizes, that is, is warm and gushing and avoidant by turns, who sometimes gives the infant what she needs and then withdraws to nurse his grievances about the responsibility, runs the risk of a child who can never fully rely on parental love and learns to cling desperately.

When you have a quiet moment today, give yourself the pleasure of remembering what it felt like to experience your intimate connection with your child as an infant. If she has passed through this stage and is on to the next or even if she is nearly grown, that attachment you and she felt for each other is still alive and undoubtedly still a source of pleasure. Your child will not need that constant physical attachment at later stages, nor will she want it. But the memory of the way you expressed your love in the face of her infant need is still a vital part of your connection, no matter how old she is.

March 23 EXPLORATION

Tell me, what is it you plan to do
with your one wild and precious life?[23]
—MARY OLIVER

At about the age of eighteen months a child begins to break away from his parents and explore the world about him. He is probably able to walk, and even in his quiet moments he is more comfortable being on his own, as long as his parents are somewhere close by. His impulse is to find out what's "out there." The shapes, sights, smells, sounds, and tastes of the world await him.

But this is the first real transition that both he and his parents are asked to go through. He may not want to be held when you want to hold him. He has a drive to break away, and some parents, particularly those who cling to their child's infancy as a golden time, have trouble allowing him his independence. They have to understand that this is not a desire to abandon them. The child is still in need of connection. Those parents who cannot adjust to this run the risk of maximizing. They find themselves reacting strongly against a child's exploring impulse, as though it reflects directly on them instead of being just part of his need to express himself in a new and important way. If a parent doesn't support her child as he begins to explore, the child may become fearful of exploration itself. He will stop seeking opportunities to break away. He may lose his curiosity and begin to see the world as a fearful place.

Some parents react to a child's entering into the exploration stage with relief. At last, the trials of early infancy are over, and the child is on his own! The child sometimes resists contact, so the parent thinks it must mean that contact and, by extension, connection are things of the past. Such a parent may become overly critical and begin to establish "rules" that a toddler is unable to understand and follow. Rules take less time and effort than being present in the moment to support and guide your child as he takes those first few steps away from you. This is a minimizing response, and it addresses the need of the parent to be free of responsibility. If it is turned into a parenting pattern, the child may become convinced that he is alone. His connection to his parents is vague, and their support is not reliably available. He can't count on his parents, so he figures he's fundamentally on his own.

How do you support your child's need to explore? Do you applaud his independence while still remaining reliably available to him when he needs your presence or advice? Remember that this impulse to explore is going to be an ongoing aspect of your child's life and that he will always tend to deal with it in the way he learned at the stage of exploration.

Today, spend some time thinking about the way you explore your own world. Do you share your explorations with your intimate other? Do you feel insecure about the world and frightened deep down when you encounter new ideas, people, or places? Is the world an inviting place for you, or does it seem menacing and unfriendly? Your answers to these questions will give you some clues about how you might seem to your child, and how you might tend to react to his encounter with new situations. To help you clarify your own approach to exploration, you can complete this statement, "When I am asked to move away from my daily routine or to reach out to other people whom I don't know very well, I feel . . . ?"

March 24 IDENTITY

For success in training children the first condition is to become as a child oneself, but this means no assumed childishness, no condescending baby-talk that the child immediately sees through and deeply abhors.[24]

—ELLEN KEY

The growth of a child is a continuing march toward individuality. The child is learning to become a whole being, connected to the rest of her world, but with a distinct personal identity. Following her initial steps to explore the world around her, at about the age of three, a child will make another transition. At this point she will begin to try on new identities as she is exposed to the possibilities offered by her environment.

The sky is the limit. Any role is fair game, as long as the child feels that there are interesting possibilities available in exploring it. One day she will be a princess of an imaginary kingdom, the next a doctor, or perhaps a cowboy or a spy. She uses new words to convey the excitement she feels at being able to become, even momentarily, a character that attracts her. The stories and movies and TV programs and toys she is exposed to spark her imagination and fuel her passion for pretending. It's a creative effort, and she wants her parents to participate in the fun.

In their unconscious fear that their children are moving into areas that are nonproductive, dangerous, or socially unacceptable, some parents make a strong effort to control the direction their children's identities take. They disapprove openly of some and ignore others. They reinforce only the identities of which they approve. This is a minimizing approach.

Other parents, who have perhaps had difficulties establishing their own identities, treat this phase as if it were relatively unimportant. Although they allow their children to explore most new identities, they have trouble supporting the activity. They do not interact with their children about their changing roles so much as they ignore them. As their children play out roles in front of them, they provide little feedback and show little interest. This is a maximizing approach.

In response to a strongly minimizing parent, a child will learn to hide those parts of her that are greeted with disapproval and respond to them in herself with denial or her own disapproval. A child who experiences a strongly maximizing parent will likely develop a diffuse sense of self, not focused or secure, and she will lose parts of herself that are not reinforced—the resourcefulness of a spy, for example, the rugged individualism of a cowboy, the skills of a doctor, the artistry of a painter or dancer.

To clarify your own responses to the identity impulse, see if you recreate how you felt when you were little and played make-believe. Old photographs can help you jog your memory. Is there a picture of you in your cowboy outfit or dressed up like a princess or swinging a slugger baseball bat? Perhaps you were an explorer or a rescuing hero or a beautiful princess. Do you remember which characters excited you the most? Do you remember how your parents responded?

It may be easier to remember your parents' reactions when you were a little older. When you expressed a desire to have a certain job when you grew up or play a certain role, were your parents critical, supportive, uninterested? Did one or both of them have an absolute idea of who you were and what you ought to become, or were they open to your fascination of the moment, enjoying along with you the story of the future your imagination was spinning?

March 25 COMPETENCE

Can you make a cambric shirt,
Parsley, sage, rosemary, and thyme,
Without any seam or needlework?[25]
—MOTHER GOOSE

The primary issue that will begin to arise for your child at about the age of four will be his competence, his ability to master skills. And this will usually take the form of competition. He will want to run faster than you and his friends; he will try to jump higher, read faster, read more books, be the tallest, smartest, most knowledgeable, powerful person he can be. You may, in fact, see him setting up competitive situations with you and with his siblings and friends that seem a little "over the top." That's nothing to worry about.

Another issue that can arise is your child's need to possess things ("This is mine!"), and the natural object of his interest will be the parent of the opposite sex—this goes for both boys and girls. But this is a possession he cannot be allowed to attain. When he says that "Mommy is mine!" and means it, you must be prepared to let him down slowly. His mother will have to say, "I am your mother, and I always will be, and I love you very much, but I am also Daddy's wife." He is trying to assert his power in the world; it is not a threat, nor is it a sexual awakening at this age. But it is important that this is a game he doesn't win. If he begins to see himself in a power position between his mother and father, this will have negative consequences later.

How do you personally feel about competition? Would you describe yourself as a highly competitive person? Is winning an issue for you? Or do you see yourself as a peacekeeper, someone for whom competition is a negative experience? Do you see yourself as one who avoids competition? The way *you* respond to your child's competitive impulse will shape *his* attitudes. Minimizing at this stage involves a highly aggressive attitude toward winning, at least winning in areas that the parent considers to be important. Being too involved in a child's sports activities, especially in their outcome, is a danger signal. Maximizing, on the other hand, involves wanting a child to avoid competition, because it is dangerous to relationships, may lose him friends, or because the parent feels he cannot win and shouldn't try.

As you can see, a parent with a child at the stage of competence needs to walk a careful line between supporting his child's need to compete while not being overly invested in which battles he picks, nor in the success of the outcome. Consider your attitudes and that of your child's other parent toward competition. How do you walk the line?

March 26 CONCERN

Of all the needs (there are none imaginary) a lonely child has, the one that must be satisfied, if there is going to be hope and a hope of wholeness, is the unshaking need for an unshakable God.[26]

—MAYA ANGELOU

One way to look at the parenting journey is to see it as a continuing release of your child. You release your child a little more with every one of her independent steps toward her individual development as a whole human being. Yet you must learn to let go at the same time that you maintain your connection. The way you maintain connection is by providing safety, support, and structure. For many parents, this is easier when children are younger and becomes more difficult as they move outward, away from family and toward friends and classmates. This is a normal development at about the age of seven.

At this point your child will start to see the world of her peers, primarily same sex peers, as her primary arena of operation. She will still be coming back to you, to the security of her home, looking for your support. But beginning now she will be revisiting and reintegrating all the previous impulses she has worked through—attaching, exploring, gaining an identity, and becoming competent—in her new framework. This is when she learns how to operate within a social rather than an exclusively family environment.

Your task now is to accept her new friends, and particularly her one or two special friends, and welcome them into your home. Usually this is an easy and delightful experience. But for parents with strong minimizing or maximizing styles, it can be harder than it sounds. A minimizing parent appears to be uninterested in his child's special friends. Either that, or he disapproves for reasons that may be important or unimportant. In the face of parental disapproval his child runs the risk of becoming a loner, isolated from others and unable to welcome social experiences. She may withdraw into a fantasy world where she is not only alone, but lonely.

But too much emphasis on making friends and keeping them at any cost reflects the opposite, equally damaging extreme. The maximizing parent is more concerned about his child's popularity than anything else. Not having strong sense of personal identity himself, he encourages his child to submerge her needs for the good of the others as a safe way to navigate socially. His child will learn that taking care of others is much more important than her own needs. Unfortunately, this is not altruistic caring, but a self-focused caring that can be filled with resentment and a sense of martyrdom.

No doubt you remember the role that friends played in your life. How did both of your parents interact with them? Was either of them welcoming and gracious while still maintaining enough distance to let you work out the details yourself? What was your other parent like? Are you comfortable in close friendships, or are you more comfortable being alone? How strong are your friendships? Do you measure your social success by the number of friends you have? What lessons can you draw from your own experience that you could use to support your child's successful socialization?

March 27 INTIMACY

I only have two rules for my newly born daughter: she will dress well and never have sex.[27]
—JOHN MALKOVICH

Many parents look upon their children's coming adolescence with emotions ranging from trepidation all the way to dread. They have heard the horror stories from other parents of teenagers, and they remember their own difficult teen years. They see how negative peer pressure, dangerous sexual exploration, and drugs sometimes create havoc in the lives of teens and their parents. The primary fear of these parents is that they will have no control over their adolescent children.

If control were the issue, this would indeed be a problem. Throughout the adolescent years children are operating in areas usually far removed from the immediate influence of their parents, both with peers, and as they begin to explore intimate friendships, with some special person of the opposite sex. This is the age of intimacy, which usually begins about the age of thirteen and continues through the teen years. It is the time when the connection between parent and child can be and ought to be just as strong as ever, but when it seems that it is most easily ruptured and most tenuous. So once again, the real issue is maintaining the health of the connection.

There are many ways for parents to deal with the problems presented by their adolescent children. But when parents react unconsciously in difficult situations with children who are budding adults, their approaches tend to separate to opposite ends of the spectrum: On the one hand, parents may attempt to control their children by setting up a wide range of rules, some of them as silly as those John Malkovich jokes about. The other approach is to assume that the child can fend for herself.

The first approach, that of the maximizer, tries to take over for the teenager by attempting to think for her in all potential situations. Structure, which includes useful boundaries and well-understood rules, is crucial at this age. But it should never be imposed arbitrarily or without real discussion and agreement. Otherwise, a child under the tyranny of too many rules runs the risk of becoming afraid of doing the wrong thing and taking appropriate risks. She will become a conformist, one who acts automatically, regardless of the requirements of the situation. She is cheated of the opportunity to develop her own judgment.

The second approach, that of the minimizer, is to be uninvolved with his child's adolescent development. He allows the child to fend for herself. Not having been given any reasonable guidelines to work with, the child will attempt to make up her own rules of intimacy, which will often be in rebellion against the norms of society.

The parents of adolescents must become adept at maintaining connection with them in the presence of challenges to the connection. Many have learned to use humor and to become more sensitive to when to talk and when not to talk. It is helpful to remember that no matter how your teenager is behaving at the moment, he needs you—for support, for advice, for continuing to believe in him, for optimism about the future. If you have a child this age, take a few moments and think about how you let him know that you are there for him no matter what, and how you help him set the limits that he needs. How do you maintain your connection? Would he be able to approach you about problems he is facing? Are you prepared to talk with him about difficult problems, like sex, drugs, alcohol, and peer pressure if he brings them up in conversation? Are you comfortable talking about these intimate subjects in a way that is relaxed and respectful, or would you just as soon run away and hide? Have you thought about these subjects enough to have a well-reasoned and reasonable point of view? Does the way you live your life express your core values, the values you believe it is important to live by?

March 28 THE CONTINUOUS LOOP

We are participatory beings who inhabit a participatory reality, seeking relationships that enhance our sense of what it means to be alive.[28]

—STEPHEN BATCHELOR

Children aren't very good at hiding what they think. Even a child who has been punished for expressing herself tells you a lot by assuming a blank mask in the presence of her punishing parent. Sometimes the words are crystal clear: "I hate you. I wish you weren't my mommy!" Or "I love you so much. You are the best mommy in the world."

Often the heart of the message is carried in the body language. "Yes. I'm glad we're going over to Mac's house to play football." These words may be rendered meaningless by the droopy face and deflated shoulders. Or "I love it when we take a walk!" from a child whose whole body is bobbing and dancing with excitement.

Some children are more expressive than others, just as some children are more verbal than others. Each child gives you information in his or her own way. You have to be attuned to their particular signs and signals. In most ways you probably already are. You know that you need their feedback. Every person in your family is part of a continuous loop of information that affects and is affected by every other part. You and your children are cocreating each other, and you will find yourself growing through the joys and difficulties you encounter through the process.

March 29 I'M REAL

Please don't let anything happen to him.[29] —SHARON OLDS

One of the secrets of conscious parenting is knowing that part of the parent's power comes from letting her children discover who she is as a person. This means sharing the struggles as well as the joys. It means not pretending that you know everything, not acting like you're always right. Like everything else, it's a balance. You can tell your children too much, and you can tell them too little.

One subject that is hard to talk about too much is your parent-child relationship. Unlike a perfect performance of *Swan Lake,* which gives us pleasure because of the illusion that it's effortless, the process of parenting doesn't have to appear easy to be effective. It's okay to let your children know that parenting them is of paramount importance to you, and that you are learning right along with them. They wouldn't believe you if you pretended otherwise.

Here is a suggestion for the kind of thing you could say to a child of yours when you have decided to let him in on the secret that you're not perfect and that you are doing your best to learn a new way of being in relationship with him:

> "You and I have talked about how important it is to me to be the best parent possible for you. Loving you is the most important part, and that comes naturally to me. Nothing you could do would make me stop loving you. But a lot of the rest of being a good parent is a matter of learning new skills. I'm in the process of learning how to be what I call a more conscious parent. That means being more aware of both you and me—what effect my reactions have on you, how I can help you sort out the choices you have—that sort of thing. It's very much like the way you are learning new skills. Sometimes you do it well and things work out great. Sometimes, you don't do it as well as you'd like. And then you keep working at it."

True, this is a lot of words. You will know how to shorten it for children who are young or impatient. Take a moment to ask yourself what effect it would have had on you if one of your parents had said something like this to you. Would you have felt more loved, more secure, more connected? When you send your children the message that although you may not be perfect, you are absolutely dedicated to their best interest, that's the most comforting message in the world.

March 30 MAKING THE MOST OF SMALL MOMENTS

The tiger in the jungle is naturally whole. . . . Only with man is it different, for in man the life process that seeks its realization must develop through a conscious personality.[30] —JOHN A. SANFORD

Every time we see or talk with our children, we are given opportunities to strengthen the connection between us. We relish the occasions where there is plenty of time to sit down together and enjoy our conversation, following the twists and turns in leisurely fashion. But a high proportion of our contact with our kids is in fragments: partial sentences, incomplete thoughts, shorthand ways of asking if everything's all right, reminders to please take your hat!

Whenever you can, it's a good idea to enter into all interactions with your children knowing what is fundamentally important. Even when you're trading jokes back and forth and being silly, you are being silly *with intention*. Even when you're not aware of having any agenda at all, you know that your default purpose is to support your child's aliveness, the expression of her aliveness, and her connection to the greater world.

There are interactions where you are aware of more specific intentions than this general one. Your eight-year-old might have lost his gloves—again—and you might want to talk to him about finding them. But your underlying intention might be to let him experience a person in authority who can express disappointment or surprise at something he has done and still treat him with respect and maintain the connection. Your four-year-old might create yet another disturbance at bedtime to distract you, and your intention might be to let her know you have limits, that you are firm. In another encounter, your intention might simply be to remain open and cheerful no matter what happens.

You probably act with more intention than you realize. Most people do. They're just not conscious of having intentions. The following simple questions will help you see how intentional you are with your children. What was your very last interaction with your child? What happened during the interaction? Were you aware of having an underlying purpose for this interaction? If so, what was it? If not, do you think you really did have a purpose, but were unaware of it? If you didn't act out of an intention, what might have been an appropriate one?

The next time you talk with your children, pause for a moment first and form a goal for the interaction. Something along these lines: I want my child to learn from me what a mature response would be to the situation he is describing. I want him to feel supported by me. I want him to learn something about how to handle angry feelings. I want him to see my excitement over our trip to the zoo. And then check in with yourself afterward and see how you did.

March 31 MAKING THE MOST OF WHAT YOU ALREADY HAVE

Often, while I sang in the choir, tears would stream down my face for no apparent reason.[31]
—CANDACE PERT

There are routines that we and our children perform every day: We brush our teeth, take showers, call each other after school, clear the table together after dinner. And then there are rituals: We read stories before bed, go out to breakfast on Sunday after church, call Grandma on Wednesday evenings, watch *Friends* on Thursdays. Both routines and rituals hold family life together. They provide structure, as well as a sense of continuity.

Some of our most important rituals occur only occasionally. Christmas only comes once a year. Your child's birthday is celebrated only once every 365 days. Thanksgiving is also an annual event. These occasions are important for children and provide a wealth of opportunities for defining family identity, conveying values, and having fun. But there are many opportunities for ritual that occur every day, if we have eyes to see them.

Meaning is what turns a routine into a ritual. A ritual is a repeated activity or action that means something to the people who are involved in it. Here are some examples:

Light candles at dinner. This ritual may simply give children the comfort of warmth and light on dark nights, or it may carry more specific meanings, which are voiced in honor of a loved one or as symbol of religious significance.

After chores on Saturday morning, take your family to a favorite "kids' restaurant." This ritual may help your children know that we do the work first and then we relax, or that those who share in the work also share in the fun.

Buy your favorite pizzeria pizza every Saturday night and watch a family movie together. What an effective way to let your children know that their preferences are important and that they can count on your good humored presence at least once in every chaotic week.

Most families have more rituals than they realize. Think about the one we have suggested at bedtime. You undoubtedly have others. It might be helpful to list the rituals that mark the passing of the days in your household. Have you found ways to add meaning to activities that would otherwise be routines? You may feel good that there are so many, or you may wish your family had more. If you wish you had more, give yourself a few minutes to look for opportunities within the chores, activities, and entertainments your family already has scheduled. Do you see any? Perhaps there is there a new ritual you would like to add to your family life. It would make sense to talk over ideas for new rituals with your parenting partner. Together you can add meaning to the life you share with your children.

Notes

1. Paul Reps, *Zen Flesh. Zen Bones: A Collection of Zen and Pre-Zen Writings* (New York: Doubleday, 1989).

2. Louis Simpson, "After a Light Snowfall," in *There You Are* (Brownsville, OR: Story Line Press, 1995).

3. Leah Hager Cohen, *Glass Paper Beans* (New York: Doubleday, 1997).

4. Judith Wallerstein and Sandra Blakeslee, *The Good Marriage: How and Why Love Lasts* (New York: Warner Books, 1996).

5. Arlie Hochschild, *The Second Shift* (New York: Viking, 1989).

6. William Shakespeare, *Richard III*, Act 3, Scene 4, in *The Complete Illustrated Shakespeare*, vol. 2, ed. Howard Staunton (New York: Gallery Books, 1989).

7. Annie Dillard, *Pilgrim at Tinker Creek* (New York: Harper & Row, 1974).

8. Allan Bloom, "The Clean Slate," in *The Closing of the American Mind* (New York: Simon & Schuster, 1987).

9. Anne Sexton, "A Small Journal," in *The Poet's Story,* ed. Howard Moss (New York: Macmillan, 1973), entry for 1 Jan. 1972.

10. Robert Frost, "Mending Wall," in *One Hundred and One Favorite Poems,* ed. Roy J. Cook (Chicago: The Reilly and Lee Co., 1958).

11. Simone de Beauvoir, *Les Belles Images,* trans. Patrick O'Brian (New York: Putnam, 1968).

12. Sidonie Gabrielle Colette, "The Priest on the Wall," in *My Mother's House and Sido,* trans. *Una Vicenzo Troubridge and Enid McLeod* (New York: Farrar, Strauss, and Giroux, 1975).

13. James Prochaska, John Norcross, and Carlo Diclemente, *Changing for Good* (New York: Avon Books, 1994).

14. Haim Ginott, *Teacher and Child* (New York: Avon, 1972).

15. Alfie Kohn, *The Brighter Side of Human Nature* (New York: Basic Books, 1990).

16. *Alcoholics Anonymous*, 3rd ed. (New York: Alcoholics Anonymous World Services, Inc, 1976).

17. Kenneth Sisam, ed., *Fourteenth Century Verse and Prose*, trans. M. Staeheli (Oxford: Clarendon Press, 1962).

18. Fran Lebowitz, "Parental Guidance," in *Social Studies (*New York: Random House, 1981).

19. Gaston Bachelard, "The Phoenix, a Linguistic Phenomenon," in *Fragments of a Poetics of Fire,* ed. Suzanne Bachelard; trans. Kenneth Haltman (Dallas: Dallas Institute Publications, 1990).

20. Bette Davis, *The Lonely Life; An Autobiography* (New York: Putnam, 1962).

21. William Wordsworth, "My Heart Leaps Up When I Behold," in *Introduction to Literature: Poems*, 2nd ed., ed. Lynn Altenbernd and Leslie L. Lewis (New York: Macmillan, 1969).

22. John Lennon, quoted in *The Playboy Interviews with John Lennon and Yoko Ono* (New York: Playboy Press, 1981).

23. Mary Oliver, "The Summer Day," in *New and Selected Poems* (Boston: Beacon Press, 1992).

24. Ellen Key, *The Century of the Child* (New York: Arno Press, 1972).

25. Edna Johnson, Evelyn R. Shields, and Frances Clarke Sayers, eds., "Mother Goose Ballads," in *Anthology of Children's Literature* (Boston: Houghton Mifflin Company, 1970).

26. Maya Angelou, *I Know Why the Caged Bird Sings* (New York: Random House, 1969).

27. John Malkovich, interviewed by *The Independent on Sunday* (London), 5 April, 1992.

28. Stephen Batchelor, *Buddhism Without Beliefs: A Guide to Contemporary Awakening* (New York: Riverhead Books, 1997).

29. Sharon Olds, "Prayer During that Time," in *Wellspring* (New York: Knopf, 1996).

30. John, Sanford, *Healing and Wholeness* (New York: Paulist Press, 1966).

31. Candace B. Pert, *Molecules of Emotion* (New York: Scribner, 1997).

April

INTRODUCTION TO THE MONTH OF APRIL

The central skill of conscious parenting is intentional dialogue. We can do so much good by how we listen and how we talk. This month we help you to focus on this process of mirroring, validating, and empathizing and remind you every day to put into practice what you are learning.

April 1 THE BEGINNING OF SPRING

He sendeth the springs into the valleys,
which run among the hills.
They give drink to every beast of the field:
the wild asses quench their thirst.
By them shall the fowls of the heaven
have their habitation,
which sing among the branches.
He watereth the hills from his chambers:
the earth is satisfied with the fruit of thy works.[1]

—PSALM 104

April is the month of rebirth and resurrection. Cloudy, turbulent skies will become calmer and sunnier by the end of the month. The earth will start to green and flower again, and the songs of birds will begin to greet the morning sun.

This is a good day to let your senses wake up to the stirrings in the land and in the air. We were meant to live our lives in tune with the changing seasons. To our ancestors the coming of spring meant the beginning of relative abundance: more food, more sun, more freedom of movement. Their survival depended on their sensitivity to these changing currents.

We shut ourselves off from the natural cycles of life, death, and rebirth at our peril. Our personalfood supply may no longer depend upon our close attention to nature, but we still carry within us the need to participate in the natural beauty around us, even if that participation is no more than enjoying the sights, sounds, and smells of emerging spring. Today, let yourself be refreshed by the weather and the quality of the light outside. Talk a walk and expose yourself to the temperature and the rain and the sun and the wind, and know that your life is filled with new beginnings.

April 2 THE MONTH OF HOLIDAYS

Therefore let us keep the feast,
Not with the old leaven, the
leaven of malice and wickedness,
but with the unleavened bread
of sincerity and truth.[2]

—I CORINTHIANS 5:8

Easter falls within April in most years, and Passover too. Sometimes they are at the same time and sometimes not. For some families these are the most sacred holidays of the year; for others, they are family holidays that may have a spiritual or seasonal significance; and for still others, they may have very little meaning. If your family observes Easter or Passover, however, it can be helpful to think about your observance ahead of time. Every holiday offers opportunities for parents and children to enjoy special rituals and activities.

It can be valuable for the two parents in the family to ask themselves some basic questions first and then to bring their children into the discussion. You and your spouse might find the time to talk for a few minutes today about what you would like to do for the holidays, and what requirements are already built into your observance. Are you expected to go to church, gather for an extended Seder meal, go out to eat, travel to visit someone else, participate in an Easter egg hunt?

These expectations set the parameters for how your family will celebrate. But within them, there is room for individual and family expression. To find out what kind of expression, you might ask yourself what you are celebrating. Perhaps the religious observance of the tradition is important to you, and your real Easter or Passover will happen in a spiritual setting. Perhaps, on the other hand, the meaning for you is found in an appreciation of spring and the ever-changing seasons.

After you and your spouse have talked about these matters enough to have a sense of direction, it's a good idea to involve your children in the discussion. Your goal is to make the celebration a participative experience for every person in the family, no matter how young or old. Given that assumption, what would your children like to do? The answer, of course, will depend on whether your family has a spiritual connection with the holiday or not and how old your children are.

Whatever you decide, we encourage you to consider at least

one activity that symbolizes rebirth and regrowth. You can plant bulbs in a planter for forcing indoors. You can bring in a branch of forsythia or some other early blooming shrub for blooming indoors, perhaps pussywillows. You can take a walk for the purpose of noticing new buds and early blooms. Your activity can be simple, but as it is anticipated and repeated throughout the years, it can become a meaningful part of the holiday for your family.

April 3 BEGINNING AGAIN

We learn to do something by doing it. There is no other way.[3]

—JOHN HOLT

It's never too late to start becoming a better, more loving person. All of us have regrets that we didn't know *then* what we know now. We're sorry we didn't have the tools or the insights that would have allowed us to handle things better than we did. We wish we had had our act together from the beginning. Depending on your cast of mind, you could say we all need to be forgiven, or you could say that we all need to realize that we are unfinished works-in-progress doing the best we can.

January is a natural month for new beginnings, and so is April. This is a good time to think about how you are doing as a conscious parent. By now you have both specific information and a general sense of where you are heading. So . . . how are you doing? Are you happy with the way your relationship is developing with your children? How about with your parenting partner?

There is an easy way to assess your progress. You can use two yardsticks. You can ask yourself whether you are gaining more insight into your own behavior, motivations, and feelings. And you can also quickly survey your conversations with family members and ask yourself whether you are using intentional dialogue more often. If the formal intentional dialogue format still feels stilted and unfamiliar, are your conversations at least in the spirit of dialogue? These are two good ways to see how your understanding of conscious parenting is deepening and becoming part of your thinking and your actions.

If your answers are not what you hoped for, remember that you can begin again where you are, right now, and go forward from here. Dialogue is always a good place to start. Even after years of practice, we all need to stop and remind ourselves to mirror, validate, and empathize. This is harder to do when conversations are running hot and emotions are intense. But that's when it's doubly important.

Today, promise yourself that you will have at least one conversation with your children and one with your spouse that includes mirroring and validating. When you see what effect this has on you and on them, you will be encouraged to keep at it.

A prayer for today: *As I allow myself to pause for a few moments in quiet meditation, I rest in reverence for the cycle of rebirth and reinvention that is evident in all of life. May I remind myself to embrace without protest the rhythm of death and rebirth that is the essence of growth in my own life.*

April 4 WITH A GOAL IN MIND

We evoke a potential that is already present.[4]

— MARGARET WHEATLEY

Yesterday, we talked about picking up from where you are now and beginning again. To help sharpen your focus, you might want to identify a parenting goal for yourself in relation to each of your children. What is one thing you would like to do during the month that would help your children become stronger and more fully themselves? Once you have formed such a goal, it will help focus your attention on an issue or a problem that you think is important.

There are many possibilities. Your goal may be simple. You may want to spend more unstructured time with your child. You may want to commit to reading one story aloud at night at bedtime. You may want to sit down and listen to your child when the two of you reunite in late afternoon.

It is also possible that you will want to tackle something more complex. Maybe you have decided that you want to allocate some energy for teaching your child the steps in the dialogue process, and then you want to be consistent about implementing it in your daily interactions. Perhaps you are ready to be explicit about your child's chores and consistent in your expectations that they will be done. Or you may have decided to help your child learn a difficult task or skill.

This is a good time to pause and see what you want to focus your attention on next. You can write your parenting goals in your personal calendar or onto an index card that can be kept in a safe place. At the beginning of May, you can take it out and review it. Today, you can close your eyes for a moment and see yourself reviewing your goals and feeling very good about the progress you've made.

April 5 THE ROCK OR THE SOIL?

Let us teach ourselves and our children the necessity for suffering and the value thereof, the need to face problems directly and to experience the pain involved.[5]

—M. SCOTT PECK

As a conscious parent, you'll find it necessary to walk the line between being too rigid and too wishy-washy. You want your children to have a firm structure of values and beliefs within which to operate, and at the same time you want them to be able to question authority when that is appropriate. Your goal is to help them be independent thinkers who can make wise decisions within appropriate limits that must sometimes go against prevailing opinion.

This requires both flexibility and firmness and an ability to modify your approach as your child grows older. This isn't easy. But it helps to have the challenge in mind: You want to be firm on matters of bedrock values and flexible when you can on everything else. This means that you need to be wise enough to know the difference. What is important here, and what can I let go?

The problem is that life often presents us with situations where there is no clear choice between a bedrock value and one that isn't so important All the options may represent values we think are important. Let's take an example. Let's say that your twelve-year-old son must choose on a school night whether to study for a math test, practice his cello for an upcoming recital, or visit a friend who is in the hospital with a broken leg.

How would you help him decide what to do? You may very well say that it depends . . . on how he is doing in math, on whether he has been practicing his cello and is prepared for his recital, and on whether he promised his friend he would visit tonight or whether he could go tomorrow just as easily.

Think about a situation with one of your children recently when you had an opportunity to be both firm and flexible: "Yes, you can go shopping, but only for one hour, and then you must come home and do your homework." "No, you cannot watch TV now, but we will choose a program for tomorrow night." "Yes, I can loan you five dollars, but let's set up a way for you to pay me back." Were you happy with the way you handled the situation, or do you wish you had done it differently? Most of us need to be reminded how important it is to walk that line between relaxed and rigid, flexible and inflexible.

April 6 MIRRORING

If you bungle raising your children, I don't think whatever else you do well matters very much.[6] —JACQUELINE KENNEDY ONASSIS

This month we are focusing our attention on the quality of our communication with our children. Although we have already talked about mirroring several times, let's resume our discussion once again. Besides helping you and your children understand each other better, mirroring helps your communication in other ways.

When you follow the format for any of the three steps of intentional dialogue—mirroring, validating, and empathizing—you are preventing other common communication problems. Mirroring, when done right, prevents you from dominating or interrupting or criticizing or withdrawing or zoning out. When you practice it adequately, you are giving your child or your spouse your full attention. And when your child participates in intentional dialogue with you, you know she is giving you *her* full attention. You can't mirror if you're only half listening.

But the real benefit of mirroring comes after some days and weeks of practice as two things start to happen. You develop the habit of deep respect for each other. And you begin to know, deep down, that your child is different from you. You begin to feel how easy it can be to let go of any tendency you had to coerce or influence your child's opinions and feelings. You stop assuming that she is just like you. For review, here's an example of a mother mirroring her sixteen-year-old daughter:

Daughter (who is the Sender here) makes a brief statement: You never listen to me. I tell you something and it's like you never hear it.

Mother (who is the Receiver here) paraphrases the statement and then asks if the message was understood: You feel like I don't listen to you. When you talk to me, it feels like I'm not understanding. Is that right?

Daughter indicates that the message was correctly received and then adds a thought: Yes. Sometimes I feel frustrated that you think you already know what I'm going to say.

Mother once again paraphrases and asks for confirmation: So you get mad when I make assumptions about how you think and feel. Right?

Daughter makes a clarification: I'm not saying I get mad. But sometimes I get frustrated.

Mother again paraphrases to find out if she understood: So it isn't that you get mad, but you would like to feel less frustrated. Am I understanding?

Daughter confirms: Yes.

Mother asks if her daughter wants to say more: Do you want to talk about this some more now?

Daughter responds: I don't think so, not right now. I just want you to know why sometimes our conversations don't go so well.

Mother paraphrases: You want us to be able to talk to each other better, and you want me to know what you think would help.

Daughter: Yes. That's right.

You might be asking yourself how any child could complain about a mother who mirrors this well. But this conversation does provide us with a clear example of the format to follow when you want to dialogue with your child. It takes some time and effort to learn how to do it, but it is definitely worth the effort.

April 7 VALIDATING AND EMPATHIZING

'Tis a wise father that knows his own child.[7] —WILLIAM SHAKESPEARE

When you validate your child, you are sending the message, "I understand how you might feel or think a particular way." When you empathize with your child you are sending the message, "I am feeling what you are feeling along with you right now." These two messages help your child know that you and he are connected, and that you don't have to agree in order to *stay* connected. You can be connected and still hold differing opinions.

Think of how powerful and sustaining it is for a child to experience individuality within connection when he is young and to carry that knowledge into his life as an adult. It means he can differ with his wife and not be afraid of compromising their marriage. He can appreciate her individuality and not be threatened. And it means that he can more comfortably participate in the give-and-take of the work place. It's okay if he and his coworkers have different ways of understanding a problem or a solution. Everybody can make a different contribution and work together toward a solution.

Here is an example of a father validating his eight-year-old son:

Son (who is the Sender) expresses his feelings: I don't want to invite Jimmy to my birthday party. He told me I was a bad baseball player and he didn't want me on his team.

Father (who is the Receiver) paraphrases the message and demonstrates that he thinks it makes sense for his son to feel this way: It sounds like Jimmy hurt your feelings and that you don't want to invite him to your party. I can see why you would feel this way. Am I understanding right?

Son confirms: Yeah, and I thought he was my friend. And he isn't.

Father mirrors: So now you feel that Jimmy isn't your friend any longer. That must hurt. I feel bad about that too.

The last sentence the father says shows empathy for his son's feelings. His son is hurt, and the father feels the hurt. In this brief dialogue, the father mirrors, validates, and empathizes with an emotional moment in his young son's life. You can see how this encounter with his dad might benefit the son when you put yourself in the son's place. How does it feel to be understood and supported in this way? Is this something you would like to provide to your own children? You can do it by making intentional dialogue part of your everyday life.

April 8 DID I SAY THAT?

He glares at his children with the eyes of an inquisitor.[8] —COLETTE

All of us react unconsciously at times in reflexive defense against what we view as an attack on us or an injustice done to us. Can you remember such an incident in your recent past, when you stuck your foot in your mouth and either had to apologize or wished you could apologize or developed a "reasoned" argument for yourself about why it wasn't necessary to apologize?

Chances are that this *faux pas* was committed either in anger or out of a sense of injury done to you. For a split second you were convinced that someone was out to hurt you or offend you or annoy you.

You very likely confused an innocent action or, at worst, a thoughtless action on the part of an "offending" person, with an intentional act designed to cause you stress or injury. For example, you may have thought that the unobservant old gentleman who cut in front of you in the supermarket line was purposely intent on insulting you.

Many incidents of "road rage" come from a driver who takes offense at what he or she thinks is a willful act of disrespect on the part of another driver. These defensive reactions against what is perceived as personal attacks happen when you have a <u>symbiotic</u> way of being in the world. You feel like an injured party because, at least in moments of crisis, you see other people as extensions of yourself. "He should have known better than to cut in front of me," you rant when you believe that everyone else should see the world from your vantage point.

A person who is acting symbiotically expects others to read his mind naturally, to have *his* best interests at heart, and to follow the same rules he follows. He is sensitive to injustices against himself, even when he has not been injured. He expects to punish. He feels the need to protect himself when there is no danger.

Parents are apt to think symbiotically when their children's behavior angers, annoys, or scares them. It's sometimes easy to take your child's behavior as a personal affront. Can you think of times when either you or your partner has acted symbiotically in this way? All of us do it, so recalling such times is not for the purpose of assessing blame, but for the purpose of seeing clearly.

What kinds of conversation, behavior, or thought processes cause you or your partner to act symbiotically in moments of stress? How do you view these triggers in moments of calm? Do you sometimes wish to retract what you have said or punishments you have inflicted? How do you explain these incidents to yourself afterward? How do you explain them to your children?

April 9 THERE'S USUALLY MORE THAN ONE BEST WAY

Suddenly a different set of answers obtains, a different logic prevails. There is more than one way to make a peanut-butter-and-jelly sandwich.[9]

—STACY SCHIFF

Part of gaining maturity involves the struggle to see situations from all sides and make judgments that allow for points of view that may be different from our own. Becoming an adult, not just being a grown-up, means learning to accept paradox and ambiguity in the behavior of others. No one is or should be perfectly consistent. Machines and computers are consistent. People are more interesting than that.

It's particularly easy as parents to become invested in how our children ought to behave and sometimes in how they ought to think about certain things. We tend to be teachers to our children, and it's not surprising that we often express our authority in fairly definite, sometimes even rigid ways. After all, we say to ourselves, we are responsible for the way they behave and think. If they don't do things the right way, it will reflect poorly on us.

Can you see how easy it is to get yourself out on a limb that way? You want to provide guidelines. You need to support your child with appropriate boundaries. And you are a teacher: you have a responsibility to show your child how the world works. But at the same time, many of the rules you set may be arbitrary. Does your child always have to have a clean room? Is it always necessary that she be quiet and respectful at dinner, even when she is bursting with life and joy?

You can learn a lot by empathizing with your child and listening to what she has to say. If you listened to her as someone who really wanted to know what she thinks about things, how would your child express herself to you? How does she feel about some of the rules you have set for her? Does she know and understand all the rules *you* use to get through life?

Make a list of all the guidelines of behavior you can think of that you use in your daily life. Now from that list check all the rules that you consider to be essential for safe, considerate behavior. Have you discussed these rules with your child and listened to how well she understands them? If you are like most parents, there are some items on your list that you don't consider to be worth enforcing all the time. Have you explained the difference between a guideline and a rule? Are there some rules or guidelines on your list that are relatively unimportant but that you insist your child follow anyway?

April 10 WHERE DID THAT COME FROM?

If the new American father feels bewildered and even defeated, let him take comfort from the fact that whatever he does in any fathering situation has a fifty percent chance of being right.[10]

—BILL COSBY

We remember a mother telling us of an incident with her twelve-year-old daughter that still makes her cringe. She and her daughter were very close. They enjoyed each other's company immensely and tried to spend as much time as possible with each other doing errands on the weekends. This particular Saturday they were grocery shopping to prepare for having company over for dinner that night. The mother told us that her daughter was full of high-spirited energy, talking, dancing up and down the aisles, making jokes, asking questions. This was the kind of time they usually enjoyed together.

For some reason, this mother remembered she felt annoyed and then she turned to her daughter and said, "Shut up! You're wearing me out." Wow! Where did that come from? These are words the mother had never said and the daughter had never heard before.

The mother said it was as if someone else inhabited her body for those few seconds, surprising her as much as she had surprised her child. When we asked her how she and her daughter handled the situation, she said that after the initial shock, they started to laugh. They told and retold the story until it finally became funny.

Humor does wonderful repair work when the relationship is already solid and when the breach is comparatively minor. Sometimes though, more serious repair and restoration work must be initiated by the parent who has just committed an unconscious act of parenting. If something more serious had been required in the above case, this is how the mother might have gone about it sometime after the incident, in the car or at home:

Mother: Can we talk for a minute about what happened at the store?

Daughter: Okay.

Mother: I'm not entirely sure what happened, but I want you to know that *I* know that I was rude when I told you to shut up. You know that I don't talk to you that way, and I don't think about you that way. In fact, I love your high spirits and your company when we go on errands. Do you know that?

Daughter: I know, Mom. We usually have fun together, and you feel bad about what you said.

Mother: That's right. I don't know what triggered it. But I know that whatever it was, it's my problem and not yours. I love you and you don't need to shut up. Okay?

Daughter: Yeah, we're okay. I forgive you [*with a smile*].

Mother: Good. And you know that if I ever do want you to settle down a little, I'll let you know in a more respectful, loving way.

Daughter: It's a deal.

By now, you can see the threads of intentional dialogue running through this apology. It's clear that saying you're sorry to a child can be an ennobling experience for both the parent and the child. The mother sends the message: "I realize that I sometimes make mistakes; it's okay to make mistakes. What counts is what you do about it." The child gets the message: "My mom sometimes screws up, so I guess I can sometimes screw up and still be a good person." Relationships can recover and get stronger as a result. What an inexpensive way to teach an important lesson.

April 11 EMPATHY

The presence of friends to one another is very real; this presence is palpably physical, sustaining us in difficult or joyful moments, and yet invisible.[11]

—HENRI J. M. NOUWEN

Empathy is the vicarious participation in the thoughts and feelings of another person. It is the deep identification with the inner life of another. You allow yourself to *be* with the person, but you don't necessarily have to *do* anything.

When you empathize with your child, you let him know that

what he is feeling is understandable enough to be shared by someone else. You let him know that he is not alone. And you keep him company while he is experiencing what he is experiencing. This is so comforting, so consoling, and so sustaining. You probably know from your own experience what it is like to plead, "Just be with me. You don't have to solve my problems. Just be with me."

Sometimes this involves physical reassurance—a pat, handholding, hugging, or holding—although sometimes the reassurance is in the form of leaning toward the person, softening your body language, and moving closer without touching. Usually, it involves eye contact. And it usually involves words and sounds of assurance and support. You understand, and you are fully present and available to your child now, in this moment.

The next time you have an opportunity to empathize with your child, let yourself participate vicariously with his feelings without saying very much. Refrain from giving advice, offering opinions, or voicing either anger or sympathy. Let your child know that you are simply with him, feeling with him, in concert with him. He is not alone. You are with him. As we have mentioned before, the few minutes you have together before bed provide a wonderful opportunity to let your child know that whatever problems she faces, whatever conflicts or difficulties, you are there understanding and participating in her feelings along with her.

April 12 THE BEHAVIOR CHANGE REQUEST

Find the real world, give it endlessly away
Grow rich, fling gold to all who ask
Live at the empty heart of Paradox
I'll dance there with you, cheek to cheek.[12]

—RUMI

The behavior change request is often used in conjunction with intentional dialogue. This is how it works. You begin with all three steps of intentional dialogue: mirroring, validating, and empathizing. After an expression of empathy, the sender (in our example it's the father) asks the receiver to name three specific behavior changes the sender might make. Any of these three changes would make the sender's frustration obsolete. The receiver gets to choose which of the three changes he or she will make. It's a good idea for the change requests to be specific, time-limited, and practical.

Let's say that a father has just initiated dialogue with his middle-school daughter about leaving her clothes on the floor of the living room and dining room. The father is the sender and the daughter is the receiver. Because the daughter is young, she may need prompting to ask her father for his behavior change requests. Let's pick up the conversation at this point.

Father: Do you want to ask me about what changes I would like to request?

Daughter: Sure. What changes do you want me to make?

Father: I would like you to choose one of the following. For the next two weeks, you can pick up your clothes every night before dinner. Or for the next two weeks, you can keep from dropping even one article of clothing on the floor at all. Or you can help me install a coatrack in the hall and only hang your coats there; everything else goes into your room.

Daughter: The three requests are [and she mirrors each one back to her father]. I'm going to help you install a coatrack and hang my coat and jacket on it. I'll keep all my other clothes in my room. Okay?

Father: Okay. Let's shake hands on it. We will go to the hardware store this Saturday and get one.

It's a good idea to have a handshake or a hug after the behavior change request has been made and accepted. Physical contact helps reinforce the connection that has just been restored. Remember, too, that your child can initiate intentional dialogue with you and make behavior change requests of you. As you become comfortable with these techniques, you will want to teach your children that they work both ways. In the beginning they may need your help to come up with requests that are appropriate, specific, and doable.

April 13 PARTNERSHIP

We-ness gives marriage its staying power in the face of life's inevitable frustrations and temptations to run away or stray.[13]

—JUDITH WALLERSTEIN AND SANDRA BLAKESLEE

What do you consider to be the most important qualities of a partner? Perhaps you might respond with a variation of the following three:

1. My partner is more interested in the good of both of us than in getting his/her own way.
2. My partner looks for ways to help me and removes barriers for me when possible.
3. My partner is open and honest with me; is both trusting and trustworthy.

Partners usually agree upon and share common goals. They may, however, not always share a common way of attaining those goals. There is always the probability of conflict. It's inherent, because partners are separate individuals. What they have in common, however, makes them want to resolve conflict in order that they may both work together effectively.

Parenting partners have extra good reasons for wanting to cooperate harmoniously. But like childless couples, they are likely to have been attracted to each other in the first place because they have complementary qualities rather than because they are alike. As we teach in Imago Relationship Theory, people who are attracted to each other as romantic partners are likely to share conflicts. They choose each other because in some specific, definable ways each represents the difficulties the other had with his or her parents growing up. Each partner seeks to resolve basic parental conflicts that were unresolved in childhood and to complete the fragmented self by restoring parts of his or her personality that were lost, hidden, or disguised.

Against this background it is important to do a lot of talking—about what you have in common and about what you do not have in common. What mutual goals do you and your parenting partner share? Have you discussed them? Make a list of the areas of agreement you and your partner share (shared) about how to raise your child. What areas of continual conflict, either large or small, do you experience with your parenting partner? If you don't currently have a partner with whom to parent, what kinds of conflicts drove you and your former partner apart?

What areas of conflict do you (did you) have about how each of you sees the parenting role? You may be tempted to think of the very large problems you deal with, but are there smaller or underlying ways in which you both disagree? Would you call your disagreements discussions or arguments? Because these questions can generate a lot of emotion, it is especially important to remember to talk with the principles of intentional dialogue in mind. Mirror each other, and then validate and empathize. Dialogue will help you heal each other's childhood wounds and work together for the good of your children.

April 14 RESOLVING CONFLICT WITH YOUR PARTNER

Western wind, when wilt thou blow,
The small rain down can rain?
Christ, if my love were in my arms,
And I in my bed again![14]
—ANONYMOUS, 15TH CENTURY

You already know that close relationships contain within them the seeds of conflict. It becomes apparent after the "honeymoon" period of a relationship. Each partner comes to the realization that the other partner is not perfect, not exactly the person that each had imagined when the relationship began. As we mentioned yesterday, we believe that a primary way to work through the conflict that arises when power struggles appear in the relationship is the use of intentional dialogue.

Because your partner is an adult, it is possible to explain the use of intentional dialogue to each other in fairly mechanical terms. You already know that the components of such a dialogue consist of mirroring, validation, and empathy, and you have some idea of how these work. The trick is now to begin to employ them. The dialogue process may seem artificial at first, especially if you are not used to speaking with each other in these ways. But that's okay. Practice makes the process work.

Intentional dialogue works best when emotion is recollected in tranquillity. The time to engage in intentional dialogue is when the heat of the moment is past. It is especially important that you, the originator of the dialogue, the sender, are calm and operating from a desire to listen and resolve conflict. You can't have an axe to grind; you can't expect to "win" an argument. Wait for a moment when you are composed and in a cooperative, listening state of mind. You have to be open about the outcome, reminding yourself that you are more committed to the process and to the connection than to a particular outcome.

Now that you have prepared yourself a little, it's time to take the plunge. Pick a subject for your intentional dialogue. Choose something around which you and your partner have conflict. Make sure, however, that you are not so polarized that engaging in the process will be impossible. The "impossible" conflicts can be saved until later when the two of you are more proficient.

To begin the dialogue, ask your partner a question about something you said or did, and then listen carefully to the answer. "How did you feel when I . . . ?" (For example, "How did you feel when I told you that you eat too fast?") As you listen to your partner's response ("I felt like a child being nagged by his mother."), think about how you will mirror this response. When you mirror accurately you signal a helpful, open stance. When you mirror *inaccurately*—by adding detail that supports your point of view or by leaving out something important in your partner's point of view—you signal that you are having trouble hearing another point of view. As you mirror, keep asking whether you are understanding correctly. "Is that right?" or "Am I getting that right?" or "Is there more you want to add?"

It is important to hear your partner's own words clearly and to let him know that you have heard. Once you've done this, the rest is easier. You can go on to validate your partner's point of view and to empathize by understanding how he must have felt in the situation.

After you feel that you have completed your first dialogue, trade places by suggesting that your partner become the sender, while you become the receiver. You can dialogue about the same issue or your partner can choose a different one. You may need to do some coaching at first, and your partner may need to do the same. Keep trying until you have a workable process. Practicing now means that dialogue will become a natural part of your relationship at some point. You will incorporate its principles into an open, questioning, and cooperative approach to life. And you will have a very effective tool for resolving conflict and solving problems.

April 15 BECOMING A TEACHER

To disapprove, to condemn—the human soul shrivels under barren righteousness.[15]
—FREYA STARK

Sometimes it is easiest to learn something well, especially if it is complex, when you have to teach it to someone else. As a parent, you are already used to teaching your child. It's part of your natural role. So when you begin to use intentional dialogue with your child, you are operating within a familiar setting.

The first time you use intentional dialogue with a very small child, make sure your expectations are appropriately modest. Remember that it is the connection with your child that is of primary importance. You don't have to explain the process in detail, you simply interact from the love and support that is already a part of your relationship. As you practice mirroring with your child, it will become a natural and comfortable part of your repertoire.

When you are talking with a small child, you want to show the same respect and intelligence that you show to other people. Your child's vocabulary is smaller, so keep it simple and brief. More important than following a script for a full-fledged intentional dialogue is simply showing that you are present and available to your child. While you may not exactly go through the stages of mirroring, validating, and empathy in the proper order or with the proper mechanics, the spirit of wanting to hear, wanting to understand, and wanting to identify with your child's feelings will come through. All the components are there; they are simply in another form.

If you are just starting to use dialogue with your young child, it is best to choose a subject around which it is easy to establish your connection. Don't start with an area of conflict between you. You want to remain calm and helpful rather than become emotionally overwrought. The subject may, however, be one where your child is having some trouble. Maybe he is unable to perform a task to his liking, or maybe he has experienced a conflict with another child, a sibling, or another adult. Any area where you observe your child acting from anger or fear is a good one.

Remember also that you are not trying to rescue your child. What you are attempting to do is to enable your child to express himself to himself and to you in a way that is consoling and helpful to him. Mirroring is centrally important. You will want to keep mirroring until your child lets you know that you've got it. It is confirming for a child when you help him verbalize what is bothering him. Validating may consist simply of moral support for his point of view, as long as it doesn't slip into complete identification with any hurt he may be feeling. A long hug may be all he needs to let him feel your empathy.

April 16 YOUR SCHOOL-AGE CHILD

. . . I would have you early prepare yourself for disappointments, which are heavy in proportion to their being surprising.[16]

—LADY MARY WORTLEY MONTAGU

A school-age child faces many challenges, and chances are many of them occur when she is not in your presence. But even when the problems take place on the playground instead of at home, your being available to talk about them with her is very important. Intentional dialogue can become a major tool for sorting out feelings, solving problems, handling conflicts, and learning new skills. She might be having problems with certain subjects; problems with friends who exclude her or make fun of her; problems with her brothers and sisters. There are endless possibilities.

As a close observer of your child, you know which situations are stressful and which call forth frustration, anger, or fear. You can use one of these situations to introduce her to the process of intentional dialogue and begin teaching her how it works.

Because your child is older, you can be a little more explicit about what you are doing. You can explain the process and engage your child's support. Again, always use language that she can understand without talking down to her. Intentional dialogue is a process of mutual support and also of mutual respect. Initiate a dialogue only when your own emotions are under control and when you are feeling calm and collected.

Watch for opportunities to follow up emotional situations with your child with dialogue about what happened and how she feels. If she needs to express anger, even if it is directed at you, you should be ready to hear her out. Sometimes the most important thing you can do is hold her and love her and save the formal dialogue for later. If so, make an appointment to discuss the subject when things have cooled down.

Your child may be able to tell you in a fairly straightforward manner what she thinks her problem is, but she may need some help putting it into words. This can be part of the mirroring process. Keep an open mind and be aware of listening. Keep asking, as you mirror, "Is that what you mean?" "Is this right?" "Is there more about that that you want to say?" Don't try to add meaning or subtract information from your mirroring. Try to give her back the same information she is giving you. When you use slightly different words, this can be helpful to her because it can help her refine her understanding of what she wants to say.

Validating is now a more complicated process than it is with a young child, and it's very important. It's not enough for you to be silently supportive, although that's important too. Your validation of the way she sees things doesn't mean that you agree with her point of view, and it's okay to say that, as long as you aren't trying to argue her out of the way *she* sees things. The primary purpose of validation is to give the child the sense that her viewpoint, given the circumstances, is a legitimate way of viewing the problem, even if it isn't the only way.

Empathy now takes the form of real, verbal support as well as hugs. It may also take the form of advice, as long as she wants your advice and as long as you give it after you identify and support the validity of her point of view. You can let her know how you might handle a similar situation yourself and refrain from telling her how she ought to feel or what she ought to do simply because that's the way you would handle it.

After you try one or two intentional dialogues, take some time to think about what happened and how things worked—or didn't work. Reviewing these early experiences and doing some analysis of them afterward will help you understand what's working and what isn't as well as how you will proceed next time. It will also will give you a sense of accomplishment as you begin to see the positive effects of the process on yourself and your child.

April 17 WORKING WITH OLDER CHILDREN

A child is not a salmon mousse. . . . Your job is to help them overcome the disabilities associated with their size and inexperience so that they get on with being that larger person.[17]

—BARBARA EHRENREICH

If you are beginning to work with establishing a habit of intentional dialogue with an older child, one who is already an adolescent or who is entering adolescence, there are some important considerations to bear in mind. First of all, this is a time when your child is farther out of your immediate sphere of influence than at any previous age. Although your connection to your child is just as critical, maybe even more critical than ever before, it may seem more tenuous to you. He is experiencing more and more the peer pressures that parents fear. So you are more likely to have emotionally charged interactions with your child at this age because of your own fears rather than your child's fears.

Second, your child may seem practically grown up. This is an illusion. Although he has the vocabulary and the emotions of an adult (and perhaps the size), he hasn't got the experience. You may be tempted to treat him more symbiotically because of your feeling that he can now understand you and respond to you as you are. Your own insecurities may be closer to the surface than they were before.

If you have already established a pattern of close communication with your child, you will not have serious problems maintaining it. If, on the other hand, you are feeling distanced from your child, you will want to be intentional in your conversation with him. Carefully select a topic for your intentional dialogue that is significant for him and not too contentious. It might make sense to suggest an issue that is stressful for him, but not for you. You want to remain on solid ground and keep your composure.

Better yet, take your cues from something that he himself raises as an issue. Maybe he has problems with a coworker at an after-school job or difficulties managing his busy schedule or worries about his social life. The things that bother you such as why he doesn't clean his room or why you don't like his girlfriend, can wait until both of you have some experience using dialogue as a means of connection.

At this age you can talk to him in detail about all of the phases in the intentional dialogue process. It's okay to explain to your child what you are doing, because you want him to be an active partner in working through the process. The most important part of the process is listening with respect, which is demonstrated by accurate mirroring. Your validation of his point of view will be critical. And the empathy you demonstrate will be obvious to him if, and only if, you allow him to verbally explore his options openly without shutting out the possibilities you don't want to hear about.

This will be a rewarding experience if you have patience. As you begin intentional dialogue with your older child, remember that maintaining your loving connection to him is the most important outcome of the process. He will be closely observing you and making note of whether you are modeling your values. You have to be able to walk the walk, as well as talk the talk. Children keep you honest. Before you initiate dialogue, think carefully about your core values and how you want to model them through this interchange.

April 18 INTENTIONAL DIALOGUE AT THE ATTACHMENT STAGE?

A child is beset with long traditions.[18] —ALICE MEYNELL

You may think it's odd to speak of using intentional dialogue with infants, but in fact the stage of attachment is the easiest time to establish such a pattern. You and your infant child already have the kind of intimate communication that is required. Your mutual attachment and her complete dependence on you is obvious. You experience the magic of cuddling and close physical contact, and you feel the awesome importance of parenting most profoundly.

Of course, your ability to use dialogue is limited by your child's early stage of verbal development. But there is no reason that you shouldn't speak lovingly and clearly to your child at every stage of her life. If nothing else, the relaxed and loving tone of your voice carries a great deal of meaning, as does your angry, stressed-out tone of voice.

At this stage, mirroring is the most significant part of intentional dialogue. It will establish the model you will use later, when verbal communication becomes more important. For now, it is important to mirror what your baby says and does as exactly as possible. You become a flat mirror, laughing when she laughs, clapping when she claps, frowning when she frowns. If she coos and gurgles, you do also. If, however, your baby is under stress, then this is obviously not the time to respond with distress but to move directly into loving physical contact. She will experience this as validating and empathizing, as you soothe and comfort her.

If your child is at the attachment stage as you are reading this, you are lucky, because you can build the connection between you steadily throughout her life. If your child is already way beyond the infant stage, don't worry; it is never too late. The next time you feel distanced from your older child, remember the wondrous love and connection you felt with her when she was an infant. It is still there, just waiting for you to acknowledge and nurture it.

April 19 EXPLORING

The world is so full of a number of things,
I'm sure we should all be as happy as kings.[19]

—ROBERT LOUIS STEVENSON

By the time your child is a toddler at the exploration stage—beginning to explore his immediate environment and branch out on his own, able to walk and accruing a vocabulary at an astounding rate—you have an opportunity to nurture the connection between you, even when the two of you are not face-to-face. His impulse to explore will lead him into areas where he is both brave and fearful. These explorations will provide perfect opportunities for dialogue.

Your own impulse at this stage may be to overprotect your child. You may be especially fearful when he starts exploring areas that raise your own fears. On the other hand, when he is safely in the care of someone else and away from you for a time, you may be glad of the peace and quiet. For his part, he may be glad to be out on his own, but he needs to know that you are there waiting to protect him when *he* needs it.

With a child this age, natural opportunities for intentional dialogue occur when your child has hurt himself or becomes fearful or begins to doubt his natural impulse to explore. Whatever the subject of your conversation, you will be supporting his impulse to explore in the best possible way if you are calm and relaxed about what he is doing at the same time that you are setting limits for his safety. If he scares you by exploring too far afield, you will want to compose yourself before you talk to him about it.

Your child is now able to understand a great deal of what you say, even if his vocabulary doesn't let him respond at your level, so you will want to speak calmly and in a straightforward way, not using baby talk, as you initiate the dialogue. Listening and mirroring will probably involve a good deal of rephrasing to help the child get to the real nature of his fears and feelings. Your tendency may be either to tell him that there is nothing to fear or to overreact to the danger. Instead, you will want to be intentional about listening and letting your child know that it's okay to be fearful. That's the validation. And as you empathize, which will probably include a hug, it is a good idea to let him decide how he feels about his injury now that the danger is past. You can both decide whether he wants to continue his exploration now or at some later time. This lets him know that you are there to support him and that his impulse to explore is fine with you as long as there is no real danger.

If your child is at the age of exploration, think about how you can use intentional dialogue to help him feel confident about new situations and deal with the frustrations that will inevitably surprise him as he learns about the wide, wonderful world. If you have an older child, take a few moments to think about how you want to continue to support his lifelong impulse to explore and try new things. Can you hear yourself supporting him through creative listening that involves mirroring, validating, and empathizing?

April 20 WHO ARE YOU TODAY?

I am a gold lock.
I am a gold key.
I am a silver lock.
I am a silver key.
I am a brass lock.
I am a brass key. . . .
I am a monk lock.
I am a monk key.[20]
—SINGING GAME

You already know that at the ages between three and four your child will be working hard to establish a separate identity for herself. Your ability to interact successfully with her will depend on your honoring the sometimes delightful and sometimes disturbing identities she will try on for size. She will need to know that you are paying attention, and at least in a limited way, entering into the game with her.

But there may be difficulties. You may tend to ignore her many changes of personality and identity. Without approving feedback she will feel unsupported and adrift, as if no particular identity catches your eye. Or you may want to strongly approve some of the things she does and strongly disapprove of others. But your role is not to guide her in her choice of trial identities but to validate and support her choices as much as you can.

This is an excellent time to set some limits in support of her role-playing. These limits usually center on issues of safety for her and others and perhaps also on the safety of property. Intentional dialogue is an effective way to help your child exercise her imagination and still keep it safe.

She may decide, for example, that she is a world explorer and head out the door with a half-stuffed suitcase before you can catch her. She may decide that she is Superman and try to fly off the roof before you know what's happening. You may love her as a scary ghost, but you may not want her using your bedspread as a ghost-sheet in your muddy backyard.

Her play-acting sometimes makes your blood pressure jump and your temperature rise. When your body physiology has returned to normal and you are calm, call your child aside and request a conversation with her. Now is the time to discuss things quietly, so she can learn both that you support her and that there are limits. Your conversation could follow this model:

- You love her so much, and you enjoy her in the role she is playing.
- You have some concerns about . . .
- What does she think about your concern?

Listening carefully, help your child articulate her feelings in as neutral a way as you can. Use intentional dialogue to discuss how she feels, not how *you* feel, about setting some boundaries so that she can explore her identity safely. Mirror her, validate her role-playing, and empathize with the creative ways in which she is expressing herself. It is possible to be supportive *and* express your own concerns.

Remember that from now on, she will revisit these questions of identity in increasingly sophisticated ways as she gets older. She will wonder who she is and how she should act when she enters elementary school and again when she enters high school, when she starts her first job, during her first dating experiences, and beyond. You are here now giving her the validation and permission to be herself that she will carry with her for the rest of her life. And you can have fun doing it.

April 21 WIN, WIN, WIN

For truly it is to be noted, that children's plays are not sports, and should be deemed as their most serious actions.[21]

—MICHEL DE MONTAIGNE

Sometime after the age of four, your child feels the impulse to assert his competence by learning skills, using tools, and mastering knowledge. He also begins to compete with others to demonstrate his competence. This impulse, which appears now for the first time, will reappear throughout his life.

Your child at this age has already developed a strong sense of self. But his connection to you is just as important as it's ever been. You may misinterpret his competitive nature as meaning that you are less important to him, but nothing could be further from the truth. Your approval or disapproval, and your interest in his competitive exploits is critically important.

During this stage you may find yourself pushing your child toward skills and interests that are important to you. That's normal and desirable as long as you don't push beyond your child's interests and abilities and as long as you allow him to express himself by learning and acting on skills in which you are less interested.

When it comes to competition, you may be overly encouraging, concentrating on winning rather than on the process of competing itself. This is an age when many parents and children become involved in Little League or soccer. Again, this is fine as long as you don't become too involved and too obsessed with winning, as many stereotypical "Little League parents" do.

On the other hand you may yourself have ambivalent feelings about competition. You may unconsciously discourage it, fearing that it leads to conflict and disappointment. But if you are sensitive to your child and alert to his signals, he will let you know what activities he is interested in and on what level. You will be able to tell whether he is subverting his own desires in an effort to please or placate you.

During this stage of development, there is one area that especially lends itself to intentional dialogue with your child. This is the area of possessiveness. The need to compete brings with it the notion that everything "is mine." This not only includes clothes, toys, and other property, but also a parent of the opposite sex. This so-called œdipal impulse is perfectly normal and something your child will grow beyond. Dialogue provides a framework for dealing with it effectively.

As always, initiate dialogue when you feel calm and ready to focus on listening and mirroring your child carefully. An important part of any conversation with your child about opposite-sex parent attraction will have to do with appropriate boundaries. It is important that your son not "win" in his attempt to become the most important person in the life of his mother. Similarly, your daughter must lose the battle to become the dominant person in her father's life. As you validate your child's œdipal impulse (which is not sexual at this stage), you must be sensitive to the child's need to lose this struggle with his or her self-respect intact.

As you empathize, be conscious of your connection to your child. You may or may not recall your own struggles in childhood with this problem. You can voice your own variation of the statement, "I am your mother, but I am also Daddy's wife. You are very important to both of us, and we also have a life of our own that is important to us." Remember that your love for your child includes helping him lose this battle gracefully, while at the same time helping him win the larger battle of becoming a secure and well-loved independent person.

April 22 BECOMING AN ALLY

A wise parent humours the desire for independent action, so as to become the friend and advisor when his absolute rule shall cease.[22]

—ELIZABETH GASKELL

Children in elementary school and older begin over time to live more and more of their lives away from home. Their parents are no longer the absolute center of their lives. Increasingly, parents become coaches on the sidelines as their children start to form close relationships with their peers. In addition to conflicts that involve only the immediate family, your child will experience many conflicts after the age of seven that take place out of your sight and even out of your knowledge. Through it all your connection with your child is still the primary stabilizing force in her life.

She will need to return home for comfort, validation, and empathy when she feels that the social whirl is too challenging for her. As she goes through the four fundamental impulses toward attachment, exploration, identity, and competence within her peer group, you can support her by welcoming her friends into your home and into your family, especially the one or two close friends that are special.

It's good to know that as your child develops a close friendship, it may take on a significance that you have trouble understanding. You may have a tendency to ignore a friend you don't particularly care for or to intrude on your child's friendships in an effort to make her more successful and more popular socially. Such tampering may be tempting, but it is a mistake. Your primary role is to validate your child's choices and to be there when things go wrong, as they inevitably will. If your daughter comes home wailing that "Brenda doesn't like me anymore," you can be ready to help her cope with the situation by helping her clarify it, making sure that she knows her concerns are important and by empathizing with her in her grief.

Often with a child at the age of concern, you will be hearing about a problem situation you don't have firsthand knowledge of. You must listen carefully in order to help your child clarify the problem. And this careful listening has to be done as much as possible without your being judgmental. Sometimes just listening to a problem and asking careful questions will be enough to help your child sort things out for herself.

When you validate your child and empathize with her, it is extremely important that you continue to see her as a person separate from yourself. This can be hard to do when she has been hurt and you feel as if it's happened to you. We all need to be reminded that our children's pain is their own and not ours. All too often we become partisans in our children's causes and then get upset when they don't do what we would have done in their place. At these times, we are being symbiotic; we are not supporting their need to solve their problems themselves.

The key is to become an ally of your child through intentional dialogue, to be a resource she will continue to feel confidence in. Because you listen to her, you let her know that her way of viewing the problem is valid and that you empathize. Sometimes she will want your advice when she is having trouble in school or with her friends. You will listen and you will help, but you will not take over the conflict yourself.

April 23 TALKING WITH TEENS

It's a sad moment, really, when parents first become a bit frightened of their children.[23]

—AMA ATA AIDOO

If you have a budding adolescent at home or a late teenager, you already know that conversation between the two of you can sometimes be difficult. If you are anticipating what it will be like when your child reaches the adolescent years, you may be forecasting imaginary problems. It's true that challenges come with every age, but they don't have to be as difficult as the popular imagination makes them out to be. During the teenage years, the intimacy stage, it will be up to you to take the initiative to maintain the connection with your child with extra careful consideration.

Your child will be starting to date, to form an intimate relationship with a peer of the opposite sex, and he will be experiencing all the difficulties that attend his first glimmerings of adult behavior. He is still in need of your support, and he will still need to retreat from time to time into the safe environment that you have established at home. Although he probably won't ask for them, he needs to feel the presence of useful, sensible boundaries that you can help him establish.

Because your teenager is almost an adult, you may have some unreasonable expectations about his level of maturity. You may tend to let him set his own boundaries, or you may conversely tend to set way too many boundaries in an arbitrary manner. In either case, he will be scrutinizing your behavior as well as his own, deciding how willing he is to let you help him out. Your adherence to the values you preach is critical. It will not be enough for you to tell him, "Do as I say, not as I do."

Intentional dialogue can be a vital tool for reestablishing your contact with your child if or when you experience problems together, or when he is troubled and needs to confide in you. You may often find yourself in the position of the initiator. You may be the one to take the first step in order to rebuild trust and confidence in your connection when it has been temporarily jarred. This may be hard for you to do, because you may have difficulty recognizing your own part in unpleasant interactions with your child. It will be important for you to be able to say sincerely, even when it hurts, "I am sorry for what I said when you and I were discussing . . . ."

It is perhaps harder than ever before for you and your child to enter calmly into a discussion of a problem that you are having with each other. Your role is, therefore, to be open about the possible outcomes of your discussion. The important thing is to keep the connection between you intact, learning not to intrude on his privacy. Whether you are just learning intentional dialogue for the first time or are an old hand at it, you can rely on the process to help you work through the hard subjects: dating and sex, drugs and alcohol, smoking, the car, responsibilities around the house, and whether you approve of his girlfriend (which you should try your best to do, by the way).

Take a few moments now to let yourself experience your teenager as he or she has grown over the years. The two of you have accomplished so much together. He is now an independent but connected whole person who is different from you. Think about all the love you have felt for your child through all his or her years of development, and be reassured that no matter what happens between you, your love is always there for you both to rely on and build upon.

April 24 A TOOL FOR RECONCILIATION

Family quarrels are bitter things.[24] —F. SCOTT FITZGERALD

In all families of any size there are opportunities to establish or reestablish conscious communication. Maybe you have had a falling out with a parent or a cousin. Maybe one part of your family has trouble dealing with another part. If you have to interact with in-laws, there are often times when you and they see things so differently that it creates problems. And sometimes problems become magnified over the years until open warfare is the order of the day.

In all of these unhappy interactions you have a role to play. It is healthy and healing and for the good of yourself—as well as your children, your partner, and your extended family—when you take responsibility for the future of a relationship that has gone sour. The spirit and techniques of intentional dialogue can help you become a peacemaker if you want to.

It will be a health-giving opportunity for you to heal yourself by taking an active role in acknowledging your responsibility for the past as well as for the future. Whether you feel guilty about the role you have played in creating problems or not is unimportant. What *is* important is to consider the future of your connectedness with your family member(s).

Rebuilding a connection by acknowledging the existence of the problem may be the most important step. Often families, like spouses, ignore problems when they are small and wait until blowups or disagreements bring them to the surface. As you enter into a dialogue with someone with whom you are disaffected, remember that the only person in the relationship whose behavior you have control over is yourself. You cannot enter into a dialogue with any expectation of successful peacemaking if your goal is to prove a point or right a wrong done to you.

Think about someone in your family with whom you would like stronger ties. Do you already have the ability to talk openly and in mutual cooperation about your relationship? Are you responsible for some of the distance between you? Consider the best qualities of the other person. As you begin to open the conversation between you, be ready to listen without prejudice. Can you envision mirroring, validating, and empathizing with this person's point of view? What steps are you willing to take to build bridges between you? After you have thought it through, take action to begin a dialogue. You really have nothing to lose.

April 25 GETTING ALONG IN THE WORKPLACE

> *A team is a small number of people with complementary skills who are committed to a common purpose, performance goals, and approach for which they hold themselves mutually accountable.*[25]
>
> —JON R. KATZENBACH AND DOUGLAS K. SMITH

We are convinced that the principles of intentional dialogue can have a powerfully positive effect on relationships in workplaces. Of course, a workplace is not a family. People work together for economic reasons, and so the connections between them are not nearly as intimate nor as strong as they are within a family or between parent and child. But the environment of the modern company allows many opportunities to listen creatively, mirror, validate, and empathize in the service of better, more effective, and more rewarding relationships nonetheless.

Coworkers are often thrown, sometimes arbitrarily, into situations where they are asked to achieve a goal to which they must all subscribe in order to be successful. Teamwork is becoming a commonplace requirement. Companies more and more recognize the power of teamwork. They seek to organize many of the efforts that used to be handled by highly structured groups—where workers operated as individual "cogs" in the machine—into more loosely structured, self-managed teams. These teams must rely for success on individuals who subordinate themselves to the mutual good of the team goals. And this can often create problems arising from unconscious behavior.

If you are a member of a team at work or if you are a manager who relies on team efforts for success, you will easily understand how useful it is when conflict is resolved calmly and mutually as it arises rather than festering and endangering the health of the work team. Besides, it's a lot easier and more pleasant to be working cooperatively with fellow workers than it is to nurture rivalries, jealousies, and resentments.

Whether or not you are currently a part of a workplace environment, you probably have opportunities to establish or reestablish a connection with others in your immediate surroundings. Perhaps you are a volunteer on a committee at your child's school or at church or in some other organization. Take some time to consider how you feel about each of the people with whom you work on a regular basis. Are there some who are easier than others for you to get along with? As you consider those with whom you have the least sense of connection, think about what you would like to have done differently in the course of your relationship. Can you see what your responsibility might be in any misunderstandings?

How would you envision beginning an intentional dialogue with someone you don't normally feel connected to or with whom close connection has been damaged? Plan in your mind a dialogue in which you initiate a calm, helpful contact. If you can remember a disagreement you may have had or construct one you might be likely to have with this person, envision listening as your disaffected coworker tells you what's bothering him or her. Can you hear this, even in your mind, without jumping into the conversation to make a point or push an argument? Can you imagine validating the complaint of a coworker against you? As you think about empathizing with this person, consider some ways you could meet him or her halfway in the future.

Now that you have thought it out, understanding that your coworkers are not likely to follow your script exactly, try out an intentional dialogue format the next time you see a good opportunity. A cool head will help.

April 26 WALKING INTO THE WORLD

Who made the world?
Who made the swan, and the black bear?[26]

—MARY OLIVER

When was the last time you gave yourself permission to take a walk? Not a walk for the purpose of getting somewhere or doing an errand, but a walk for the sheer pleasure of it, for the pure joy of walking outside in the fresh air.

If it's been a while, you might set aside a half hour or so today or tomorrow. Prepare to enjoy yourself by letting your senses come alive to the sights, smells, and sounds around you. Tell yourself you are going to feel the air, register the quality of the light, and feast your eyes on what you can see. Let yourself feel thankful for the miracle of being able to move your feet, bend your knees, and swing your arms freely and smoothly as you wish. Fill your lungs with fresh air and breathe deeply. You are alive, and your body works so well!

You may glory in a walk by yourself, or you may want to take your children with you. Certainly their young age can't stop you. We see determined mothers and fathers pushing one and sometimes two babies ahead of them in strollers when they go out for their daily walk or run, so you can do it too.

Walking is a very good time for thinking, but it is also a good time for being present in your moment-by-moment experience. In half an hour you can clear your head, improve your mood, and do something nice for your body. Why not give yourself this gift today? You deserve it.

April 27 REST

Did Susan rise up from her bed,
As if by magic cured?[27]

—WILLIAM WORDSWORTH

There is no doubt that walking is one of the best things you can do for yourself. Another is getting enough sleep. Are you rested? Do you have the energy and enthusiasm you want to have for your children and the rest of your life? Spend some time today thinking about your sleep patterns. Some busy parents have trouble going to bed at a reasonable time because the late night hours are the only ones they have to themselves. While it is certainly delicious to read mysteries or other page-turners, short-changing yourself on sleep can make you feel groggy the next day.

We know several working parents who find ten minutes or more after lunch to nap or rest. If you find yourself tired in the afternoon, you might ask yourself if there is a way you can lie down or sit up with your eyes closed for a few minutes in the early afternoon. Many people say that the nap habit allows them to function much better on into the evening.

If a siesta is not possible for you, and you are tired, see if you can find a way to adjust your schedule to get some extra sleep. It is possible that an extra half hour might make a big difference. If you want to change your bedtime schedule, decide when you want to say good night and turn off the light. And keep to your plan for one week. See what happens. Do you feel better in the morning? A consistent sleep schedule is important for both you and your children. Mixing cranky kids with cranky parents does not make for a good time.

April 28 WHAT DO YOU THINK?

Inquiry means asking questions, over and over again. Do we have the courage to look at something, whatever it is, and to inquire, what is this? . . . Questioning, questioning, continually questioning.[28]

—JON KABAT-ZINN

In the spirit of intentional dialogue, set yourself a fun task for the day. Find at least one occasion during the day to ask each of your children their opinion about something. It can be an issue that you are thinking about that is in the current news—maybe a political issue or a social policy issue or a matter of international interest. It can be something of a more personal, psychological nature. Or, perhaps better yet, it can be something suggested by your child herself. Every day your children bring you gems of stories about what they have seen and heard.

No matter how old your children are, or what their level of verbal skill, it is possible to let them know that you are interested in their reactions to things. Instead of immediately pronouncing your truth, you can draw them out a little and encourage them to form their own opinions.

"What did you think when Jessie pulled Tommy's hair?" "Do you think your teacher did the right thing?" "Can you think of a better way the bus driver could have handled this situation?" "I was thinking we might go camping for spring vacation. What do you think?" "Sounds like you were upset over that. Is that right?" "That sounds wonderful to me. Are you happy about it?"

The way these examples are worded, they sound cooperative and interactive rather than unilateral. They are said in the spirit of give-and-take and leave the impression that you value what your children think and want to know what's going on inside their heads.

When you treat your children this way, they find it natural to deal with their friends and older people the same way. You are teaching them the spirit of intentional dialogue. You are sending the message that you are open, ready to hear what other people think, flexible, responsive, and interested in maintaining a strong, positive connection with other people.

April 29 CELEBRATING YOUR ROOTS WITH NEW RITUALS

"Where have I come from, where did you pick me up?" the baby asked its mother.[29]

—RABINDRANATH TAGORE

Rituals are the glue that holds families together. They organize interactions, activities, and turn them into meaningful exchanges. They help children understand what parents think is important, and make it easier to grasp elusive temporal concepts that need to be made concrete to be understood: "once a week," "once a month," "once a year."

We have already talked about taking regular activities and recasting them as rituals. Now let's talk about adding a ritual that your family can enjoy. People often wonder where new rituals or traditions come from. If you are ready to enrich your family life in this way, think first about your own family history. There may have been things you did as a child that you had forgotten about that would be fun for your own children. If not from your childhood, then perhaps from your spouse's or partner's. If nothing comes to mind, look a little deeper into your family history. Ask your parents, your grandparents, or your aunts, uncles, or cousins about their daily lives when they were children. Without a doubt, there are rituals that they may never have talked about and you may never have heard before.

Another source of inspiration is your ethnic heritage. Even if you are multinational, you can pick up an ethnic thread and learn more about how your ancestors lived. Every nationality is rich in traditions. Food is a good place to start. How about Irish soda bread, or English bangers 'n' mash, or Moroccan humus, or Mexican tea cakes, or Asian pot stickers?

You can take your children to the library and find one book that describes traditions and rituals from your ethnic and cultural heritage. Together, you can choose one or two to incorporate into your lives. Keep in mind that whatever you choose will increase in richness and meaning as it is repeated. Every time you eat a special meal or repeat special words or play a special game, you make it more your own. Your children will remember when you did it last year and the year before, and the memories become part of what they remember about you, their other parent, and their brothers and sisters.

If you don't already have a rich fabric of family rituals, you can create them. All rituals come from somewhere. By the time your children are doing them with their children, it will feel as though they have been part of your family's life forever.

April 30 RITUALS, CELEBRATION, AND FAITH

Not twice this day . . . this day will not come again. Each minute is worth a priceless gem.[30]

—ZEN SAYING

Your family may or may not be religious. Religious observance may be an integral part of your life, providing texture, context, and meaning to your thoughts and actions. Or, you may have other spiritual, philosophical, and ethical guidelines that provide texture, context, and meaning to your thoughts and actions.

Whatever guides and inspires you, near the heart of your beliefs must be the ethic of love. Loving your neighbor, however verbalized and interpreted, would certainly be included in most people's descriptions of what to do to live a good life. Some parents are comfortable talking freely about love. They speak openly and naturally about loving each other and their children, and they have no problem talking about love in a more abstract, less personal general way. Other parents find it harder to talk about love and let their actions speak on their behalf.

If your children were asked about the essential meaning of religion for you or about your most important value, would they know how to answer? If they did answer, would they know how important loving is in your life?

Give yourself permission today to be as open as is comfortable for you in talking with your children about love and showing them what loving means to you in real life. Your children are smart, and they are sensitive to you. They will learn a great deal about loving when they see you doing it in situations that are frustrating or disappointing.

A prayer for today: *In the silence of my own heart, I approach the essence of the spiritual life, and wordlessly commit myself to the power of love in the great and small things of my life.*

Notes

1. *Holy Bible*, King James Version (Cambridge, Eng.: Cambridge University Press).

2. *Ibid.*

3. Julia Cameron, *The Artist's Way: A Spiritual Path to Higher Creativity* (New York: Jeremy P. Tarcher/Perigree, 1992).

4. Margaret J. Wheatley, *Leadership and the New Science* (San Francisco, Brett-Koehler, 1990).

5. M. Scott Peck, *The Road Less Traveled* (New York: Simon & Schuster, 1997).

6. Jacqueline Kennedy Onassis, quoted in: Theodore C. Sorensen, *Kennedy* (1965).

7. William Shakespeare, *The Merchant of Venice,* Act 2, Scene 2, in *The Complete Illustrated Shakespeare,* ed. Howard Staunton (New York: Gallery Books, 1989).

8. Sidonie Gabrielle Colette, *My Mother's House and Sido,* trans. Una Vicente Troubridge and Enid MacLeod (New York: Farrar, Strauss and Giroux, 1953).

9. Stacy Schiff, "The Runaway Mother," *The New Yorker* (November 10, 1997).

10. Bill Cosby, *Fatherhood* (Boston, MA.: Prentice-Hall, 1987).

11. Henri J. M. Nouwen, *The Genesee Diary* (New York: Doubleday, 1989).

12. Rumi, *Speaking Flame*, re-created by Andrew Harvey (New York: Meeramma Publications, 1989).

13. Judith Wallerstein and Sandra Blakeslee, *The Good Marriage* (New York: Warner Books, 1995).

14. Anonymous, *Introduction to Literature: Poems*, 2nd. ed., Lynn Altenbernd and Leslie L. Lewis (New York: Macmillan, 1969).

15. Freya Stark, *Traveller's Prelude* (London: J. Murray, 1950).

16. Lady Mary Wortley Montagu, "Letter," 19 Feb. 1750, to her daughter Lady Bute, *Selected Letters,* ed. Robert Halsband (Harlow, Longmans, 1970).

17. Barbara Ehrenreich, "Stop Ironing the Diapers," in *The Worst Years of Our Lives* (New York: Pantheon Books, 1991).

18. Alice Meynell, "The Illusion of Historic Time," in *Essays* (Westport, CT: Greenwood Press, 1970).

19. Robert Louis Stevenson, "Happy Thought," in *The Literature of England,* ed. George K. Anderson and Karl J. Holzknecht (Chicago: Scott, Foresman and Company, 1953).

20. Edna Johnson, Evelyn R. Shields, and Frances Clarke Sayers, eds., *Anthology of Children's Literature* (Boston: Houghton Mifflin Company, 1970).

21. Michel de Montaigne, "Of Custom," in *Essays,* trans. John Florio (New York: AMS Press, 1967) bk. 1, ch. 22.

22. Elizabeth Gaskell, *North and South* (St. Clair Shores, MI: Scholarly Press: 1971).

23. Ama Ata Aidoo, "The Message," in *Fragment from a Lost Diary and Other Stories*, eds. Naomi Katz and Nancy Milton (New York: Pantheon Books, 1973).

24. F. Scott Fitzgerald, "Notebook O," in *The Crack-Up,* ed., Edmund Wilson (New York: New Directions, 1993).

25. Jon R. Katzenbach and Douglas K. Smith, *The Wisdom of Teams: Creating the High-Performance Organization* (Boston: Harvard Business School Press, 1993).

26. Mary Oliver, "The Summer Day," in *New and Selected Poems* (Boston: Beacon Press, 1992).

27. William Wordsworth, "The Idiot Boy," in *Selected Poetry* (New York: The Modern Library, 1950).

28. Jon Kabat-Zinn, *Wherever You Go There You Are* (New York: Hyperion, 1994).

29. Rabindranath Tagore, *The Collected Poems and Plays of Rabindranath Tagore* (New York: Macmillan, 1962).

30. Paul Reps, *Zen Flesh. Zen Bones: A Collection of Zen and Pre-Zen Writings* (New York: Doubleday, 1989).

May

INTRODUCTION TO THE MONTH OF MAY

For most people parenting is a cooperative enterprise. Even parents who do not have partners can benefit from alliances with other adults who are supportive. This month we will focus your attention on the partnership aspect of parenting; you will learn how the quality of your relationship with your partner is directly relevant to the quality of your parenting.

May 1 THE MERRY MONTH

About the Maypole new, with glee and merriment . . .[1]

—THOMAS MORLEY

In all the northern hemisphere, spring is definite presence. It's time again to be outdoors, working in the garden, playing sports, going on excursions to the country, barbecuing, and wearing light clothing on your walks.

The beginning of warm weather and the shift in routines are the kinds of seasonal changes that you and your children have learned to adjust to. By now you know that change brings disruption, but it also brings opportunity. If your kids are in school, it's time to think about how you want the summer months to unfold.

You can't stop summer from coming, but you can learn to dance to its tune with ease and grace. You do need to think ahead and make some conscious preparations, however. Now is a good time to ask yourself how you feel about the beginning of a new season. Are you looking forward to summer, or does it feel burdensome?

Think of your summer experience as a stream rather than a series of compartmentalized boxes, fluid rather than static. The stream has many currents that come together and mix in beautiful ways: sometimes you and your children are enjoying activities together; sometimes your children are in structured situations apart from you; sometimes you are away from home working or socializing; and sometimes each of you is pursuing private goals apart from the others.

Now is a good time to sit down with your parenting partner, if you have one, and your children, as soon as they are old enough to participate, to see how you want your summer to flow. Most families plan a vacation and look ahead to special day-care arrangements. While you don't need to structure all of your time, the possibilities of summer camp or summer school may be a good starting point.

Ask each member of your family how they want to spend part of the summer. By letting each person have their say, you increase the possibilities for a creative and relaxing three months. Children and adults get to follow their own pursuits while the family as a whole remains connected. All of you together create a summer stream that tumbles and spills into quiet pools of quiet reflection.

May 2 WHAT BROUGHT YOU AND YOUR PARTNER TOGETHER?

I lie here thinking of you . . .[2] —WILLIAM CARLOS WILLIAMS

Remember what it was like to first be in love . . . the thinking, the yearning, the dreaming? You envisioned a life together; first just the two of you and then with the children you both wanted and would love. Even before it happened, you knew that becoming pregnant and giving birth within a loving relationship would be one of life's most beautiful experiences.

What you couldn't have known is all the ways that having children would change your romantic relationship. In many ways it deepens your attachment to each other and your sense of being a family. The bonds of connection extend in more than two directions. You have gathered others into your circle. Your loving energy isn't just for each other but spills over into the lives of your children to nourish and sustain them.

And the two of you now have to try a little harder and schedule a little more carefully in order to nourish and sustain each other. To keep the intimacy and excitement of your marriage alive when your children need so much care requires more conscious attention. You must remember every day to say and do the things that will continue to build your relationship.

A simple place to start is to indulge yourself with memories of how much you enjoyed each other when you were first together. When you close your eyes, you can see again the two of you having fun—laughing, crying, and loving each other. You can remember what you both looked like and reexperience the physical attributes and the emotional characteristics that first attracted you.

Your partner would probably love hearing you talk about your romantic memories and the things you fell in love with. Can you see yourself sharing a conversation of this sort? After you talk about why you fell in love, you can talk about what you love now about your partner. What do you still love and admire, and what do you love and admire that's new since your beginning?

Couples engaged in the hard work of raising children need to share positive feelings with each other as much as possible. "Love talk" helps them know they are a unit, facing the joys and difficulties of life together. It gives them the energy to do what must be done.

May 3 YOUR FAMILY VISION

One not necessarily very beautiful man or woman who loves you . . .[3]

—LAWRENCE FERLINGHETTI

Visions—how beautiful and powerful they can be. The right cup of coffee . . . the perfect sunny day at the beach . . . a bookshop in Paris. People who create rich fantasies of the future are sustained by them, and sometimes they are guided by them.

Private fantasies are wonderful, but it may not have occurred to you that family fantasies can be also. Let's use today as a time for thinking about family visions and how they can be helpful in creating a rich and satisfying family life.

What if we assume that it is one year from now. You and your family have awakened on a Saturday morning to beautiful weather. You have the whole day in front of you. You can now construct your ideal family day. There is no schedule, and there are no obligations, no errands. How would you like to see you, your partner, and your children spend this time? Where do you go? What are your activities? Can you describe your interactions? Do you spend all your time together, or do you spend some time apart from each other?

Allow yourself a leisurely number of minutes to really develop your ideal family Saturday. Give yourself the pleasure of imagining the details of the clothes you wear, the food you eat, and the feelings you share together.

Now, imagine that it is three years from now. Your children are three years older. In this fantasy they are bigger and more competent than they are right now. Imagine yourself spending the day together in an ideal way. Again, allow yourself the freedom to dream and luxuriate in the details. What are you doing, and how does it feel to be in each other's company? Spend several minutes creating and elaborating your vision.

Such daydreaming is pleasurable, and it serves an important function. It can give you information about what you wish for. It can help you clarify what you want for yourself, your children, and your partner. What does your one-year vision tell you about yourself and the other members of your family? What feelings are present? How are you independent from each other, and in what ways do you remain interdependent?

Ask yourself the same questions about your three-year vision. What has changed and what has stayed the same?

After you have completed this exercise, tell your partner about it. Without being specific about the details, let your partner know how much you enjoyed the exercise and suggest that he or she do it also. Then you will be able to combine your separate visions into a family vision that represents your mutual desires. Becoming aware of what you want for yourself and your family will help you get it. If there is a disparity between your vision and your current reality, seeing the distance between them will help you traverse it. Tomorrow you will have the chance to take pencil to paper and use what you have learned from this daydreaming exercise to write some family goals.

May 4 SETTING GOALS TOGETHER

The more conscious your decision, the more conscious the outcome.[4]

—STEPHEN LEVINE

Yesterday, when you were daydreaming about your ideal Saturday one year from now and three years from now, you ended up with a vision of how you want your family to think, feel, and act together. Hopefully, your partner also went through the same exercise and came up with his or her vision for the family's future. When you talked together about what you learned, it was probably obvious which things you envisioned in common. These qualities, characteristics, or activities can now be turned into specific goals that you can work on together.

Here's how you can do it. Schedule a time today for you and your partner to sit down together for the purpose of identifying some family goals. Start by writing down those positive desires that were present in both of your separate visions and then turn them into goal statements. Your goals should be possible and desirable. Then decide which specific tasks you will accomplish together or separately that will help you achieve your goals. These tasks should be detailed and set within a specific time frame, so that you know who has to do what and when.

If you feel your children are old enough, you can share much of this process with them, given their age and ability to comprehend. You want your children to be included because you want them to feel attracted to your vision of family life. You also want them to understand that creating a family takes the motivation and effort of everyone in the family, not just the parents.

Here's is an example of how one family turned an element of a vision into a goal: The mother wanted her family to "enjoy doing things together." The father wanted "the household to be peaceful." They figured that a common theme might be finding a few activities they could do together that were enjoyable and possible for them and their two children. This became a goal.

They decided to work toward the goal by having an "activity hour" every Saturday afternoon for two months where each member of the family got to choose (within limits) what activity they all engaged in. Their six-year-old son chose finger painting for his first Saturday. Their nine-year-old daughter chose a board game.

They also wrote down a second goal of keeping Saturdays as relaxed and unscheduled as possible, because they realized that in order to enjoy their family activities, they had to be rested and unhurried. You can see from this family's example how daydreams and visions can be both pleasurable and useful when they are transformed into practical planning in the here and now. They can also be simple in concept and scope and easy to put in place.

May 5 MIXED MESSAGES

I wish either my father or my mother, or indeed both of them, as they were in duty both equally bound to it, had minded what they were about when they begot me.[5]

—LAURENCE STERNE

Every child learns who he is from his environment. He is constantly picking up clues about how he is doing and whether or not he is okay. His primary concern is to survive, and he must rely on subtle messages from parents and others close to him to let him know whether he is on solid ground or shaky ground. Sometimes their messages to him are direct and obvious, but most often they are unconsciously sent and unconsciously absorbed.

In the next few days we want to help you uncover some of the messages you may have absorbed as a child about who you were and your place in the world. They are important because some of them undoubtedly continue to operate internally in your life today. They may still be a strong influence on who you are and how you parent.

Without a doubt, many of the messages you received were positive. And many of the negative ones were useful for your growth and safety as you developed into an adult. But some of them didn't help you as a child and don't foster your success as a person now.

Today, let's see if we can understand more about the messages you received that relate to your *core self*, that part of you that either lets you feel good about your very being and your acceptance by others or doesn't let you feel good and doesn't let you feel accepted.

We suggest that you allow yourself to consider the issues we are raising during ten or fifteen minutes when you are going to be undisturbed. Close your eyes, and let yourself once again be a small child, living in your childhood home with your parents. Call forth an image of your mother, and then let yourself see your father. Take time to reexperience what they looked like, how they talked, what it felt like to be in their presence. Recall a time when you experienced total acceptance and approval from each of them. Now let yourself recall a time when you experienced their disapproval. Reconstruct as many of the details as you can. Can you recall other approving times and other disapproving times?

Their approval and their disapproval are still with you in some way today. You may have had occasion before to think about how your parents influenced your sense of self. Or this kind of exercise may be new to you, and it may be difficult to uncover this information from your past.

Some of the basic positive and negative messages that parents give their children are listed below. When you read through them, do any of them strike you as definitely true?

Positive Messages	**Negative Messages**
It's okay to be you.	Don't be you.
You are a gift from God.	You are a bother.
You are just the boy/girl I wanted.	If only I had had the boy/girl I wanted.
I love you. You add to my life.	You will be the death of me.
I am so happy I had you.	I don't know why I had you.
Children are a blessing.	Don't ever have children. They'll ruin your life.

As you think about how you each of your parents viewed you as a child, what was the most powerful, positive message you received from each of them? What was the most powerful negative message? Can you tell what difference these opposite messages of approval and disapproval continue to make in your life today? Do they continue to affect you? This kind of self-examination is often difficult, but the benefits are worth it. If these long-ago messages about you and your worth are still alive in you, you will want to know it. You don't want your unfinished business to unnecessarily contaminate your children and their sense of their own worth.

May 6 MESSAGES ABOUT THOUGHT

I have seen men in real life who so long deceived others that at last their true nature could not reveal itself.[6] —SØREN KIERKEGAARD

It's worth taking a moment to consider the received notions that underlie our assumptions about the world. Where do our ingrained ideas, our beloved prejudices, and our pet peeves come from? Many of them come from home. Some of the strongest messages children receive from their parents concern what kinds of thoughts are permitted and what kinds are not really all right to think. This kind of message is often very explicit. You may have no trouble remembering some of the pronouncements you heard at the dinner table about politics and religion, the way people ought to view diversity of race or national origin, how people ought to view class or taste in clothes and speech, and which kinds of speech are acceptable and which are not.

The way children are exposed to ideas has a great deal to do with how they learn to accept new information. It also affects the way they think about themselves. As a child were you expected to see the world in very clear, unambiguous ways? Was the world a place of clearly defined good and bad? Or were you given a lot of freedom in your thought? Was the world a complex place where you were encouraged to perceive many sides of issues?

As you scan your memory for clues to the messages you might have received about the way your thoughts were allowed to form, consider whether you might have heard or inferred any of the following messages, positive or negative, from each of your parents:

Positive Messages	**Negative Messages**
It's okay to think.	Don't think, or don't think certain thoughts.
It's okay to express your thoughts.	Don't express certain thoughts.
I am so impressed by your clear thinking.	You can't think straight. You are really dumb sometimes.
It's good to be creative.	How could you think that?
You are very clever.	Don't act or be very smart.
Education will broaden your mind.	You don't need to go too far in school.
Girls can think as well as boys.	Girls don't think as well as boys.

Many boys find intelligence in girls attractive.	Boys don't like girls who think too much. Never act smarter than a boy you want to impress.

What was the most powerful positive message you received from each of your parents? What was the most powerful negative message? How do you relate to each of these messages today? Do you feel complete freedom of thought today, or are there some restrictions you place on yourself? Do you know what messages you are sending to your own children?

May 7 ARE MY FEELINGS ACCEPTABLE?

"I am so grieved, Davy, that you should have such bad passions in your heart."[7] —CHARLES DICKENS, DAVID COPPERFIELD

It is often hard for adults to express feelings, especially about some subjects. Some people grow up with a sense of shame about the expression of strong feelings or emotions, such as tenderness, anger, or fear. You may remember the words of Mr. Murdstone in *David Copperfield,* who, whenever David's mother expressed any tenderness toward her son, was fond of saying, "Clara, be firm."

On the other hand, many children learn from an early age that an appropriate expression of feelings is healthy and normal. In our society it is more common for girls than boys to be allowed to express feelings freely, as if the boys' repression was an indication of "manliness." In families where a parent values control above most other attributes, like Mr. Murdstone, the expression of emotion may be clearly or subtly discouraged.

One of the most lasting legacies for a child who has not been allowed to express his or her feelings and who has the internal sense that such expression is a sign of shameful weakness is the inability of that child to trust feelings in adulthood, either her own or those of others. As you examine memories of your childhood experience and think about each of your parents, how do you relate to the statements, positive and negative, listed below? Does any of them feel familiar?

Positive Messages	Negative Messages
It's okay to feel.	Don't feel. Don't feel that feeling.
Tell me about your anger.	Don't show your anger around here.
So you are experiencing a lot of feelings now. That's okay.	You are too emotional and sensitive.
You are feeling sad right now. It's okay to cry.	Boys don't cry. Don't be such a crybaby.

As you remember certain feelings you had as a child and imagine how each of your parents responded to them, can you recall the most positive things you heard? The most negative? Does any of this legacy remain with you today, as an adult? How do you react to your children when they express their strong feelings? Are the boundaries you draw for them around their feelings appropriate?

May 8 A LIFE OF THE SENSES

Our sense of smell can be extraordinarily precise, yet it's almost impossible to describe how something smells to someone who hasn't smelled it.[8]

—DIANE ACKERMAN

It is common for people today to consider that the late twentieth century is a time when bodily senses have achieved full play, when we are, in fact, bombarded with sense experience. We have lived through the so-called sexual revolution; there has been a good deal of experimentation with drugs; music of one sort or another is free and overflowing out of our homes and into many public places; whole industries have grown up to provide products to scent our homes, our bodies, and even our automobiles. A sizable proportion of our economy and our energy goes into gratifying our senses.

On the other hand, we are also a society that has done much to deaden and devalue our senses. We do this partly by creating a kind of pollution of the senses, bombarding ourselves with stimulation of all kinds. Why do we do this? To begin with, we become less sensitive to sound, touch, smell, and taste as we age. And because so many sense experiences are available at our fingertips, we overload our systems, requiring more stimulation to reach the same level of pleasure: stronger tastes, more vivid colors, music all the time. In the end, there may be many sense experiences from which we exclude ourselves or to which we are no longer sensitive. Or we may have forgotten how to appreciate subtleties.

Some children are taught to think of their bodily senses as sinful, trivial, or in some other way irrelevant. But children are not born with jaded senses or a notion that their bodies are sinful vessels. The simplest things—the smell of sun-dried laundry, freshly mown grass, flowers without strong scent or the streets after a hot summer rain, the sound of mourning doves early on a warm spring day, nursery rhymes, the soft fur of a kitten's coat—all seem new and marvelous to small children, and sometimes even to adults when they stop to experience them.

As you think about yourself as a child, try to remember how you experienced every sense you had, from the hugs you received to the music you heard to the food you ate. Did you feel encouraged to experience your senses, or did you experience them furtively, certain that something about this kind of pleasure was not acceptable? Did you feel compelled to rebel against the dampening of your senses or fear or suppress certain bodily sensations, or did you experience the full joy of sensual exploration? One way you can answer this question is by asking yourself how you positively support the early exploration of all the senses that you see in your children today.

May 9 MOVING AND GROOVING

> Misha [the ballet dancer Mikhail Baryshnikov] was one of those children who cannot sit still. Erika Vitina, a friend of the family, says that when he ate at their house you could see his legs dancing around under the glass-topped dinner table.[9] —JOAN ACOCELLA

All of us know what it's like to be with a child who's having a hard time sitting still. Children often use bodily movement, including singing, whistling, giggling, bouncing around, and jumping up and down, as ways of expressing their aliveness. Of course, there are some children who have a physical inability to concentrate except for brief moments and who suffer from involuntary physical movement. But we are not speaking here of children with attention deficit disorder or hyperactivity.

Normal children spend a lot of time in motion. It's part of how they are learning to experience the world, part of their heightened awareness of life and their surroundings. Most adults, on the other hand, have learned to suppress or to redirect their physical energy into sports, dancing, organized musical activities, or partying. They also spend a lot of effort "keeping the lid on" their children's movement.

How do you feel about yourself now as an active person? Do you allow yourself a full range of movement, or are you always conscious of maintaining decorum, limiting your physical self-expression? Do you have to have a couple of drinks before you lose your physical inhibitions? Do you feel insecure about how you appear to others when you dance, sing, play at sports, or act silly?

Take some time to think about yourself as a child. What messages do you think you heard about using the muscles of your body? Do you think of yourself as graceful, at home in your body, satisfied with the way it moves? What messages do you sense you might have received from each of your parents about your physical being? Were your parents more likely to encourage you to move around, or did they spend a lot of energy helping you act "more grown-up?" How do you, in turn, support your child's expression of physical aliveness?

May 10 YOUR DOMINANT BELIEF PATTERN

For you were love who could tell
A man's thoughts—my thoughts—though I hid them. . . .[10]

—PATRICK KAVANAGH

In loving but reticent families, a lot of unspoken love gets communicated, as in the poem above. In truly dysfunctional families, however, when love is present, it is distorted by secrets and lies. The message from the parents is: "Don't see. Don't tell. Don't know." It is very common for adults to say or to imply, "We don't talk about that." And it is very common for them to rebuff or refute their children's accurate observations and conclusions. "No, that's not what happened." "You're crazy if you think that way." In other words, the child is told that he can't trust his own capacity for thought and discernment. The message, spoken or unspoken, is: "Don't trust yourself to know what is true."

To a lesser degree and with less harmful consequences, even parents who are competent and caring will inadvertently give their children the message that some part of their normal functioning is off-limits, distressing to the parent, or downright dangerous.

In the last four days, you've had the opportunity to think about the messages you received as a child with regard to thinking, feeling, sensing, and moving. Today, you can summarize your insights and observations by responding to the following:

When I was a child, my parents gave me the message that:
It was okay for me to use my intelligence and to think.
It was *not* okay for me to use my intelligence and to think.
It was okay for me to have feelings and to express those feelings.
It was *not* okay for me to have feelings and to express those feelings.
It was okay for me to enjoy the sensory experiences around me.
It was *not* okay for me to enjoy the sensory experiences around me.
It was okay for me to exult in the power, beauty, and motion of my body.
It was *not* okay for me to exult in the power, beauty, and motion of my body.

It will be obvious to you which functions your parents supported and which they tried to repress. You can probably see that their negative reactions to you and your functioning must have stemmed from the negative messages that they themselves received when they were young. This is one of the primary ways that wounding is passed down from parents to children.

After you have answered these questions in reference to your own childhood, think about how your children might answer when they are adults, in reference to *your* parenting. As you guess what their answers might be, it will become clear whether or not you think you may be sending your children negative messages about their natural functioning. If you think you may be, it can be comforting to remember that it is never too late to do something about it. You can begin today to give your kids permission to be who they are and to enjoy their full range of natural gifts for thinking, feeling, sensing, and moving.

May 11 WHEN I FALL IN LOVE

I am no good at love . . .[11] —NOEL COWARD

Romantic attraction can seem like a mystery, and our own behavior in the flush of first love can seem nonsensical. Why do we fall in love as we do? Imago Relationship Theory maintains that the answer to this question usually lies within our lost selves, the part of us that is missing and not integrated into the recognizable behavior we identify as our own. We want our prospective life partners to complete us, to make us whole, as we embark on what we hope to be a permanent love relationship, one that will include the raising of children.

When we marry and have children, whether the marriage lasts or not, we most likely enter into a permanent commitment, if not a permanent working relationship, with our parenting partner. If nothing else, our children carry both sets of genes.

Even if you are no longer married to your children's other parent, you can learn something by considering the choice that you made. What was it that originally drew you to your parenting partner? Do you think your original attraction was based on attributes that have endured, or has your partner surprised you by doing, feeling, and thinking things differently from how you saw them at first? For most people, it's a little of both. Unfortunately, it's not uncommon for us to see the differences as deficiencies, although when you are honest, you can probably find strengths in your partner that you don't see in yourself. In many ways, you complement each other.

When we say that two people complement each other, we mean that their strengths and weaknesses, skills and aptitudes, tend to balance. When they work together, they become a fully functional team. Can you see ways that you and your current or past partner complement each other? A good deal of your lost self can be seen in your partner's strengths, and your partner's lost self can be seen in yours.

May 12 WHAT IS THERE ABOUT YOU?

We've made a great mess of love
Since we made an ideal of it.[12]

—D. H. LAWRENCE

It should come as no surprise that long-term romantic partnerships often result in conflict at some point. In most marriages, the ideal love of the honeymoon frays into disillusion. If you were super insightful and articulate, you might express it this way: "This person is NOT like me. What I saw as a possibility for resolution of many of my own deficiencies has become a power struggle. My own way of being in the world is in conflict with this *alien* way of being!"

However alien your partner may seem, it is important to continue to see and believe in the positive attributes of this person to whom you have made a commitment. Together you are parenting children, and you must be able to make conscious choices together about how to help them navigate childhood and become fully functioning adults. This is not always easy, because, as much as you love your children, raising them can exacerbate the areas of conflict already inherent in your relationship.

When you discover a parenting issue that causes conflict, it can help for both you and your partner to make an effort to focus on your child and her needs, rather than on the long-standing grievances between you. Ask yourself what is best for your child now. As together you attempt to see her accurately, remember to respect each other. This is part of your commitment to become conscious parents even when issues in your own relationship divide you deeply. When you mirror, validate, and empathize with each other you will be respecting each other. The respect is built into the dialogue process and acts as a safety net when your own emotions are too intense to be trustworthy.

May 13 YOUR PARTNERSHIP CHALLENGE

Now my heart
Turns towards you, awake at last.[13]
—KENNETH REXROTH

You already know that every marriage or long-term partnership has challenges. All of us are sometimes lonely, sometimes disappointed, sometimes hurt. We don't always do the things we should, and we often do things we should have left undone. We all learn that challenges and difficulties are as much as part of our relationship as joy and generosity. We learn a great deal from them. These difficult places are where we start growing.

You probably already know where these places are in your marriage or long-term partnership. Can you name them? We're not talking about whether you can name your partner's weaknesses and insufficiencies, but whether you can identify areas that the two of you need to work on together.

If you're not sure or if it feels like everything is difficult for you, then you probably need to think about this question calmly and in some detail. Set aside some time today for the purpose of thinking about your recent interactions with your spouse. Can you remember what your last argument or disagreement was about? How about the one before that? And the one before that?

When we asked one wife about her recent altercations with her husband, she recited, without hesitation, "Money . . . money . . . and money." You, too, may have no trouble seeing a pattern in your difficulties. Do you think your partner would see the same pattern? How would he or she answer when asked to name two areas of challenge in your relationship?

Since we know that every challenge is also an opportunity, let's consider what you can do to start addressing the areas of difficulty in your marriage right now. Our suggestion is simple: *Resolve to stop all criticism around the issue or issues that are causing you and your partner problems.* We are not suggesting that you make this a casual resolve or an inconsequential vow. Consider what we have just said very carefully. You will want this decision to be well-considered and serious. *I resolve to stop all criticism around these issues today.*

Healthy, loving relationships cannot survive in the poisoned air of criticism. Starting today, you will be working toward a relationship where criticism has no place at all, ever. For most couples this is a mighty big step. If you want, you can start your no-criticism policy with a somewhat smaller focus, concentrating on those places where the two of you are having the most trouble. For the previously mentioned woman who had money worries, it would mean that she does not criticize her husband in any way around the issue of money. She can continue to express her feelings. She can share her concerns. She can draw up a budget. She can get angry. But she can't accuse or denigrate or belittle or find fault. For her, as well as for many others, this would be a big change. It is a big change that can bring big results.

We strongly encourage you to start working toward a criticism-free marriage. When you do, as part of your initial resolve, let yourself indulge in the anticipatory happiness that will result. Feel your body let go of the tension and turmoil that a critical stance produces. You are about to set yourself free from the burden of fault-finding and replace it with more productive and loving strategies for change.

A prayer for today: *As I breathe in the air of the Infinite, I fill my body and my soul with the healing power of love.*

May 14 VALIDATE AND EMPATHIZE WITH YOUR PARTNER

Recall his sorrow and his deep distress,
Recall his loneliness.[14]

—JAMES AGEE

Working to create in your home an environment free from criticism and filled with confirmation is a major achievement, one of the most important gifts you can give your partner, your children, and yourself. Each person in your family will learn that it is permissible to offer an unpopular opinion, try something new and not succeed, or take an emotional risk—all without fear of attack.

To achieve a criticism-free household will take vigilance and dedication. You may have to concentrate on just this one goal for a while in order to begin to eliminate old, automatic critical reactions. When you feel you are satisfied with your progress, you can take the next step toward consciousness by, not only outlawing criticism, but replacing it with validating and empathizing.

Instead of retaliating or counterattacking the next time your spouse does something that bothers you, you can focus on the second and third steps of intentional dialogue and respond with your verification and understanding of his or her point of view. The issues that have been difficult for you and your spouse are the areas where one or both of you has been wounded and where you have wounded each other. An appropriate response to a wound is tenderness and gentleness. It's natural to do what you can to help the healing.

The next time your partner begins to get upset or angry over something, instead of matching the heat, pause for a moment and put yourself in his or her place. Let yourself feel what your partner is feeling and validate those feelings out loud. It can be simple. "I can see how you would feel that way." "I know you're feeling . . . ." "It worries you when I do . . . , I know, and I'm sorry that . . . ." "I know I may have sounded like I was blaming you. And when a person is being blamed, it's easy to strike out."

Try it. You will be amazed at the softening effect it has on your spouse and how much faster the two of you can talk about the problem and come to terms with your differences.

May 15 WHAT YOUR PARTNER COULD DO FOR YOU

Not beautiful or rare in every part,
But like yourself, as they were meant to be.[15]

—EDWIN MUIR

All of us can benefit from positive reinforcement, whether it come wrapped in the words of poetry or not. When someone close to us speaks from the heart with authentic praise or validation of who we are, we are buoyed up. Suddenly the whole world seems brighter. Difficult tasks seem possible to do. We operate with inner strength and courage. When we understand that someone whom we love also loves us, we are happy.

Give yourself the pleasure, today, of taking some time to think of how someone close to you could be supportive of you. What could this person do or say that would give you new hope and energy? We're not thinking of material gifts, but gifts of the soul, simple expressions of love and confidence in you as a person. Perhaps a simple compliment, deeply felt: "You are looking especially beautiful today." "I really appreciate how hard you work and the energy you give whatever you do."

What could your partner say to you that would be most satisfying and most likely to cause you to feel joy and self-confidence? What, in turn, could you say to your partner? Set the stage for a dialogue during which you reveal some of the supportive actions you would like your partner to take. Think of things that would make you feel especially loved and appreciated. This is a good conversation to have during a relaxed evening at home or some other leisurely time when you are alone together. As part of your dialogue you may need to coach your partner about mirroring you exactly. Ask your partner to validate any requests you might make, and give him or her the opportunity to empathize with you.

Hint: This is, of course, not a time for the faintest trace of criticism or recrimination. Starting off with a sentence like, "You never tell me. . ." or "You always are so . . ." is probably not the best way to accentuate the positive. Your goal is to arrive at mutual understanding. And after your partner has heard you out and understands what your requests are, it would be a good idea to reverse the procedure and allow your partner to seek something from you.

May 16 TALKING THINGS OUT

> My Dear Father—I am aware that I have been a great expense to you in spite of my scholarships, but you have ever taught me that I should obey my conscience, and my conscience tells me that I should do wrong if I became a clergyman.[16]
>
> —SAMUEL BUTLER

Clearly the young man in Butler's novel is doing his 1824-version of intentional dialogue, at least his letter is in the *spirit* of dialogue. One of the main ideas in *Giving the Love that Heals* is that, through conscious effort, the spirit of intentional dialogue can become part of every family interaction you have. Today and tomorrow we will talk in more detail about what this spirit is.

You may not be able to define the spirit of dialogue precisely, but you probably recognize it when you hear it. You can tell when two people are listening to each other—not interrupting or coercing or thinking about something else. They are looking at each other, giving signals that they are following what the other person is saying, and waiting for each other to finish before beginning to talk.

In addition, you can tell that they are being nonjudgmental and nonintrusive. Their stance is, "I want to understand what you are telling me, and I respect you and what you are saying, whether I agree with it or not." They don't undercut or belittle each other. They don't make assumptions that they know what the other person is thinking and feeling.

This spirit of "recognition of separateness within connection" can become the ground of family life. You can enjoy each other, enrich each other's lives with your differences, and carry on your daily business with respect and affection. And this is true whether you happen to be agreeing with each other or not. Sometimes the specific words of intentional dialogue will be spoken, but whether they are or not, the spirit of intentional dialogue can be manifest in both words and body language.

May 17 WHAT YOU CAN SHARE

Love is life. All, all that I understand, I understand only because I love. All is, all exists only because I love. All is bound up in love alone.[17]

—LEO TOLSTOY

It wouldn't be too far-fetched to say that the spirit of dialogue is the spirit of love. And sometimes it makes sense for two people to look at how they are loving in the spirit of love. Most of the time when you and your partner use intentional dialogue, you will be talking about people, issues, and events, rather than about how the two of you are talking together. But using your communication skills occasionally to evaluate your communication skills can be valuable and rewarding. Even if you began reading this book recently, you probably have had a chance to learn about the process of intentional dialogue and to begin practicing its techniques.

Today you can suggest to your partner that the two of you spend a few moments talking about how the dialogue process is working for the two of you. Here are some questions you can consider:

1. When was the last time we used intentional dialogue when conversing with each other?
2. Did we use it the last time we had a heated discussion?
3. If we did, how did it work? If we didn't, why not?
4. What comments or observations do we have about the way we dialogue together? Are there things we would like to do better?
5. Do we want to set a goal that will facilitate our using it more often? If we do, what is the goal?

Learning a new skill requires persistence and intentional effort. It's easy to drift back to old habits and patterns. Most people find that they need to remind themselves and each other about intentional dialogue quite often until it becomes a permanent part of their functioning. You and your partner can help each other to mirror, validate, and empathize by working on this goal together. Then, when you need or want to use it with your children, you will find yourself gravitating toward it naturally and easily.

May 18 BEGINNING A PERSONAL GROWTH PLAN

The soul has no room to present itself if we continually fill all the gaps with bogus activities.[18]
—THOMAS MOORE

Pausing long enough to express appreciation is an important part of conscious family life. When your children and your spouse say nice things about you as a parent, what do they say? Or if they don't verbalize their approval and gratitude, what do their actions and attitudes say about your positive attributes as a parent? Do you get feedback that you are good in a crisis, patient as a teacher, a good provider, or a gentle companion? If you can answer this question immediately, then you and your children are lucky. There is a lot of open, warm communication between you.

Would you be able to say as readily which aspects of parenting you still need to work on? Do your spouse and children help you see more clearly which parts of yourself are undeveloped, unexpressed, or perhaps undiscovered? It can be hard to see those parts of ourselves that are hidden from us, but the people closest to us can help if we observe more carefully how we react to them in the course of daily interaction.

You can get clues about which parts of you are still undeveloped or suppressed by asking yourself which functions you try to inhibit or suppress in your spouse or your children. Do they do things that are part of normal functioning that make you uncomfortable or distressed? Does your spouse talk too openly about feelings? Do you feel that open inquiry into certain subjects is "off-limits?" Do you feel that creative projects are annoying or a waste of time? Are you uncomfortable with your body or the bodily aspects of life in general? Are you uncomfortable when your children sing at the top of their lungs or run wildly in joyful abandon?

If you can identify with any of these feelings or with other things that your spouse and children do that you don't like, you may have discovered a part of you that was not allowed to develop normally. When you make such a discovery, it can be helpful to pause and consider the possibility that your spouse and kids may be fine, but you may have stumbled upon a part of yourself that was suppressed as a child and needs to find expression.

Because one of the goals of becoming a conscious parent is to become as fully present and as fully functioning as you can, this is a golden opportunity. Ask yourself what you can do to develop this forgotten part of yourself and restore it to fuller functioning. What can you do to ease your automatic negative reaction when you see it in others and begin to explore it for yourself?

May 19 SEEKING INFORMATION

My friends are my "estate." Forgive me then the avarice to hoard them! They tell me those who were poor early, have different views of gold. I don't know how that is. God is not so wary as we, else he would give us no friends, lest we forget him![19] —EMILY DICKINSON

It is always useful to look to others for information about yourself that you can't see. When we are too close to something, we can have trouble seeing it. As we've already discussed, there may be several important traits you possess that others can see, but you can't. We have called this collection of traits the rejected self.

Undertaking to learn more about your rejected self can be traumatic to contemplate. You might get information that you will have trouble accepting. One response is to invent rationales that prevent you from asking for or accepting feedback. ("They don't know what they are talking about." "Their experience is limited." "They can't be correct; I'm not like that at all." "They are misinterpreting.").

Today we are going to suggest that you to do something that takes great personal courage: Find out what people think about you. Remember that when you actively seek information from others, you want to be able to trust both the person and the information in advance. First, for your own benefit, write down a list of the traits that you think describe you best, both positive and negative. You might also include in a separate list those traits you admire most in your family members and among your closest friends.

Now, select a few people whom know you well and whom you trust to tell you the truth caringly. Your present or former parenting partner may fit this description. Ask each one of them to write in a column a list of adjectives that describe you as a parent. Then ask each one to place either a plus or a minus sign next to every adjective, depending on whether the person sees this descriptive word as a positive or a negative trait.

It is important to leave these friends feeling that it was okay for them to be truthful about what they think. Assure them that you appreciate their honesty and that your feelings will not be hurt. Making them feel that honesty is what you are looking for is your way of repaying their trust in this process. And when they give you information that is true but less than positive, don't feel betrayed. You haven't been.

After you have completed this process, compare the lists from your friends. Are there adjectives that appear on the lists that you wouldn't have suspected? Which adjectives, both positive and negative, do you react to most strongly? If you don't agree with all of these descriptions of yourself, don't worry. It is to be expected that different people have difference perceptions.

You now have some information about some of the things that you have rejected in yourself. You may also tend to reject them as negative traits in others, especially your partner(s) and your children. Perhaps this makes more understandable the strong reactions you express when someone exhibits these traits. Although this process may be difficult, it helps you dispel the illusions that keep all of us unconscious. You can rejoice that you are beginning to become conscious of what makes you the person you are.

May 20 REJECTING POSITIVE INFORMATION

This is hard to say
Simply, because the words
Have grown so old together.[20]
—DAVID WAGONER

One of the most pleasant kinds of feedback you can receive is an unexpected compliment, something that makes you feel truly valued. The ability to give and receive this kind of sincere positive feedback is a strength that partners in a parenting relationship need to nourish. It is a benefit to their relationship and to their working well together as a team. Yet it is a rare person who accepts compliments positively all the time. Why is it that all of us sometimes have trouble accepting positive information about ourselves?

Sometimes we just can't fathom that we are good-looking, competent, sensitive, or skillful. For one reason or another, we have rejected a particular positive aspect of ourselves and may not be able to see that it is part of us.

Even though it seems punishing to turn away the good words that come our way, we do it anyway. If a woman has a negative view of her physical abilities, for example, even though a person she normally trusts compliments her on her grace and coordination, she may say, "You can't mean that. I'm one of the clumsiest people around."

Sometimes two people who live together for a long time learn to keep quiet about the positive traits of their partners, primarily because their positive feedback has been continually rejected or received with cynicism. Eventually, they give up. It's not worth the hassle.

You have already given some thought to the concept of your rejected self, which we discussed yesterday. Given your openness to feedback from others about these parts of yourself, can you now envision accepting compliments more graciously? Can you let down your guard and believe the nice things people say about you? Can you remain open to the possibility that they describe something about you that you may not have seen before? If you reward your intimate friends by believing the best things they tell you about yourself, you will not only learn more, but you will begin to accept rather than reject those traits you never knew existed in you.

You might also be aware, as you embark on this quest for positive data about yourself, that your partner has the same need to learn wonderful things about himself or herself. He or she may have blind spot too. We suggest that you share your quest for sincere, positive feedback with your partner. If both of you spend time looking for and providing positive feedback to each other, you will have new information to share and the beginning of some interesting conversations. You will both appreciate the positive support you give each other as you begin to integrate these unfamiliar new aspects of your personalities together.

May 21 WHAT I REJECT ABOUT YOU

"... Don't stand around
my bedroom making things cry
any more![21]

—FRANK O'HARA

What are the things that upset you the most about your partner or ex-partner? Maybe you are fanatically punctual and your partner has trouble being at the appointed place on time. Maybe you are a diligent housekeeper and keep an orderly work area and your partner is a "slob," someone who seems to enjoy navigating through life with a lot of disorder. Maybe you are careful about spending money and your partner is extravagant by your standards. Whatever the case, be assured that in any long term relationship both partners have traits that drive the other nuts. And what if your child is a failure because of the negative things you see in him, and it reflects badly on you?

If you were to make a list of undesirable traits in your partner and your children, you would be approximating a description of your rejected self. As we know, people often project both positive and negative traits onto others, whether they really have them or not. Since this is common human behavior, you undoubtedly attribute some of your own thoughts and behaviors to your spouse and children, and they attribute some of theirs to you.

If you and your partner have a trusting relationship, the best thing you can do is talk about these issues. You can begin a conversation with him or her, observing the spirit of intentional dialogue, by asking for feedback: "If you were to make a list of the things that bother you the most about me, what would be on the list?" This may seem like a dangerous thing to do, but what you are really looking for is another perspective. If you feel able to begin this kind of conversation, you may both gain some clues about subjects for further discussion, as well as a new opportunity to help each other work through unconscious judgments and achieve a new understanding.

May 22 A JOINT BODY OF WORK

Though much is taken, much abides . . .[22] —ALFRED, LORD TENNYSON

A partnership is a joint venture, and the body of work that partners do together requires them to understand the ground rules, the basis for the partnership. As two people grow together they usually have to reexamine those ground rules from time to time to make sure they are still in agreement. So often we see long-term partners who have lost the ability to do this, and it means that part of the work they have to do together in order to continue is rediscover the basis for their relationship.

It often happens that two people who live together for many years develop ways of interacting together that are less than supportive, although they go unchallenged. Perhaps a husband constantly interrupts his wife. Perhaps a wife makes a habit of speaking for her spouse without consulting him. Maybe they ignore each other or otherwise undercut each other's individual self-expression.

If this is happening in your home, you now have a tool to help you raise these difficult issues with your partner and begin resolving them. Intentional dialogue can bring such problems into awareness and provide a strategy for both of you to tell your side of the story. Doing this work together causes you to focus on the "we" in your marriage and discourages you from retreating into separate "I's."

Today, think about whether there are annoying or destructive habits that you and your partner have fallen into that you feel ready to examine and change. If you decide that there are, plan when you would like to dialogue about them, and prepare yourself to approach your partner in a calm, positive, and receptive state of mind. Remember, you are sowing the seeds of a better marriage and a healthier environment for your children. So for today, concentrate on this "we" that constitutes the understanding of your partnership. The work two adults do together to move past their individual, unconscious inheritance is what will make their successful parenting possible.

May 23 OUR CHILD

Say of him what you please, but I know my child's failings. I do not love him because he is good, but because he is my little child.[23]

—RABINDRANATH TAGORE

Chances are that he is also someone else's little child. Unless you are a single parent, with no participating partner, you are loving your child in the company of another involved adult. The two of you must cooperate and coordinate your efforts to provide safety, support, and structure as your child grows up. You do not want to argue over your parenting. You want to meet each other halfway. Yet it is also true that parenting provides many areas for conflict. Being forearmed with an understanding of what areas of conflict are likely to arise can help you avoid making your child a battleground.

It is highly likely that you and your partner represent two different styles of parenting, which we call maximizing and minimizing. One of you may pursue and be overly involved with your child. The other may tend to withdraw and be relatively uninvolved, avoiding conflict by being absent. Both of you may tend to see your child as an extension of yourselves, rather than understanding the child's need to become a person in his own right.

As partners, you have the ability to meet on common ground. Both of you can rally to the call of what is best for your child. You both care about his well-being. So how do you learn to discern together what is best for your child? The first step is to consciously agree with each other that neither of you has a lock on the truth about who your child is. Each of you has part of the truth, and you need to learn from each other.

It would be a wonderful world if each time a conflict arose between you and your parenting partner, you could act rationally and consciously to resolve it. But until you have a great deal of practice, it is wise to assume that each of you will be bringing unconscious feelings to the conflict. Hopefully, you already have an idea about what these unconscious feelings are and what triggers them. Even so, occasionally in the heat of the moment you may say or do things that you wish you hadn't.

When you find yourselves regretting an interaction, schedule some time together, when some of the emotion has passed away, helping each other reconstruct through intentional dialogue what went wrong. The object is to coach each other on how to dissect an unpleasant interaction so you can learn from it. After you have both had a chance to express your injury, anger, and fear and understand each other, you want to come back to what your child needs from you. Support each other both in front of your child and in the privacy of your relationship together. When you mirror, validate, and empathize with each other, neither of you will lose a battle, and both of you will win understanding on behalf of your relationship and the health of your child.

May 24 A CHALLENGE

By wisdom a house is built,
and by understanding it is established;
by knowledge the rooms are filled
with all precious and pleasant riches.[24]
—PROVERBS 24: 3–4

Tracking your children's emotional and physical health, cultivating a deeper knowledge of yourself and the hidden springs of your behavior, nurturing your primary romantic relationship, and building a satisfying work life is a lot to manage at once. You can keep only so much in mind at one time.

Fortunately, the human brain is so complex that we can perform several tasks simultaneously, and we can keep on learning new things no matter how old we are. When our cognitive and emotional load is heavy, as it is for most parents, our inborn capacity for complex tasks almost always allows us to find ways to accomplish them all.

Whenever you feel overwhelmed by the demands of your life, it's wise to be extra sensitive to the possibility of emotional overreaction. You can train yourself to follow a simple rule at such times: Whenever you feel a powerful urge to react with anger, self-righteousness, or fear to something or someone, pause before you react. The purpose is not to stifle your emotions, but to give yourself time to examine your internal turmoil before you decide what to do.

This is an especially useful strategy when your kids push your hot buttons. The very next time one of them triggers a red-hot reaction in you, you can pause and ask: "Is there something I need to do now, or would doing nothing be the best course?" "Is this one of my issues or does it belong to someone else?" "Am I trying to make *my* problem someone else's?" "What can I do to support my child in this moment?" These questions are also useful during disagreements with your partner as well.

And remember, if you forget to pause next time, there is always the time after that and the time after that. Developing the habit of intentionality during times of stress is a learning process. It takes a while. If you keep at it, you will find yourself thinking before you speak more and more often until it becomes automatic.

May 25 CONTINUE THE PERSONAL GROWTH PLAN

Parenting is a mirror that forces you to look at yourself. If you can learn from what you observe, you just may have a chance to keep growing yourself.[25]

—JON KABAT-ZINN

On May 18, we talked about beginning to understand which aspects of your own functioning are underdeveloped and impeding your ability to respond fully as a parent. Because these aspects of yourself are "lost," they are hard for you and other people to see. As we discussed, a way to begin to recover them is to closely observe when you have a tendency to suppress traits or behaviors in your spouse and children. Chance are that these are the very same characteristics that you were not allowed to develop when you were young. Once you have identified one or two places in yourself that have been constricted, here's how you can proceed with your own healing.

First, let's acknowledge that these are not weaknesses; they are places where you were wounded. Whatever behaviors you have adopted to compensate for the loss of full functioning, you did the best you could. These behaviors helped you survive. Second, it is helpful to describe how you would like to see yourself functioning now, as if you had never been wounded in the first place. Third, you can decide which specific, loving actions you can take to heal your wounds and begin to restore a full range of options for yourself.

Let's consider an example of how this might work. Let's say that you notice that you start fidgeting when your children express a desire for something they cannot have; something like, "I wish I had a real horse," or "Why can't we go to Disney World?" After observing your impulse to stamp out this kind of talk, you suspect that you may not have been allowed to express wishes and desires of your own as a child. So you didn't. When you ask yourself what benefit this silence might have brought you, you conclude that not wanting things protected you from the pain of not getting things. You didn't have to feel disappointment. But after thinking about it now, you realize that what you would like is to be able to allow your children a free range of expression, including wishes for things you both know you can't afford. You'd like to be more relaxed. To help yourself develop a more mellow frame of mind, you decide to be warmly accepting when your kids express their wishes and, more than that, to indulge in some fantasy wish-making of your own. Because your spouse is your healing partner, you tell him or her what you've been thinking and ask for support.

Are you ready to start on your own healing journey right now? The process we have described is not difficult, although it may initially take some time for you to begin to unearth those parts of yourself that have all but disappeared from view. Take a few moments to feel what it would feel like for you to live as a free, fully functioning person. Can you imagine the effect this would have on your children? They, too, would live as free, fully functioning people. That's the vision that provides energy for the healing journey.

May 26 SEEING YOUR CHILDREN THROUGH DIFFERENT EYES

My only daughter, my dearest child:
Fair Swanhild sat in my hall
As beautiful to behold as a beam of the sun.[26]

— OLD NORSE POEM

All of us get into ruts. We wear grooves into our relationships by assuming we already know what the people close to us will say and how they will act. We blunt the freshness of the moment by enacting old scenarios over and over again.

But the father in the poem above was able, for a golden moment, to see his daughter in all her radiance. What if you, too, could see your children through new eyes? It would be wonderful if there were an easy way that you could understand more about them from the inside—what bothers them, what delights them, what makes them laugh. We have found that there *is* an easy way. You can ask them a question that will give you new information about how your child operates. As a result, you will see your child with new eyes, guaranteed!

Find a time when the two of you are relaxed, unhurried, and

feeling close. Then ask, "What is it like living with me?" Wow! That's a question that hardly anybody has a chance to answer because nobody asks.

Your child may ask you what you mean. And then you can explain that you want to know, "What is it like, for you as a child, having me as a parent?" Such an open-ended question is fertile ground because your child has complete freedom in responding. But if she needs still more help, you can ask more specific questions, such as: What do you like the most; what do you like the least; what do you want me to do to make it better for you?

You will want to receive whatever answer you get with calm equanimity. No need to defend or explain yourself. You simply want to hear what your child has to say. This is a time when mirroring to make sure you've understood is important, as is validating and empathizing. At the end of your conversation you can let your child know that you are glad for the chance to talk about this with her and that you support her desires. You can say something like, "I'm glad you could tell me how you're feeling. It is helpful to me. And I want you to know that I think you deserve to have what you've told me you want. I love you and want the best for you." There is no doubt that this conversation will change your relationship for the better, especially if you begin to act positively on the information.

A prayer for today: *Today, I create for myself a few moments of sacred space in which to refresh my capacity to see the people around me as they really are—not as damaged, but as whole people struggling to regain their wholeness. Slowly, and with intention, I breathe on them the air of sweetness that will help them grow strong.*

May 27 WHEN YOU CAN'T SEE THE FOREST

Their hearts held cravings for the buried day.
Then each applied to each that fatal knife.[27]

—GEORGE MEREDITH

We know there are times when issues arise between two people that they can't resolve on their own. There may be a serious rupture of their relationship that they simply can't get past without help, or there may be a combination of issues that make it difficult for them to step outside of their individual points of view in order to stand on common ground.

There are also times when single parents can benefit from outside guidance. It isn't always easy to step outside your own way of seeing things without help from another person. Often an experienced professional can be more helpful than a close friend or family member.

Through the course of reading this book, you have had the opportunity to spend time thinking about yourself, your partner if you have one, and your children. You have gained understanding that you didn't have when you began. Now is a good time to think about how well you are doing.

It may be that this process is encouraging you to seek counseling alone or with a partner. If you decide professional help would be a wise step, you are already way ahead. You will be beginning the process with some knowledge of the origin and meaning of the issues that are giving you trouble. You will already have done a great deal of productive soul searching, rather than empty churning. You already have a basis for developing real solutions, rather than a sense of despair over your future.

May 28

TIPS AND REMINDERS: PARTNERS TAKE CARE OF EACH OTHER

Give all to love;
Obey thy heart . . .[28]

—RALPH WALDO EMERSON

Conscious parenting is built on a conscious marriage where each partner nurtures the other, and both of them strengthen and protect the marriage itself. Today, let's focus on nurturing your partner in the spirit of Emerson's poem, the spirit of free and open giving to the other.

You live with your partner. You undoubtedly know him or her well. You go to bed together; you wake up together; you work for the good of your children together. There are many, many things you do to please each other. Even so, it would be a mistake to assume that you know everything about your mate, or that your mate knows instinctively what to do in every instance to make you happy. You may have a good deal of experience to the contrary.

Both of you can learn more by asking than by assuming. Today, give yourself and your partner a gift by asking him or her to tell you one simple thing you can do that would delight and please. The request should be a simple, everyday request, something that can be done easily once the desire is voiced.

Here are some examples. One husband wanted his back scratched just before he went to sleep. One wife wanted to be able to choose the next movie they saw together in a movie theater. Another husband wanted his wife to greet him with a loving hug when he walked through the door at the end of the day. Another wife wanted her husband to draw her a bath in the evening. Other examples: "take turns saying a prayer at dinner," "ask me how my day was after work and mean it," "take your cups and glasses back to the kitchen after you use them," "offer to make dinner once a week," "take me back to that Japanese restaurant," "don't talk so long on the phone after dinner."

We are certain that your partner will be pleased (and perhaps surprised) that you are asking for a request. It's fun, and it shows that you really want to give pleasure. We suggest that you offer this gift to your partner in the selfless, other-focused spirit of giving. Don't be too intent on making it reciprocal. But don't be surprised if your partner asks what he or she can do for you in return.

May 29

TIPS AND REMINDERS: PARTNERS ESTABLISH AND MAINTAIN THE "WE" IN THE RELATIONSHIP

Love and harmony combine,
And around our souls intwine . . .[29]

—WILLIAM BLAKE

Combining, mixing, and entwining—that's the essence of a successful marriage. One of the biggest challenges is learning how to nurture each other and, at the same time, learning how to nurture the relationship as a whole. The marriage itself is almost like a separate entity. It is more than and different from the two people who make it up. There are decisions that benefit primarily the wife or the husband or the marriage (which benefits everyone).

Although the idea is new to many people, it can be very valuable to get into the habit of asking, "How can we act to benefit our marriage?" Or "What can we do that would be good for *us*?" Each couple strikes a different balance between individual and couple concerns, but all healthy marriages have some sense of identity, some invisible circle around them that sets them apart as a unit and makes them recognizably different from those around them.

Today, ask yourself what you do to reinforce the idea and the reality of the "we-ness" of your marriage. Often, you can tell if couples have a sense of the "we-ness" inherent in their relationship by listening to them talk. Do you use the "we" instead of just the "I"? Do you let your children know that you and your spouse are a cooperating, working unit? Equally important, do you both confer before making decisions that would affect the family? Does each of you act and talk as though the other's opinion is important?

Another sign of "we-ness" is the kind of support you give your spouse. Do you support him or her in public? Do you sometimes compromise your own wishes for the good of the family order? Do you refrain from complaining to mutual friends about him or her when to do so would be hurtful?

What is one thing you could do today that would promote the strength and health of your marriage? How can you underscore your commitment to the loving and working partnership that you and your spouse have established? It could be as complex as setting aside time for the two of you to set family goals for the future, or it could be as simple as using a few moments of private time to contemplate the beautiful qualities of the new entity that the two of you have created from your own separate selves.

May 30 FAMILY RITUALS

They stopped suddenly and stood as silent as tree-shadows, listening. There was a sound of hoofs in the lane, some way behind, but coming slow and clear down the wind.[30]

—J.R.R. TOLKIEN

One of the most enduring and beautiful rituals a family can enjoy is reading aloud to each other. It can be satisfying, no matter how old your children are. If they are too young to know how to read, then parents can take turns reading aloud and showing the pictures. If, however, your children are old enough to read, then they can take their turns as the book is passed around from person to person.

One family we know read several classics aloud when their youngest was about six until she was nine. They read *A Christmas*

Carol two years in a row, until they got tired of it. They read some of Madeleine L'Engle's wonderful books. And they read both *The Hobbit* and *Lord of the Rings* by J.R.R. Tolkien.

It is important to accurately gauge the level of comprehension and the attention span of your children and to choose books that are of real interest to them. A short period of reading every evening on a consistent basis is better than long, inconsistent bursts.

Reading aloud sets the stage for a rich variety of accompanying rituals. You can drink hot chocolate, warm milk, or herb tea as you read. Your children can snuggle up in their pajamas and sit in favorite places during the reading. You can develop favorite ways of deciding who gets to read first and how to decide which books to choose.

If you think this sounds like fun, why don't all of you make a trip to your nearest library and ask the librarian for suggestions about which books would work well for your family. Even when your children are teenagers and are no longer interested (*if* they are no longer interested), they will remember these reading evenings with great fondness.

May 31 LIVING VALUES

What I had meant was, that when I came into my property and was able to do something for Joe, it would have been much more agreeable if he had been better qualified for a rise in station.[31]

—CHARLES DICKENS

One of the values parents often identify as important for their children is "giving to others." They want their children to learn to feel empathic with people in difficult circumstances and to act generously to help when the opportunity arises. Sometimes, however, they feel at a loss about how to put this value into practice.

Perhaps the most important way to teach this (and other) values is to live it yourself. That means being generous whenever you can and also telling your children about what you are doing. When you write a check to a charitable organization, let your kids know you have done so. When an opportunity comes up to give a coworker a ride or to donate time to a nonprofit agency or to offer to take over someone's else's workload while they are sick, tell your children what you are doing and why you think it's important.

Aside from these occasional opportunities, there may be some activities your children can participate in that happen more regularly and can therefore become rituals. Perhaps you can donate clothes and household items to the Goodwill once every three months. Maybe your children can offer to help out at Sunday school a couple of times a month. Maybe you and they can volunteer to serve meals at a homeless shelter one or two evenings a month. You may have an elderly neighbor who needs grocery shopping or lawn mowing every week. Your local hospital undoubtedly has opportunities for services that your children could help perform. Don't push, but do let them see how much satisfaction these acts of helping and compassion bring to you.

If this value is important to you, then you will find suitable rituals of caring that your children can participate in. You will know that they have learned a generosity of spirit that truly began at home.

Notes

1. Noah Greenberg, ed., *An English Songbook* (Garden City, NY: Doubleday Anchor Books, 1963).

2. William Carlos Williams, "Love Song," in *Selected Poems* (New York: New Directions Publishing, 1963).

3. Lawrence Ferlinghetti, "Recipe for Happiness in Kavarovsk or Anyplace," in *Endless Life* (New York: New Directions Publishing, 1973).

4. Stephen Levine, *Meetings at the Edge* (New York: Anchor Press, 1984).

5. Laurence Sterne, *Tristram Shandy* (London: J. M. Dent, 1991).

6. Søren Kierkegaard, *Either/Or*, in *A Kierkegaard Anthology*, ed. Robert Bretall (Princeton, NJ: Princeton University Press, 1946).

7. Charles Dickens, *David Copperfield* (Harmondsworth, Middlesex, Eng.: Penguin Books, 1972).

8. Diane Ackerman, *A Natural History of the Senses* (New York, Random House, 1990).

9. Joan Acocella, "The Soloist," *The New Yorker* (January 19, 1998).

10. Patrick Kavanagh, "In Memory of My Mother," in *Collected Poems* (Old Greenwich, CT: Devin-Adair, Publishers, 1964).

11. Noel Coward, "I Am No Good At Love," in *Collected Verse* (London: Methuen, 1985).

12. David Herbert Lawrence, "The Mess of Love," in *The Complete Poems of D. H. Lawrence* (New York: Viking Penguin, 1971).

13. Kenneth Rexroth, "Loneliness," in *The Collected Shorter Poems of Kenneth Rexroth* (New York: New Directions, 1956).

14. James Agee, "Epithalamium," in *The Collected Poems of James Agee* (New York: Ballantine Books, 1970).

15. Edwin Muir, "The Confirmation," in *The Collected Poems* (New York: Oxford University Press, 1965).

16. Samuel Butler, *The Way of All Flesh* (New York : Knopf, 1992).

17. Leo Tolstoy, *War and Peace,* trans. Louise and Aylmer Maude (New York: The Heritage Press, 1938).

18. Thomas Moore, *Care of the Soul* (New York: HarperCollins, 1992).

19. Emily Dickinson, "Letter to Samuel Bowles, August, 1858," in *Major Writers of America*, eds. Perry Miller *et al.* (New York: Harcourt, Brace, & World, 1962).

20. David Wagoner, "The Old Words," in *Collected Poems, 1956–1976* (Bloomington, IN: Indiana University Press, 1976).

21. Frank O'Hara, "A Rant," in *The Collected Poems of Frank O'Hara*, ed. Donald Allen (New York: Knopf, 1971).

22. Alfred, Lord Tennyson, "Ulysses," in *The Literature of England,* eds. George K. Anderson and Karl J. Holzknecht (Chicago: Scott, Foresman, 1953).

23. Rabindranath Tagore, "The Judge," in *The Collected Poems and Plays of Rabindranath Tagore (*New York: Macmillan, 1962).

24. *The New Oxford Annotated Bible* (New York: Oxford University Press, 1994).

25. Jon Kabat-Zinn, *Wherever You Go There You Are (*New York: Hyperion, 1994).

26. "Gudrun's Inciting," *Norse Poems*, trans. W. H. Auden and Paul B. Taylor (London: Faber and Faber, 1983).

27. George Meredith, "*Modern Love*, No. 50," in *The Literature of England,* eds. George K. Anderson and Karl J. Holzknecht (Chicago: Scott, Foresman, 1953).

28. Ralph Waldo Emerson, *Selected Prose and Poetry*, ed. Reginald L. Cook (New York: Holt, Rinehart & Winston, 1962).

29. William Blake, "Song," in *Blake, Complete Writings* (London: Oxford University Press, 1969).

30. J.R.R. Tolkien, *The Fellowship of the Ring* (Boston: Houghton Mifflin Company, 1965).

31. Charles Dickens, *Great Expectations* (New York: The Heritage Press, 1939).

June

INTRODUCTION TO THE MONTH OF JUNE

This month we are flavoring our meditations with some good ideas. Over the years we have learned much from our own experiences and the experiences of other families about how to think about the common issues that come up between parents and children. Perhaps these thoughts will help you see more clearly the light you are seeking in your own parenting.

June 1 WHO MADE THE WORLD?

I do know how to pay attention, how to fall down into the grass, how to kneel down in the grass . . .[1]

—MARY OLIVER

As June begins to heat up the earth, we feel our spirits rise with the sun. The increased light helps us feel hopeful and energetic. We get up easier in the morning and dawdle outside longer in the evening. The air around us begins to sound and smell like summer.

This can be a day for soaking up the sensual delights of this time of year. Instead of hurrying along with our world already inside us, we can slow down a bit and enjoy the real beauty of the world we live in, a world that functions quite independent of our concerns and preoccupations.

Today, let yourself breathe the fresh air of the natural world. Let the sights and sounds of June be your soul food. Feast your eyes on the purples and reds and yellows the month offers us. Let the breezes touch your face.

Earth is ever hopeful in her renewal, and we can be too. We know that worries form and dissolve, problems rise and fall, difficulties come and go. We can be hopeful about ourselves and the children we love. We can continue our efforts to become conscious and loving people who meet the challenges of life with the wisdom that comes from having lived through many Junes. What are the special gifts that are offered for you today?

June 2 LET NATURE BE YOUR TEACHER

Come forth into the light of things,
Let Nature be your teacher.[2]

—WILLIAM WORDSWORTH

Let the generosity of Nature be our teacher. This time of year, she is open-handed with her gifts. She paints the world around us with a full brush. May we also be both generous and thankful. May we give what we can today to the people around us: listen when we'd rather not, stay a minute when we'd rather hurry off, affirm when we're really not so sure.

And may we spend some moments counting our many blessings, especially those we take for granted. If we can stretch our legs and walk, we are blessed. If we can think and talk, we are blessed. If we have children, we are blessed. And if there is love in our lives, we are doubly blessed.

Let us take our cue from Nature and become a renewing source of wisdom and cheerfulness for the people we see on the street and around the dinner table today.

June 3 THE PAUSE

"Wait," said the Frog. "Do not let your fear and anger blind you. What did you see?"

"I," Mouse stammered, "I, I saw the Sacred Mountains!"[3]

—NATIVE AMERICAN STORY

This month our orientation is toward resolutions and positive outcomes. In a manner of speaking, we will be spending more of our time "living in the solution." Today, and for the next five days, we will explore a simple process that you, as a parent, can learn when you are confronted with a perplexing, maddening, or sensitive moment with your children. The purpose is very simple. We are showing you a way to slow down, think about what just happened, and refer to the guidelines of conscious parenting before deciding how to respond.

The steps go like this: pause; consider whether you need to do something to address your child's behavior; ask yourself whether there is something you need to do to provide safety, support, or structure; and then continue in the spirit of intentional dialogue. Although this process takes some effort in the beginning, you can imagine how it will become automatic and speedy with practice.

Let's talk about the first step now: learning to pause before proceeding. We are talking about practicing the skill of pausing or "taking time out" in your children's presence. We are suggesting that you learn how to say, "Ahhh" and "Oh?" in response to emotionally charged or surprising news,

This is the opposite of the hair-trigger, unthinking, jump-right-in reaction we are all so good at. This is the stance of thoughtful consideration. It shows you are still listening and that you are not yet making judgments. Your soft murmuring will make you appear wiser than you may feel. But the basic benefit to you is that it gives you time to think. . . . What's going on here, and do I need to do anything about it?

That's all you have to do for today. Just practice, in your imagination and in reality (if you get the opportunity), the wise parent's gentle and hopeful pause the next time your child does something outrageous or unexpected.

June 4 TO SPEAK OR NOT

Words cannot describe everything.[4] —PAUL REPS

Yesterday, we talked about mastering the art of the pregnant pause when confronted by something that would ordinarily cause you to react negatively. That's a critical first step. Now we're going to address what you do, if anything, after that.

After you have indicated to your child that you are listening without having yet taken a stand, you can check in with an internal question, "What is the best response I can make right now?" This is a more complex question than it might appear. "Best" here means best for facilitating your child's ability to learn what he needs to learn, feel alive, express his aliveness, and experience his connection to other people and to that which is greater than himself.

Surprisingly often the best response is a neutral one. Better to encourage him to tell you more or let him go on a little longer before you decide what to say or do. Let's say that he's just confessed to cutting his little sister's hair. You know you are going to have to reset some limits and work with him a little more on appropriate behavior, but in the moment the best thing to do might be to find out how much hair he cut off and what he was thinking. In this case your neutral request for more information is a prelude to responding.

Sometimes, your neutral request for more information is a prelude to doing nothing but remaining interested. For example, if your seven-year-old daughter is furious and threatens to pack her bags and leave home, you might decide the best response is to let her know you heard her and you know she is angry; then do nothing while her fire burns itself out.

Listen today for opportunities to observe your own reaction to your children when they surprise or anger you. See if you can slow down your reaction so that it includes a pause and a rational consideration of what to do next. Tomorrow and in the next few days we will talk about what to do if a quick response is called for.

June 5 SONG OF SAFETY

This song of mine will wind its music around you, my child, like the fond arms of love.[5]

—RABINDRANATH TAGORE

All of us wish we could sing a song of love to our children that would keep them safe forever. But safety requires constant vigilance. Many times we are called upon to act quickly in the moment to keep our youngsters from harm's way. Examples with young children are obvious and fairly constant. You grab your toddler before she steps out in front of a car; you take away the matches before she starts a fire; you react like a madman when she disappears for a moment at the shopping mall.

Older children, too, need you to be there insisting on safe behavior. You insist that your twelve-year-old wear a helmet when he rides his bike; you don't allow him to swim out beyond the buoy line at the lake; you insist that he stay home from football practice when he has the flu.

With teenagers, as well, you continue to be a firm voice for health and safety, although you are less often acting in moment-by-moment emergencies and more often setting boundaries and limitations for behavior that will occur outside your sight. You sign a contract with your teenager that she will not get into a car with a driver who has been drinking; you insist that she come home from downtown before dark; you educate her about responsible sexual behavior.

These examples are fairly straightforward. But they make the point. When your child does something upsetting and you are giving yourself time to respond, ask yourself first whether you need to act to ensure her safety. If this is a safety issue, then you will know that your words and actions must be built upon the message that you and she must work together to assure her protection. That doesn't mean that you can't be relaxed and open, but it does mean that you are resolved to act firmly in her behalf.

June 6 SONG OF SUPPORT

I felt as if
I was nothing, no one, I was everything to her, I was hers.[6]

—SHARON OLDS

From the first moment we hold our babies, we are captivated. We pledge ourselves to love and support them forever. As they grow older, and they annoy us in unimaginable ways, we remind ourselves again of our pledge to support them no matter what.

When your child has angered you, the question isn't *whether* you want to support him, but *how* you want to support him—even when he has done something outrageous and offensive. Supporting him doesn't mean you are condoning his behavior; it means you are supporting the person he is underneath his mistakes and misdemeanors.

So, in the process of figuring out how to respond in the heat of the moment—after you have paused, asked yourself whether a response is called for, and considered whether the issue is one of safety—you can then ask yourself if there is something you need to do to be specifically supportive. If you have decided to do nothing but allow your child to provide you with more information while you maintain a neutral response, that is a form of support.

But, today, let's also consider more targeted kinds of support. We remember hearing a mother talk about what it was like for her to have been involved in an accident where her brother broke his collarbone. She was six years old, and her nine-month-old brother was playing with her on the top bunk of her bunk bed. When she realized that he was too close to the edge, she lunged for him, causing him to topple over backward and break his collarbone. What she carried with her from this incident was the loving reassurance from her parents that this was not her fault and that everything was going to be all right.

This little girl hadn't misbehaved, but even if she had, it would be appropriate for her parents to ask themselves how they could support her sense of herself as a good person and maintain a strong sense of connection between her and them.

As conscious parents we must continually ask ourselves, in the midst of all of kind of interactions (pleasant and unpleasant), how we can support our children's sense of themselves as worthy people who can learn and become competent and compassionate individuals with something important to contribute. For the next day or so, notice all the ways you support your children and the opportunities for supporting them that slip by unobserved.

June 7 SONG OF STRUCTURE

Discipline is the basic tool to solve life's problems.[7] —M. SCOTT PECK

The last question to ask yourself before you decide how to respond to something unexpected or unpleasant that your children have done is to ask yourself whether they need more structure. Has this heated moment between you arisen because your child needs help with guidelines or boundaries?

Let's say your young son has just spilled spaghetti all over the living room couch. Anger is certainly one reaction. But before you blow your top, pause and ask yourself why this accident has occurred. Does he know that he is to eat only in the kitchen at the table? Does he know that having a bowl of leftover spaghetti before dinner is not allowed?

What if your fifteen-year-old has stayed out past curfew for the second time in a row? It is appropriate for you to insist on a conversation with her about this matter. But you need to know whether your expectation that she be home before midnight was absolutely clear to her. And if your rules have been a little wobbly in the past, she may need to find out from you that you definitely mean what you say when you say tell her when you want her home. If her excuse involves a complication, such as being with friends who didn't have to be home and who didn't listen to her protests, then you can help her set guidelines for what to do when such complications arise in the future.

The world is a complex place. Children look to their parents for guidance about how to negotiate the complexities. Knowing how to provide structure without being overly preachy or too lax is a skill you will develop with experience and with the help of your children themselves. When you listen, they tell you what they need.

June 8 IN BETWEEN THE WORDS

All rational beings, angels and men possess two faculties, the power of knowing and the power of loving.[8] —THE CLOUD OF UNKNOWING

You may have noticed that the process we have just been talking about—pausing, asking yourself whether you need to respond, and then asking whether your response could well be focused on the providing of safety, support, or structure for your child—this process contains echoes of intentional dialogue. It requires that you get more information before you say or do something, and it points out the importance of responding with conscious intention to what is happening rather than reacting in automatic ways out of your own unconscious needs.

In addition, intentional dialogue is part of this response process in an even more integral way. If you decide to address safety, support, or structure with your child, you can do so using the techniques of intentional dialogue. You can let your child know that you want to respond to what she is doing or saying by talking about (name your subject), ask her if this is a good time, and if it is, deliver your message as you would in any other dialogue.

On a deeper level, a parent who cultivates this way of responding to an emotional situation with her child is able to act according to her values and intentions and demonstrate respect for her child at the same time. With practice this can become a way of being in the world that is loving and effective.

Now that you are introduced to these ideas, see how often you can use them in your life. If you need to refresh yourself, you can reread these last few days' entries to recapture the concept. And then take every opportunity you can to put it into practice and make it your own.

June 9 THE SAME FOR MY PARTNER

All language is therefore shared language. Even the most intimate and hidden conversation with ourselves is in words we have learned from speaking with others.[9]

—JAMES P. CARSE

Pausing before you react can be an effective way of improving communication with your partner as well as your children. The pause is full of possibilities. If your partner has just said something startling or upsetting, you can pause to determine whether you need more information, and then ask for it. You can clarify in your own mind how you want to handle this situation. You can decide whether to initiate a full discussion or simply acknowledge that you have heard what your partner is saying. You can slow things down.

Even better, though, is when couples learn how *not to* approach each other in anger or high emotion in the first place. No one likes to be "attacked" when they first walk in the door or to feel accused of something without warning. But when such moments do occur, or when real emergencies arise, it is liberating to know that you can pause, consider what you want to do, and then respond accordingly.

As you think about this idea and how it applies to you and your partner, you can ask yourself whether your interactions have this measure of self-control. If they don't, and the two of you tend to form chain reactions of tiny explosions together, you can take the initiative to introduce a little softening to the process. You can begin to remove the extraneous emotion from your conversation and train yourself to respond to what is happening right now with dignity, patience, and mutual respect.

A prayer for today: *In my quiet time alone, I honor the sacred stillness that is within me and between me and others. I believe in the healing power of my positive thoughts and intentions. I have no need to rush in and fill the space with words that are superficial and distracting.*

June 10 MAKING TIME

Time for you and time for me,
And time yet for a hundred indecisions . . .[10]

—T. S. ELIOT

It's no secret that the coming of a new baby raises the question of time. We worry about whether we will have as much time as we need to nurture the new life we have created. We have the idea that there was a time when parents could count on long stretches of unstructured time in which to immerse themselves in parenthood. Whether or not this is a romanticized fiction, most of us agree that nowadays such immersion would be a luxury. More and more families are headed by one overworked parent or by two parents, both of whom need to work to make ends meet.

It's true that there have been adaptations on the part of some companies to accommodate working parents. Some "family friendly" companies allow family leave arrangements for new parents and flexible working schedules and have developed day-care facilities on site. But most parents don't have this kind of workplace support. They keenly feel the conflict between raising children and making a living. Child care is often less than satisfactory. When it is available, it's drastically expensive and often unreliable or temporary.

The demands of both work and home can wear people out. Some parents respond by spending even more time in the refuge of the workplace, where relationships are less emotionally ambiguous.

Whatever your particular work-home situation, these are questions that you as a parent almost certainly continue to face. How can you give your children what they need, meet your other obligations, and still have a life of your own? For every parent this is an ever-changing challenge that requires different answers at different times. Our task is to help you stay focused on the needs of your child. If you are gently reminded on a regular basis that your role as a parent is primary, you will find creative ways of finding the time that will allow your children to flourish.

Keep in mind that the unstructured time you spend with your child—holding him, listening to him, just being available to him—is as important to the quality of your life as it is to his. Is there a way to make this kind of time a priority in your life? You can schedule and structure work to some extent. You can often schedule time away from work. But you can't always *structure* the time your child needs to spend with you when you have scheduled time with him.

Rather than worry alone about how you are going to meet these challenges, it can be helpful to discuss them with your parenting partner or a trusted friend if you don't currently have a partner. As you think about these issues, make the distinction between what is important and what is urgent. A telephone call, for example, is urgent: You probably feel a need to answer the phone when it rings. But is it necessarily important? The need your child has for your presence and attention may not seem so urgent. It can probably be put off. But it can be vastly more important.

June 11 QUALITY TIME

Quality time . . . But this, too, is a way of transferring the cult of efficiency from office to home.[11] —ARLIE HOCHSCHILD

You can be sure of one thing about parenting. It does not lend itself to efficiency. More than a set of tasks, parenting is a process where the value lies at least as much in how you get there as where you end up. If you have trained yourself to operate on a strict timetable with almost every moment scheduled, you may have real trouble with this. When your child needs you—and we don't mean just to take her to an appointment or to nurse her when she is sick, but to be there for her—you can assume that her need won't fit easily into your schedule. Children don't function on calendar time, especially little ones.

A child doesn't always have to be attended to when she demands your attention. But her request for your time always has to be weighed against your other priorities. Sometimes they are more important than your child's need, but not often. When your schedule conflicts with your child's need, take a few moments to consider what is really important before you make a decision. Is it more important to follow your own task schedule, or can your plans be flexed to accommodate your child?

Perhaps it is helpful to think of being guided, not by your "to do" list, but by your deep commitment to the kind of person you are. And you can be guided by what you are growing *toward*, which, as we've discussed it in this book, is becoming more aware. When you are aware of who you are and the kind of parent you want to be, you are better prepared for the unforeseen responsibilities and unexpected tasks that can take you by surprise. You can't control all the events that impinge on your life, but you can respond with intention to new information and act consciously as a result.

Quality time is the time you are fully available to your child. Whenever you cut a conversation short or interrupt the telling of a story or ignore a request, you are meeting your own needs for efficiency and not attending to the needs of your child. Sometimes such hurrying is unavoidable, but sometimes you can slow down and ask yourself who needs you most—your child or your job. Ten years from now will you be glad that you took that extra phone call or read an extra five pages of your report, or will you be glad you stopped what you were doing to tell your son about the time Babe Ruth pointed his bat where he was going to hit a home run and then hit it?

June 12 MOM OR DAD TO THE RESCUE

When, therefore, anyone provokes you, be assured that it is your own opinion which provokes you. Try, therefore, in the first place, not to be bewildered by appearances. For if you once gain time and respite, you will more easily command yourself.[12]

—EPICTETUS

During the past school year your child may have had his first real opportunity to experience another adult, a teacher, in an authority role. For some children and their teachers, this connection is made happily and easily, and for others, it's not so easy.

Whether last year was his first school year or not, if you have a school-age child, parent-teacher conferences are now part of your life. Usually these conferences happen like the seasons of the year, on a regular schedule. It may happen at some point, however, that you get a call or a note that the teacher wants to see you because there is some difficulty. Such a summons can strike fear into a parent's heart. Parents generally don't want to hear that their children are having problems.

Your son may have been disruptive; he may have fallen behind in his studies; his teacher may perceive an adjustment problem; or there may be some other information that he is less wonderful than you want him to be. On the other hand, you may have called for a conference because your child came to you with a problem he was having with his teacher.

It is sometimes tempting to ignore what the teacher is saying or to defend against it. It's also easy to blame your child or his teacher instead of listening. Because the content of the conversation is emotional, you know it is especially important to prepare yourself to use the tools of intentional dialogue: mirroring, validation, and empathy. They will help you understand how both your child and his teacher perceive the problem. After you've understood, you can work on developing a plan that will help your son and his teacher deal constructively with the problem.

Your attitude toward school and your child's teachers will influence your child. Your role here is to help your child retain his respect for the teacher and to help the teacher understand him as well. You might want to think back over the last school year. What opportunities were there for you to discuss your child with his teacher(s)? How did you handle these discussions? When your child begins school again in the fall and you are called into a parent-teacher conference, you can prepare yourself to value and use his or her insights as an aid to your own efforts in raising your child.

June 13 NO MORE PENCILS

"Then, my good friend," I said, "do not use compulsion, but let early education be a sort of amusement; you will then be better able to find out the natural bent."[13]

—PLATO

As school lets out for the summer, your child envisions an endless opportunity for fun, uncontaminated by the usual responsibilities. No more homework, no more teacher. Three months seem like a lifetime. The routines of the school year can be left behind until fall.

This summer you may already have helped your children plan some organized activities for the season, perhaps summer school, a summer job, or a family vacation. Private music lessons, dance classes, and organized sports can continue after school is out if your child is interested in them. They provide structure within the welcome freedom of the summer months.

The summer interlude also provides an opportunity for more reading. It's a chance for your child to read the books she enjoys instead of being compelled to read homework assignments. In the laid back atmosphere of the summer, she can take her time to explore fantasies, detective stories, historical dramas, humor, adventure, and biographies that she might not have time for during the year.

You can encourage her reading by going with her to the public library. The library is ideal, because if she doesn't like a particular book, she can always turn it in and get another. The whole system is set up to encourage experimentation and curiosity. Without putting pressure on her by monitoring what she reads, you can establish the pleasant ritual of regular library visits. If she is interested in talking about the books she reads, the two of you will have some interesting conversations.

Reading is an ideal summer activity: loosely structured, openended, full of variety. Your child can learn at her own pace, taking advantage of the freedom to follow some new interests and let go of others. Maybe the two of you can also choose some books for you at the same time, and you can read along with her throughout the summer months.

June 14 FAMILY VACATIONS

Let there be spaces in your togetherness.[14] —KHALIL GIBRAN

You may be familiar with the National Lampoon series about family vacations. In this series of movies we see the hopelessly inept and naïve Clark Griswold and his family try to have an "ideal" family vacation in a variety of settings: motoring across country, going to Europe, creating an at-home family Christmas, and in Las Vegas. Each of these movies pokes fun at the various hopes and desires we all have about how wonderful two weeks together as a family is going to be.

As we watch their sincere efforts at togetherness, we can see that these four people may be part of the same family, but they are definitely not in sync. They embarrass each other, they can't agree on where to go and what to see; their plans fall apart; they loose their luggage, the weather is lousy. They may not be having fun, but we are. We get to see what happens when two parents and two children who love each other try to accommodate four different sets of interests and preferences in close quarters.

But the Griswolds notwithstanding, families all across the country continue to take vacations together and enjoy them. In most cases there is a backlog of good feelings to carry everybody through the inevitable but temporary frustrations. In fact, after enough time has passed, the frustrations almost always become fodder for future family stories that are told with affection and humor.

Some difficulties do seem to get magnified on vacation. Bickering between brothers and sisters can seem intolerable when you are stuffed into a car traveling through the four hundred miles of flat grasslands of the Great Plains. Fortunately, the intensity of the feelings provides ample energy for attempts at resolution and reconciliation. Everyone has a strong incentive to resolve conflict, so that peace can be reestablished. Parents learn from experience that "vacation" doesn't really mean that they are completely off-duty. They still need to be patient and sensitive to the physical and emotional limits of their children.

Here are some things that might lead to more pleasant interactions on your family vacation:

- Plan in advance but stay flexible while the vacation is actually happening.
- Budget enough extra money to allow yourself to take care of unforeseen expenses and not sweat every dollar.
- Give everyone in the family a chance to have some time alone each day.
- Try pairing up in different combinations: sometimes Dad with younger brother, sometimes with older sister, sometimes with Mother alone, etc.
- Allow for serendipity. The experience of encountering something interesting and unplanned may be the highlight of the vacation.
- If you're driving long distances, allow for frequent stops, especially if you have small children.
- Provide lots of snacks and drinks throughout the day.

Family vacations are fun. Really.

June 15 EXPLORING

Goosey, goosey gander,
Whither shall I wander?
Upstairs and downstairs
And in my lady's chamber.[15]
—MOTHER GOOSE

Summer is a golden time for exploring new territory. When faced with a new situation children can either be somewhat adventurous and welcoming, or somewhat cautious and reluctant.

The impulse toward exploration first appears in small children, around the age of eighteen months. They become intent on expanding their horizons, always keeping an eye out for their parents or other trusted caregivers. They wander into corners and cupboards, pulling things off shelves and exploring nooks and crannies. Through this process they learn to trust their own curiosity and to be confident that they can operate in a safe world.

As a parent, you play a critical role in your child's developing sense of trust and safety. You want to set guidelines that allow for freedom within limits. For example, you could say to your two-and-a-half-year-old son: "You can stay in the backyard, but don't go outside the fence without me for now." Or "You can play in the basement, but stay away from the stairs for now. If you want to climb up the stairs, let me know, and we can climb them together." You may need to reinforce these guidelines several times, but eventually your child will come to see his world as a welcoming place with room for him in it.

This early pattern of exploration will set the tone for all his future explorations. Does he feel confident starting school, trying out for the school play, getting a job, graduating from college, getting married, raising a family, setting off in a new career direction? Children who haven't been supported in their early attempts to learn about their world can learn these skills later, but they get a head start when conscious parents support their earliest impulses to explore the world around them. Throughout his whole life, this toddler will be exploring new territory as he matures from one stage of development to the next.

Spend a few minutes today thinking about how your child approaches new experiences. Think about how you want to support him as he begins his next adventure. Ask yourself what he needs from you in order to get the most out of the experience. By thinking about it now, you are preparing yourself to act in his best interest later.

June 16 WHILE SHE IS EXPLORING

And green and golden I was huntsman and herdsman, the calves
Sang to my horn, the foxes on the hills barked clear and cold . . .[16]

—DYLAN THOMAS

The world beckons, and your child is ready to take advantage of her many opportunities to learn and grow. When your child lights up at the possibilities the world offers her, you know you have been a good ally in her attempts at exploration. She has the tools she needs to explore safely and with a sense of security.

There are some children, on the other hand, who resist anything new, preferring to remain in safe and well understood environments, wanting you to be there all the time. That doesn't mean that you have not been a supportive ally for your child. Adventurousness, like all other characteristics, is partly a matter of inborn temperament. There may be many reasons for her timidity. It could just be that she needs to take things slower and needs to progress in a very patient atmosphere

But if you find that your child is afraid to step out into the world, among the questions you can ask yourself is whether she is picking some of that up from you. Are you somehow stifling her impulse by maximizing, giving her the idea that the world is dangerous and that you need to be there at all times to protect her? If you are, she will develop a dependence on you and a reluctance to explore. On the other hand, your approach may be to minimize and send her the message that you are remote from her explorations, that they are of little interest to you, and that you would just as soon have her examine the outer world on her own. In that case you may be substituting a set of rules and guidelines in place of your availability and involvement. Children who are strongly influenced by a minimizing parent may be forced into independence too soon.

You can gain insight into your own attitudes by asking yourself how good an explorer you are. Does the world call to you to learn and grow by examining new things? Or does it frighten you and push you back into the safety of the familiar? When you know how you support yourself in new endeavors, you will know more about how your support your children. Having this knowledge allows you to do something different.

June 17 I DON'T RECOGNIZE THIS CHILD

> Most children at the tender age of six or so are generally full of the most impractical schemes for becoming policemen, firemen, or engine drivers when they grow up, but when I was that age I could not be bothered with such mundane ambitions.[17] —GERALD DURRELL

Have you ever found yourself wondering, "Who *is* this child? I hardly recognize him." Maybe your four-year-old son is speaking and acting in a way that you haven't seen before. That may be a pleasant surprise for you, or you may want him to go back to the default position and return to his more recognizable self. All of a sudden, he's become a stern, disciplinarian parent, lecturing his little sister about her behavior. Or this quiet little boy of yours may have become the leader of a pack of wolves rampaging through the house with his friends.

As an adult who has both crafted and discovered a solid identity for yourself, you may be a little uneasy at the chameleon nature of your child at this stage. It's easy to make the mistake of assuming that exhibiting a range of shifting identities presents the same problem for your child as it would for you. After all, you have spent a lifetime establishing an identity. Your confidence in your ability to work and get along in the world has been built step-by-step through years of effort. What if your beloved child gets frozen in an ineffective, disappointing, or difficult identity that dooms him to incompetence for life?

You don't need to worry. Your child is doing what he is supposed to be doing now. He has many years in which to establish an adult identity. But in order to do so, he needs to be able to experiment, try things out, and learn which things work and which don't. This impulse begins early in life and will reappear later whenever he asks himself, "Who am I?" This primary question rises to consciousness throughout life, including even middle age, when biological, sociological, and personal changes cause people to reassess who they are and how they are living.

Living well depends upon the ability to continue to grow and change. As a parent you can support the earliest manifestation of this impulse by participating in your young child's attempts to discover what feels right to him. Your positive response, along with rational guidelines, will let him know that he has permission to explore his intuitions and ideas about how he can best live in the world.

June 18 WHY IS SHE SO DISAPPOINTING?

Oh, high is the price of parenthood,
And daughters may cost you double.[18]
—PHYLLIS MCGINLEY

All of us carry at times the burden of being disappointed in our children. We are afraid that our children will become people we don't like very much or that their behavior signals some deep character flaws. We feel partly responsible for the problem and unhappy that we haven't done something to correct it. Most often these feelings are short-lived, as our son or daughter once again becomes delightful and rewarding. But, on occasion, parents live with fears that can grow like a sickness inside them, undercutting positive feelings and creating guilt in themselves and in their child.

You are probably aware by now that a good deal of what you fear in your child belongs to you. Chances are the fears you have about your child are ones you harbor on your own account or on your partner's account. Knowing that, we need to ask how parents can get past their fears and avoid overreacting to normal behaviors that trigger them.

One thing we know for sure. If you constantly label your child, you are in danger of creating a self-fulfilling prophecy. You reinforce her awareness that she has a certain problem. You present the world to her in this way, and sooner or later she *will* have the problem to wrestle with herself. Your job is *not* to create her identity for her, but to support her efforts to create her own. When she occasionally looses her way, she needs to know that you love her no matter what, and that you are there to help her hold the flashlight as she finds her way back.

The first instant you sense that she has done something to trigger alarm or anger in you, you can pause and let the moment pass. The more time you give yourself between what triggers your unconscious fear and your reaction to it, the better able you will be to step back and assess what is really happening. If you want to, you can see this situation as a test. The test is to see whether you can separate your child's *behavior* from who she is. The test is to determine whether you can support your child by allowing a range of behaviors, some of which disturb you, in order to avoid labeling your child in your own mind and forcing her to label herself in hers.

A prayer for today: *With my whole being, I ask for the strength to see my children as You see them. May I see with Your eyes and feel with Your compassionate heart.*

June 19 YOUR CHILD WON'T TRY

Most people live dejectedly in worldly sorrow and joy; they are the ones who sit along the wall and do not join in the dance.[19]

—SØREN KIERKEGAARD

Have you ever come upon your child sitting along the wall instead of joining in the dance? He is with a group of other children, for example, and they are playing a game, but he is not participating. Or he is learning to swim or dive off a board into the water, and he is acting as though he is terrified. Or he is supposed to be part of a play at school, and he gets stage fright and won't go on.

As you observe you child hanging back, you could be thinking many things. You could be saying to yourself, "He's so shy and timid. This won't do. He has to get in there and give it a try." You could be saying, "I was just like that as a child. He's just like me, so I understand and won't push him," or "I was never like that. I always gave it my all. What's wrong with him?"

All of these are reasonable first reactions. Once you're aware of them, you can decide what you want to do. You may decide *not* to express any of these thoughts. First, you want to remind yourself to understand, accept, and move past your own embarrassment or disappointment in your son. This is going to be his battle to fight, not yours. While still remaining connected to his feelings, you want to distance yourself enough to see that he is a different person from you, and it is not appropriate for you to judge yourself by his behavior.

At this point you can either dialogue with him, or simply accept his behavior and reassure him that you love and believe in him. If you decide not to talk with him at this moment, you could have an imaginary dialogue with him as a way of gaining more understanding of why he is acting the way he is.

You might imagine him telling you something like this: "The last time I tried something like this, I wasn't very good at it." Or "I am afraid this will hurt." Or "I am not comfortable with these people. I don't think they like me." Or "I'm afraid I won't do it well enough and I'll be embarrassed." When you stop to think about it, it may be fairly easy for you to decide how he might answer. You can then envision yourself validating his feelings and empathizing with them.

Regardless of whether you actually have this conversation, you will want to express your validation and empathy with the fear he is feeling. He needs this in order to know that you love him and accept him and are there to help him move beyond his fear when he is ready.

June 20 IT'S NOT WHETHER YOU WIN OR LOSE

> If you can meet with Triumph and Disaster
> And treat those two impostors just the same, . . .
> Yours is the Earth and everything that's in it.[20]
>
> —RUDYARD KIPLING

We live in a society that loves competition. In business, striving for success is called "playing the game," and competition is a basic component. Even in jobs and professions where competition is not so explicit, it can be an important element of success. Obviously, you want your children to be able to develop the skills and attitudes of healthy competition. Sometimes, though, as you watch your child play games or participate in organized sports and observe his anguish over losing or the ferocity of his desire to win, you wonder just what healthy competition is all about.

Most parents would agree that healthy competition is valuable in part because it teaches children how to lose graciously. This is an essential life skill. Most of us—and our children will be no exception—experience defeat at least as often as victory. To behave as if winning is, in the words of Vince Lombardi, "the only thing" is to set ourselves up for a great deal of pain. Anyone with a favorite team has a chance to practice this skill, since nobody wins the Super Bowl all the time.

For a child, losing can be terribly traumatic. He may need help accepting defeat in board games or casual pickup games at home in order to let go of the need to always win. When he loses, you can help him see that not only is he the same person he was before, but you love him in a way that is completely independent of how well he plays the game or how often he wins. Intentional dialogue is a good way to do this. The question is, can you help your child compete and go on, even in defeat, with no loss of self-worth? It is critical that he learn to strive and to play again another day, win or lose.

It is also very important to model in your own behavior gracious winning and gracious losing. This is a good time to examine your own attitudes toward competition. Are you someone who needs to compete and win often, and for whom losing is a sign of personal failure? Or are you someone who fears competition and steers clear of it, because you have difficulty handling the strong emotions that it releases? If either of these extremes sounds familiar, you may need to step back from your worry over your child's behavior and take a look at your own.

June 21 MY FRIEND DOESN'T LIKE ME ANYMORE

Adversity tests the sincerity of friends.[21] —AESOP

As soon as your child goes off to school and finds herself in new social situations, you can be sure that she will begin to experience the joys and traumas of close friendships. And sometimes things will seem more tragic to her than they do to you. How do you help her through the pitfalls, the disappointments and betrayals, of close friendship?

It can be helpful to remember your own ups and downs with friends. Take a few moments right now, close your eyes, and call to mind what it was like to be in grade school and pre–high school. Can you remember times when you felt abandoned, cheated, or misunderstood by friends that you counted on for support? This childhood drama is the stage upon which adult social skills are learned, and the feelings were no doubt as real to you as any you have felt since. Remembering this early cast of characters and the intricate plots that occupied center stage in the past can help you be empathic with your child's tales of woe.

Therefore, when she tells you the difficulties, the answer is not to tell her to lighten up, nor is it to get in there and try to fix everything for her. Your compulsion to fix the situation may send her the message that your opinion of her is tied up in how well this situation turns out; that if she doesn't take drastic action to keep her friendship on an even keel, you may be severely disappointed in her.

She needs you to listen to her, not take sides, affirm your love for her no matter what, and help her to come up with some alternatives. If your child is young, you may be able to take an active role. But the older your child is, the more you will need to stand on the sidelines, help her draw some boundaries, and cheer her on as she figures out how to solve the problem herself.

Standing back and making yourself available for moral support can be difficult for a concerned parent. But as your daughter develops into a fully functional person, this is a role you'll be called upon to play more and more often.

June 22 THE SOLSTICE

Some people say there is a new sun every day, that it begins its life at dawn and lives for one day only.[22]
—BYRD BAYLOR

On or about this day every year in the northern hemisphere, the sun is directly overhead at noon at the tropic of Cancer, and summer officially begins. This is the summer solstice, which celebrates the longest day and the shortest night of the year.

Do your children know about the summer solstice and what it means? Whether they have been exposed to this concept in school or through other means, you can discuss it with them again. They can know that this is a special day. It has always been a special day, for all people, all over the world. Until very recently people lived in harmony with the changing seasons. They were more aware of the sun and the moon and the stars. The movement of these bodies across the heavens had great meaning in preindustrial cultures, and celebrations and religious rites marked this day as distinct from all others.

The summer solstice is a wonderful excuse to spend some time talking with your children about a variety of subjects the event suggests. If you plan ahead and go to the library for books, then you will have plenty to discuss with your children. But it isn't necessary.

Here are some questions that are intended to suggest the richness of the conversations you can have with your kids on this day. You don't have to have special knowledge of astronomy or anthropology; you can simply be carried by your interest in exploring new ideas with them.

Many years ago, when people lived on farms, and without electricity, what do you think they did on the longest day of the year when it was too light to go to sleep? Why do you think people would celebrate the coming of summer, which is signaled by the solstice? What happens to the earth when there is more sunlight shining on it, or less?

When you share your interest in the natural world, your children are able to make connections they have no way of making on their own. This is a perfect opportunity to help them enlarge their understanding of the world and have fun using their imaginations.

June 23 MIDSUMMER

Once I spoke the language of the flowers,
Once I understood each word the caterpillar said . . .[23]

—SHEL SILVERSTEIN

We believe in taking as many opportunities as you can for celebration. The summer solstice is one that is built into the natural rhythm of the year. If you go to the library, you will find a richness of books on myths and celebrations that have occurred in many cultures all over the world. But even without special references to guide you, you can use the solstice as an excuse for a "sun" party.

Your theme is the long-lasting daylight. Depending on the age of your children and the weather in your part of the country, you might consider staying up outside until the sun finally sinks in the west. You can note the time and marvel at how late it actually is. Your kids can help you prepare foods that are sun-centered. You can drink sun tea from tea bags soaked outside in water warmed by the sun and then cooled in the refrigerator. The food can reflect your imaginative associations with sunny themes: deviled eggs as miniature suns; salads from farm-fresh vegetables that have just come in season: sun-dried tomato pasta; dried fruits; "hot climate" ingredients such as lemons, olives, avocados, and tropical fruits; a big, round sun cake with yellow frosting for dessert.

Whatever you choose, you are helping your children see that the length of the day makes a difference; the temperature and the amount of sunlight still have a direct effect on our lives. On a more symbolic level, you are helping them celebrate the coming of light and the eclipsing of darkness. When you celebrate the winter solstice in December, you will be helping them see that the cold, dark days are also part of the natural cycle. We need both the light and the dark, and we can appreciate both for the richness they bring.

June 24 RULE BREAKING

They [adolescents] are struggling hard to figure out how to behave, what to do, and why . . .[24]

—ROBERT COLES

You are now into the summer, and everyone is spending as much time as they can outdoors. If you have school-age children, they are glorying in the prospect that summer will never end, while you, on the other hand, may be *afraid* that it will never end.

The concern, if you are a working parent, is how to help your child cope with all that unstructured time during the day. If you have young children, you will arrange for child care, and that's that. But if your kids are too old for a baby-sitter, the problem can be more difficult. You worry about what your older children are going to do with their unsupervised, "hanging out" time. As a precautionary measure, you may be thinking of all the ways you can make sure that your presence is somehow part of your child's consciousness, whether you are actually in the house or not.

Clearly, you and your child will want to spend some time discussing each day's schedule. Part of that discussion will center on expectations and appropriate rules of behavior. For example, you may not want your fourteen-year-old son to have more than two friends over when you're not there. Or you may not want your daughter to spend all day at the mall. Or you may want both of them to spend the afternoon doing yard work after they swim in the pool that morning. Whatever your expectations and limitations, you want to be sure that you communicate them clearly and that your children have the opportunity to respond. They may want to negotiate the details or influence you to compromise in one way or another. That's fine as long as you discuss it and the decisions are clear to everyone.

But what happens when the boundaries you agreed upon are not being observed? The transgression of household rules is something you will want to think about and take action on. Some parents find themselves reacting in anger and then reaching for a standard punishment, such as "grounding." The problem is that punishment tends to be an ineffective tool for facilitating new behavior, and the punishment you reach for may have no relation to the transgression. You may establish momentary control, but, unless you have a very strong, positive connection with your child and she understands and agrees with the punishment, the solution is short-lived.

Instead, think in terms of connections. You want your response to be connected to the violation, and you want to reestablish your personal connection with your offending child. Be assured that your child has a strong moral sense and a desire for guidance. This is not done by establishing guilt and shame in your child, but through long-term positive contact characterized by listening, being available, and establishing mutual trust. The question you might ask yourself after she has disappointed you is how you can keep your long-term conversation going despite your disappointment over what she has done.

June 25 QUESTIONS ABOUT SEX

Questions are never indiscreet. Answers sometimes are.[25]

—OSCAR WILDE

When children first ask about sexual matters, parents have a sense of how important their answers are. What they say next will be remembered. Although some parents feel compelled to deflect, ignore, or disapprove of their children's inquiries, most want the opportunity to shape their children's attitudes and behaviors in this area. They aren't content to leave it to friends or the popular culture.

Perhaps you remember how your mother or father interacted with you when you began to feel sexually curious. Your memories have no doubt helped shape your ideas about how you want to respond to your own children. If you are in touch with what you wanted to know when you were young, you can use that awareness to guide you now.

A general guideline is to respond to questions about sex as honestly as you can with enough information to answer the questions as completely as possible without elaboration. Your child is looking for information, not a moralizing lecture that conveys your fear or distaste. If your child is receiving some structured sex education in school, it is important for you to be supportive of that information; if he is getting information from his friends, it is important to make sure that the information is accurate.

Parents of older children will notice a shift from questions that sound like, "What is this all about?" to questions that imply, "What should I be doing? How do you feel about this?" Older children expect and need their parents to help them deal with human sexuality from both an informational *and* a moral and ethical standpoint.

As always, before you can provide good guidance to your children, you will need to be on speaking terms with your own attitudes on the subject. Although your sexuality is a deeply private matter, how you respond to questions, what you say about sex, and what you convey through nonverbal messages will greatly impact your children. Now is a good time to begin thinking these issues through so you are prepared to be a positive factor in your child's developing sexuality.

Here are some questions that can help you order your thoughts. As a parent who has a need for a sexual outlet yourself, how do you present your own sexuality to your child? Do you pretend it doesn't exist? If you are a sexually active single parent, how do you interpret your behavior for your children? If you are sure of the rules for sexual behavior that you want to communicate to your older children, how well do you follow those rules yourself? How firmly do you believe what you are saying?

June 26 TELEVISION

> *. . . he had a thousand and one basic reasons for being bored, the slightest thing, like pushing a ball with a billiard cue, will be enough to divert him.*[26]
>
> —BLAISE PASCAL

Pascal couldn't have imagined the role television would play in our lives as a diversion. And now that summer's really in full swing, your children may be diverting themselves in this way more than ever.

You may have seen the bumper sticker that says, "Kill Your Television!" For some families eliminating the TV is a reasonable option. But for most, it is not. Whether we like it or not, television is a major force in our society. It not only provides us with information and entertainment, but it strongly influences our attitudes, values, and perceptions. And whether we admit it or not, television is a satisfactory child-rearing aid for busy, exhausted parents.

It is worthwhile to think about what role you want television to play in your life and your children's lives. As the parent, you have the right and the obligation to determine, in consultation with your children, which societal influences hold sway in your household.

We would like to suggest that you read through the following statements and think about how much you agree or disagree with them. Focusing your thoughts in this way will help you come up with a television policy that is intentional and consistent:

- Television ought to be balanced with other forms of learning or entertainment that involve more participation and interaction.
- Television viewing should be restricted to specific times and specific programs.
- Parents need to know what their children are watching.
- Parents need to watch commercial television with young children to help them distinguish between the program itself and the ads that are trying to sell products, since small children are not able to make these distinctions themselves.
- Parents should avoid using the television set as a babysitter for long stretches of time.

Reviewing these ideas will help you understand more clearly your own approach toward television viewing. If you want to cut down on the amount of TV your children watch, be sure to discuss the change with them first. It works for some families to go "cold turkey," but most will want to restrict viewing gradually, allowing their children as many choices as possible.

You can let them know that one reason you are suggesting less television is that you want to spend more time with them doing other things, and you want them to have the pleasure and satisfaction of engaging in a whole range of activities. Not just one.

June 27 WORK AND MONEY

I remember a wise old gentleman who used to say, "When children are doing nothing, they are doing mischief."[27] —HENRY FIELDING

You may already have settled the question of allowances in your family. If you haven't, or if you're not satisfied with your current policy, you might want to think about it further. As is the case with television viewing, this issue requires some good thought.

Some parents believe that children need spending money, and they provide it in the form of an allowance. Others want their children to learn the value of money early and expect their children to earn their money by doing household chores or holding a part-time job. Still others give money to their children on an as-needed basis. By the time your children leave home, you might have found yourself exercising some combination of these options or all of them at different times.

In summer the question of spending money can be especially important. For one thing, your child has more unstructured time, and that usually means more opportunities for going to the movies, shopping, and eating out. Teenagers are often anxious for the extra freedom and buying power a summer job brings.

Talking about work and money with your children can be very rewarding. You can discuss what it means to live in a mass market, commercialized culture. This is a society that asks kids to buy a great deal. There are clothes, computers, sports equipment, entertainment, food, cosmetics, and the list goes on. When you talk about these issues, your children get an opportunity to hear about your experiences and your views. There are opportunities to explore the relationship between money and status, and money and worth. And there are specific learning opportunities to teach them about budgets and financial management.

Wherever you are in your parenting cycle, this is a good time to pause and ask yourself how you are handling your own financial responsibilities and opportunities, and how you are teaching your children to handle theirs. This is a subject that requires full and frank discussion as well as all your listening skills and loving support.

June 28 TAKING CARE OF YOURSELF

What I call innocence is the spirit's unself-conscious state at any moment of pure devotion to any object. It is at once a receptiveness and total concentration.[28]

—ANNIE DILLARD

We are made happy by many different things. This is a good day to ask yourself what you need to lift your spirits and make you happy. Since an important part of becoming a conscious parent is becoming more aware of your own desires and needs, this is a meaningful question to ask on a regular basis. Even if you are not able to gratify your desire today, you can enjoy identifying what would make you happy, along with the prospect of fulfillment in the future.

If you can think of simple things, you will be more likely to attain them. Here are some simple ideas, suggested to us by people to whom we asked the question, "What is a simple thing you could do for yourself today that would make you happy?"

- Take a half-hour nap after lunch.
- Have a cup of Chai tea in the afternoon.
- Eat a chili dog with sauerkraut.
- Go see a movie after work.
- Buy a new lipstick.
- Spend an evening alone with my wife, without the kids.
- The Sunday *New York Times.*
- Curl up with a trashy book.
- Indulge in a half-hour of yoga stretches.

You get the idea. We have found that people don't have trouble thinking of things that would make them happy. And it seems that many of these pleasures are within reach. Can you find a way to give yourself a treat today and bring a smile to your lips?

June 29 SPEAKING A LOVING TRUTH

The environment in which we experience new information has a strong influence on our actions and reactions to that information.[29]

—JENNIFER JAMES

One of the most profound ways we take care of ourselves is to say what needs to be said. Is there something you need or want to say to someone close to you, perhaps something you've been thinking, but haven't found the right words for? It could be something loving and supportive, or it could be something difficult.

Spend a few moments thinking about the people in your life who have recently done something nice for you. Perhaps you want to thank them for an act of kindness. Or maybe someone has done something that you appreciate for its beauty of competence. A coworker may have done a good job on a report or a presentation. Your daughter may have done a nice job setting the table. Your spouse may have surprised you by how well he or she soothed your crying child. Letting people know that you see and appreciate their efforts helps them and makes you feel good too.

Perhaps what comes to mind is that you need to honestly express your feelings to someone close to you, even though your message is bound to cause some pain. Maybe your wife needs to know that you don't want a surprise party for your birthday, or your friend needs to know that you can't spend so much time talking on the phone at work, or your son needs to know that you are uncomfortable giving him more money until he gets a job.

You can use this opportunity to see whether there are feelings and thoughts you have that will be both good for you to express and good for the other person to hear. If you think there are, you can rehearse what you want to say ahead of time, so your message is delivered in a positive and constructive way. When you are honest with yourself and lovingly honest with those around you, you are taking care of yourself in a profound way. And you are building positive relationships with the people around you.

June 30 HALFWAY THROUGH THE YEAR

This you must always bear in mind: what is the nature of the whole, and what is my nature, and how this is related to that, and what kind of part is it of what kind of whole.[30] —MARCUS AURELIUS

Instead of looking ahead to the rest of the summer, let's spend some time looking back. Whether or not you have been reading this book since January, this is a good time to take stock. We are halfway through the calendar year. Give yourself the pleasure of allowing some time to reflect on yourself as a parent and as a person. In what ways are you a different person today from who you were on January 1 of this year?

As you review the last six months, the big events will no doubt claim your attention first. Perhaps there were trips, a death, a move, a promotion at work. Your family's financial situation may have changed for the better, or for the worse. There are countless internal and external occurrences that have changed you. Apart from the big events, there is the slow accumulation of influences that hardly alter your daily routine, but that affect your internal world. If you have been reading this book, you will have spent many hours by now thinking about your past, your family, and your intrinsic nature. You know more about yourself than you did in January.

In addition to looking at the changes in yourself, you may be able to detect changes in your significant relationships. If you are part of a committed relationship, how has that changed? Do you find that you discuss problems more easily with each other than you once did? Do you find yourselves in agreement about how to facilitate the growth of your children? Where do you still have areas to work on between you?

As you have observed your children over the course of the last six months, you can undoubtedly pinpoint obvious changes in each of them. Can you more easily recognize their stages of development? Can you see underneath the mask of behavior to the needs and motivations that generate that behavior? What do you know about each child that you didn't know in January?

As you pause at this midpoint in the year, you can bring to mind a vision of where you want to be when the year finally ends six months from now. How do you want to be feeling about your children, your partner, and yourself? What will you *have* that you don't yet have now? How will you *be* in a way that you aren't yet being now?

Notes

1. Mary Oliver, "The Summer Day," in *New and Selected Poems* (Boston: Beacon Press, 1992).

2. William Wordsworth, "The Tables Turned," in *Selected Poetry* (New York: The Modern Library, 1950).

3. Steven Foster and Meredith Little, *The Roaring of the Sacred River* (New York: Prentice Hall, 1989).

4. Paul Reps, *Zen Flesh, Zen Bones: A Collection of Zen and Pre-Zen Writings* (New York: Doubleday, 1989).

5. Rabindranath Tagore, *The Collected Poems and Plays of Rabindranath Tagore* (New York: Macmillan, 1962).

6. Sharon Olds, "First Birth," in *Wellspring* (New York: Knopf, 1996).

7. M. Scott Peck, *The Road Less Traveled: A New Psychology of Love, Traditional Values, and Spiritual Growth* (New York: Simon & Schuster, 1978).

8. Anonymous, *The Cloud of Unknowing,* section 4, trans. Clifton Wolfers (London: Penguin, 1978).

9. James P. Carse, *Breakfast at the Victory: The Mysticism of Ordinary Experience* (San Francisco: HarperSanFrancisco, 1994).

10. T. S. Eliot, "The Lovesong of J. Alfred Prufrock," in *Reading Modern Poetry*, eds. Paul Engle and Warren Carrier (Glenview, IL: Scott Foresman, 1968).

11. Arlie Hochschild, *The Time Bind* (New York: Henry Holt, 1997).

12. Epictetus, *The Enchiridion*, trans. Thomas W. Higginson (New York: Liberal Arts Press, 1948).

13. Plato, *The Republic, Book VII*, in *Five Great Dialogues*, trans. B. Jowett, ed. Louise Ropes Loomis (Roslyn, NY: Walter J. Black, 1942).

14. Khalil Gibran, "On Marriage," in *The Prophet* (New York: Knopf, 1983).

15. Edna Johnson, Evelyn R. Shields, and Frances Clarke Sayers, eds., *Anthology of Children's Literature* (Boston: Houghton Mifflin, 1970).

16. Dylan Thomas, "Fern Hill," in *Modern Poetry*, ed. Maynard Mack, *et al.* (Englewood Cliffs, NJ: Prentice Hall, 1963).

17. Gerald Durrell, *Menagerie Manor* (London: Penguin Books, 1964).

18. Phyllis McGinley, "Homework for Anabelle," in *Times Three* (New York: Viking, 1960).

19. Søren Kierkegaard, *Fear and Trembling*, in *A Kierkegaard Anthology*, ed. Robert Bretall (Princeton, NJ: Princeton University Press, 1946).

20. Rudyard Kipling, "If," in *One Hundred and One Favorite Poems,* ed. Roy J. Cook (Chicago, IL: The Reilly and Lee Co, 1958).

21. Aesop, "The Travelers and the Bear," *Aesop's Fables,* selected and adapted by Jack Zipes (New York: Signet Classic, 1992).

22. Byrd Baylor, *The Way to Start a Day* (New York: Aladdin Books, 1978).

23. Shel Silverstein, "Forgotten Language," in *Where the Sidewalk Ends* (New York: Harper & Row, 1974).

24. Robert Coles, *The Moral Intelligence of Children* (New York: Random House, 1997).

25. Oscar Wilde, *An Ideal Husband*, quoted in *The Portable Oscar Wilde*, ed. Richard Addington and Stanley Weintraub (New York: Viking Penguin, 1981).

26. Blaise Pascal, *Pensées*, trans. A. J. Krailsheimer (London: Penguin Books, 1995).

27. Henry Fielding, *Tom Jones* (Watford, Herts., Eng.: Taylor Garnett Evans & Co., 1960).

28. Annie Dillard, *Pilgrim at Tinker Creek* (New York: Harper & Row, 1974).

29. Jennifer James, *Thinking in the Future Tense* (New York: Simon & Schuster, 1996).

30. Marcus Aurelius, "Meditation No. 9," in *Marcus Aurelius and His Times*, trans. George Long (Roslyn, NY: Walter J. Black, 1945).

July

INTRODUCTION TO THE MONTH OF JULY

Conscious parenting is a multifaceted experience that emphasizes the different needs children have at different ages. This means that you as a parent grow along with your child. During this month we take a closer look at the challenges your children face at different developmental phases and how you can continue to express love, caring, and respect for each child at every age and in every circumstance.

July 1 IN THE *GOOD OLD* SUMMERTIME

After a little I am taken in and put to bed. Sleep, soft smiling, draws me unto her . . .[1]

—JAMES AGEE

July brings many of the summer traditions we have grown to love. It's a month full of national holidays like Canada Day (July 1), Independence Day (July 4), and Bastille Day (July 14). The baseball season is about half over, and the All Star game is coming up. It's a time for swimming outdoors, for family picnics, for crickets rhythmically chirping in a darkness that comes very late. It's a season for mosquitoes and, for some, the curse of allergies. And across the Midwest, the South, and the East, it's a season for hot, humid days and nights punctuated by powerful electrical storms and cleansing, torrential rain.

Like James Agee's small boy in Knoxville, Tennessee, during the summer of 1915, children all over the country are accumulating memories of summer and of the leisurely time spent with their families, and of learning who they are. For them these will be the good old days of their childhood. In later years they will tell tales of how it was in their family, what the weather was like, who the main characters were in their lives. As all children do, they will feel that there was something mythical about these characters. They will survive in stories as somehow bigger, funnier, more loving, more loved than they actually were.

When your child tells stories of his childhood summers many years in the future and you are an important character in this faraway landscape, how do you think he will describe you? What will he know about you? Think of your own summer days as a child. Can you feel what it was like again? What stories can you tell your own children that convey the magic of a summer's evening with your family?

A prayer for today: *Remembering the times of peace and contentment I felt at times as a child causes me to value the memories my own child is creating now. May I honor each day as an opportunity my child and I share together.*

July 2 GIVING THANKS

> It is good to give thanks to the Lord,
> to sing praises to your name, O most High;
> to declare your steadfast love in the morning
> and your faithfulness by night.[2]
>
> —PSALM 92

It is a good thing to give thanks every morning and every night. Spend a few moments alone in contemplation of the blessings your family brings. Let your attention rest on each of your children, your mate if you have one, and other relatives you may feel close to: mother, father, sister, brother, nieces, nephews. Allow yourself the pleasure of seeing in your mind's eye each of these special people, and then become aware of how your feelings of love, respect, and gratitude register in your body. Do you feel warmer, softer, more energized, more open, less tense? As you focus on each person, give yourself the time to fully appreciate their unique qualities.

This ritual of gratitude can be done even when other, negative feelings are present in your consideration of others. We are complex creatures. Our responses to people are tinted with many different colors. This exercise simply asks you to bring your positive feelings to the foreground, helping you develop a more profound understanding of the ways that both positive and negative experiences can contribute to your personal growth. If you make giving thanks part of your daily life, you will come to see how annoyances and grievances with others can make you stronger and more loving. They, along with the happy times, add texture and meaning to your life.

As you enjoy this fine summer day, remember to thank the Giver of All Gifts, and resolve to use your gifts well.

July 3 RELATIONSHIPS WITH EXTENDED FAMILY

Why is our image of the ideal family so far from the common reality?[3]

—SALVADOR MINUCHIN

Tomorrow is one of the biggest extended family holidays of the year. You may be planning trips, vacations, or picnics that extend into the evening fireworks. Not only will you and your children be spending the day together, but you may be planning to widen your circle to include other relatives as well.

Before you find yourself in the thick of the family drama, spend a few moments now thinking about the people you will be sharing chicken and potato salad with tomorrow. Is there someone who stands out as a little harder to get along with, more irritating, or more flawed than the others? You know what we mean: the aunt or uncle or mother-in-law who truly gets on your nerves. You tell yourself that if you have to listen to the stories or the complaints one more time, you'll scream.

If there is such a person, then you have been given an opportunity. The opportunity is to prepare yourself now to be tolerant, attentive, and forgiving when the two of you are actually face-to-face. To do this, you can practice these attitudes right now. Let yourself call this person to mind as fully as you can. Now visualize him or her surrounded with a warm, golden light. This is the light of your non-self-centered love. It contains within it tolerance, affection, and forgiveness. It overlooks petty and annoying personality traits and holds the whole person up to the light, knowing that there are hidden wounds and sorrows that mar the perfection of all of us, including yourself.

This visualization will help you feel differently about crabby Aunt Alice or selfish Cousin Bob when you sit down to eat together tomorrow. You know that you don't have to approve of their way of being in the world, but you can approach them with a new sense of compassion. Regardless of what your Fourth of July celebration is like, you can rejoice in your private celebration of personal reconciliation.

July 4 CELEBRATING THE FOURTH

Humanity with all its fears,
With all the hopes of future years,
Is hanging breathless on thy fate![4]
—HENRY WADSWORTH LONGFELLOW

Sometimes we are left with the feeling that the Fourth of July is just a day to have off from work. Maybe you're planning a picnic and fireworks with the family, or a couple of hours indoors watching the latest summer blockbuster movie. It is also a day for national celebration, and this means you have an opportunity to share something deeper with your children, in addition.

Democracies embody some important features that we tend to take for granted. They are conscious embodiments of the will of the people. They are all founded upon a three-legged stool: respect for law, tradition, and reason in equal measure. They derive their authority from the consent of the governed, so that they can learn and profit from past mistakes rather than being forced to perpetuate mistakes and then reverse them.

The democracies of the western hemisphere all share an atmosphere of multiculturalism. With the exception of native peoples, all of our ancestors arrived here looking for a fresh start, unburdened by Old World social or religious barriers. No nation, however, is free from mistakes. It is important to remember, accept, and integrate these too. Nations as well as individuals suffer from dysfunctional legacies, and the United States is no exception with its legacy of slavery, dislocation of native peoples, and distrust of immigrants.

Nevertheless, we have some unique things to celebrate on Independence Day. You live in a great country. You live in a country that celebrates the ability to accept the rule of the majority in freely elected legislative bodies, while at the same time respecting the legitimacy of minority opinions. In a way, we live in a country that is always trying to become conscious rather than allowing itself to be controlled by its darker nature.

How will you and your family be celebrating Independence Day? What values do your country and community represent for you that you want your children to understand? How do you model for your children a respect for law, tradition, and reason?

July 5 PHYSICAL FITNESS

The real bottom line hasn't changed: you still must eat right and exercise to maintain a healthy weight.[5] —ENVIRONMENTAL NUTRITION

Physical inactivity has serious health consequences. According to this same article in *Environmental Nutrition,* more than one-quarter of a million deaths occur each year from obesity-related health problems, making overweight the second leading cause of preventable death in the U.S. after smoking. This means that one of the most valuable lifelong gifts you can give your children is the gift of involvement in physical activities.

You can instill the value of being active in many ways. Most obviously, you can become a physically active person yourself. When your children see you looking forward to a walk after dinner, it makes an impression. When you and your spouse play tennis, ride your bikes, take ballroom dance lessons, or hike on the weekends, you are also sending a message. When, through the years, your children witness your pleasure in yoga, aerobic, or stretch classes, they absorb your enthusiasm and come to think of their bodies as important elements in their overall well-being, to be enjoyed and cared for. They learn these attitudes from you.

In addition to enjoying these activities yourself, you can go out of your way to make physical activity part of your *family* life. You can not only eat together, read together, and go to concerts together—but you can enjoy exercise together.

If sports, exercise, and body care are not now part of your everyday life, it is not too late to add them. Studies show conclusively that exercise can be successfully introduced in to the lives of people of any age. And chances are you aren't even close to old age yet! If exercise is new to you, you can start with the simplest and most effective exercise we know: walking. If you are out-of-shape, start by walking five or ten minutes and very gradually work up from there. Invite your children to come with you. Or sign up for a class that will allow them to come along. For every person, there exists some form of physical movement that is just right.

Our bodies were meant to move. They break down when we don't breathe deeply and use our muscles. If your children have been sedentary, do what you can to coax, invite, and expect them to participate in physical activities. When they are seventy-five and healthy, they will thank you.

July 6 WHEN YOUR CHILDREN ACHIEVE AT DIFFERENT LEVELS

Come my beloved,
consider the lilies.[6]
—ANNE SEXTON

We are aware of a family where an older son publicly overshadows his younger brother. The older boy, whom we'll call Bob, is a high achiever in science. He is also something of an athlete and is active in high school student government. The younger brother, Sean, although he is intelligent and popular with other kids in middle school, is an average student. He seems to just putt along without being particularly interested in academics or sports. He does, however, show some interest in drawing.

The mother in this family is especially anxious to assure her younger son that he, too, is appreciated and loved. She sees him as an "underdog," and that means that she tends to overprotect him in order to compensate. We'll reconstruct a conversation she had with Sean at a point when he was showing her one of his drawings:

Mother: Wow! That is outstanding! That drawing of a horse is just about the best one I have seen by someone your age. You should do more with art. Maybe that's where your talents lie.

Sean: Oh, Mom, it's not that great. Lots of kids I know can do better.

Mother: No, really, it's very good. Would you like to take some art classes? Maybe you should try watercolors.

Sean: Well, okay. I guess I could do that if you want.

This younger child is intelligent enough to know that, one, his drawing is okay, but nothing special and, two, that his mother is worried about how much he is achieving. She tends to inflate Sean's accomplishments, attempting to equalize her appreciation so that both sons feel equal. As a result Bob doesn't feel properly rewarded for doing what he does well, because his mother is very sparing in her careful praise of his accomplishments.

This mother is having trouble seeing that it is her own conflicted relationship to achievement that is at the root of her actions. The message she is sending here to Sean is: "You are something of a disappointment to me. I feel that you are able to accomplish more than you have done. High achievement is very important to me, but since you can't really compete with your brother in important ways, I am going to help you find a way in which you *can* compete and achieve. That would be a relief to me."

This mother, though well-meaning, isn't playing fair with her children, and both of them can see it. The older child feels that his accomplishments are being ignored: The harder he tries and the more he achieves, the more frustrated he is that his mother values his achievement equally with his brother's. The younger child learns that his mother is worried about him and that her judgment of him is in some sense a lie. He is also being let off the hook by not being allowed to find his own way without his mother running interference for him. He is learning not to trust the information she gives him. Although he feels duty bound to try to please her, he is really humoring her rather than satisfying his own interest.

It is difficult to find fault with this mother's motives. She is trying to smooth the way for the son who isn't quite "measuring up." But she needs to take a different approach. Can you see some ways in which you could advise her to interact with her two sons so that each of them feels valued and supported for who he really is?

July 7 A QUESTION OF MOTIVATION

Here and there is born a Saint Theresa, foundress of nothing . . .[7]

—GEORGE ELIOT

If you have more than one child or if you grew up in a family with more than one child, you can probably relate to inequalities between children in the same family. Of course, siblings are often very similar, but, depending on age, gender, and many other factors, they may also be very different. As we saw yesterday in discussing two levels of achievement, one may seem to be highly motivated, while another may seem to have no particular direction. This is another way in which children can develop differently. But it may have less to do with the children themselves than with the attitudes their parents take toward them and their birth order.

One child, often the oldest, may accept and integrate easily the value a parent places on performing well, especially in the areas where the parent is highly invested. Another child of the same parent may see, quite rightly, that her sibling is already so far ahead in the areas that count that there's no point in competing in those areas. What is important to note, however, is that both children are responding to the parent and the parent's ideas about what is important. One is successful in pleasing the parent; the other is less so. One learns that she is going to do well in life, because she is doing what her parent expects; the other does less well and therefore fears that she is inadequate.

It's a dangerous thing for parents to be too invested in the interests and achievements of their children. A parent can force a child to value what he values, but such coercion, even when it is skillful and subtle, doesn't accomplish his goals. Manipulation, coercion, and every other kind of undue influence create more problems than they solve. Besides, his child's interest or lack of interest in art, music, sports, computers, dance, or any other activity is not a "problem" at all. But if it were anyone's problem, it would be his child's.

While it is important for children to compete successfully in the world as adults, the subjects they choose to be interested in and the ways in which they choose to compete can be various and complicated. As you think about your own children or yourself in a family with more than one child, can you step outside the system you have carefully constructed for yourself that defines success and failure?

Does her direction please you? In that case, she may have chosen the same battleground you yourself chose: sports, music, science, the liberal arts, or social acceptance, for example. Are you worried about her ability to compete and do you feel a need to motivate her in other directions? In that case, she may be receiving the message from you that her own personality and interests are a disappointment to you.

What ways can you support your child as she chooses or does not choose to be motivated in a particular direction? How can you relax your need for her to "be" in a certain way and not to "be" in others?

July 8 BEING AVAILABLE AND INVOLVED WITH A YOUNGER CHILD

. . . a quick wash of feeling signaled for the children and for me that a poem or story had happened, regardless of whether we wrote it down or called it so.[8]

—WILLIAM STAFFORD

This father is a poet, so he gives his children small stories that might be poems. He is present for his children and gives them what he has to give. This is what children need. They need to know that you are *reliably* warm and available to them. This may be what everybody needs, but older children and adults learn to make allowances, to wait their turn, to understand extenuating circumstances, and not to expect the people around them to drop everything and attend to their needs. Young children, however, flourish when their early years are spent in a world made safe and caring by parents who love and attend to them.

Common sense tells us that real life gives us the chance to flexible with this idea. There are many times during the day when children have to be patient. Even very young children can learn to wait a little before you drop everything to turn to them. When you are on the phone or driving or changing the baby's diaper, there is a lapse of time before you can pick up your two-year-old and give him a reassuring hug.

Waiting a little is a good thing for him to learn, as long as he knows that he can count on you. Through you and your responses to him he forms his expectations of life and his own sense of self-worth. Every moment you're with him you are sending him messages about how the world works. Your curiosity and interest in his treasures, your support when he's uncertain, your love freely given, help him enter the world with confidence and energy. The time and devotion you invest now will reap countless rewards for him and for you later.

It's worth pausing for a moment and letting yourself think about the messages you want to send your child during those routine moments every day when nothing much seems to be happening except the two of you are in the moment together.

July 9 ACTING AS COACH TO YOUR OLDER CHILDREN

Advice for Coaches:

1. Become a communicator.
2. Recognize the needs of your kids and balance your needs with theirs.
3. Develop perspective: remember what you were like at their age and what you could do then; don't judge the kids by what you can do now.[9]

—AMERICAN YOUTH AND SPORTS PARTICIPATION

As your children grow, and become more capable and independent, your role changes. While you are still reliably available and warm, you find yourself flavoring your support with more coaching—the best kind of coaching. You are ready to share your experience and your belief that your child can learn and do things and be happy. And you expect her to do more of the work herself. She has to remember to take her lunch to school *and* keep track of homework assignments *and* ask her friend to her birthday party. You are there teaching her how to accomplish these tasks, standing by to offer encouragement and advice if she asks for it.

We all know what bad coaching looks like. It often wears an angry face. The coach cares more about the performance than he does about the individual development of his players. He will pass up opportunities to let his kids learn from experience in favor of micromanaging their actions. Often he expects too much and pushes too hard.

As parents it is possible to make some of these same mistakes. You can be so busy or so distracted or so symbiotic that you pass up opportunities to teach your children about life's important lessons.

If your children are nine years old or older, give some thought to what it would mean to *coach* your child about how to handle a problem or meet a goal. Would that look and sound different from how you usually handle problem situations?

July 10 YOUR YOUNG CHILD IS DEPRESSED

> It is no wonder that her brown study
> Astonishes us all.[10]
>
> —JOHN CROWE RANSOM

When this poem was written in 1924, a blue mood was called a "brown study," and such moods were remarked upon and puzzled over in the literature of the time. Even today our moods are somewhat mysterious to us. We know they are influenced by many different factors. For example, when you open the pages of this book, sometimes you are in thrall to the beauty and joy of the world. Other days you feel dull and listless, and still others you may feel really down.

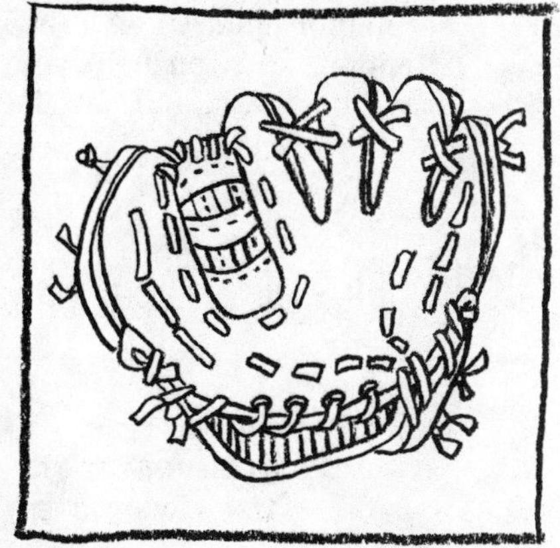

The science of mood and emotion is still in its infancy, but there are some things we know. On the physical level, a person can elevate his mood with exercise, sunlight, proper nutrition, and adequate sleep. On the emotional level, he can elevate his mood through relaxation and visualization, supportive human relationships, meditation and prayer, and loving, generous actions.

As an adult you may be aware of these factors and intentionally take steps to do the things you know will help. And as a person who has lived in the world awhile, you know that you can brighten your mood by completing a task that has been weighing on you or by engaging in creative work that captures your full attention. So you have some knowledge and some resources.

But what about your children? How can you help a young child under ten who seems to be depressed? First, you have to be tuned in to your child's moods. Take a moment now and review your observations of your child for the last week. Could you say what her outlook on life has been and what her energy level has been?

Whenever you notice that your child is unresponsive and exhibiting changes in eating and sleeping habits, it's time to do some investigating. If there has been a disruptive or disturbing event in her life, you may need to look no further. Whether the unhappiness involved her directly, or someone else she is close to, her feelings of sadness or worry may be perfectly natural.

If nothing has happened that you know of, you can always ask her how she is feeling. One mother we know of who asked her five-year-old daughter about her moping was shocked to discover that she thought her father was going to die. She had overheard a conversation about the poor health of her grandfather, who happens to have the same name as her father. It was a simple problem to resolve.

If your questions don't yield any information either, then you may be witnessing a blue mood of undetermined origin. Your approach in this case can be the same as it would be if there were a specific problem. The best response is more loving contact with you and with other caring people in the child's life: more time talking, more time doing things together, more time laughing and playing. Feeling down and slightly depressed is normal for children, as it is for adults. If you are there, paying attention, you can help your child know that all feelings are okay, they pass, and she doesn't have to face the hard times alone.

July 11 YOUR OLDER CHILD IS DEPRESSED

In the deserts of the heart
Let the healing fountain start.[11]

—W. H. AUDEN

Keeping track of the moods of your teenagers can be a roller-coaster ride for you, as well as for them. It's as if they are in a hurry to explore all the human territory before it's too late. But if you notice that your child seems depressed, and the mood seems to be lasting, you can initiate a dialogue with him to see if you can learn more about what is happening.

You: Jake, sometime today when you have about fifteen minutes, can we talk?

Jake: Sure, right now's okay.

You: Good. I've been noticing that you seem a little down this week, and I wondered whether there was something bothering you, and whether you wanted to talk about it.

And then you are off and running . . . It may be that there *is* something bothering Jake, but he doesn't want to talk about it with you. If that's the case, you can simply let him know that you are warmly and reliably available to him if he does decide to come to you later. Additional words of support are always welcome: "I think you're a great person." "Whatever's bothering you, I know you'll be able to straighten it out." "I'm here for you." "I love you."

If you have a teenager whose normal pattern of behavior is significantly and persistently disrupted, then you may have a problem that needs attention. The tendency toward depression is to some degree a matter of individual neurochemistry, and there are people who need medication to function well. In the teenage years, there are also endless possibilities for psychological problems or hormonal imbalances that may need professional help.

The best way for you to know what you are dealing with in an unhappy teenager is to stay close. In this case, staying close means maintaining a strong connection while encouraging all possible freedom. When your child does have a problem, he will be more likely to bring it to you if he knows that your response will be neutrally supportive of what is best for him, not overly emotional and not judgmental. Your unshakable belief in him and your genuine desire to be with him will sustain him as he faces the considerable challenges that modern adolescence brings.

July 12 APPROACHING A PROBLEM

The Wu Li master does not speak of gravity until the student stands in wonder at the flower petal falling to the ground.[12] —GARY ZUKAV

There will be times when you think that your child is having problems. If she is in trouble with teachers, other kids, or even the law, then you *know* there is a problem. But there are other times when, because you are used to observing how your child usually acts or seems to feel, you see that she is struggling with something, is depressed, or is generally "not herself," at least not the self you have come to expect.

It may not be possible or even advisable for you to intervene to solve her problems for her. But you naturally want to give her the support she needs to work through her difficulties and return to her normal, happy self. As an example of how you can do this, let's look at a child who is behaving differently than her father expects. It's not that he is acutely worried or that her behavior is causing him personal distress. He just wants to help her through her difficulties by lovingly supporting her:

Parent: Are you okay? It feels to me like you may be unhappy. You seem . . . [out of sorts, depressed, grouchy, uninterested in things you normally like to do]. Is there something you would like to talk about?

Child: No, not really.

Parent: Okay, but I am here if you need me.

Child: Well, all right. It's just that I'm having trouble with Amy.

Parent: Did something happen that makes you think that?

Child: Well, Amy has taken some things out of my locker without telling me. I think she is stealing things. She shows me things she has taken from other kids too.

Parent: She is taking things from you and from others. Does she want to include you in this?

Child: Yeah.

Parent: And it makes you feel worried? I really understand that that could make you feel uncomfortable. Have you talked about how you feel with her?

Child: Yeah. She won't admit she took my things. And she thinks stealing is cool.

Parent: You know that I love you and would like to help. I am glad you understand that stealing is wrong, and I am glad you are letting her know that you don't want to do this with her. Is there anything you would like me to do [*gives her a hug*]?

At this point, the parent has assured his daughter that he (1) understands her problem, (2) understands why she might be upset, (3) that he is there to help *if she needs advice*, (4) his love for her is independent of whether she and Amy resolve this problem and continue their friendship, and (5) she can trust her dad not to take any action without consulting her, despite the seriousness of the problem.

Can you think of a situation where your child had a real problem and where you could have used some of these ideas to make her feel your love, support, and connection? How did the situation resolve itself? Did you let your child solve her own problem? How invested were you in any solution you suggested; that is, how important was it that she follow your advice?

July 13

APPROACHING A PROBLEM YOU EXPERIENCE WITH YOUR CHILD

There is a taint of death, a flavour of mortality in lies—which is exactly what I hate and detest in the world—what I want to forget.[13]

—JOSEPH CONRAD

Yesterday we discussed the kind of problem that any child might have with one of her friends. Today, let's talk about an instance when the child is having a problem with her parent. This time the mother of a nine-year-old girl is not just a helpful observer. She is really upset with her daughter's behavior. The mother is a single woman in her late thirties. She works hard and attempts to keep her house in good order. But the little girl, Beth, refuses to clean her room. The room is such a mess that the mother rages to her friends, "Only a crazy person would have a room this messy. You can't believe it!"

The messy room makes the mother afraid that her daughter is basically "as lazy and uncaring as her father is." Feeling that way, the mother has pushed her daughter hard about this issue. At first she tried to reason with Beth. Later there were threats and loud accusations. Then she tried waiting to see when Beth would reach such a level of disgust with the condition of her room that she would clean it up herself. "Let her stew in her own juice until she can't stand it anymore." None of this has worked. The room has become a major source of anger between them, and neither will budge.

Breaking the deadlock will be up to the mother. She has already made some mistakes. What mistakes has she made? Without meaning to, she is treating her daughter as an alien "enemy," a kind of fifth-column reenactment of her father, the mother's much despised ex-husband. There is a kind of symbiosis at work here in which a loving mother has begun to treat a common problem, a child's messy room (even a very messy room), as a personal assault. Because she has cast this problem as an issue of primary control, she is determined to win "for the good of the child, so that she will not become like her father." In seeing the room as the room of a crazy person, she is disconnecting herself from Beth. After all, she herself is always neat and clean. The child's fear, anger, and confusion has resulted in her stubborn attempt to retain control over her own space.

Something must be done to change this situation. But what?

This mother can lovingly back off, apologize, and attempt to reconnect with her child. She can reestablish her daughter's right to be in charge of her own space and, at the same time, let her know her thoughts about the importance of some semblance of order. It won't be easy, and it won't be done in one conversation, partly because there may be other control issues that are muddying the waters.

After Beth and her mother reconnect, the mother might ask her daughter if she would like to make an appointment for the two of them to work on the room together. Beth may be leery and turn her down, or on the other hand, she might accept the invitation. Then the mother can use the work party as an excuse to have fun together. However they handle their reconnection, it is important that Beth not see her mother as an enemy to her developing sense of self *and* that her mother not come to believe that her child is out to sabotage her. This mother must re-vision her child in order to step outside her symbiosis.

If you were in charge of writing the reconciliation part of this story, how would you have Beth and her mother interact? You can refer to your own experience if you have had similar conflicts with your child. Thinking about these issues gives you an opportunity to consider what you would do if you began to view your own child as alien, defective, or profoundly different from you in a way that scares you.

July 14 A CHILD WHO HAS TO MAKE NEW FRIENDS

> Such a friend is someone whom we can trust to refine our understanding of what it means to live, who can guide us when we are lost and help us find the way along the path, who can assuage our anguish through the reassurance of his or her presence.[14]
>
> —STEPHEN BATCHELOR

Americans are a people on the move. We live in a highly mobile society, and it is likely that at some point you and your children will face the problems as well as the satisfactions of learning to cope with a new community. Perhaps you've been laid off at work and need to go where the jobs are. You may be looking for a new school system for your children. You may be moving into a new neighborhood as you move up in the housing market.

It is easier when your children are younger, because they have not yet reached the age when most of their development occurs outside the home. But if your child has reached the stage of concern, which begins at about age seven, it can be challenging for him to integrate into a new social group at school. Your child has already become comfortable in his old setting and may be leaving behind one or two very close friends, separating from whom feels like personal disaster. Not only must he face his fears of not being accepted by his new group, but he experiences the personal loss of his dearest friends. He will feel isolated and alone—a problem that you as his loving parent must take seriously.

Recognizing that your child will be in crisis during the adjustment period in a new setting, you can do several things:

- Remember that you, as the responsible adult, have decided to make this move for good reasons. His discomfort is not an indictment of your decision. You have to avoid being defensive about the move you have just made.
- Remind yourself that this lesson in learning flexibility will increase your child's sense of self-confidence and his willingness to try new things in the future. He will learn that he can do it.
- You can increase support from within the family by spending more time on family activities.
- You can make yourself available to discuss your child's worries and fears, rather than forcing him to view only the positive aspects of the move. You can allow him a full range of expression, even if you don't want to hear about the negative parts. You can share your own feelings of strangeness in this new setting and perhaps tell him about similar experiences you have had adjusting to new circumstances in the past. This is a time for empathy.
- You can help your child maintain contact with his old friends, if possible.
- You can begin to include new friends in your family circle as soon as your child is willing to bring them home. By being open to his choices and accepting of how he handles this transition, you are helping him discover who he is.

If you are anticipating the possibility of a move in the foreseeable future, it is helpful to prepare your child ahead of time. As you view your child now, can you guess how he will handle such a transition, and what he will need to help him strengthen his sense of self?

July 15 PROBLEMS OF SINGLE PARENTS

The number of single parents . . . averages out to a truly unprecedented 6 percent increase each year, reaching 12.2 million by 1996.[15]

— STEPHANIE COONTZ

Today, we want to pay homage to the courage and dedication of single parents. Whether you are a mother or a father raising children on your own, you work hard every day to be there for the children who depend on you. Both of us have been single parents ourselves and remember the challenges and the satisfactions.

Parenting by yourself can be complicated. There is more work on your shoulders, and there are often emotional complications that come from the divorce. You want your children to get the benefits of your union with their other parent, but you don't want them to suffer the consequences of the split. You want to be both mother and father to your children, manifesting the whole range of character strengths that are usually divided by gender, but it's difficult to extend beyond the limits of your own personality.

If you are a single mother and you have boys, you worry about providing a male role model. If you are a single father with girls, you worry about providing a female presence.

Whenever you are in danger of becoming overwhelmed by the task, you can come back to rest in this reality-based perspective: No one raises children in perfect circumstances. Many married parents cause their children difficulties that they can't avoid in spite of being married. You and your children find yourselves in a particular set of circumstances. Accepting them will help you get on with the job at hand. The safety, support, and structure that children need can be provided by either a mother or a father and by only one parent rather than two. You make an important contribution to your children's future happiness when you teach them how to cope with difficulties rather than misleading them by letting them think it is possible to live a life without problems.

Our intention here is to validate the challenges of being a single parent. We know how hard it is. And we want to express publicly how important your efforts are and what a difference it makes to you and your children and to the rest of us who live in the same neighborhood with you. So on this day, if you are a single parent, you can pause to give yourself the appreciation you deserve. You can go about the day's business, warmed from the inside by your satisfaction in the loving and tireless devotion you show to the children who are part of your family.

July 16 RESOURCES OF SINGLE PARENTS

Out of which door do I go,
Where and to whom?[16]
—THEODORE ROETHKE

One of the challenges of single parenthood is managing to get your own emotional needs met through appropriate adult contact and activities, rather than slipping into the error of relying on your children. You and your children may naturally feel a safeness and closeness in each other's company that reinforces the sense of separateness from others. While it is important to feel and act as though you are a family, with an identity and a history, you want the boundary around you to be permeable. You want all of you to benefit from infusions of energy and interest from the outside.

As an adult and a parent, you have interests, needs, and desires that you will want to meet apart from your children. If you have a strong sense of yourself as an independent, worthy person and a strong sense of the world as a place of possibility, then you will look for opportunities to exercise and enjoy your capacities in many different ways, even if you do not have a romantic partner.

First, of course, you will cultivate opportunities for adult conversation and stimulation. Friendships can be the mainstay of life, and they can be the spice. They often last longer than romantic alliances, and for many lucky people they extend well beyond the child-rearing years. There seems to be a magical alchemy to some friendships, but you are more likely to ignite the right chemical reactions if you are interested in other people and vividly alive to the possibilities in your own life. Then you have more to share.

Second, you have interests of your own. You may justifiably complain that you have little opportunity to exercise them, but they are still there. Maybe its a good idea to take an inventory of what you feel passionate about: raising roses, quilting, playing the bass, Celtic music, flea markets, the homeless, saving old-growth forests, the rings of Saturn! Are you in touch with your own flickers of interest? And if you are, how do you manifest your desire to know more and do more about them?

Third, you can encourage yourself to find meaning in everyday life. Do you like poetry, music, art, reading inspirational and sacred books? Do you allow yourself any time to reflect on your experiences and make the connections that give depth and meaning to what you are experiencing? There are many rituals that help people anchor to the deeper significance that runs underneath the chaos of making a living and raising children. People can meditate or pray or write in a journal or do daily devotional reading or walk in pristine natural settings as a way to prepare themselves to be open to the deeper meaning of their lives.

Fourth, you can exercise. Exercising brings benefits beyond the physical. It's true that you need to exercise to keep your body healthy and your weight under control. But exercising also results in better mood, more inner calm, and a sense of accomplishment. These sound like important benefits for people trying to raise children alone.

You may be tired and short of time. But don't forget to take care of the person who takes care of the children. That person is also a child of the universe, worthy of your tender love and consideration.

July 17 TROUBLE WITH AUTHORITY

For as pressing milk produces curds,
and pressing the nose produces blood,
so pressing anger produces strife.[17]
—PROVERBS 30:33

You have a child who is breaking rules. She is openly flaunting authority. You have gotten feedback that she is violating the rules. One of the first things you feel is anger, either at your child for being in this situation or at the person who has questioned your child's behavior. You may also experience fear—fear for the long-term well-being of your child or fear that somehow this "transgression" reflects on you.

Authority is usually represented either by a set of rules or by a person who embodies those rules. Sometimes authority is embodied in a set of traditions that have attained a level of acceptance that makes them difficult to question. They are, in effect, the standard of behavior within a particular community.

Sometime breaking the rules is a positive response on the part of your child, who cannot, in good conscience, abide by rules that make no sense to her. When you talk with her calmly and reasonably about her actions, you may discover that you can understand and in some sense agree with her "rebellion." You then have the duty to discuss the next steps, including any reparations she may need to make.

On the other hand, a child who breaks rules primarily because he refuses to recognize any authority but his own momentary impulse is a more serious matter. When this happens, you can bet you have an angry child. It is your task to understand that anger.

Having trouble with authority can be a natural outgrowth of a child's being subjected to too many arbitrary rules, which are set for him without his cooperation. Especially in later stages of growth and particularly in adolescence, the child expects to be able to make most of his own decisions, based on what he has been taught and what he has learned. Rules that are set arbitrarily and without much explanation cause rebellion. A parent who has made a habit of substituting rules for personal interaction with his child runs the risk of this kind of rebellion.

What authority do you represent to your child? Do you see yourself as someone who must be obeyed without question? Do you have a habit of explaining the rationale behind the rules you set? Do you usually set rules *with* your child rather than *for* your child? Do the rules you set rely on the values you hold? Does your life reflect the kind of values you teach your children?

July 18

WHAT KIND OF CONTROL SHOULD YOU HAVE OVER YOUR CHILD?

> You have your play and your playmates. What harm is there that you have no time or thought for us![18]
>
> —RABINDRANATH TAGORE

You already know that as your child grows and develops into an independent person, she will be, in some profound sense, moving farther and farther away from your sphere of influence. That's what being a parent is about: the preparation of your child for a life of her own. Naturally, part of your task is to help her integrate the best and most useful lessons, so that when you are not there, she will have some guidelines and experience upon which to make decisions and act successfully.

But that doesn't mean that you ever leave your child to flounder on her own without the benefit of your wisdom and love. It means that throughout your life together you will be helping her to establish boundaries and learn to discriminate between safe, successful social and moral behavior and those behaviors that are unsafe, unethical, or unsuccessful.

So the issue of control is a faulty one. You are never in control of your child. She is moving away from early childhood, where boundaries are more likely to be explicitly detailed by her parents. She will graduate to points along the way where the boundaries and rules become increasingly more implicit and general and where there is a lot of room for her to exercise her own identity, judgment, and skills.

Depending on how old your child is, you may begin to see her stretching or even breaking the boundaries you have already set. This can be disturbing. Try stepping back and asking yourself whether it's time to relax a rule that may have outworn its usefulness. You may have said, for example, when your child was four years old, that she would have to wait until she was in third grade before you would let her stay overnight with a friend, but now you feel a need to be more flexible. You may have a set rule that your family will always eat Sunday dinner together. Wait till you try to enforce this one on an active teenager with lots of weekend interests.

Part of the work a parent has to do in letting go is to learn how and when to relax rules and boundaries. What boundaries are currently in force for each of your children? Do you feel that you can relax any of these boundaries? If your child moves over the line or asks whether she can, do you feel that you can ease up without feeling as though you have lost a battle? Can you instead feel as if your successful parenting has given her the ability to move away?

July 19 ACTING OUT

One must face the fact that "good intentions" are only good as long as they are faithfully re-examined in the light of new knowledge, and in the light of their fruits.[19]

—THOMAS MERTON

When an older child rebels against authority, this society tends to take it seriously. Sometimes it is an indicator of antisocial behavior and may even become a question of the law, in which case, the parent is aided or replaced by civil authorities. But when younger children rebel openly, it is the primary responsibility of parents to figure out what is happening.

We can assume that there is always a reason for a child's "acting out." Maybe he's tired or hungry. Maybe he's experienced a severe frustration and instead of internalizing it, he has a tantrum. All of us are familiar with the kid in the supermarket who is screaming and creating as big a disturbance as possible while his embarrassed mom looks helplessly on or smacks him right in front of everyone. In public, she feels compelled to do something to quiet the disturbance by exerting control. If she doesn't, she fears the judgment of strangers and the condemnation of her child and her parenting skills.

Children are smart. A three-year-old may learn that it is really bad news when he acts out in public, but he can go crazy in the privacy of his home environment. Or he may have learned that it is dangerous to act out at home, but safe to do it in public.

No matter how conscious a parent you are, you will experience this kind of behavior from your child. It's part of the growing-up process. It is wise to remember that the continual repression of anger can lead to an explosion of greater force later, sometimes directed outwardly in angry behavior or sometimes directed inwardly in self-destructive behavior.

When you have an experience like this with your child and you have had some time to collect yourself, you can spend some calm energy investigating the cause of the disturbance. Is he angry for a specific reason, or do you need to look for a pattern of behavior? How does your child feel about his display when he has had time to calm down? After the storm has passed, is he looking for some kind of support, forgiveness and understanding? As a <u>conscious parent</u> you are looking to give support by <u>mirroring</u> back his explanation of what was bothering him, <u>validating</u> his right to feel upset (whether you agree with him or not), and <u>empathizing</u> with his situation.

How you react to your young child's anger will influence how he handles intense feelings when he grows up. You can let him know that it is normal and reasonable to feel anger and that he can make a *decision* about how to express it or *whether* to express it. Now is the time to work with him to revise any patterns of overreaction to everyday frustration. He can learn that you accept his feelings and are available to help him channel the energy from his anger into constructive solutions. As always, you can examine your own response to anger and see if you accept your own feelings, and then make reasonable decisions about how to express them.

July 20 WHEN YOUR CHILD GETS INTO REAL TROUBLE

In the darkness he saw visions of a thousand-tongued fear that would babble at his back and cause him to flee, while others were going coolly about their country's business.[20] —STEPHEN CRANE

Gangs proliferate around the country. Children can become involved in dangerous and destructive activities that formerly threatened only older teens. Sometimes a situation arises where parents have to become suddenly and dramatically involved to set their child on a different path. At this point they can no longer sit on the sidelines and offer support. They have to take steps.

Although such a situation may never arise in your family, it surely will for someone in your extended family or for friends and neighbors of yours. For this, if for no other reason, we do well to think about the issues involved in being a conscious parent in the midst of crisis.

We know of one family who had to go through a difficult time with their fourteen-year-old daughter. This was a supportive family, where both parents were highly involved with their two teenage daughters. Their younger daughter, Melissa, was a normally loving, intelligent, and curious child. One Friday night, Melissa was sleeping over with three other girls. When the host's father was called in to handle an emergency at work, the girls were left unsupervised, without Melissa's parents knowing about it.

Melissa's parents were awakened early on Saturday morning by a call from the police. The girls, who had apparently been drinking, had been caught breaking into a local store that had been closed for the night. They had not stolen anything, but they had vandalized the store. Melissa had been with them.

This incident galvanized the family. Their precious daughter had been involved in a serious offense, and they had to figure out why it had happened. As it turned out, Melissa *had* been involved but had not participated in the vandalism. The ringleader had been a girl named Alicia, whom Melissa's parents knew to be experiencing some difficulties. They had no idea the difficulties would result in this kind of problem.

What would you do if this situation had occurred within your family? Melissa's parents did the following:

- They assured Melissa that they loved her and that they would support her through this difficulty. They repeated their unshakable conviction that she was a good person.

- They spent a good deal of time learning from her how she came to be involved in this mess and discussing with her the gravity of the situation.
- They went with their daughter to her appointments within the legal system and developed a program of reparations with the store that had been vandalized. They supported the importance of her sentence to community service at a local convalescent home for the elderly.
- They reviewed the rules and boundaries they had agreed to in the past to determine what changes ought to be made, but they did not install any specific punishment. They did, however, tell Melissa that she could not associate with Alicia again until they gave their approval.

But, primarily, they refused to give up on their daughter, even though they were clear about the unacceptability of her behavior. Melissa appreciated her parents' intervention, because this crisis demonstrated to her that she really needed them to work with her.

When a problem like Melissa's arises within a family, there are no real guidelines but these: Love your child, get as much professional help as you need, and work to reestablish connection and mutual trust so that you stay in touch. Be courageous in confronting circumstances that need to be changed. Remember, that it is through your child's connection with you that she will work through the difficulties and develop the personal strengths she needs to be successful in the future.

A prayer for today: *Now is a time for me to give thanks for the moments of Grace I have been given in my life, even at times I have not asked for it nor deserved it. It's time for me to allow this Grace to cover me and my child.*

July 21 STANDING ON PRINCIPLE

In the turmoil of world affairs no universal principle, no memory of similar conditions in the past can help us—a vague memory has no power against the vitality and freedom of the present.[21]

—GEORG WILHELM FRIEDRICH HEGEL

Every adult has principles he lives by or tries to live by. Most of us also admit to principles we think we ought to live by but don't. Some of the latter have been handed down to us by tradition or

have been instilled in us by guilt, either as a result of our upbringing or through some externally imposed source.

On July 4, we discussed the basis of a successful democracy: the principles of adherence to law, tradition, and reason applied in equal measure. Conscious parents, too, need to base their behavior and attitudes on principles and pass them along to our children. Short of being rigid and adhering to the letter of an established principle rather than its spirit, it is our duty as parents to stand our ground from time to time.

Suppose your child is lying to you about something you consider to be important. This requires your attention. It may mean that your son feels that you cannot deal dispassionately with some kind of information and that he needs to protect himself from your disapproval. In fact, so dangerous do you appear to your child that he will take the risk of lying to you, rather than face you over this particular issue.

Maybe, because you fear loss of control, you are too rigid about adherence to a particular rule. Maybe you have a habit of intruding on your child in matters she considers her own business. But even if you have made these mistakes, there are still times when you must intervene to indicate that this lie—or other breaking of a rule—should be confronted *on principle.*

Can you think of a time when you were a child when your parents confronted you as a matter of principle? How did that feel at the time, and how do you see it now? Can you think of a situation in which you had to act on principle with your child? It's worth remembering that confronting on principle is not the same as punishing on principle. With your own child, were you calm? Did you attempt to learn what was really happening before you acted? Did you love your child throughout the confrontation?

July 22 A YOUNGER CHILD'S SEXUAL EXPERIENCE

. . . I suddenly notice that our child's hope and thighs have swelled so they taper to the knee. And her flesh is more liquid than it was.[22]

—SHARON OLDS

Last month we suggested that conscious parenting involves having enough self-control to pause before reacting when something upsetting occurs with your child. This gives you time to get more information and/or review your options for responding intentionally in the best way.

Now it's about a month later and a good time to remind ourselves again of this strategy. As you look back over the last week or so, has there been an instance of upset with your child? If there has, did you remember to pause and take stock before reacting? Again, the steps are: pausing; asking yourself whether you need to do something or nothing at this moment; asking yourself whether your response needs to focus on safety, support, or structure; all the while, keeping in mind the principles of intentional dialogue.

A common and often upsetting episode for many parents occurs when their young child demonstrates overtly sexual behavior. We remember one mother telling us how upset she was when the teacher in her daughter's second grade class called to say she was concerned because her daughter was sexually stimulating herself in class. Other stories of young children showing their bodies to each other—playing "doctor"—are common.

This is the kind of occurrence that gives conscious parents a chance to practice their positive intentions. It helps if you know that sexual feelings are present in children at a very young age and that self-stimulation is common in five-, six-, and seven-year-olds. And it helps, when you get an upsetting teacher phone call or happen upon evidence of sexual curiosity yourself, to pause long enough to construct your response carefully. If such behavior is normal, you may want to educate your child about the importance of privacy, rather than make her feel bad for sexual feelings that come built into the equipment.

Your everyday life with your child is filled with chances for you to do more listening and more thinking before you do more talking.

July 23 AN OLDER CHILD'S SEXUAL EXPERIENCE

If sex were all, then every trembling hand
Could make us squeak, like dolls, the wished-for
words.[23]

—WALLACE STEVENS

Sexual encounters are common at an earlier and earlier age these days. Social norms have shifted to accommodate this younger exposure. As a conscious parent, you will want to think about these issues ahead of time. Your middle- and high-school-age child will be living in a social environment where sexual experiences with other kids are prevalent.

Sexual information is everywhere. Your children will be required to learn certain kinds of information in sex education classes. The school will attempt to educate them about the facts of conception, contraception, pregnancy, and sexually transmitted diseases. These are important technical matters you will want your children to be familiar with.

But the equally important questions of what a loving relationship is like and what role sexual desire and sexual interaction play in loving relationships will have to come from somewhere else. Your children will pick up many of their ideas about love, romance, and sex from the popular culture. They will absorb even more from the adventures of their friends.

You might ask yourself what information are they getting from you about these very important matters. What messages do we send our young people about what it is like to be married and how to handle the inevitable problems and what the satisfactions are? What messages do we send them about the role of sex in personal growth and commitment?

You may be struggling with these questions yourself. Your own marriage may feel unfulfilling and more difficult than happy. You may be unsure about whether a satisfying sexual relationship is possible after the first blush of high romance. For your own sake, you may want to begin to work on these issues in yourself and with your partner. These relationship problems present opportunities for personal and spiritual growth.

But in addition, you may have another reason to seek answers. Your children will learn a lot of what they know about love, sex, and marriage from you. You don't have to be perfect to teach them well, but you do have to have an approach, a way of understanding intimate relationships that will draw your children toward their possibilities and help them know that difficulties sometimes lie at the center of these possibilities. It's through the difficulties that we expand into the solutions. That's the way it has to be.

July 24 WHEN YOU HAVE CONCERNS ABOUT YOUR CHILD'S FRIEND

Our minds and feelings are trained by the company we keep, and perverted by the company we keep.[24] —BLAISE PASCAL

As soon as your child begins to talk about friends at school, your ears prick up. Who are these children? Will they be fair and friendly to your child? Do they have bad habits that you and he will have to deal with? Will these children recognize how special your child is? This is the beginning of a long process where friends become increasingly important in your child's life. You will remain the central influence, but other people will balance and sometimes conflict with the power you have. And there will be times when a group of twelve-year-olds or sixteen-year-olds will appear to carry more weight than you do.

So what happens when you begin to realize that your child's best friend, this unformed soul, may have serious behavior problems? The only way you will know for sure is to spend some time with this friend. It's always a sound strategy to include your child's friends in your family activities as much as possible. This, in a noninvestigative and nonintrusive way, allows you to know each of your child's friends as a person.

You may have all your fears put to rest, or you may find that this friend presents real problems. But no matter what your assessment, you have to remember how important he is to your child. If you broadcast your negative comments, your child may become defensive and close down.

You can, however, remember that your son may be uneasy about his friend also. After all, he has absorbed many of your values. If at all possible, it's a good idea to do what you can to help him come to the conclusion that he would rather not spend time with this person. In the process, you can stand aside, ready to support him, see that he is safe, and see that, to the best of your ability, he observes the structures you have worked out together.

As you think about the friends your child has brought home for you to meet, ask yourself how you feel about each of them. What is there about each that you like and find positive? What worries you? Is there something you can do to put your dislikes, fears, and disapprovals aside, or do you really need to listen to your inner voice and raise, calmly and supportively, your concerns with your child?

July 25 FRIENDS

Come you indoors, come home.[25] —GERARD MANLEY HOPKINS

There are times for almost every child when friendship seems elusive. Being friendless is a major theme of childhood, and one we can all relate to. Years into successful adulthood, people still tell painful stories about birthday party invitations that were ignored or declined. Or they talk about particular kids who were isolated and picked on. Anyone who was ever betrayed and deserted by a best friend still remembers the sting. Even the girlfriend who steals your boyfriend is a cliché of adolescence.

Realizing that these experiences are common does not make them easier for parents to deal with. Very few things hurt the heart as much as watching your beloved child struggle with real or imagined rejection.

If your child, or children, has already had such experiences, you know what we mean. As you think about these times, can you remember how you handled them? How did you support your son when he was bullied? How did you express continued confidence in your daughter when she was left out by her classmates?

You can ask yourself what you would need in a similar situation. When you think about it, you will probably conclude that you would want someone in your life to listen to the hurt without becoming too emotionally involved. And you would want this person to let you know that you will not be alone and forlorn forever, that everybody goes through such times, and that things work out. Last on the list, you may want some specific help. You might want help with what to say. Do you know where to find it?

Your belief in the okayness of your child and your steady conviction that she will be able to have what she wants while being authentically the person she is will help her develop the inner strengths she needs to handle those times when reassurance and support are in short supply. What a gift.

July 26 WHICH PARENT RULES?

They were both ashamed of the evil natures they exposed in each other; each in the first days of their love had hoped to be the ideal image of the other.[26]

—KATHERINE ANNE PORTER

As we know, issues of control between child and parent are common and are a normal part of growing up. Equally important to a child are conflicts between her parents about who is in control and how the power in the marriage is used and abused.

Let's take a look at an example of a common conflict between spouses that affects the children in the household. We are aware of a couple who have decidedly different ideas about the meaning and use of money, especially where it concerns their two children. The father, Roy, is a prototype-engineering manager in a small, high tech company. His wife, Susan, is a social worker. Their children, a girl in high school and a boy in middle school, do not have a formal allowance. Roy feels that allowances are a bad idea and that any money his kids get should be earned by working around the house or at after school jobs. So he allows them to earn small sums by doing dishes, mowing the lawn, and taking out the garbage. And he would prefer to have his daughter work after school the way he did when he was in high school. As far as he is concerned, aside from cash for school lunches and an occasional movie, they don't really need extra spending money.

Susan wants her kids to have more free, relaxed time when they are not in school or doing homework. She thinks there is time enough for getting jobs once they're in college. She would prefer to give them a regular allowance, but she is paying lip service to the idea that they have to earn it. She ends up giving them extra money on the side, despite Roy's objections that there is no budget for that kind of thing. A lot of Susan's extra goes for clothes, but a lot is "frittered away," as Roy is constantly complaining.

This situation has continued for some time, causing both parents and their children a lot of low-level anxiety. The kids feel guilty about spending too much money. Roy feels that a principle he and his wife have ostensibly agreed on ("spending-money is to be earned") is constantly being subverted and that too much money is being wasted. And Susan feels that she has to continually override Roy's wishes to give the kids the money they need to survive in the current social scene. No one is satisfied with the status quo, but there is not enough pain being caused for a crisis to emerge. So until there is a crisis, or until this problem becomes part of a list of difficulties that require serious attention, nothing may happen. Roy and Susan go on creating unhappiness for themselves and guilt and confusion in the minds of their two children regarding money.

This little story can give you the opportunity to think about a similar situation you may be facing in your family. Can you think of a problem that is going unrecognized between you and your parenting partner that may be confusing to your children? What can you say about the problem and why it exists and what you have done to solve it? Do you think it is worth working on between you, so that you can face your children's needs as allies rather than as secret adversaries?

July 27 GOING IT ALONE

Once in their youth the light shone for them; they saw the light and followed the star, but then came reason and the mockery of the world; then came faint-heartedness and apparent failure; then came weariness and disillusionment, and so they lost their way again, they became blind again.[27]

—RUMI

There are going to be some times when you and your family make decisions that receive very little social support. The network of people you normally rely on to advise you—or maybe the people who advise you whether you want them to or not—doesn't seem to agree with you. It could be the way you are handling your health, your finances, or your career. You are always assessing the feedback you get from other people regarding how you handle these important matters. And it's no different when people around you offer opinions about the decisions you make regarding your children.

As we have said before, it's a good idea, whether you accept them all or not, to pay attention to the comments people offer you about your parenting. Your mother-in-law thinks you are too relaxed with your child. Your friend at work thinks you will spoil your child. Your younger sister thinks you are too uptight. What data do they have that leads them to conclude that?

Many people offer advice based on tradition, on hearsay, and on faulty information. Their advice could be classified as <u>symbiotic</u>. It reflects what they have done or would do in your place, as though one size fits all. But they don't really know you or your child. And while it is always advisable to listen for new information and to keep an open mind, there are going to be times when you need to feel the rightness of your own conviction about what is best for your child.

Are you someone who arrives at decisions easily and who has very few second thoughts? Do you always know exactly what you are doing? It's true that you could be an exceptional person with extraordinary powers of observation and judgment. Or you might need to remind yourself to listen very carefully to others. You may have a tendency to filter out information that disagrees with your view of things. On the other hand, are you someone who has difficulty making decisions because you are plagued by second thoughts? If so, you may need to listen most carefully to your inner voices. You may need reassurance that it's your job as a parent to follow the advice of your heart, provided that you really have the well being of your child at the center of thoughts.

In either case, parenting is an opportunity to develop flexibility. You learn to be willing to change your mind about a course of action you have decided on or about a rule you have made. You learn to watch your child to see what effect you are having and to disengage from your dependence on pleasing or displeasing the adults around you who are anxiously giving advice.

July 28 SHIELDING YOUR CHILD

The things that can really break your heart are romance and children, compared to which losing your job is no big deal.[28] —GARRISON KEILLOR

Every family goes through crisis. It could be the death of a grandparent or a close family member. It could be the threat of financial difficulties through the loss of a job or the accumulation of debt. It could be marital unhappiness that threatens to tip over the happy family vision everyone wants to hold on to. The temptation of many parents is to shield their children from problems until the stress works itself out. And when their children ask questions, they deny the difficulties or offer the vague assurance that "everything's going to be okay."

This kind of reassurance is not reassurance. Kids absorb emotional vibrations like dry sand absorbs water. They know something upsetting is happening. Even very small children are able to pick up on the vibes generated by parents in crisis. Older children generally grasp the nature of the problem, but they feel excluded when no details are forthcoming. To be left completely in the dark is to fill the space with monstrous imaginings in which they see themselves as responsible.

If you decide to share information with your children about a crisis you are confronting, think about how you want to do it ahead of time. Spend a few moments alone focusing on your love for your children and your commitment to do what you can to help them understand what is happening. Envision the connection of love and support that exists between each member of your family. It is a spiritual bond that will survive, no matter what worldly problems you are facing.

Picture with yourself in the center of your family and let your love radiate out toward each person until it enfolds each of you in love. Experience for yourself the sense of internal forgiveness you can generate for each child and adult in your family circle. Know that your connection can survive whatever changes are in store for you. You may not be able to control the events that bring this trouble upon you, but you can change the person you are, so that you can help everyone face it together.

When you talk to your children, you will want to exercise good judgment. There may be details you want to withhold, especially if you and your partner are experiencing severe marital problems. Your goal is to help them understand the situation, to say explicitly that you and other responsible adults are doing everything you can to solve the problem, to let them know that they are not responsible, and to tell them that you will stay in touch with them about what is happening.

July 29 FAMILY EVENTS IN THE MIDST OF SUMMER

Summer time, and the livin' is easy.[29] —DU BOSE HEYWARD

At the end of July, summer is at its height. And the warm days conjure visions of all kinds of trips, and excursions with the children. There are hours in the park, or at the local outdoor pool. There are visits to the zoo and the art museum. There are out-of-the-city trips to the countryside, the mountains, the farm country, or the beach. The mood is relaxed and the pace is leisurely.

Have you done the summer things you wanted to do with your children? If you would like to do more, there is still plenty of time. Why not involve your children in the planning? Where would they like to go? What special picnic would they like you to pack? You can think in terms of places you've been and adventures that would be new. Talking with other parents and looking in the newspaper will give you ideas.

Even relatively mundane excursions can become special when a simple treat is built into the schedule. An ice cream after the Saturday errands. A picnic at the local college campus on Sunday afternoon. Frisbee with the dog after work. Throwing the ball around in the evening until it gets too dark to see.

These are the small moments that you and your children will remember. They fit exactly into the summer season and make for delicious summer memories long after summer has faded away.

July 30 SETTING EXAMPLES

The common problem, yours, mine, every one's,
Is—not to fancy what were fair in life
Provided it could be—but, finding first
What may be, then find how to make it fair
Up to our means: a very different thing![30]

—ROBERT BROWNING

We want our children to know that happiness and fulfillment don't depend upon the good luck of having perfect companions and perfect circumstances. But, rather, on how people can take the less than perfect and make it into something better. A child who sees his parents working out their problems with him and with each other through love, mutual respect, and calm consideration will be comfortable both rejecting violence in settling disputes and in adopting similar conscious behavior, at least in principle.

A child who is used to seeing one or both parents overreacting to frustration through verbal or physical violence also learns a lesson. The lesson is obvious. Being visibly upset and shouting or striking out seems to be normal and is expected. The child learns how to do the same with parents and friends. It doesn't make much difference whether or not his parents tell him that his outbursts are unacceptable. They themselves don't seem to have learned the lesson very well.

Children who see their parents' abusive behavior followed by abject guilt and apology are also learning something about how life is supposed to work. They are learning a cycle of overreaction and remorse that can seem appropriate when institutionalized within a family.

And there are many other models of behavior that parents set for their children. It is within the family that children learn about personal integrity, obedience to community laws and regulations, ways of solving interpersonal conflicts, respecting the environment.

Stand back a little from your relationships within the family. Observe how you agree and disagree with others and how you make your wishes known. Remember, your children are watching and learning from what you're doing.

July 31 AS I DO

Acquire knowledge. It enableth its possessor to distinguish right from wrong; it lighteth the way to Heaven . . .[31] —MOHAMMED

It is as natural for teenagers to judge their parents as it is for younger children to observe and learn from them. After all, teenagers are approaching the age of independence. Increasingly, more of the important aspects of their lives are occurring outside the direct influence of their homes. Friends and sometimes love relationships are their primary focus, and parents are included in their teenagers' lives only if they're allowed in.

Parents are also likely to want to set boundaries. But at this age, your child needs to understand and cooperate if boundaries are to have any meaning. Stamping your feet and yelling are not effective ways to gain compliance. Even if they do work temporarily, they will backfire in time.

There are many areas where teenagers continue to need guidance from you. Two of the most important are sexuality and drugs. Your older child is dealing with his or her sexuality alone or with others, no matter what your preferences or your comfort level. You will want to support her with accurate information, honest discussion, and relevant personal experience. Your own attitudes and problems with sexuality may get in the way of frank and open discussion, and your sexual behavior ought to reflect the values you want your child to learn from you. It is not only what you say that counts but what you do.

With regard to drugs and alcohol it is even more important that your actions be as responsible as your warnings to your child. The social environment we live in convinces them that both drugs and alcohol are natural recreational adjuncts to the lives of healthy, normal adults. If you want your child to experience where you stand on this question, you simply must set an example yourself.

Your children may not have reached the age when sexual behavior and the use of drugs are serious issues yet, but they will. Teenagers all across the country report them as important issues where they go to school. How will you prepare yourself to be ready to support your pre-teen's or teenager's interactions with a helpful attitude and wise advice? How will you work with her to set boundaries that give her safety and structure when she is out of your immediate influence? What will you have to do to square away your personal life in order to set an example worthy of emulation?

Notes

1. James Agee, "Knoxville, Summer,1915," in *A Death in the Family* (New York: Bantam Books, 1969).

2. *The New Oxford Annotated Bible* (New York: Oxford University Press, 1994).

3. Salvador Minuchin, *Kaleidoscope: Images of Violence and Healing (*Cambridge, MA: Harvard University Press, 1984).

4. Henry Wadsworth Longfellow, "The Building of the Ship," in One Hundred and One Famous Poems, ed. Roy J. Cook (Chicago: The Reilly and Lee Co., 1958).

5. "Surgeon General's Report," *Environmental Nutrition,* October 2, 1996.

6. Anne Sexton, "From the Garden," in *Anne Sexton: The Complete Poems* (Boston: Houghton Mifflin, 1981).

7. George Eliot, Prelude to *Middlemarch* (Boston: Houghton Mifflin, 1956).

8. William Stafford, *Reading Modern Poetry: A Critical Anthology (*Glenview, IL: Scott, Foresman, 1968).

9. *American Youth and Sports Participation,* brochure, sponsored by Athletic Footwear Association, North Palm Beach, Florida, 1991.

10. John Crowe Ransom, "Bells for John Whitesides' Daughter," in *Selected Poems* (New York: Knopf, 1924).

11. W. H. Auden, "In Memory of W. B. Yeats," in *The Collected Poetry of W. H. Auden* (New York: Random House, 1940).

12. Gary Zukav, *The Dancing Wu Li Masters* (New York: Bantam, 1979).

13. Joseph Conrad, "Heart of Darkness," *Heart of Darkness and The Secret Sharer* (New York: New American Library, 1950).

14. Stephen Batchelor, *Buddhism Without Beliefs: A Contemporary Guide to Awakening* (New York: Riverside Books, 1997).

15. Stephanie Coontz, *The Way We Really Are: Coming to Terms with America's Changing Families* (New York: BasicBooks, 1997).

16. Theodore Roethke, "The Lost Son," in *The Lost Son and Other Poems* (New York: Doubleday, 1948).

17. *The New Oxford Annotated Bible* (New York: Oxford University Press, 1994).

18. Rabindranath Tagore, "The Gift," in *The Collected Poems and Plays of Rabindranath Tagore (*New York: Macmillan, 1962).

19. Thomas Merton, *Conjectures of a Guilty Bystander* (New York, Doubleday, 1968).

20. Stephen Crane, *The Red Badge of Courage* (New York: Pocket Books, 1957).

21. Georg Wilhelm Friedrich Hegel, *Reason in History: A General Introduction to the Philosophy of History*, ed. Robert S. Hartman (New York: The Bobbs-Merrill Company, 1953).

22. Sharon Olds, "Twelve Years Old," in *Wellspring* (New York: Knopf, 1996).

23. Wallace Stevens, "Le Monocle De Mon Oncle," in *The Collected Poems of Wallace Stevens* (New York: Knopf, 1951).

24. Blaise Pascal, *Pensées*, #814, trans. A. J. Krailsheimer (London: Penguin Books, 1995).

25. Gerard Manley Hopkins, "The Candle Indoors," in *Poems of Gerard Manley Hopkins* (New York: Oxford University Press, 1976).

26. Katherine Anne Porter, *Ship of Fools* (New York: The New American Library, 1963).

27. Rumi, *The Sufi Path of Love: The Spiritual Teachings of Rumi,* trans. William C. Chittick (New York: State University of New York Press, 1983).

28. Garrison Keillor, quoted in "A Return to Lake Wobegon" by Ellen Emry Heltzel, in the Portland *Oregonian*, November 10, 1997.

29. Du Bose Heyward, "Summertime," *Porgy and Bess*, libretto by Du Bose Heyward (New York: Columbia Masterworks, 1951).

30. Robert Browning, "Bishop Blougram's Apology," in *Browning: Poetical Works, 1833–1866*, ed. Ian Jack (Oxford: Oxford University Press, 1970).

31. Sir Abdullah al-Mamun alSuhrawardy Alamma, trans., *The Sayings of Muhammad* (London: John Murray, 1949).

August

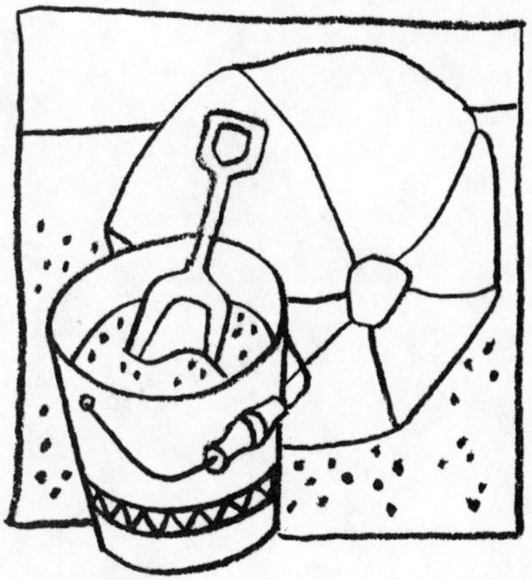

INTRODUCTION TO THE MONTH OF AUGUST

This last month of the summer, we are turning our attention toward one of the most important realities for many of today's families. We are placing emphasis on what it is like when one parent and child(ren) decide to combine and form a new unit with another parent and child(ren). Blended families are not unusual. They are everywhere. And they bring with them refreshed energy and new hope for creating the kind of life together that will inspire and nurture all its members. Much of their success depends upon their ability to meet the challenge with patience, courage, and conscious attention.

August 1 DOG DAYS

From a dark country sky, one can observe around a dozen meteors per hour any night of the year.[1]

—DAVID H. LEVY

The summer is past its prime, the leaves are looking a bit shopworn, the corn is high and tasseling, and the air is heavy and hot. You tend to take the warm weather for granted and look forward with a little longing for the rich, cool days of early autumn. It seems a long time since school let out. Even children who could not wait for the summer to begin may be yearning for the start of school so they can see their friends.

These are the "dog days," a term that may have originated with the prominence in the night sky of the Dog Star, Sirius. Another night-sky phenomenon you might see during August is shooting stars. And in the northernmost states or in Canada you might even catch a glimpse of the northern lights.

Our ancestors were intimately familiar with these nighttime occurrences. The night sky was a full map of constellations: the Milky Way and stars beyond stars that could easily be seen with the naked eye. It is unfortunate that the bright lights and pollution of our big cities now cloud the view that was so important to our forefathers. As consolation, this city atmosphere does at least make the rising of the full moon an awesome sight.

There is still magic in the night sky. Can you pick out the Big Dipper and find the North Star, which remains fixed at due north throughout the night? Can you locate Orion's belt or Leo or Cassiopeia? On these warm summer nights, when darkness is beginning to come just a little earlier, you can share these sights with your child.

Night-sky viewing is an opportunity to remystify the world with your child during her bedtime ritual. After all, there is a magnificent natural world to present to her, and not all lessons need to be learned from science programs on PBS. A simple book on astronomy can help you pass on an appreciation of the beauty of this world, which is silently and inexorably moving through the universe.

August 2 BLENDING

. . . yes, I am willing to be
that wild darknes. . . .[2]

—MARY OLIVER

Have you ever seen aerial photographs of the Amazon River flowing into the Atlantic Ocean? The brown sediment of the world's most powerful river billows into the blue of the ocean, but the two waters don't mix for more than a mile. You can see a distinct line of brown and blue separating them, even in their confluence. And then, gradually, the line starts to dissolve and they become one, with a color and composition made from both.

If you are a part of a blending, or a blended family, you and your mate will never dissolve completely into each other. You will retain your separate identities, although the life you make together promises to be richer and more interesting than one either of you could make separately.

It may be that, in the beginning, when you and your partner and all of your children are together, you don't mix very well at all. Some of you are brown and some of you are blue. You have had other relationships and other experiences. Your past mistakes inform your sense of what you want loving to be like this time. You know how you want to raise your children.

Today, as you think about the task of creating one body of water out of separate rivers, you can pause to celebrate the many miles you've traveled so far. No matter what the terrain has been, you have traveled a long way, past many obstacles. You can be sure that experience will continue to be your teacher. As was true in the past, experience will continue to teach you dear and wonderful lessons through both the loving and the challenging moments of family life. Only now you have a partner, and a new family, to help you learn them.

A prayer for today: *I am silent before the beauty and power of the Divine. May I feel the sacredness of my own life and approach the patterns of my life with the reverence that is due.*

August 3 BETTER THIS TIME

By learning to bring your awareness to past experiences and conditioning—memories stored in the very receptors of your cells—you can release yourself from these blocks, this "stuckness."[3]

—CANDACE PERT

You are determined that into *this* relationship and *this* family, you are going to bring what you have learned from the past. You are lucky enough to have another chance with someone you really care about. You want it to work! Just knowing something about the possible difficulties and having the absolute determination to do whatever it takes to create your new family will help you be successful. Attitude is all.

Here are three fundamental attitudes, or approaches, that will help you achieve your goals. Our experience with couples over the years has taught us the importance of these three factors in creating satisfying relationships. We briefly state them here as food for thought. As you read them, take your time thinking about them and decide how you want to use them to build conscious relationships with your partner and his or her children, as well as with your own children.

The attitude of consciousness. The more conscious you are of how and why you act and feel the way you do, the better partner (and parent) you will be. Develop the habit of asking yourself about your intentions in the present moment, and pledge to find out what you can about how you are being affected by past experiences and interactions that might not now be entirely clear to you. Self-awareness helps you change behaviors that no longer serve you well.

The attitude of healing. Your intimate family relationships present you with a unique opportunity to heal wounds from your past. You now have the opportunity to do things differently. You don't have to be a mindless slave to the overreactions you may have had in previous relationships. It *is* possible to stop criticizing, blaming, and defending and to become a more listening and accepting person. Relationships are the best context for healing.

The attitude of dialogue. Intentional dialogue is the most powerful tool you have for improving your communication. When you mirror, validate, and empathize, you are making yourself understood and doing what you can to understand the other person in an atmosphere of mutual respect.

Go ahead and enjoy your feelings of hope and enthusiasm for

the future. You have a special opportunity to be an agent of happiness and fulfillment in your new family. We're celebrating the creative possibilities of the future right along with you!

August 4 ALL YOUR CHILDREN

Day after day, year after
year I dressed our little beloveds . . .[4]
—SHARON OLDS

Each of the children in your household is a gift. Each one, even in difficult moments, is one of God's children. Each one represents a potential that is much more wondrous than any we could imagine. When you approach your children with this sense of awe at their very existence, you will be preparing yourself to see what is beautiful and unique in them. And they will be more likely to show you the treasures of their personality.

Set aside some quiet time today to focus on each of the children who now live in your family. When you are alone and undisturbed, you can begin to let yourself relax by breathing deeply and letting go of whatever tension you feel in your body. Let distracting or distressing thoughts float in and out of your awareness and begin to gather your attention to one of your children. Take your time in calling forth an image of this child in as much detail as you can. Register what she looks like, what she is wearing, and how you feel in her presence. Imagine yourself gazing at her with love. Now let arise in your mind an awareness of the gift she brings. Perhaps she has the gift of laughter or empathy or intellect or movement or tender feelings or peacemaking. Of course, she brings more than one gift, but see what one quality comes to mind. And then let yourself inwardly celebrate your child and the gift she gives to you and the world.

Go through this process of inward celebration for each of your children and your partner's children. The more often you do this meditation, the more you will keep in the forefront of your thinking an appreciation for the unique and wonderful qualities your children possess. You will be amazed at how your ability to see what is beautiful in them will bring forth what is beautiful in them.

August 5 QUESTIONS OF PRIVACY

The Enemy, who wears
Her mother's usual face . . .[5]

—PHYLLIS McGINLEY

Everyone has their own definition of privacy. Each of us has a personal range that is comfortable, beyond which we feel threatened or violated. This sense of personal space, whether defined physically or emotionally, is not only an individual but a cultural matter. What would be quite normal and within an acceptable range for someone from India or Africa or Italy or China, for example, might be beyond the comfort level for a northern European or an American and vice cersa.

Within families, too, norms are established. In some homes, a parent's bedroom is a place for children and parents to join together on Sunday and read the paper; on the other hand, sometimes, a parent's room is an inner sanctum which children are not encouraged to enter. In some families various states of undress are normal, while in others there is a strong consciousness of personal modesty that makes undress in almost any form unacceptable. Some parents are comfortable entering their children's rooms without knocking, and some parents maintain the same strict boundaries of privacy for their children as they do for themselves. There is a range of behaviors that support both the individual development of each family member while maintaining their connection.

If you are now in a family whose members have recently begun to live together, you may be astounded either by your lack of personal privacy or by the barriers against familiarity that you feel have been erected against you. It takes time to establish a workable family style that incorporates different preferences and expectations. Here are some solid general rules that may help you establish a healthy sense of privacy in your family:

- All children deserve to have their privacy respected. Their thoughts and feelings are their own business, except when they ask for or seem to want your involvement. (The exception would be when you have strong reason to believe their behavior is destructive.)
- The existence of healthy parent-child bonds helps you and your children know where personal boundaries are and to let others know, without guilt or recriminations, when they are transgressed.

- All family members deserve a place in the home where they can be alone and have their individual thoughts and property to themselves.
- Everyone in a family, including parents, has a right to the privacy of their own bodies. Even younger children need to develop a sense of their parents' privacy as well as their own.
- Parents should never intrude into their children's space and possessions looking for hidden thoughts and behaviors. If you suspect a problem, talk it out rather than engaging in spying.

How do these guidelines sound to you? Are you easy with the norms of privacy you have established within your marriage and for your children? Are your children comfortable with those norms, both for themselves and with respect to you and their siblings?

August 6 THE GREEN-EYED MONSTER

Jealousy is always born together with love, but it does not always die when love dies.[6]

—LA ROCHEFOUCAULD

During the Middle Ages the Catholic Church named envy as one of the Seven Deadly Sins, so seriously was it taken. Envy refers to the desire to possess something belonging to another. Jealousy, very close to envy, refers to the feeling of resentment that someone else has something, particularly love, that should belong only to you.

Sometimes it seems we humans are born jealous. How many toys are sold at Christmas, for example, simply because children want what all their friends will be getting? In sibling rivalry, too, we see children jealous of each other within a family. It's so common we take it for granted. We marvel when two siblings are *not* particularly jealous of each other.

It is common for both boys and girls who have reached the stage of competence, at around the age of five, to compete for the attention of the parent of the opposite sex and to have feelings of jealousy toward the same-sex parent. In families who have not grown up together, jealousy can be a problem when a child resents the attention paid by his biological parent to a new mate or the mate's children. The opportunities for jealous feelings are everywhere in a newly blended family.

These feelings of jealousy are normal, but they still need to be attended to. It helps to understand that jealousy derives from insecurity and is related to symbiosis. It rises up in us when we see other people as extensions of ourselves who are necessary for our self-definition rather than as separate individuals. It subsides to lower levels in us as we begin to mature into self-defined, whole individuals.

Children have difficulty understanding that there is enough love for everyone to have as much as they need. Until they have experience to the contrary, they tend to see love as a finite resource that can be depleted. How do you help your child deal with feelings of envy or jealousy? Do you take it seriously enough to pay attention and soothe your child into an understanding of your unconditional love?

Envy of others or fear of betrayal is based on a sense of personal inadequacy. How do you handle this fear in yourself? Are you learning how to be a whole person who can take care of your own needs with a sense of calm and personal strength?

August 7 EXPECTATIONS

And so she changed, while other folks
Never tried nothin' at all.[7]

—SHEL SILVERSTEIN

You have the courage to change, the courage to try for happiness. If you didn't expect it to be happy in your new family, you wouldn't have committed to it. Besides happy, you undoubtedly also expect to be financially viable and to provide a nurturing environment for your children to grow up in. These are basic and reasonable benefits to expect from your blended family. In addition to these, do you have any others? What else do you especially want to achieve and receive in your relationship with your partner?

There may be a part of you that can't help but indulge in good old-fashioned wishing. "I wish for a conflict-free marriage." "I wish for my partner's children to love me totally." "I wish for a family with no problems." If only such wishes were possible. . . .

We have found that the most useful kinds of expectations have to do with processes rather than outcomes. We are thinking here of such things as expecting that we will discuss financial matters on a regular basis and deal swiftly with any problems that come up. Other important process-based expectations involve being able to handle dissatisfactions through dialogue, or being able to talk about setting limits for the children through mutual discussion, or being able to build a family identity through fun family activities.

You will notice that these expectations center constructing both on ways of dealing with problems *and* positive ways of being together. They do not depend on the unrealistic hope that new beginnings will banish all difficulties. They assume that difficulties will arise and that we will be able to deal with them when they do.

What expectations do you have for your new family? Are they based on process or outcome, or both? If you were to identify some process-based expectations, what would they be? Take your time to think about this question, because how you answer will indicate where you and your partner might want to put some effort into planning. For example, if you have the expectation that you and your partner will be able to talk honestly about your feelings, you might ask yourself what the two of you have done to make that happen. Your expectations say a lot about who you are.

August 8 FLEXIBILITY

I like to have a man's knowledge comprehend more than one class of topics, one row of shelves. I like a man who likes to see a fine barn as well as a good tragedy.[8]

—RALPH WALDO EMERSON

People generally begin new enterprises with a great deal of hope. Whether it is a new job, a new school, a new city, a new home, or a new relationship, we usually have an expectation that things will be different with a new start. Certainly, it was with such high hopes that pioneers crossed the Great Plains in the nineteenth century looking for a new home in the West.

Although we bring many of our old problems with us when we begin anew, there is every reason to hope that we will be given an opportunity to change for the better. Amid the nervousness in confronting a new situation, there is the excitement of discovery. This is true for whole families as well when the winds of change bring the possibility for new happiness

If you are part of a newly blended family, or even if you have just changed or are about to change your living situation in an important way, you can be sure that there is an adventure ahead of you. But there will also be a new set of challenges. Inevitably, your expectations will be modified by your actual experience.

Not everything you wanted or expected will turn out as planned. This is a hard lesson for children to absorb, and sometimes it's hard for their parents too. Most children are conservative by nature and have trouble dealing with changes and disruptions in routine. To begin with, they may not share your view of the big picture and the positive changes your greater experience allows you to envision. They may simply see that their everyday lives are going to be different. It is your task to be empathetic and affirming when things don't go their way.

As you think back over some of the great life changes you have made, do you remember what you expected going into them? In the instance when things didn't go as you expected, can you still see positive elements that resulted? How have you become a wiser, more complete person as a result? What rewards have you gained from even some of the generally disappointing changes you have made?

Perhaps if you had known what problems lay in front of you, you might not have taken some of your more important leaps into the unknown. But how narrow might your life have been without the adventures you've had! Are you prepared to support your child as he leaps and bounds into his future?

August 9 A NEW CONNECTION

Marriage has become an option rather than a necessity for men and women, even during the child-raising years.[9] —STEPHANIE COONTZ

Today, we will begin to explore how you can be a conscious parent to your children if you are beginning a new relationship with a significant other or a new marriage. These matters can add to your understanding of conscious parenting, even if you are part of a long-term marriage. At the very least, you can increase your sensitivity to those parents who *are* in this situation.

As a single parent who has been unmarried for some period of time, you may have had several romantic relationships that have already influenced your children, or you may have had only one, or you may have been uninvolved the whole time. If you are at a place now where you are making a commitment to a romantic partner, you are full of hope for the future. Your new partner, together with any children he or she brings to the relationship, is about to embark on an important learning experience.

You are no doubt aware of the primary need to develop a lasting and healthy connection with each other. You know you need to establish new routines within an environment that nurtures your love relationship and allows you to deal effectively with children and all the other concerns that everyday life brings.

The children in your new family are of primary concern. The connections they establish with you and your partner can follow as many patterns as there are people. Some children adjust rather easily; others have trouble adapting to new people and new ways. For most children the ride is bumpy, at least in the beginning. There are stops and starts and unexpected turns which require that you and your partner proceed slowly and with a great deal of support and love.

We know of one family in which the son of the newly remarried mother had formed a strong attachment to his mother's previous boyfriend. They had spent a great deal of time together and had become fast friends. This boy had difficulty accepting that this past relationship was over and that his mother had chosen to marry someone else. As you might expect, he showed his disappointment and frustration in countless ways. Only the continual understanding and support of both his mother and her new husband were able to tip the scales in a positive direction.

If your child is still deeply attached to her biological father or mother (or another parent surrogate), this may present the same kind of challenge to you. If you are in this situation, think about each child who is part of your family. Can you understand who that child is and what her needs are going to be? What problems is she experiencing in the adjustment? You will want to spend time with your new partner talking about each of your children and working out strategies for handling difficulties. You will also want to reassure each other that new connections require time and cooperative effort. It is important to be patient with children who act out their frustrations.

The ties of familiarity and affection required in a family cannot be decreed or built quickly. You will have to go through difficulties together as well as good times in order to establish trust and mutual understanding. But parents who truly love their children and respect their individuality will act firmly and consciously during this adjustment period, ignoring their own impatience in order to make small, positive contributions that strengthen their bonds of affection.

August 10 THE OLD AND THE NEW

what if a dawn of a doom of a dream
bites this universe in two. . .[10]

—*e. e. cummings*

It is human nature to believe in the transformational qualities of new relationships. We envision ourselves free from the old obligations and constraints, free to enjoy (at last) our true, best selves. Our visions are more than infantile wish fulfillment. There is something real to this notion of transformation through new love. There is no doubt that we are changed by the complex chemistry that ignites us when we interact with someone new. Novel characteristics show themselves, while old ones drop away. The possibilities of our personalities are reshuffled.

But these possibilities are not endless. Our personalities and our temperaments are, to some extent, fixed. That's what makes us recognizably and consistently different from everyone else. All of us have an operating range within which we can hope for improvement.

New situations often call forth new behavior, especially when we are happy. But new situations can also call forth old behavior. There is nothing wrong with established patterns of thought and action that work well for you and are a fulfillment of your authentic self. Old patterns that keep getting you into trouble are another matter.

If you were a complaining person before you met your current partner and you find yourself to be a complainer still, then that merits some attention. If you were quick to anger then and you are quick to anger now, then that also merits your attention. What can you do when you find yourself in the same ruts you've always been in?

There are many things you can do, of course. So many books are written to help people change everything about themselves from how they get up in the morning to how they go to bed at night. What we want to focus on here is just one part of the change equation. We think it's the most important part.

The responsibility for changing you belongs totally to you. You are the only one who can effect the interior transformation of perception, attitude, and feeling that will lead to observable behavior change. You know the old joke that asks, How many psychologists does it take to change a lightbulb? Answer: Only one, but the lightbulb has to want to change.

If there is something about the way you interact with your partner or your children that you don't like, then know that it is up to you to change it. This will probably involve a period of reflection, an attempt to understand why you do the things you do, a gathering of resources to help you see a better way, a commitment to do things differently, and then persistent day-by-day effort to make the change.

Don't forget that the whole process rests on your acceptance of personal responsibility and your own desire to live a better way.

August 11 A NEW SET OF HABITS

How use doth breed a habit in a man![11] —WILLIAM SHAKESPEARE

Any time people with different origins, experiences, and ages come together in a new living arrangement there are going to be small, irritating habits that disaffect or bother one or another. Like seeds, these irritations have the potential for ripening into a fully mature form, and then they can become real problems. You may demand a calm, quiet, orderly home, for example, while others in your new family may like more noise, more mess, and more irregular comings and goings. You may like soft, easy-listening music to soothe your nerves, but someone else in your new family may like lots of loud rock or rap music on a steady basis. You may be very careful about letting everyone know where you are and when you will be home, while to others such logistical considerations are no big deal.

Even in a family with long-established habits, some family members can drive the others crazy. Think of how much more difficult it is when you don't yet have a history of loyal and affectionate association. If these conflicts aren't resolved, laundry lists of minor irritations can become declarations of war.

The key is to defuse as you go. This requires an ability to

bring up problems in a reasonable manner as they occur. And it also requires the practice of tolerance. If your children have complaints, it will be your task to teach them how to deal with problems and to model the tolerance you wish them to show toward others. Start with the things that drive you crazy. Ask yourself what you want to do about your reactions. Can you adjust, or do you need to speak out and try to develop some boundaries around certain habits or behaviors? How can you turn your partner into an ally for your efforts, instead of an enemy?

When someone in your new family does something that is seriously problematic for you, ask yourself why you are having such a big reaction. Without realizing it, you may have become used to running your own show without having to take into account other ways of doing things. Or the behavior that bothers you may feel like a reenactment of some distressing incident in your past. It helps to keep the concept of symbiosis in mind and to remind yourself that other people are separate from you and entitled to their own views and their own style. You cannot expect everyone, particularly those who have had very different life experiences, to act the way you would.

Intentional dialogue is a powerful tool, both for understanding other people and for confronting difficulties. Behavior change requests are a safe way for people to convey what they would like family members to do differently. In whatever you do, especially involving your children, cooperation between partners is critical. And if your problem is with your partner's "bad" habits, it will be important to work this out with him or her in private without carrying your complaints to your child.

As a start, you could compile a list of habits or behaviors that bother you in the people you live with. Which things do you think you could or should learn to tolerate, and which things do you need to address? Does your partner have a similar list? Do you have habits you could or should change? If you were to explore these lists with your partner, how would you approach the discussion in a spirit of real, loving cooperation?

Learning when and how to confront and when and how to practice tolerance is a skill that new families develop over time in the trenches of everyday living. But once learned, they bring continuing benefits to the practitioner throughout life.

August 12 TIME ALONE WITH YOUR NEW PARTNER

Yet they never get tired of each other; they are a couple.[12]

—CARL SANDBURG

You are a couple, and you are both parents. Have you ever talked to a parent who wasn't busy? Stay-at-home parents are busy; working parents are busy; parents with one child are busy; parents with six children are busy; and so are those who are single and those who are partnered.

As you know, it is easy to put your adult relationships on the bottom of a long list of obligations. Romantic dinners just don't seem as important as dentist appointments and grocery shopping. Our experience with couples, however, tells us that when time alone with your partner appears only on the once-a-month checklist there are going to be negative consequences.

The irony is that at the very time when we most need to be connected with our partner in order to meet the demands of family life, we have less time and less emotional energy for making the connection. When we don't connect, things get harder. And when they get harder, we're less likely to connect. It can become a descending spiral.

Remember how it was when the two of you were first together and in love? Nothing kept you apart. Being together was life itself. Being apart felt like dying. This tells you that obstacles aren't the only reason you don't spend more time together. These obstacles can be overcome if the desire is strong enough.

The difficulty is that the craving for each other tends to diminish over time. You don't feel delight in each other as keenly, and each of you becomes for the other associated with an accumulation of disappointments and dissatisfactions. In order to maintain your time commitment to each other, you have to decide that time alone, away from the children, is important. You need to remind yourselves that it is personally renewing and vital for the health and happiness of your children. Their future is heavily influenced by your outlook and the decisions you make about your personal life as a couple.

If you are running a deficit in personal time as a couple, you have some catching up to do. Your goal is to get beyond just taking care of the business of life and enjoy some unstructured experiences that focus on the two of you as people. You want to be able to talk, make love, and just be together. When you are in each other's company, paying attention to each other, sharing intimate experiences over dinner, in the theater, or the bedroom, you are laying down the foundation of your marriage and your family. Can you think of a better investment?

August 13 ACCEPTING THE ROLE OF NEW PARENT

There are lots of things that you can brush under the carpet about yourself until you're faced with somebody whose needs won't be put off.[13]

—ANGELA CARTER

Sometimes a new family relationship starts off on the right foot and just keeps building from there. At other times there is a period of adjustment during which things go less than smoothly. The two adults in the family are very much in the process of developing their relationship, at the same time that they are creating parenting roles with each other's children and helping their own kids to adjust to a new parent. The connections can be tentative. And each person may be carrying heavy baggage from past relationships.

If your connection with a child is recent or in process, you may often ask yourself, "Just how should I relate to this child? What is the best way for me to fill the role of parent?"

A parent-child relationship is inherently unequal. The child looks to a parent to satisfy his needs for safety, support, and structure. The parent is available to the child to supply these things within a loving framework. Anyone expecting to step into a parenting role must be able to establish a strong connection before being able to satisfy these needs without hitches.

A younger child will probably be able to adapt quicker to his mother's or father's new partner as a real-time parent. An older child may have more trouble. No matter what the age of the child, the parenthood of a stepparent has to be earned, even if both the child and the biological parent are willing and supportive.

It makes sense to begin creating a new parent-child relationship as early as possible, with both partners acting jointly and lovingly to share the decision making. The parent and new partner should be allies and comrades in parenting in the same way they would be if the child were the biological child of both. That doesn't mean they always agree, but they have a way of working out their differences for the good of the child. As long as a stepparent is loving and consciously respectful of the child's sense of self, there is no reason to expect that their relationship won't develop as well as if they were biologically related.

Taking on the role of active parent to an older child, a teenager, for example, can be more challenging. There is a lot of catching up to do, and it can't be done all at once. The child has a history the new parent hasn't been part of, and behavior patterns and attitudes have had many years to set.

For an older child, a full parenting role may not be possible or necessary. Establishing mutual respect may be all that is needed at first. The important thing is for you and your partner to concentrate on the integrity and closeness of your adult relationship while at the same time behaving fairly and openly with your teenager.

As long as mutual respect nurtures and maintains the connection, real contentment with each other's company, trust, friendship, and deep affection will grow in time. Your new family will grow into its sense of comfort and intimacy based on long association. Expect the best, and expect that it will take time.

August 14 NEW DAILY ROUTINES

Help me to avoid every sin,
And the source of every sin to forsake;
And as the mist scatters on the crest of the hills,
May each ill haze clear from my soul, O God.[14]

—CELTIC PRAYER

All families rely on routines to get them efficiently through the day together. Think of those first few moments in the early morning when you first wake up. You lie in bed and work up the energy to get going. You stagger into the shower or put on the morning coffee or tea. You get the morning paper and move through the sections that interest you most. Maybe you turn on the radio to get the news or maybe a morning TV program. You wake the kids and get breakfast started. These things are so familiar to you, and so comforting, that you are on remote control while you do them. Your children also have their own morning routines. When you *don't* go through your morning routine as planned, you can get grumpy and complain to your friends at work that you got up on the wrong side of the bed.

Whenever parents take their kids on vacation, for example, or when their college student returns home for the holidays, or when school is about to start, they scramble to reestablish a sense of normalcy by instituting new routines as fast as they can. Routines are important, because you don't have to think about them. You don't have to make any decisions. You already know the steps to *this* dance. And when a routine is broken, it can feel like a real disruption.

Consider how important your child's bedtime routine is to both of you. Being together at the end of the day—perhaps with a favorite story, song, or prayer—is the way you both expect to bring things to a happy, connected closure. And when that doesn't happen, it is sometimes hard to finish the day properly.

Think about your family's morning and evening routines. How useful are they to your family? How do you react when you are jolted out of your regular routines? If you feel disrupted and react accordingly, one of the best things you can do for the people around you when you get grouchy is to say, "I'm sorry for being a little grouchy. I guess I'm just not connecting this morning/evening." Then you make amends.

August 15 NEW CELEBRATIONS

According to Navajo thought, our task as humans is to find the harmony between the orderly and predictable world, represented by Black God, and the unpredictable, represented by Coyote.[15]

—JEAN GUARD MONROE AND RAY A. WILLIAMSON

Look for as many opportunities as you can for creating occasions, celebrations, and rituals in your family. They are the silver thread that holds your family together and gives your shared life meaning: occasions, such as graduations and promotions; celebrations, such as anniversaries, Christmas, and the end of school; rituals, such as bedtime stories and prayers and Saturday morning brunch.

Each member of a blended family comes with some celebrations intact. Everybody has a birthday. Almost everybody celebrates Christmas or Hanukkah. Every family with children marks the end of one school year and the beginning of the next. If you are living with new people, these celebrations will probably retain some of their old flavor at the same time that they add new elements. Birthdays for a child who was previously an only child will take on new shades of feeling and meaning when celebrated in the midst of two or three new stepsiblings.

But don't stop at important occasions. Take advantage of naturally occurring events that can be seen through the lens of ritual and celebration. Some of these, like family vacations, can involve everybody. And some of them can single out individual family members for special honor and recognition: one child's acceptance on the basketball team, another child's violin recital, yet another's decision to let go of an activity or interest he has outgrown.

And then there are the bread-and-butter rituals of daily life. These are ways of accomplishing the tasks of living with a special sense of their meaning and importance. Setting the table with the good dishes on Sunday evening. Going to the park after Saturday morning housecleaning. Shopping downtown for birthday presents instead of going to the local mall. Saying good night to each other at the end of the day. Greeting each other in special ways at the beginning.

Life is hard for adults and children. Each day brings challenges. You can make your home a place of rest, reflection, and laughter by paying attention to the small moments as well as the large ones—and catching what you can of their beauty and their significance.

August 16 THINKING TOGETHER

She bid me take love easy, as the leaves grow on the tree;
But I, being young and foolish, with her would not agree.[16]

—WILLIAM BUTLER YEATS

It is always difficult when two parenting partners disagree on some fundamental level. One of you may see a certain behavior as disruptive or unacceptable, while the other is not concerned by it. One of you may react strongly and wish to punish, while the other, though agreeing that the behavior should be dealt with, does not believe in punishment for this kind of problem. One of you sets the rules and expects them to be adhered to strictly; the other is open to looser guidelines and some bending.

Disagreement over "discipline" is a special concern for blended families, where different norms, habits, routines, and understandings are still trying to work themselves out. It can take a while before you coalesce into a unified parenting effort. If you are part of a blending family, you may already be aware of this. You know that you will have to find working solutions to most of your disagreements. You don't have the option of simply agreeing to disagree when you are considering matters of importance in your children's lives. Your mutual cooperation is critical to the well-being of your family.

It can be helpful to consider common points of disagreement before they are actually a problem in your household. To that end, here are some situations where parents often have different approaches as well as some questions for you and your partner to consider:

- Your child's room is a mess. She is apparently unconcerned, but the mess is a concern to one or both of you. How will you discuss this problem with your child? If you have set a goal with her for straightening things up, and she doesn't meet the goal, how will you react?
- Your child does not come home when he said he would. Later, you discover that he was not where he said he would be. What kind of expectations would you set up to help him get accurate information to you and to get him to be home on time? What will happen if he doesn't meet your expectations in the future?
- Do you feel comfortable talking with your child/stepchild about behavior that is troubling you? Let's say that you don't like the way she reacts when you outline your expectations for her behavior. She has a smart mouth, or she ignores you, or she is sarcastic and disrespectful. Conversely, does your child/stepchild feel comfortable discussing problems he/she is having with you? What could you do to ease the situation? What role would you like to see your partner play in this situation?
- Do you feel that you are a strict or a relaxed disciplinarian? Do you feel that your partner is a strict or a relaxed disciplinarian? Can you define what you mean by these terms? How do you handle differences between you in this regard? Are you willing to change anything in the way you handle discipline?

After you and your partner review these questions, either together or separately, make time to get together to discuss your responses. If the questions or situations need some modification to fit your particular circumstances, feel free to tinker with them or add to them. Use them as "essay" questions, as starters for conversation between you. When you feel that you have discussed a situation or question thoroughly, before you go on to the next one come to a consensus on what action you would take. Try to use this exercise as a way of understanding yourself and your partner better, and as a way of reaching a working agreement about how to handle the real-life the conflicts you will inevitably face together.

August 17 ACTING TOGETHER

No matter how calmly you try to referee, parenting will eventually produce bizarre behavior, and I'm not talking about the kids. Their behavior is always normal.[17]

—BILL COSBY

Adult partners usually display different styles when they interact with each other in unconscious moments. In stressful situations, they each choose different courses. What upsets one may not affect the other. During an argument, one may pursue by seeking contact and reassurance, while the other may withdraw by seeking solitude and refuge. As parents, they usually have different styles too, which can lead to real conflict when they are under pressure with their child. It is a revelation to new parents that they can have such serious disagreements.

There are many ways a parent can unconsciously undercut his partner. He can ignore his partner's point of view ("Go ahead, but don't let your Mom know I said yes."); he can withdraw from the decision-making process ("I don't agree, but my opinion doesn't carry any weight around here, so go ahead and do what you want."); or he can attack his partner in front of their child ("You don't know what you are talking about."). In these ways, and many more, parents can subvert their ability to act together in their child's interest.

We are not suggesting that parents have to agree about everything in order to be conscious parents. We assume disagreement. But we *are* suggesting that creating an atmosphere of cooperation, where disagreements are worked out with mutual respect, is an important part of conscious parenting. One way to establish such an atmosphere is to follow the guideline that points of serious disagreement will be discussed by mirroring, validating, and empathizing *before* action, rather than afterward. This is an especially urgent need if the partners have not had a great deal of experience parenting together and if the child in question has a greater experience with and loyalty to one parent than the other.

Dealing with a child whose behavior is disruptive, dangerous, or disrespectful of the rights of other family members requires parents to check in with each other before any action is taken.

When you and your partner agree about what is best for your child in such a case, then one or both of you can feel empowered to interact with the child according to your joint decision.

But if you and your partner find yourselves in strong disagreement about the action to be taken, it is imperative that you come to an understanding before either one of you acts on your own. Otherwise, you undercut your relationship and your effectiveness with your children when similar problems arise in the future.

Come to such a difficult discussion as openly as you can. You have chosen each other as life partners. You can learn from each other. No one person has all the answers. The way you handle your differences, even apart from the specific action you decide to take, will influence your children a great deal. Show them that they don't have to be afraid of differences and that every person deserves to be heard and respected. *And* that solutions are possible.

August 18 YOU'RE NOT MY REAL MOM/DAD

"Why, he looks just like my old Bunny that was lost when I had scarlet fever!"

But he never knew that it really was his own Bunny, come back to look at the child who had first helped him to be Real.[18]

—MARGERY WILLIAMS

Most parents have read or will read Margery Williams's wonderful story *The Velveteen Rabbit.* It is about a beautiful rabbit toy that becomes old and shopworn and is inadvertently thrown out in the trash only to become a real rabbit because of a little boy's love. If you haven't read it to your children, we urge you to get a copy. It is a moving metaphor for the creative power of love.

It's a story that conveys how love grows into something real only after the glitter and glamour have worn away. The power of love wears away what originally seemed important but is really superficial. What matters are the heart and soul that are left. This is a good story for stepparents, because it can help them teach their stepchildren that accidents of birth are not as important as the reality of the flesh and blood love that they now share.

But for many stepfamilies, there is a time in the beginning before that love feels very "real." Their connection may be institutionalized by marriage or some other commitment, but time hasn't yet ripened the heart into real affection and affiliation. Until it does, the stepchild may say, or think, "You're not my real mom [or dad]." And the stepparent may be appalled to catch herself thinking in return, "You're not my real child."

All of us cherish the notion from time to time that there is a perfect, "real" parent who will understand us perfectly and anticipate our every need. (This is the person we hope we've found when we first fall madly in love.)

It is hard to confront our disappointment in each other and to put away our fantasies of perfect love and perfect family life. But we are consoled by the reality that everyday, mundane caring builds upon itself over time until a deep affection characterizes the way we interact with each other. In the end, real parenthood is not the result of a biological condition. It is the outgrowth of long support through the good times and the difficult ones.

Finally, when love rubs away the beautiful coat of the velveteen rabbit and the shopworn, scruffy fabric beneath shows through, we know that we are real parents of real children, and the bond between us is too strong to be disrupted by superficial things.

August 19 WATER AND FIRE

What a conflict of water and fire there must have been here! Just imagine a river of molten rock running down over a river of melted snow. What a seething and boiling of waters; what clouds of steam rolled into the heavens![19]

—JOHN WESLEY POWELL

One of the hardest things to cope with is the unhappy intrusion of ex-partners and old business into your new family relationships. This may not be a problem when a previous marriage has been satisfactorily resolved and/or enough time has elapsed for wounds to heal or to diminish. But sometimes divorced couples continue to wrangle over visitation schedules, custody rights, financial obligations, and other on-going emotional issues for many years.

This means that you are dealing with difficult issues that are made more difficult by intense feelings of anger—and perhaps betrayal. It is not uncommon for people to feel cheated by former mates and betrayed by a legal system that is inadequate to dispense any real justice. It can be hard to keep these feelings from contaminating your present life.

If this describes you or your partner, then you will want to take extra time and care in reading this book. You will want to be especially committed to the process of understanding your own journey to this point and dedicated to becoming conscious in your dealings with your new partner and your children.

Your guideline will be to do whatever is in the best interests of your children. Although only *you* can determine what that is, we can say with some assurance what we know it is not. Your children will not benefit from hearing you complain about their other biological parent. They will not flourish when you share with them your innermost fears about money. They will not prosper in a home that is filled with anger, suspicion, and blame. They will not experience joy when your own view is narrowed by bitterness.

They will learn from you about life by how you handle your difficulties. A matter-of-fact explanation of circumstances that affect them, a personal perspective that is hopeful and ready to see the good, an investment of positive energy in life as it is now—these are attitudes that will heal you and heal them and prepare them to love and be loved in the future. Such attitudes are yours to adopt. It's up to you.

August 20 THIS KID IS NOT LOVABLE

All God's children are not beautiful. Most of God's children are, in fact, barely presentable.[20]

—FRAN LEBOWITZ

There are times we parents have a lot of trouble seeing our children with loving eyes. They do, in fact, seem barely presentable. We may be reacting negatively to something our child has said or done, or to our child's defensive response to something *we* have said or done. Every parent knows the feeling. And every married couple, regardless of how long they have been together, experiences times when they don't even see each other as presentable, much less lovable. These are the times when you look around and wonder how you landed in the middle of these people.

What do you do if you are in the process of blending your family with someone else's and you must admit to yourself that you don't find your newly acquired child very lovable or even likable? First, you can recognize that these feelings are probably temporary. When you think about it, there's hardly been even one single person in your life that you found lovable *all* the time. Your commitment to this child is strong, and short of a catastrophic failure, positive feelings will either grow or reassert themselves in time. Second, recognize that giving love is sometimes an act of will. Love is a decision. You decide to love this child and bring your behavior in line with your decision. Acting in a loving way will help you feel more loving.

What we are saying is that you are required to act consciously to understand, care about, and love this child here before you. Part of this process can involve examining your own negative feelings, your own predisposition to judge. Why do you feel so negative? Perhaps you feel no love coming *back* from your new son or daughter. You feel rejected. If this is true, then you can be extra vigilant against becoming symbiotic. A symbiotic viewpoint might go something like this, "This child doesn't care about me. She is out to get me. She is ungrateful for the things I have done for her. It's not fair to me, and I won't stand for it. Why should I do all the work?"

The answer, of course, is that you must do the work because *you are the parent.* You may have trouble holding on to this thought in the heat of the moment. If you are inclined to say or do something you'll regret, then you can remember to remain neutral in the face of the perceived insult and rejection and step back for some moments to compose yourself. Review what just happened, review your conscious commitment to care for this child and give yourself time to lower your blood pressure. When you have tapped into your own sense of peace and security, you can reaffirm your efforts to care consistently for this child who is being so difficult.

Part of being a conscious parent is knowing that you don't always get the appreciation you deserve at any given moment. You don't have to limit yourself to a tit-for-tat world. The love you give doesn't have to be instantaneously returned to you on the spot. You give because it's the right thing to do.

If you can truly feel that, then you have freed yourself from a great burden. In the end you may receive the love and admiration you want for yourself, but in the meantime you are inoculating yourself against a symbiotic need to be personally comforted by someone else. You are learning to comfort yourself and take care of your own needs. And you are helping your child understand the nature of loving at the same time.

August 21 THIS KID IS A REAL PROBLEM!

There is no appetite for parenthood; there is only a purpose or intention of parenthood.[21]

—R. G. COLLINGWOOD

Yesterday we discussed those times when you feel less than loving toward your child. Today we feel it is only fair to discuss what may be happening when, despite your love, you are facing a child who is in real crisis or who is chronically unable to function within your family. Children grow up today in an increasingly hostile environment. From peer groups to family circumstances, today's children are under increasing pressure from all sources. And there may be a child now living under your roof who has been exposed to difficulties you don't even know about.

Whether you are the child's natural parent or not, you may be in a position to observe a pattern of wounding in your child that requires professional help. There are resources that can help. Possibilities include your medical care provider, county health professional, church or school counselor, or a private therapist. But before you make a decision to seek outside help, you will want to clarify for yourself what you are observing and what role you want to play in addressing the problem.

As difficult as it is, you will want to examine your own motives and insecurities. On what basis are you concluding that this child is in trouble? Is your decision based on your love and understanding of your child? Or are you observing a situation that you just don't want to deal with? Are you in over your head? Are you willing to become involved in partnership with whatever helper you choose to contact? Are you and your parenting partner in agreement about the seriousness of the problem?

If you and your partner decide to seek professional help for your child, you will have to put aside embarrassment and any sense of personal failure. They don't serve any purpose except to prevent you from getting the help you need. There isn't a person alive who couldn't benefit from good professional help at one time or another. You need not fear that you will be abandoned and left alone with your problem, provided that you continue to nourish your connection with your child and to stay in close touch with the professionals with whom you are working.

And if one agency or counselor doesn't feel right, you always have the option of going somewhere else. The important thing to remember is that help will come if you are persistent. You, your partner, and your child may feel isolated now, but every problem is an opportunity for growth if you approach it in a spirit of confidence and hope for the future.

August 22 WHEN DISSENSION RULES

Your little hands were never made
To tear each other's eyes.[22]
—ISAAC WATTS

Sometimes you may feel more like a referee than a loving parent. Your kids just don't like each other. You know this because they hit, kick, and bite each other, and wound each other with words. You close your eyes and hope and pray for a truce while you cheerfully prepare a nice Sunday dinner or take the family to a movie or begin some other activity you've planned to bring everyone together. But you have the nagging feeling that all your energetic and careful preparations will blow up in today's version of the Sibling Wars. We've all been there.

Sometimes you reach your limit. And when your worst fears *are* realized, you blow up. Even conscious parents loose their cool on occasion. You may reach your limit and let fly with whatever pops into your head. All of a sudden, your attention shifts from the particular battle of the moment and focuses on the injustice they are doing to you. That's the style of a maximizer. Or on the other hand, you may feel that there is no use dealing with these idiots and clam up, walk away, and refuse to connect. That's the style of a minimizer.

However you act when you are disappointed or outraged by others in your family, you are convinced that life is unfair and, most particularly, that *your* life is unfair. When you start feeling this way it's time to slow down, calm yourself, and seek your own inner support. Only by recapturing your inner calm in some way can you assert your independence from the nasty scene spilling out in front of you.

You may not become calm right away, but as soon as you understand what you need to do, get back on the right track and start repairing your interpersonal connections. Attempt to revitalize your sense of humor. You may need to apologize for your outburst or your withdrawal. By taking these steps you are further defusing your bodily uproar and capturing the high ground. It is even likely that your return to calmness will have a soothing effect on your children and on your partner. You are on your way back to recapturing those feelings of love and support that will enable you to be of service to yourself and your family.

A prayer for today: *I recognize my yearning for the peace and quiet of conflict-free relationships, realizing at the same time that I must learn to accept the times of disquiet and cultivate my capacity for faith.*

August 23 NEW RIVALRY

> Now Jacob looked up and saw Esau coming, and four hundred men with him. So he divided the children among Leah and Rachel and the two maids. . . . He himself went on ahead to them, bowing himself to the ground seven times, until he came near his brother. But Esau ran to meet him, and embraced him, and fell on his neck and kissed him, and they wept.[23]
>
> — GENESIS 33: 1–4.

You are already aware, if you have more than one child, that siblings commonly see each other as rivals for their parents' attention. It is often hard for them to understand how a parent can truly love every child, each in his or her own way, in equal measure. You are also aware from previous discussions how a child who has entered the stage of competence may become a rival for the attention of his opposite-sex parent and at that point may also see a same-sex parent as a rival.

In a newly blended family, however, there may be a new twist. At the same time you and your partner are putting together a lasting relationship, your child or your partner's child can easily fall into the pattern of rivalry with his parent's new partner or with newly acquired brothers or sisters. This is normal, but it requires some careful handling.

Just as you would if you were calming normal sibling rivalry, you stretch your capacity to give attention to all the children in the family in a lovingly impartial manner. You may feel more strongly drawn to your own child than to your partner's child, but you can learn to deal fairly with both.

There may be some days when it seems that everyone, your partner included, has become a needy child, and it may seem that you are the only one who can satisfy their needs. You may start to feel sorry for yourself, because, after all, you have needs too. Who is going to take care of *you*?

Whenever you begin to detect these feelings of persecution, overwork, or overwhelming pressure, you can use them as a reminder to slow down and take some time out. These are situations that require extra effort in order to think and act consciously. Unless you practice stepping back, taking time to soothe any symbiotic feelings that are surfacing, you run the risk of reacting in an unconscious way.

Someone in this family has to be an adult, and it may as well be you. This is a conscious position. The inverse, unconscious position, is to expect that others will have to pick up the slack, since it's not fair to expect you to do so. Probably, no one else will. You can use these occasions to practice calmly expressing your support for those who need it, while taking care of your needs, as far as possible, through intentional dialogue. Whether you believe it now, or not, your new family is helping you grow and become more tolerant, more understanding, and more loving. Over time you will see how lucky you are!

August 24 VISITS

But the second piece of advice is not to be scared off. Most stepfamilies do well . . .[24]

—STEPHANIE COONTZ

Your partner's children are coming to visit, and you may harbor a whole range of feelings about seeing them, all the way from horror to out-and-out excitement. How you feel, of course, depends upon what they are like, what happens to your partner in their presence, and how you feel in their company. The answers may all be positive or all negative or anything in between. The only thing we know for sure is that their visit is important and you want it to go as well as it possibly can.

Since this is the case, it's worth spending some time preparing and planning for it. Start by asking your partner how he is feeling about being with his children and what he wants to have happen. You are really asking what he wants in terms of the emotional aspects of the visit and what he wants in terms of the schedule.

Then share with him any ideas you may have for helping him achieve his goals and any concerns or problems that you think may need to be addressed. This is the time for the two of you to talk honestly without being rushed. If you are on the same wavelength, then you won't easily be thrown off by uncooperative, undisciplined children or by plans that go awry.

Many parents in this situation want to do too much or buy too much. It's important to keep your children's ages in mind and their capacity for scheduled activity. But even more important, you can keep in mind that what all children really want is their parents' affectionate attention. The greatest gift we can give our children is the quality of our attention.

Adjusting yourself to their level, listening and being responsive, offering encouragement and support, being willing to engage in activities they enjoy, setting reasonable limits—these are the ways you can let them know that you are there for them and that you care about them. No matter who they are, or what their circumstances, they deserve this much.

August 25 FINANCIAL CONCERNS

... if a man had twenty pounds a year for his income, and spent nineteen shillings and sixpence, he would be happy, but ... if he spent twenty pounds one he would be miserable.[25] —CHARLES DICKENS

Many marriages hit the rocks over the question of finances. Not having enough money is a big problem. But just as great is the continual disagreement over how an adequate amount is to be spent. What one partner sees as extravagance, the other may see as essential. How to spend money on children can be a source of some of this discontent. School is starting again soon, for example, and the question of school clothes, books, and supplies may be beginning to draw your attention.

It is common in an era of two-income families and late marriages for partners to keep their finances separate. They may agree that one partner will pay some expenses, and the other partner will pay other expenses. Obviously, this requires detailed discussion if it's going to work. Deciding to share all expenses is more common, but even this requires detailed discussion.

Couples owe it to themselves and their children to discuss and review expenses on a regular basis, even when it doesn't seem necessary. That avoids sudden surprises and recriminations later. Ask almost any divorced couple, and you will find out that ignorance of financial matters or inability to deal with financial difficulties is a recipe for disaster. Nasty surprises involving money reverberate in relationships through a pattern of shock, accusation, and argument and are hard to recover from.

If you are part of a blended family, it is even more important to consider the question of how the family's money will be made and spent. If there is a great income disparity between you and your partner, it can be difficult, if not impossible, to share expenses equally. And differences in the amount of discretionary money available can lead to questions about who gets to buy what and from which pocket.

How have you and your partner chosen to deal with family finances? Is the way you are handling money an open book to both you and your partner? Are you in agreement with your partner over all major expenditures, such as house, car, schooling, food, and clothing? Do you make and follow a budget, and do you allow each other some agreed upon discretionary spending? If you regularly have arguments over money, how is this affecting your relationship and your children's attitude toward money? Is it time to get a handle on this problem?

As with all other challenges in family life, this one can be seen as an opportunity for improving your communication, clarifying your values for your children, and working more closely toward common goals with your partner. It all depends on how you deal with it.

August 26 DIFFERENT LIVING STANDARDS

I saw him once literally bleed from the bottoms of his feet, a man who came here uneducated, alone, unable to speak the language, who taught me all I needed to know about faith and hard work by the simple eloquence of his example.[26] —MARIO CUOMO

We live in a materialistic society. As someone once said, "How much is enough? Well, just a little more than I have now." Sooner or later, all of our children feel the siren call of brand-name clothes, action-packed vacations, traveling abroad, first-rate schools and colleges, and lots of spending money. Despite how much your children have and how hard you are working to give them what they want, the popular culture will push them to want more. And they, too, will embrace materialism if you don't step in to help them replace it with a more important set of values.

During the years that children are living at home, many families undergo profound changes in their earnings. Sometimes the change means that there is a lot more money to spend, but often it means there is less. Either way, parents need to decide how to help children handle the new circumstances.

Job loss and divorce are among the common events that can pitch a family in comfortable circumstances into circumstances that are more straitened. If your family has undergone this monetary transformation, then you have some figuring to do. You need to think about how you can change your living standards to match your resources—and how you can help your children adjust to new circumstances.

It may be natural for your children to envy their more comfortable friends and neighbors. It's what you and your children do with these feelings that really counts. Begin by asking yourself how you handle whatever feelings of envy *you* may have. Your children will learn so much from your example. If you are fun, energetic, creative, and loving regardless of the size of your salary, your children will learn perspective about what money can buy and what it can't buy.

When you and your children spend time together having fun, working, supporting each other, and cultivating a spiritual life, then the amount of money available for buying things will seem much less important. They will have a chance to learn firsthand that material fortunes ebb and flow, but what remains are the affections of the human heart. Reassure them that you will be all right, and they will be all right. You will all survive intact with the things that count most.

August 27 THE NEW BABY

Both culture—the traditional way of doing things in a particular society—and individual experience guide parents in their tasks.[27]

—MEREDITH F. SMALL

We have a good friend who married an older man when she was twenty-two. He had two children from a previous marriage who were eight and ten. They had a baby together two years after they married. They divorced, and our friend got married again at age thirty-nine. A year later, she and her second husband had a baby together and another two years later. Since she had functioned as a mother to all five of these children, you could say that her involvement with young children spanned thirty years! Even if you count only her biological children, her oldest and youngest were eighteen years apart.

All of these children were wanted and much loved. Each was very different from the others, having been born to her at very different ages and in very different social and financial circumstances. It was almost as if she had two or three different families, although in her mind they were all one.

If you find yourself in something like this circumstance—or if you have had an early and late family with only one husband—then you know the blessings that can come when a new baby is born into a family with older brothers and sisters. Not only can they be helpful with housework and baby care, but they are less likely to feel jealous and competitive.

You, too, will have more energy for one baby than you would have for two or three born close together. You and your partner may feel that you've had a chance to "practice" on your older children and are ready to buckle down and be devoted to a late baby in a way you weren't when you were younger. How wonderful that we are all free to make our families any way we choose!

August 28 THE JOY OF PETS

If I had a donkey that wouldn't go,
Would I beat him? Oh no, no.
I'd put him in the barns and give him some corn,
The best little donkey that ever was born.[28]

—MOTHER GOOSE

Pets and families often go together. Unless there are strong objections from their parents or living conditions or allergies that simply won't permit it, children glory in the company of dogs and cats and birds and fish and an assortment domesticated rodents. Over half of all American homes have a pet of some kind. Learning to love and take care of another living, breathing being is a great teacher of life's most important lessons.

It's true that there are unconscious pet owners in the same way that there are unconscious parents. There seems to be a human predisposition to love *the idea* of a pet, while finding the reality often tedious or downright irritating. If you've offered shelter to an animal, you probably know how scarce your children can make themselves when the puppy makes a mess in the house or the cat needs to be fed or the birdcage needs to be changed. And if you suddenly inherit an older pet, you may feel the brunt of previous, dysfunctional ownership when you observe the bad habits this poor, old dog carries into your household.

We have an acquaintance who recently remarried after several years of living as a single parent. Her dog, an old American cocker spaniel, came with her into the new marriage. It was a package deal. The old problem is that her new husband hates the dog. Although she has had many years of companionship from her beloved dog and views it as a member of her family, he cannot bear the dog's habit of jumping up on the furniture or stealing food from any dish it can reach. When he looks at the dog, he sees a crotchety, spoiled irritant. When his wife looks at the dog, she sees only her loyal old friend.

Pets, especially dogs, easily become the object of the strong feelings their owners project onto them. A lonely child can easily see her beloved dog as being left out or unappreciated by other members of the family. A little boy who is much loved by his parents can practice loving the dog in return. A frustrated child can quickly redirect the anger he feels for you or other people in his life toward his trusted canine companion. Parents soon learn that they can tell a lot about what is happening in a child's life by watching closely how he interacts with the family dog or cat.

Getting a family pet is a big decision. Dogs and cats easily live ten years or more. Think about how old you will be and how old your kids will be in ten or fifteen years. If you already have a dog or cat, you know the joy and comfort they can bring. You also know the lessons in personal responsibility they can teach children. If you don't now have a pet or are planning to add another, think long and hard about whether you have the financial and emotional resources required to neuter, train, and keep them in good health. You will want to consult with other members of your household to make sure that everyone understands what their rights and obligations are. Then prepare yourself to become deeply involved in loving one more member of your family.

August 29 MISSING ASPECTS OF YOUR OLD LIFE

What is precious is never to forget
The essential delight.[29]

—STEPHEN SPENDER

Human experience is very complex. There are shades of feeling and shades of meaning in everything we do. We never find ourselves totally in heaven or totally in hell except for very brief, relatively rare moments. These moments are often unforgettable and exert a much greater influence on us than their brevity might suggest. But they remain punctuation marks, adding excitement to the gentle murmur of our ordinary days.

There may be times, even in your present happiness, when you find yourself yearning for aspects of your old life. There may be things you miss about your previous partner and moments you remember with pleasant nostalgia. Even the behavior you once found unbearable may appear to you now through a lens that softens with romantic focus. Maybe his obsession with his ride-around tractor wasn't so bad. Maybe now you see her determination to make you happy as sweet and touching.

One could argue that a good life is one that is deeply felt, that to be present and alive to the feelings of the moment means you are living well. If that is true, then whatever threads of sadness or regret for the past run through your life can add richness and depth to your experience. If they overpower you or paralyze you, you need to find a way to let them go. But if they flavor your life rather than dominate it, then you know you are alive and living well.

August 30 FAMILY NIGHT

If you think that peace and happiness are somewhere else and you run after them, you will never arrive.[30] —THICH NHAT HANH

No doubt your family is closely scheduled. If both parents are working in a household where there are school-age children, then by definition, you don't have a lot of throwaway time. Even if your family is different from this, you are probably busy. You have to schedule a time to be unscheduled.

What would it be like if you scheduled a "family night" once a week or once every two weeks? This would be an evening when all of you would be home together and free from other concerns for an hour or two. Your time together could be longer or shorter, depending on the age of your children and the realities of your outside obligations. But the point is, that for some period of time on a regular basis, adults and children would know that you will have a chance to enjoy each other's company undisturbed.

Some families have family meetings during this time, when the business of running their family enterprise is discussed. Grievances, complaints, praises, and appreciations, all get voiced in an orderly fashion, under the wise facilitation of one of the parents.

For many families, this helps family logistics and relationships work more smoothly. But this is not an essential component of family night. You *can* just get together for the purpose of passing the time pleasantly in each other's company. Some advance planning is probably a good idea, but it can be very simple.

You can talk while you enjoy a favorite snack. You can play family games. You can do a crafts project together. If you make cards or simple, handmade gifts, then you are killing two birds with one stone: being together and accomplishing a necessary task. You can make music together. You can *listen* to music together. You can cook together. You can learn a new skill, like growing seedlings or learning to knit. You can be active by taking a walk, or if you are more ambitious, you can skate or bike ride. You can read aloud. . . .

Obviously, there are endless possibilities. The important thing is that you are together, doing something other than the necessary work of keeping the business of life on track. You are interacting, laughing, learning, refreshing yourselves at the well of the commitment and affection you have for each other. Think about it. Do you think such benefits are worth a couple of hours every week?

August 31 KEEPING YOUR SENSE OF HUMOR

Family jokes, though rightly cursed by strangers, are the bond that keeps most families alive.[31]

—STELLA BENSON

Okay, the summer is almost over and school is about to begin. Your kids are both bored and frantic as the summer winds down. The need to shop for new school clothes is becoming a preoccupation as your kids count the days until the First Day of School. As always you are wearing many different hats: breadwinner, lover, housekeeper, chauffeur, patient counselor, athletic director, and certainly tired-out parent. Let's hope you've kept your sense of humor alive, along with everything you've accomplished this season.

Being able to laugh at yourself and the world around you is probably the single most useful skill you can apply to parenting and learn from parenting. There are so many opportunities to take note of the silly, absurd, and ridiculous aspects of life when you are a mother or a father.

As we've passed through these summer days, we have frequently asked you to step back and pause before reacting to something that upsets you. Nothing helps put things more in perspective than a sense of humor. Laughing helps you get some emotional distance from the part of you that is feeling sorry for yourself, and since it's contagious, it helps your children and your partner to step back and relax too.

Humor is a complex human response, with all kinds of emotional colorations. Sometimes it is a caress, and sometimes it's a weapon. The most effective kind of humor in family life is gentle and has the ability to defuse tense situations by reminding everybody that they don't have to take themselves so seriously.

Can you laugh at yourself, even when you are frustrated, or self-pitying—perhaps most especially then? If you can, you've already gone most of the way toward becoming an effective parent. Every time you step away from self absorption, you open the door for good feeling. You get yourself out of your rut, and everyone else moves right along with you into a more cooperative, optimistic space.

Notes

1. David H. Levy, *The Nature Company Guide to Skywatching* (Alexandria, VA: Time Life Books, 1995).

2. Mary Oliver, "Whelks," in *New and Selected Poems* (Boston: Beacon Press, 1992).

3. Candace Pert, *Molecules of Emotion* (New York: Scribner, 1997).

4. Sharon Olds, "Socks," in *Wellspring* (New York: Knopf, 1996).

5. Phyllis McGinley, "Fourteenth Birthday," in *Times Three*, (New York: Viking Press, 1968).

6. La Rochefoucauld, François, duc de. *Maxims*, No. 361, trans. L.W. Tanock (New York: Penguin, 1967).

7. Shel Silverstein, "Alice," in *Where the Sidewalk Ends* (New York: Harper and Row, 1974).

8. Ralph Waldo Emerson, "Journal Entry, Ralph Waldo Emerson," in *Selected Prose and Poetry,* ed. Reginald L. Cook (New York: Holt, Rinehart, and Winston, 1962).

9. Stephanie Coontz, *The Way We Really Are: Coming to Terms With America's Changing Families* (New York: BasicBooks, 1997).

10. e. e. cummings, "what if a much of a which of a wind," in *Poems 1923–1954* (New York: Harcourt, Brace & World, 1955).

11. William Shakespeare, *Two Gentlemen of Verona*, Act 5, Scene 4, in *The Complete Illustrated Shakespeare*, ed. Howard Staunton (New York: Gallery Books, 1989).

12. Carl Sandburg, "A Couple," in *Good Morning, America* (New York: Harcourt, Brace & World, 1928).

13. Angela Carter, interview in *Marxism Today* (London; Jan. 1985).

14. "Thanksgiving," *The Celtic Vision: Selections From the Carmina Gadelica*, ed. Esther de Waal (Petersham, MA: St. Bede's Publications, 1988).

15. Jean Guard Monroe and Ray A.Williamson, *They Dance in the Sky* (New York: Houghton Mifflin, 1987).

16. William Butler Yeats, "Down By the Salley Gardens," in *Collected Works,* vol. I, *The Poems,* ed. Richard J. Finneran (New York: Scribner, 1997).

17. Bill Cosby, *Fatherhood* (Boston, MA: Prentice Hall, 1987).

18. Margery Williams, *The Velveteen Rabbit* (New York: Barnes and Noble Books, 1991).

19. John Wesley Powell, *Down the Colorado: Diary of the First Trip Through the Grand Canyon, 1869* (New York: E. P. Dutton, 1969).

20. Fran Lebowitz, "Manners" in *Metropolitan Life* (New York: Dutton, 1978).

21. R. G. Collingwood, *The New Leviathan: Or, Man, Society, Civilization, and Barbarism*, pt. 2, ch. 23, aphorism, (New York: Crowell, 1971).

22. Isaac Watts, Divine Songs, *Attempted In Easy Language for the Use of Children,* no. 16, ed. J. H. P. Pafford (London: Oxford University Press, 1971).

23. *The New Oxford Annotated Bible* (New York: Oxford University Press, 1994).

24. Stephanie Coontz, *The Way We Really Are: Coming to Terms with America's Changing Families* (New York: Basic Books, 1997).

25. Charles Dickens, *David Copperfield* (New York: The Modern Library, 1950).

26. Mario Cuomo, Address to the Democratic National Convention, July 16, 1984.

27. Meredith A. Small, "Our Babies, Ourselves," *Natural History,* October 1997.

28. "Mother Goose Nursery Rhymes," no. 41, *Anthology of Children's Literature,* eds. Edna Johnson, Evelyn R. Shields, and Frances Clarke Sayers (Boston: Houghton Mifflin Company, 1970).

29. Stephen Spender, "I Think Continually of Those Who Were Truly Great," in *Collected Poems* (New York: Random House, 1955).

30. Thich Nhat Hanh, *The Long Road Turns to Joy* (Berkeley: Parallax Press, 1996).

31. Stella Benson, *Pipers and a Dancer* (New York: Macmillan, 1924).

September

INTRODUCTION TO THE MONTH OF SEPTEMBER

Have you ever thought to yourself that there has to be a quieter, simpler way to live? Our theme this month is simplifying, and our purpose is to encourage you to reflect on ways you can simplify your routines and your activities Over and over again, people find that their quality of life goes up when they learn to moderate their spending, say no to unnecessary commitments, make their daily routines more efficient, and focus on the human and spiritual values that give life joy and meaning. We hope these thoughts will inspire you to do the same.

September 1 LONG AT THE FAIR

There is something memorable in the experience to be had by going into a fair ground that stands at the edge of a Middle Western town on a night after the annual fair has been held.[1]

—SHERWOOD ANDERSON

They're almost over, those lazy days of summer. State fairs and county fairs are either in full swing or wrapping up. Leaves are looking pretty shopworn, and everyone anticipates the Labor Day holiday which spells the end of the line for summer vacation. Children will be beginning a new school year, and things are about to change. They look forward to the start of school with a mixture of excitement and regret. They may be bored by the experience of so much leisure time, but they may not look forward to getting back to schoolwork either.

This is a time to focus on your child. She is thinking about new teachers, new friends, new learning challenges, and new routines. And you are there to be her stage manager, confidant, and supporter. You will listen to her excitement and trials as you prepare her to face each day with a sense of readiness.

It makes sense to think about how you can simplify your child's life as well as your own as you all plunge into a new school year. How will this school year be different from those of the past? How will you help your child develop a schedule that leaves your family less stressed and frantic than it was last year? How will you reduce the demands of carpooling and after school activities down to a healthy level? How can you set a pace that is appropriate for you and your children? How will you and your partner balance your other obligations with the responsibilities that come with your child's schooling?

We leave you with these questions, on the first day of September so that you can begin to turn your attention to this new, but ever-returning cycle in family life.

A prayer for today: *As I move into my time of quiet and relaxation, I ask for the serenity to both re-create and watch the re-creation that is taking place in front of me. May I have in equal measure the energy and the quiet to be part of the flow of my life.*

September 2 GETTING READY TO GO BACK TO SCHOOL

Our behavior is a function of our decisions, not our conditions.[2]

—STEPHEN R. COVEY

Even after you've put your school years behind you, you can still feel the gentle tug of September, and the bracing promise of a new start in a new school year. The crisp air, the new clothes, the unmarked pages of notebooks that haven't been used yet—all these cues beckoned you toward your dreams of a better future. This idealized future featured you as a central character, only you were magically better-organized, more popular, and better dressed!

Now your children are going through their own version of this ritual that is part hope, part determination, and part sweet illusion. This is a good time to talk to them about putting in place the mechanics that will help the school year run smoother. You can ask yourself, and them, what needs to be done to make things easier and simpler. Simpler is important because you want each member of your household to do as much for themselves as they are capable of doing. Children are more likely to act independently when systems are simple. And you want the running of the household to be as efficient as possible, so that you can spend valuable time and energy on things that deserve it, like educational activities or just having fun together.

"Simple" requires advance thinking, detailed planning, cooperative labor, consistent effort, and a periodic evaluation of how things are going. That sounds like a lot of work, but what it means is that if you spend some time up front making sure that the mechanics and the logistics work well, then you don't have to rethink them every single day. Here are some questions you, your partner, and your children might want to talk about now, before school actually begins:

- What are the transportation needs on school days, and how are we going to meet them?
- What are the food needs on weekdays, and how are we going to meet them?
- How will we meet the needs for parental participation, schedule coordination, and child participation that are generated by student activities outside of school?
- Who is responsible for what, and when, at home during the week?
- How are we going to keep track of what's going on?

This is not an exhaustive set of questions, but it's probably enough to begin with. Ask yourself how you can simply and consistently meet these requirements. Then you will have a good idea of your schedule and a reasonable plan for a division of labor that teaches your kids responsibility and helps you keep your sanity.

September 3 STARTING AND ENDING THE DAY

In any reform effort, the hardest change is the inside work, the emotional work.[3]

—PETER BLOCK

Do you remember how you were rousted out of bed to go to school? Were you awakened in some gentle Ozzie-and-Harriet kind of way? Your mom musically called your name up the stairs, you cheerfully got up, and eagerly tumbled down to the prepared breakfast and the loving smiles that awaited you? Or was your morning routine something different?

Such memories might influence how you get your family going in the morning. Parents exercise this particular privilege of parenthood in any number of ways. There is the let-them-fend-for-themselves school, the drill-sergeant school, the efficient-stopwatch school, the barely-functional-myself school, and the nurturing-and-organized Mom school, to name but a few.

Certainly, there is a certain amount of stuff that needs to get done in order to get everyone successfully out the door. But something even more important than efficient organization needs to happen.

You and your children are greeting the day and beginning the miracle of waking life all over again. The spirit in which you do it makes a difference. Whether or not you are Harriet Nelson, you want to interact with your children in as positive, calm, and optimistic a way as you can. Do whatever you can to keep things simple and organized, including putting in extra time the night before. You don't want last-minute glitches to spoil the positive mood. You want to send your children off with smiles and love, instead of cranky complaints.

All of this is worth repeating at the end of the day. Bedtime rituals are a golden opportunity for closeness and sharing. You can wrap your children in stories of beauty and rich imagination as you send them lovingly to sleep. Keep it simple and keep it loving, and your children will carry these feelings inside them as they transition into the waking and sleeping part of their days.

September 4 DETAILS, DETAILS

Generations have trod, have trod;
And all is seared with trade; bleared, smeared with toil . . .[4]

—GERARD MANLEY HOPKINS

Oh, there are so many details in family life. The putting on and the taking off . . . . Organizing them into routines will reduce the chaos and teach your children good lifetime habits. And your initial efforts at organization will reward you with increased peace of mind.

Getting started in the morning, for example, can be a much easier process if some of your morning tasks are done the night before. You can also think about which of them could profitably be shared between family members. You have to factor in, of course, that you may have different requirements on different days of the week. Here are some ideas that might help:

- Make school lunches the night before. If your children are old enough, they can make their lunches themselves or at least help you do it. Make sure that they have a range of choices and that they understand that they are to choose one vegetable, one fruit, one sweet treat, and so on. Lunch is a balancing act. You want them to eat it, but you don't want their teeth to rot out or their only vegetable to be corn chips.
- Have your child lay out school clothes the night before. Some kids can pull any old outfit out of a drawer and be ready to go. Others agonize over their choices, taking up valuable time in the morning. Rounding up hard-to-find items like shoes and socks can forestall the last minute hunt as the school bus is about to pull away.
- Set out the breakfast things the night before. Some food has to be left in the refrigerator, but some foods, like cold cereal, and bread, and dishes and silverware can easily be set out in advance.
- Make sure your children complete their homework during the previous evening, when there is enough time to read that

passage in the encyclopedia or check the math. Early morning "homework panic" is not conducive to starting the day off right.

- Check with your kids the night before to determine whether there are any unusual driving or school requirements for the next day. Do the gym clothes have to be washed, do you have to sign any permission forms, are your kids going on a field trip, does someone have an appointment with the doctor or the orthodontist? Best to think about these responsibilities the night before.
- Allow an extra ten minutes to get your children to the bus or the carpool on time. If you have little ones, you may want to wait for the bus with them. If they miss their ride, you will spend extra time and emotional energy to get them to school yourself.

This doesn't mean that you have to act like a drill sergeant. If your children aren't cooperating with your morning efforts, you will have to take the time, preferably after the day is over, to discuss the problem calmly. Allow older children to help you with younger ones. Ask your parenting partner to lend a hand. And remember that no matter how organized you are, not everything will be under your control at all times. Life just isn't like that. But, hope springs eternal . . . maybe tomorrow.

September 5 SIMPLE WORDS

I will not play at tug o'war.
I'd rather play at hug o'war . . .[5]

—SHEL SILVERSTEIN

The most magical, transforming words in the English language are: I Love You. They couldn't be simpler, and yet they echo forever inside our hearts, long after they've been spoken.

If these are the last words your child hears as he runs to catch the bus in the morning or climbs into bed at night, you are giving him a great gift. And you double the impact when you say them with a smile and a hug. Even if there comes a time when he shrugs away from the hug, you can be sure he still needs to hear and feel that you love him.

The simplicity of the message leaves you room to be creative. There was a period in our children's lives when "I love you" was translated into Spanish (Yo te amo), French (Je t'aime), and German (Ich liebe dich). We said it this way for fun and because our kids were enchanted by the power they had to make themselves understood in the languages they were learning in school.

There have also been other phrases during the years that have stood in place of the more conventional three words. "Go get 'em, tiger" once filled the bill. And then there was the sweet game that lasted many years, of, "I love you more than [*fill in the blank:* all the stars in the universe, all the bugs in the backyard, all the fleas on the dog, all the grains of sand at the beach, etc.].

Other people's endearments always run the risk of sounding silly or ordinary. But, we urge you to let yourselves go and say daily good-byes to your children with simple and loving affirmations that don't leave any doubt about how you feel about them. Leave them with "I love you" ringing in their ears and in their hearts.

September 6 DON'T DO EVERYTHING YOURSELF

What if Woman were to allow herself to trust her own unhappiness and to make life changes—changes that would allow time and place for her to experience her life as it lives itself out slowly, moment by moment?[6]

—JUDITH DUERK

Mother is almost always the captain of the family ship—and the CEO and the Principle Therapist and the Chief Housekeeper. There may be some fathers who also feel responsible for seeing that everything gets done, and done right, but generally, any imbalance in this regard favors the mother.

We can debate all the complex reasons why women end up doing the lion's share of the work within the family, but some of them are obvious. Women have traditionally been the keepers of hearth and home. Their mothers tended the home fires, and so did their grandmothers, while the men in the family worked on farms or in factories or fought in wars. Nurturing patterns are passed on to daughters with their mother's milk.

Culturally women are also programmed to care about clean sheets and clean toilets. If you doubt this, go to your nearest newsstand and pick up a copy of any men's magazine, and then compare it to any randomly chosen women's magazine. Now, imagine the genders reversed: the men getting advice on fashion, beauty, and home decorating, and the women getting encouragement for more effective functioning in business and on the golf course.

There may very well be biological reasons to help explain most women's instinct for nurturing detail in the home. Women get pregnant, have babies, bond with those babies, and give over their lives, at least for a time, to keeping their babies safe and happy. And it's a good thing that they pay such close attention. Being obsessed with your children when they are young helps ensure their survival.

For many women, organizing and keeping a well-run home and family is so much a part of their identity that they are not aware of how one-sided their appropriation of this territory can be. They may feel tired and taken advantage of, but the question is are they willing to give up anything to get help.

If you are a mother who feels burdened by a larger share of the work, allow yourself some time today to think about these questions: What am I doing that someone else in the family could do instead? Am I prepared to have others do the work their way, whether it meets my standards or not? How would it feel to have my partner or my children take over some of the home chores that I have always considered to be part of my domain?

In our experience, many women are conflicted about asking for help, at the same time that they are complaining about having so much to do. Any change in this pattern begins first with a change of heart, *your* heart, and a growing determination to let go of some of the pleasures and obligations that have always defined what it meant to be a woman and a mother.

September 7 KEEPING TRACK

A calendar, a calendar! Look in the almanac; find out moonshine, find out moonshine.[7]

—WILLIAM SHAKESPEARE

Most of us swear by our calendars. We know when family birthdays are coming up and have a good idea of how we're going to celebrate. We keep track of the big things. We are aware of the major holidays and mark down when the kids have time off from school. But there may be more you can do to use calendars effectively and keep surprises from knocking you off balance.

Have a large calendar posted in the kitchen or family room with some writing space available for each day. At the beginning of each month conduct a five- to ten-minute planning session with your family. Take longer at the beginning of the school year. Write down all the events that you and your children know about. If you want, you can write individual commitments in different colors for each member of your family or put initials beside each entry. As the month goes along, you can add any new information as it crops up. It's important to add new obligations as soon as you know about them. You may think you'll remember the emergency finance committee meeting, but don't count on it unless you write it down.

Why is keeping track so important? Because we are human and we forget and because life is unpredictable. You don't want to add panic, anger, and disappointment to your family life, just because you don't write things down on the calendar. It's true that you can't control everything, but you can at least eliminate the no-brainers from the equation.

Calendars are great visual tools. You may be able to pace yourself better if you see that events are starting to cluster around a particular date. You will be able to schedule transportation when you see who needs to use the car when. You will be able to see which dates are already taken so you don't add anything new. Family scheduling meetings also allow you to talk about which activities take priority and require preparation or group involvement. As much as possible, you want to develop a no-surprises policy with regard to family schedules.

One way to begin to eliminate extra busyness is to think of your calendar as a family time-budget. Like your financial resources, your family's time is a commodity that has limits. When the limits are exceeded, you start running a debt. Sooner or later, it will have to be repaid.

September 8 THANK GOD IT'S FRIDAY

In all our efforts to provide "advantages" we have actually produced the busiest, most competitive, highly pressured and over-organized generation of youngsters in our history—and possibly the unhappiest.[8]

—EDA J. LE SHAN

All of us who work during the week look forward to Friday, because it signals the beginning of what we hope will be two "unstructured" days when freedom reigns and we have fewer demands. But for many of us end of the week celebrations are bogus. What we imagine will be free time is already spoken for.

The unstructured time we yearn for may simply be no more than *unplanned* time.

In the midst of these weekend chores it may be especially difficult to find time for the family to be together enjoying each other's company and building important family rituals and memories. Weekends have become little more than a catchall for the things we didn't get to during the week—haircuts, housework, washing the car, yard work, and shopping. There is no doubt that these chores have to get done, but if we plan ahead and think of them as potential points of connection, we can do some of them together rather than separately.

Not that we advocate the entire family move in lockstep from task to task throughout the weekend. It's also a good idea to plan *relaxed* family time on the weekends where family members can be truly present to each other. Depending on the age of your children, these times don't have to be long or elaborate. You can share a bagel for breakfast or check in with each other for half an hour in the afternoon.

Along with the togetherness, you can give yourselves a break from all the social contact of the rest of the week by encouraging some alone time. Both time together and time alone makes for a truly restful weekend that sends parents and children alike back into the weekday routine feeling re-created.

It can be useful to think about how your family members have spent each weekend for the last month. Does one weekend leap out as being especially satisfying? What made it that way? Our guess is that during that weekend you found a balance between the pleasures of family togetherness and the pleasures of your own company. Perhaps you can plan another that incorporates what you have learned about maintaining this delicate balance.

September 9 THE CLUTTER OF THINGS

With regard to whatever objects either delight the mind or contribute to use or are tenderly beloved, remind yourself of what nature they are, beginning with the merest trifles: if you have a favorite cup, that it is but a cup of which you are fond—for thus, if it is broken, you can bear it.[9]

—EPICTETUS

As you look around your house, you may be able to write a long list of things you would replace if you had the money, either because you want to add to the convenience of your home or because you want to add to your enjoyment. At the same time that the list is a measure of your current dissatisfaction with things as they are, it can also be seen as a measure of the potential pleasure that stirs your imagination

As you look around your child's room, however, you may register mostly dissatisfaction. You may be amazed by the mess. Part of the reality is that your child is growing and her tastes and needs are changing. Most of what she needed to support her care and her interests a year ago may already be outgrown. But they're still in evidence, nevertheless! Old sweaters fight for space with new ones. Toys she no longer plays with are stacked in the closet or around the room "just in case."

All children need a space where they can make a private mess. And it makes sense that some of the stuff is kept because of their emotional attachment to it, regardless of its practical value. But how about all the things that qualify as just plain clutter? And what do you do about your child's desire for new things when the old things still work just fine?

It can be useful in this regard to think about your own attitudes toward desiring, possessing, and discarding material things. No doubt you occasionally lust for some item: a new car, a bigger house, a more fashionable suit or dress, the latest gear or accessories. But where have you learned to draw the line? By now, you've probably had the experience many times of buying something to make yourself feel better or to satisfy a dissatisfaction and then having the thrill be short-lived. You probably have some perspective on both the pleasures and the emptiness that comes from the pursuit of material things.

How will you help your child learn this lesson? The key, we continue to discover, is in moderation. You don't have to deprive your child in order to make her aware of the dangers of materialism. But neither should she be deluged by too many clothes, toys, or opportunities to amuse herself. You don't want her to get the idea that such bounty substitutes for the rewards of a life of caring, personal effort, and service to others.

You can talk with your child about what possessions she really uses and values. Which toys does she really play with? Does she need all these jeans and this entire pile of shirts? How would it feel to give some things away to children who are less fortunate? And, finally, you can help her keep her "want" list to a reasonable length by sharing with her your own deepest feelings about moderation, balance, and sharing.

September 10 ELIMINATING CLUTTER

Ah, am I still imprisoned here, alone? . . .
With instruments, together hurled,
Ancestral stuff, heaped up and stacked—[10]

—JOHANN WOLFGANG VON GOETHE

Yesterday we began to talk about your child's clutter, and you spent some time examining your own values about the acquisition of material things. Let's continue today with further ideas about how you can help your child clear the decks and prevent his possessions from multiplying in the night until they take over every horizontal surface of his bedroom.

One way to remove clutter is for you and your son to sweep through his room, letting him choose things that can be given or thrown away. This tactic may work every so often, especially if he is truly sick of some of his stuff and agrees that he will never wear a particular shirt or pair of pants again. Most of the time, however, you may find him reluctant to part forever with his beloved treasures.

Perhaps a more effective idea is to create a rotating collection of belongings, which can be reevaluated on some agreed-upon schedule. Assuming the permanent nature of big items—like furniture, computers, and wall decorations—ask him to identify which clothes, toys, and personal gear he wants to use in the coming week. Everything else gets stored on shelves, in closets, or down in the basement.

Games, for example, can always be stored until there is a need for them. Clothes can be stored away or given away depending on the season of the year and how fast your child is growing. At the end of the week, the two of you can check in together again and see what he wants to exchange for the coming week. Things that aren't going to be used get put away to make room for current needs and interests. In this way you have a relatively constant supply of stuff in his room, rather than a growing proliferation of objects. Every so often it will be obvious that some items are rarely if ever going to be used again and they can be discarded.

As you help your child develop a habit of using some toys and storing some away, you will also learn which kinds of toys and games your child really plays with. Then, as birthdays and opportunities for buying things arise, you will have a good idea about what items to buy or to suggest to others.

The point behind this exercise is twofold: You want your child to get a sense of how much he really needs, and you want him to experience the benefits of at least minimal neatness.

Too many toys, clothes, and play opportunities not only add to physical clutter; they also add to emotional clutter. Not surprisingly, a child with too many material things and an excess of indulgences is more likely to be bored than a child who has learned what truly interests him. And he is more likely to want to own new things in order to remove that boredom rather than relying on his own inner resources.

September 11 READY TO CLEAN

What do girls do who haven't any mothers to help them through their troubles?[11]

—LOUISA MAY ALCOTT

In the last few days we have talked about ways to tame the clutter in your child's bedroom. Today we will give you some suggestions for simplifying the furniture of a room, so that there are fewer surfaces and pieces to keep track of. Before we start, though, it's valuable to spend a couple of minutes thinking about your own philosophy of freedom and control.

How much latitude you allow your child in her own private space says a lot about who you are as a person and as a parent. We are referring to both actual space and emotional space. If you are a very neat housekeeper, for example, do you expect your daughter to meet your own standards? Or are you able to make allowances, both for her youth and for the fact that she is a different person from you? If you do make allowances, how to know where to draw the line? How big a circle do you draw for what is acceptable? The way you answer these questions will give you insight into how comfortable you are in letting your children be who they are, even as you still set standards that teach limits.

As for physical space, you can arrange to provide her with simple, sturdy furniture—a bed, a dresser, and a desk, for example—

that create as much empty floor space as possible. It's also important to provide sturdy shelving or cabinets where she can store the toys, books, and games she isn't using. We don't recommend she have her own TV, however. Her room should be a private place, but it doesn't have to be an isolated island that supplies all her wants.

We have a friend whose eight-year-old daughter enjoys rearranging her room every few months. The opportunity and ability to rearrange gives her a sense of control and allows her to exercise her imagination. It's also a good excuse to clean things up in the process. The parents sometimes feel that such "renovations" are a hassle, but they know it's exciting for their daughter.

Asking your child to talk to you about her desires for her private space is a good way to let her know that you are interested in her thoughts and want to cooperate in her plans. Together you can agree on the help you can give and how she can meet whatever guidelines the two of you have set up.

September 12 TAKING RESPONSIBILITY

All systems of morality are based on the idea that an action has consequences that legitimize or cancel it.[12] —ALBERT CAMUS

Now that school has begun, your child has assumed a new set of responsibilities. He has to get himself ready each day, prepare his homework, and interact with his peers at school, as well as encounter many new subjects and skills. And in doing this, he is learning bit by bit to accept responsibility on his own. No matter how fast a learner he is, however, he will sometimes slip up: He forgets to hand you the note from the teacher, he leaves his lunch on the counter, the homework doesn't get done. Sometimes having fun means more to him than being prepared.

Throughout this daily drama, you are doing the best you can to see that he is competitive with his peers, that he is ready to begin the day, that he has his lunch taken care of, and that he is on time for school. Reluctantly, you come to the conclusion that you can help him be prepared, but as much as you'd like to, you can't accept his responsibility for him.

You can help him by holding him accountable for his actions. Like many grown-ups, children will learn to excuse their mistakes and failures if they are allowed to do so: "He made me do it." "I had too much to do." "I didn't have time." "She hit me first." "The cat ate my homework." Whether you smile at any of these bluffs or not, you can support your child by letting him know that empty excuses are not going to cut it, especially when he is blaming something else or someone else for his own inattention or inadequacy. You don't have to punish him, just don't let him get away with it.

Along with this no-blaming policy, you can encourage him to ask for help when he needs it. It is a smart person who knows enough to use the wisdom and experience of the people around him. Asking questions is a sign of lively intelligence, not stupidity. In addition, you can let him know that some things are not anyone's fault. They just happen.

You will want to be explicit about these matters, and you will also want to monitor your own behavior and attitudes. Set an example as a person who accepts responsibility and asks for help when *you* need it.

September 13 THE PLACE OF GOOD MANNERS

Saint Bridget was
A problem child.[13]

—PHYLLIS McGINLEY

You may wonder what a discussion of good manners is doing in a chapter on living simply. Good manners are more than fancy clothes to be trotted out only for special occasions, like evening gowns or a tuxedos. They really do have a purpose. Among other things, they are meant to simplify relationships. They reduce the misunderstandings and miscommunications that so easily occur between strangers, acquaintances, friends, and even family members.

Saying "Good morning," "Thank you," "Please," and "You're welcome" is a way of acknowledging the presence and intrinsic value of other people, while reducing the chances that there will be problems, resentments, or the need to make repairs. It demonstrates a respect for others. Holding the door for someone coming through behind you, whether you are a man or a woman and whether the person behind you is a man or a woman, accomplishes the same task. So does writing a thank-you note for a gift from an aunt or grandparent. Examples are as numerous as the pages in a book by Miss Manners.

In practicing good manners, both you and your child will come across people who respond positively and reinforce your actions.

But you will also experience people who are not paying attention or who are rude or clumsy. When that happens, it's natural to have a strong, negative, unconscious reaction. It feels like a personal rejection of your attempts to be pleasant and courteous. All we can say is that these occasions are an opportunity to practice your most conscious behavior by stepping back and reminding yourself that nothing personal is intended. Your ability to soldier on, doing the right thing, will be an important lesson both for you and for your child. It will help your children learn that good manners are not only a gift you give to the people around you but a gift you give to yourself.

How careful are you to teach your children the appropriate thing to say or do to demonstrate that they are attentive to and respectful of others? As you teach them, are you careful to set them a good example? You can get a sense of how you're doing by the number of times your child does or says the right thing without being reminded. Good manners can become ingrained very early in a child if you are careful to remind him kindly and quietly and treat him with the same courtesy you are teaching him in his relationships with others.

September 14 LISTENING ATTENTIVELY

Falstaff: *Very well, my lord, very well; rather, an't please you, it is the disease of not listening, the malady of not marking, that I am troubled withal.*[14]

—WILLIAM SHAKESPEARE

All of us have experience with the disease of not listening. You know what it's like when people finish your sentences for you or wait for a microsecond pause to jump in with their own thoughts. They step all over your words, interrupting you to say something they consider more important.

It's hard to admit that we may, on occasion, be guilty of the same offense. But all of us are careless once in a while; it is a rare person who listens so well to others that he picks up all that is said to him and responds directly to what others have said.

But listening attentively is something that can be learned and practiced by everyone. One of its biggest benefits is that it simplifies your life. When you train yourself to pay attention to the words and body language of the people you are communicating with, your interactions are cleaner, more compassionate, and more to the point. You waste less time mired in misunderstanding.

A good way to begin to raise your level of awareness about your own listening skills is to spend a day listening to yourself as you converse with the people around you. You may be pleasantly surprised, or you may be embarrassed by how often you intrude or ignore. As you attempt to improve your skills, you can remember that every time you intrude on someone's speech or ignore their words, you are fraying the connection between you. Conversely, every time you pay attention and are careful to respond to the conversation at hand instead of the one inside your own head, you are building a positive relationship. When you listen carefully to your child, you are teaching him how to develop a skill that he will be able to use to his advantage all his life.

September 15 BE CONSISTENT

If our children deserve a thousand chances, and then one more, let's give ourselves a thousand chances—and then two more.[15]

—ADELE FABER AND ELAINE MAZLISH

One of the most important ways to simplify your family life is to have consistent policies in place for routine matters. You can cut down on the amount of negotiation or emergency fixing you do every day when everyone knows ahead of time what they are expected to do and what they are not allowed to do. As we've said, this means periodically spending time planning and discussing family systems; things like, who does which chores, who takes which responsibilities, and who goes where and when.

A list of family activities that lend themselves nicely to consistent routines and roles might include: getting up in the morning, eating breakfast, making provisions for lunch, after-school schedules, preparing and eating dinner, getting homework done, getting into bed at night. Your children would know, for example, how much television is permissible on any given night and when their bedtime is. They would know, without asking, whether they are expected home in time for dinner and what their responsibilities are for the meal.

Having said all that, however, we must emphasize that along with being consistent, it is also important to be flexible. At first glance, these two qualities may seem to be opposite. But actually, they work hand-in-glove together.

Flexibility allows you to take into account special circumstances and also helps you see when your consistent policies need to be updated and modified. After all, a family is a living, growing organism. It never stays the same for long. And you have to be able to come up with new routines and expectations to fit changing realities.

A flexible attitude allows you to see that your daughter can be relieved of washing the dishes when she isn't feeling well or that your son needs to put off tuba practice until tomorrow, because he needs to rehearse for the school play, which is next Saturday. Being a martinet and relying on rules instead of your own judgment is counterproductive in the long run.

Generally, though, you can organize your family so that there is a default position. Everybody knows what to do and what to expect during most days. If you're shaking your head at this point and mumbling that there are no ordinary days, that every one is a unique disaster unto itself, then it's time to ask some serious questions about how you are living. Your questioning will need to go beyond how to set up efficient family routines.

September 16 OH, THAT TELEPHONE AGAIN!

Take a red book called TELEPHONE,
size eight by four. There it sits.[16]

—ANNE SEXTON

If your child is a teenager, you probably have very intense feelings about the telephone. To your fourteen-year-old, it is a lifeline, a passionate connection to the things that *really* matter. To you, it may be an intrusion and a source of wonder. "What in the world is there to say after two straight hours of talking?" you sometimes ask. It can also be an object of frustration when your simple desire to get or make a call is blocked by an endless stream of words and intonations you can't understand.

Parents deal with this low-grade irritation—or open conflict—in different ways. Some simply pay for a separate phone line and ignore the problem. Others feel that unrestricted use of the telephone may be damaging in some way and attempt to institute guidelines. If you find yourself in the latter camp, here are some suggestions for taming telephone madness:

- Restrict the hours during the day when your children can have lengthy conversations on the phone. You might want to insist on no early-morning or late-night calls. You get to define the hours.

- Discuss with your children ahead of time how much time is appropriate for telephone talk in any given evening. Let them know that telephone conversations cannot be allowed to take away from other priorities, such as family dinners, school work, music practice, and so on.
- Limit incoming calls to five minutes or less, unless homework is done.
- Turn off the ringer on your phone at night when your children are home and in bed.
- Encourage your children to coordinate long phone conversations, so each sibling has a chance to talk and no one child dominates.
- Install the "call waiting" feature on your line. That way, if you or other callers are trying to get through to give or receive information, your child can interrupt her call to take the message.
- Install a separate business line if you conduct business out of your home.
- Always be courteous and understanding with your child's callers. That's how you want her to learn to deal with situations that may be annoying. And that's how you would want her treated if she were calling a friend's home.

You may have additional guidelines that make sense in your family. Make sure that your communication about them is clear, uncomplicated, and well understood. This will simplify what can otherwise be a very inconvenient convenience.

September 17 SHARING RESPONSIBILITY

There's not a breathing of the common wind
That will forget thee; thou hast great allies . . .[17]

—WILLIAM WORDSWORTH

On September 12, we stressed the importance of teaching your child to take responsibility. Today we are going to encourage you to do something that might at first seem contradictory: share responsibility for parenting your children whenever you can. Parents need all the help they can get. Sometimes that help is available in the form of dentists, doctors, coaches, school counselors, and teachers, who can back up or augment themes you are sounding with your children.

Your kids may think that brushing their teeth is one of *your* weird ideas until they also hear it from their dentist. They may consider you a fossil for insisting on eight hours of sleep until their coach reinforces it at practice. Limiting the junk food gains legitimacy when the same message is papered on walls, presented in videos, and stressed in classrooms.

Skillfully using an authority to bolster your argument brings the broader community into the discussion. Your child has to admit that he isn't just performing according to your whim, but that you, along with the very best professional opinion, have his best interests at heart. That should simplify your discussion and clarify the argument.

Of course, other people can't do your job for you. We are talking here about *sharing* your responsibilities. It's pretty ineffective to say something like, "I don't have a problem with this, but your teacher [father, grandmother, doctor, *etc.*] wants you to do it this way." That really *is* passing the buck. Neither is it effective to refer all conflicts back to cultural tradition as the ultimate authority. You probably don't operate this way yourself, and in the end this approach will seem irrelevant to your child, because it is impersonal and doesn't take current circumstances into account.

Think for a moment about how you set behavioral guidelines with your child. Do your discussions often involve argument? If so, how do you represent your views? Are your guidelines well reasoned, and do you listen carefully to your child's point of view? Do you have opportunities to share responsibility with legitimate authorities such as the ones we have cited?

September 18 HEALTHY EATING

So I commend enjoyment, for there is nothing better for people under the sun than to eat, and drink, and enjoy themselves, for this will go with them in their toil through the days of life that God gives them under the sun.[18]

—ECCLESIASTES 8:15

In the midst of the abundance most of us enjoy in our lives, it is important to remember that not all children in North America go to bed with full stomachs. Any discussion of healthy eating must take place with the recognition that there are those among us who are too poor to pick and choose what they eat. We must acknowledge the problem of hunger and do what we can for those who are struggling. Food is the gift of life. May we never forget to give thanks for what we have.

Having said that, we know that the question of what, when, and how to eat is a major concern for many American families. With the burgeoning variety of foods we now have available, comes the quandary of how to make a healthy diet part of your family's everyday experience.

We are certainly bombarded with information about what *not* to eat. Anyone who has been paying attention knows that supermarket shelves are stuffed with foods that contain empty calories, tooth-rotting sweeteners, saturated fats, added chemicals, and preservatives. We are addicted to fast food as well as convenience foods. The overconsumption of sugars and fats and the habit of cyclical dieting have made us into a population that's getting fatter every year.

Parents can either accustom their children to such eating patterns or establish patterns that are healthier. Eating habits are a legacy that spans generations. Your children are learning a taste for the foods they will want to eat for the rest of their lives. Keep in mind that today's convenience may lead to problems in the future.

If you start with consistent, healthful eating habits from the time your kids are small, food choices don't have to become a major issue. You don't have to become a health-food fanatic. Moderation, consistency, flexibility, and a relaxed attitude built around a solid commitment to healthy food will get you where you want to go. Although it is by no means a comprehensive list, here are a few guidelines we have found to be helpful:

- No matter how busy your family is, develop the habit of eating together as often as you can for breakfast and dinner. It may not work all the time, but instill the expectation of family meals early, and it will easier when your children reach the middle-school years.
- Plan out your meals once a week, so that you have a good idea of what will be served each day. Make a big grocery shopping trip once a week, so you'll know you have what you need to carry through the week's plan.
- If you are not a vegetarian, develop the habit of using red meat as a *part* of a main dish instead of as a main course itself. Substitute chicken, turkey, and especially fish as often as you can. See if you can occasionally introduce tofu into the repertoire.
- Use any means you can to reduce the fat in your cooking. When you *do* use oil, use mostly olive oil and canola oil, which are healthier overall than other kinds of fats and oils.

- Look for alternatives to the usual high-fat, high-salt, high-sugar snack foods. Fresh and dried fruit, low-fat chips, whole grain breads and cereals, yogurt, low-fat cottage cheese, and low-fat spreads do the job. If you don't buy the other stuff, you won't have it around as a temptation.
- Serve your children modest first helpings with the opportunity for seconds later.
- Serve desserts only rarely, as a special treat rather than as a regular part of your meals.
- Discuss sharing the cooking and clean-up chores with your family. Your children can learn to help with some of these chores at an early age. Both parents in a two-parent household should share the burden of planning and preparing meals.

It could be that the biggest problem you will face in developing healthy eating habits for your children will be overcoming the bad habits you and your spouse already have. This is a good excuse to clean up your act a little.

A prayer for today: *Every day I am sustained by abundance in my life. I am sustained by the fruits of love and the fruits of the table. I pray for the wisdom and the determination to share what I have with others that they may know the healing power Your love.*

September 19 BIRTHDAYS GALORE!

I celebrate myself and sing myself,
And what I assume you shall assume.[19]

—WALT WHITMAN

In the elementary school years, birthdays and birthday parties multiply as fast as dandelions on a spring lawn. They may taper off in middle school, but until then, you will be buying presents, wrapping them, and driving to parties—a lot. You have no control over what happens in other families, but you can give some thought to how to make your family's birthday parties fun and manageable.

Contrary to what you might hear from your children, parties with more kids, more gifts, more games, and more food and entertainment are not necessarily the best. Young children can handle only so much stimulation. One friend of ours uses this rule: Never invite more children to a party than your child has years; for example, if your child is four years old, invite no more than four other children to the party. It will make the excitement and chaos much easier for you and your child to manage. Older children often express a preference for de-escalation. A memorable event with one or two special friends is much more memorable and enjoyable than a trip to Wendy's with a crowd.

If you are the party planner, you can think in terms of a simple theme that will tie the whole thing together. Scavenger hunts, dress-up, space aliens, arts and crafts— these come immediately to mind, and you can no doubt think of more. Whatever you plan, don't lose sight of what is really important. Your child will want to feel special from morning to night. He will want to be "in first place," with his preferences and desires taking precedence, at least on this one day of the year. All of this is more important than presents. Gifts have an important role to play, but they don't make up for the creative touches that show that you are paying attention to him, loving him, wanting him to feel special.

Birthdays often make for emotional memories. They are like snapshots that capture the feelings and circumstances of that particular time. When you think back over your own childhood, do any birthdays come to mind? Can you remember a favorite birthday? How did you celebrate? We're guessing that you can remember what you did, but you probably cannot remember what presents you received. What can you do for the members of your own family that will help them feel loved and cherished and help them remember?

September 20

BEING ACTIVE IN YOUR CHILDREN'S EDUCATION

Character education is a moral imperative if we want today's youth to have the self-esteem, stamina, and support they need to survive and become successful, productive, and responsible citizens.[20]

—THE CHARACTER EDUCATION COALITION

Make a commitment to do whatever you can to be active in your children's education. If you have this explicit intention, then you will find ways to be involved, no matter how busy you are with other concerns.

Some parents are fortunate to have the time to volunteer as room mothers in their children's classes. This gives you firsthand knowledge of the classroom environment and allows you to be aware of the opportunities and problems your child is experiencing.

Other parents serve on parent committees and participate in special projects in the evening or on the weekends when they have more time. This doesn't get you into the classroom, but it does expose you to your child's teachers and friends, and it gives you a taste of the atmosphere of the school.

At the very least, you will want to meet your children's teachers and establish the expectation that you will stay in touch with him or her throughout the year. You can find out from the teacher what level of outside homework your child should plan for and how you can reach the teacher when you have questions or concerns.

Your involvement in your child's school life will underscore the importance of education for your children. It will also make it easier for your child to share experiences with you, since you know the people and places he is talking about. The more aware you are of how your child is doing academically, the more likely it is that you can provide good counsel about which classes or activities to pursue, and how to handle the inevitable difficulties that arise in the natural course of being a student.

September 21 HOMEWORK

The importance of concentration is no surprise; it is essential to any good performance to be able to focus on a specific target and resist distraction.[21]

—JAMES LEOHR AND PETER MCLAUGHLIN

Your child has a job, just as you do. Her job is to be a student. Your role is to help her establish the habits that will allow her to become a successful student and to provide a home environment in which learning can flourish. How you do this evolves over time as your child gets older.

As we know, children learn their most important lessons from us, based on the kind of people we are. If we have inquiring, searching minds, they will absorb a desire to learn about the world from the way we ask questions and find out about our world. If we appreciate good writing and public television, they probably will too. If we go to science lectures and concerts and plays, they will grow up with an appreciation for the finer aspects of our culture. Exposure to educated discussion, good books, and quality artistic experiences goes a long way toward forming an orientation toward learning.

But we must do more than that. From the very beginning, we need to set up the daily routines that make schoolwork a priority. These routines need to support the educational process as we find out what assignments are to be worked on every evening, provide the physical space and quiet that our students require, make ourselves available as helpers in the actual work, and reinforce the priority of homework on a list of other activities. The ideal routine allows you and your children to know how and when homework will get done every night, so that you don't have to discuss and negotiate with them about it constantly.

Children of different ages need different kinds of help from parents, and the help that parents offer needs to be adjusted for each child. It is not unusual to have one child who rarely needs help and is a great student, while a sibling may need double the amount of motivation and monitoring. Everyday homework routines can make your job easier and give your reluctant student a better chance of doing well.

A reminder: School performance can bring out <u>symbiotic</u> impulses in parents. All of us need to remind ourselves that we are not our children and our children are not us. You cannot do your child's work for her, as much as you may want to. She will find her own way in the world. Your job is to do everything you can to provide a supportive learning atmosphere in your home and to encourage her to set and meet high educational standards for herself. The rest is up to her.

September 22 WHAT IF YOUR CHILD STARTS SLIPPING

Send to us power and light, a sovereign touch.[22] —W. H. AUDEN

It's hard to know what to do if you start noticing that your child isn't doing as well in school as she has in the past. Living through that experience can be confusing. There is so much going on that it can be hard to see important patterns. And then, if you see a definite pattern of decreasing performance, it can be hard to know what to do about it.

So let us start out by admitting that this can be one of the most complex and difficult parts in the already challenging job of being a parent. Let us say next that it is a rare parent who hasn't had to deal with this kind of worry about a child. If you are concerned about your child's school performance, you have lots of company.

First, try to see clearly what is going on. Is your child missing assignments, not doing required reading, tearing through writing assignments without much thought or effort, letting his grades slip? If the answer is yes, then arrange time to talk with your child about what you are observing. Remember to use the tools of intentional dialogue to help you understand what is happening. Concentrate on getting information about how your child is feeling about school and why homework isn't being done.

After you have some idea of what is happening, make appointments to talk with his teachers. They may not have as much of the picture as you do, but they will have pieces of the school picture you cannot possibly have. After an initial teacher visit, it is probably a good idea to involve your child in the discussion between you and her teachers. You will want to put together a plan that will allow your child to make up missed assignments and get back on track in class.

Throughout this process you will be looking for the underlying reasons why he is letting things slip. It could be that he is having difficulty learning; he could be having social problems that have nothing directly to do with academics; he could be experiencing psychological difficulties due to personal or family troubles; or he could be engaging in destructive behavior that needs immediate attention.

You are a detective, trying to piece together an accurate picture of what is happening and why it is happening. Once you have some understanding of the "what" and the "why," you can start crafting a solution. Sometimes the solution is simple—your child needs more time and more help with her homework. Sometimes the solution is not simple—he is attracted to kids whose behaviors do not support your family values.

All you can do is be sensitive to the signs that things aren't going well and dedicate your efforts to finding out why and what needs to be done to get your child back on track. Keep in mind that children continue to be profoundly influenced by their parents, well into their teenage years. Even when it seems that your efforts are fruitless, you can be assured that they are not. Your steady, kind insistence on what is important will help your children blossom, if not right at this moment, then sometime later.

September 23 VALUES BREED SUCCESS

My research has shown that it is the process of helping, without regard to its outcome, that is the healing factor.[23]

—ALLAN LUKS AND PEGGY PAYNE

When we ask parents to talk about their definition of successful children, we hear a lot about caring for others and being trustworthy. Parents want their children to become people who exhibit integrity, courage, responsibility, diligence, service, and respect for the dignity of others.

The decline of such values and virtues is of great concern to all of us who care about the society we live in. And it is apparently of great concern to young people themselves, who sometimes experience their schools as amoral and violent environments.

If building character is part of your definition of success, then you have a focus for your parenting. You will do whatever you can to teach your children how important these virtues are. When you are clear that it is more important for your child to be honest and not cheat than to get good grades through cheating, then you will parent accordingly.

Values simplify your life. They shine a light on what is important in situations that might otherwise be confusing. You'll notice that we didn't say that they necessarily make your life easier. It has always been challenging to live up to a set of principles, especially in the face of opposition or lack of support. But they do direct your efforts and clarify your goals.

September 24 THE OVERSCHEDULED FAMILY

Just as some people seek to reduce sensory stimulation, others go to great extremes to increase it.[24]

—ROBERT ORNSTEIN AND DAVID SOBEL

When parents talk about being overscheduled, they may be expressing any number of dissatisfactions and conflicts. Most likely, they are experiencing some dissonance between all the things they do and their level of satisfaction in doing them. And almost certainly, they mean to say that they feel like they are doing too much. Increasing numbers of people are yearning for a quieter, simpler life, and are actively seeking such a lifestyle.

Simplifying starts in the heart with a firm sense of who you are and what your purpose is in living. It moves on from there to an inventory of how you spend your time and what activities draw your energy and attention. Then you are free to see whether what you do reflects and expresses you, as a unique person with a unique purpose. As a final step, you can decide which changes to make—what to let go, what to keep doing, and what to add to your life—as a way of living a more congruent, harmonious lifestyle.

Today and tomorrow, let us ask some questions that will help you make an inventory of how you spend your time and energy. Here are some simple questions to help you start getting a more accurate picture of your life. The more time you spend thinking about them, the fuller picture you will get.

Work—How many hours a week do you work at paid employment? On a scale of 1 to 10, with 10 being the most, how satisfying is your work?

Housework and Other Maintenance—Approximately how many hours (or minutes) do you spend on routine housekeeping chores? These are tasks that help you maintain the quality of home life you are comfortable with, such as making and serving meals, housecleaning, yard work, home maintenance, laundry, etc. How many extra hours do you spend a month on other tasks that are not part of your daily routine, such as paying bills, car repair and maintenance, carpet cleaning, etc.?

Volunteering—How many hours do you spend a week or a month on volunteer activities, such as church, civic, or school commitments?

Personal—How many hours do you spend every week on activities you do for yourself and your own personal pleasure and satisfaction, including such things as taking classes, exercise, meditation, journal writing, making music, reading, arts and crafts, and other hobbies?

This is probably enough for one day. Tomorrow, we will take a look at children, family, and partnership commitments.

September 25 THE OVERSCHEDULED FAMILY (CONT.)

We may imagine that history will be revealed as a continuum, an advance, an opening like the tree of life. What one often finds, however, is very far from a majestic unfolding, and very far from being a continuum in any sense.[25] —OLIVER SACKS

Yesterday, you began an inventory of activities that will help you see how you are spending your time. You have to see what you are doing before you can know what to change. Let's continue today, by asking you to consider the following questions:

Your Children—How much time do you spend every day on parenting activities, such as sitting down and talking; on recreational activities, such as throwing a ball, playing a computer game, or doing crafts; and on morning and/or bedtime rituals? How much time do you spend on helping your children with homework or school projects?
What extra organized activities are your children involved in, in addition to school and unscheduled family time?
Your Partner—How much time alone do you and your partner spend together each day?
Your Family—What activities does your family enjoy together every day, every week, or every month?

How much "free" unstructured time does your entire family have together each week? This means time when you are not trying to do homework or chauffeur to the next activity or do chores?

Now that you have finished pondering these questions, you can let yourself reflect on what your answers say about you and your life. Here are some additional questions that will help you interpret your responses:

- What would somebody who didn't know you say about your priorities and values, based on the information you have provided?
- What can *you* learn from this exercise?
- Do you feel that this brief profile is a true reflection of your true self? Or, another way of putting it: Are you living the way you were meant to live?
- Can you identify any mismatches between what you are doing and what you think is important? Between what you are doing and what you *wish* you were doing?

A most useful next step is to share these pages with your partner and invite him or her to answer the same questions. This is an effective nonthreatening way to begin talking about if, and how, you may want to simplify your family life.

September 26

USING THE SCHEDULE TO SIMPLIFY YOUR FAMILY'S LIFE

If we real-life mothers have a secret, it is that this relay team we have assembled so that we might simultaneously love and work has about it all the grace of a three-legged race.[26] —STACY SCHIFF

There is no doubt that children used to have more naturally occurring unstructured free time. There was time after school to kick around the neighborhood, playing with the other kids on the block until you were called in for dinner. There were casual softball games and roaming play in backyards and vacant lots on and street corners. And there was time alone, when you were expected to find things to do to amuse yourself. On Sundays, your family may have piled into the car and gone for drives in the country after church, before Sunday family dinner.

There is not much point in bemoaning the loss of our slower, simpler past—except to notice its rhythms of activity and nonactivity, structure and nonstructure, time with friends and time alone. These patterns of bygone childhoods can help us see how very organized today's children seem by comparison.

If you want to rebalance your family life so there is more unstructured time, more alone time, and more time for your entire family to do things together, the chances are that you will have to schedule them. The irony is that you have to schedule time to be unscheduled. You have to plan for time alone.

Why not schedule two weekend afternoons every month for family excursions? They can be simple, and they can be short. A picnic in the park, a drive to the farm country to buy produce, a walk through a new part of town. One idea that works well in families with different ages and interests is to have everybody take turns choosing how the time will be spent together.

To encourage your children to learn how to be alone and inner-directed, you may have to find pockets of time in your schedule when everybody goes to their rooms, and engages in a project or an activity that is self-motivated. You can help by making art supplies, books, and other creative materials available.

An important factor in the earlier, simpler childhood we have been recalling is that there was no television. If you want your kids to play outside more or interact in informal ways with other family members, you may have to plan for times of the day when the television is off. In order to provide an environment that stimulates the imagination, encourages the development of inner resources, and develops an appreciation for the natural world, you will have to consider these things important, and give some thought to the conditions under which they flourish.

September 27 KEEPING TRACK

They went to sea in a sieve, they did;
In a sieve they went to sea;
In spite of all their friends could say . . .[27]

—EDWARD LEAR

When your child is small, you almost always know where she is and what she is doing. Most of her time is spent around you, and you are in charge of her time in almost every important way. But as she grows older, she moves away from you. By the time she is a teenager, your child is conducting her life almost on her own. You are there, of course, but for her you are more like a safe refuge to return to than a constant presence. And from then on your need to know where she is may be greater than her need to let you know.

So, like all parents, you will be practicing the art of letting go, trying to find a balance between your child's need for independence and your need for reassurance that she is safe and secure.

She may be sleeping over at a friend's house or downtown at the arts festival. She is out there somewhere under someone else's supervision; sooner or later, she will be on her own. At this stage when she is semi-independent, you are continually setting up and readjusting boundaries and guidelines that will keep her both safe and independent.

Basic to this process is teaching her to let you know where she is, what she will be doing generally, whom she is spending time with, what arrangements have been made for adult supervision, if any, and when you can expect her home. You want her to call you when plans change or if something goes wrong and she needs your help.

You have to trust her to keep you informed, and she has to trust you to accept information without reacting unconsciously in a negative way. Once again, the task is to remain connected, however tenuously and whatever the distance. When boundaries are overstepped, as they may sometimes be, that connection is what you retain in order to start the communication and the trust flowing again.

How do you react when your child is away from you, even if you know where she is and roughly what she is doing? Are you perpetually anxious? If so, you may want to work on that. Your anxiety will not strength your connection and will not help you remain stable, conscious, and detached enough to be of assistance when necessary. How do you react when your child has stretched a boundary or guideline too far? Do you overreact, or do you respond in a way that maintains connection while allowing for growth?

September 28 EATING OUT

No man can tell but he that loves his children, how many delicious accents make a man's heart dance in the pretty conversation of those dear pledges.[28]

—JEREMY TAYLOR

Eating out can be the best of times for families—or the worst. It is both entertainment and respite. You get out of the house for a while, and you don't have to fix one meal at least. But it's also something of a gamble. How will the children behave? Will the baby cry throughout dinner? Will Mom and Dad be able to have an adult conversation over their meal? Can we all have fun together?

When your children are small, it's a good idea to go to a "family restaurant," where the special requirements and tastes of children are easily accommodated. Lunch is less formal than dinner, so if you're not sure about your kids' stamina, this is a good meal in which to try things out. You can have a lot of fun trading stories, memories, and family in-jokes and developing a sense of camaraderie.

Your first restaurant meals together can be for teaching and learning. You are teaching your children manners and broadening their social experience, and you are learning how much your children are capable of at this particular age. Even if it doesn't go smoothly right now, no real harm is done if you maintain your sense of humor and are willing to try again. Remember that practice makes perfect: the experience of eating out together becomes pleasurable and successful only with time and energy. As your children have a chance to practice public deportment, they can graduate to more formal surroundings, and you will see how much they have benefited from the skills they have developed.

What kind of standards do you set for your children when you are in a restaurant together? Are you able to accept a less than perfect evening together in the spirit of adventure? Do you and your partner feel a sense of being in this together? Now that you're thinking about it, would it make sense to do anything differently—go to a different place to eat, or go at a different time, after the kids have their naps, for example? For this kind of experience, you get to choose what is easiest, most educational, and most fun.

September 29 CONSIDERING WHAT IS IMPORTANT

Who are we? Are we what we do? Are we what others say about us? Are we the power we have?[29]

—HENRI J. M. NOUWEN

Spend a few minutes every morning thinking about what your focus is for the day. After you get up, but before you get busy, find a place where you can be alone to gather your thoughts. You will want to spend a minute or two relaxing your body and quieting your mind. Ask yourself what idea, feeling, or image you want to carry with you into your day today. Pause for a minute or two and let yourself incorporate this idea, feeling, or image into your body and soul in a deep way. Then, allow yourself some time to visualize the people, places, and tasks you are expecting to encounter. See yourself meeting the day's events with your focus firmly in mind. Use your imagination to make your visualization real, so that you can experience yourself feeling, acting, and looking the way you have decided is important to you. During the last few moments of your meditation, let yourself feel the satisfaction you will experience when the day is actually over and you have done what you wanted to do. This whole process can be done in five to ten minutes of undisturbed time.

Your focus can be any positive thought, image, or feeling that you are powerfully attracted to. Here are some examples:. You may want to be more peaceful, so you visualize a stream emptying into a quiet, deep forest pool. This image elicits certain feelings of peace and beauty in you that you want to capture and retain throughout your day. You may want to be more energized, so you come up with the affirmation, "I have unlimited energy." You may want your focus to be on becoming a better listener, so you present a brief argument to yourself about why listening is important. You may be facing deadlines on the job and want to focus on the importance of working at a steady, undistracted pace.

This is a simple tool for clarifying your values and streamlining your functioning. By spending time each day meditating on what is important, you can see more quickly what to do and what to stop doing. Try it. You'll be surprised at what a difference it makes.

September 30 TIME FOR YOURSELF

. . . mothers are divided from each other in homes, tied to their children by compassionate bonds; our wildcat strikes have most often taken the form of physical or mental breakdown.[30]

—ADRIENNE RICH

Yesterday, we talked about the value of taking a few minutes at the beginning of the day to fix in our minds and hearts a focus for our thoughts and actions. The truth is that a few minutes in the morning is great, but why not take mental rest breaks as often as you can throughout the day? Any parent who has daily responsibility at home with children needs frequent breaks. Whenever you possibly can, it's a very good idea to take some time—it doesn't have to be a long time—in which you collect yourself and center. As we have seen, if you are alone and undistracted, even five or ten minutes can make a difference. A best case would be time alone at the beginning of your day, at the end of your day, and periodically throughout your day as you transition from one challenge to another. We are thinking of a few minutes before the kids get up from their naps or before they come home from school or before you enter the house at the end of the day.

The purpose is to physically relax and mentally let go of worries and thoughts so you can "clear the slate," so to speak. You will be amazed at how quickly you can refresh yourself in this way. The more you practice letting down and letting go, the more benefits you will gain. You will be able to retreat into yourself and gather strength and energy for the next phase of your day.

Here is one way to structure your centering breaks: Close your eyes and breathe slowly and regularly. Let go of muscle tension, starting with your toes, your feet, your legs—and let go all the way up to the top of your head. Pay particular attention to relaxing your face and jaw. As you continue breathing, imagine your breath entering your body at the soles of your feet and flowing through your body all the way out your nose. Feel your feet and hands becoming warmer.

As you begin to relax, think about the safest place you can imagine. Your safe place could be outside beside a mountain stream or inside a room where you have felt most comfortable. It could be anyplace where you have been particularly happy and loved. Let yourself stay in this safe place for a while, enjoying the feelings it stirs in you. As you begin to rouse yourself and come back into the here and now, know that this safe place and your feelings of peace and serenity are now inside you. You carry them with you as you reenter the stream of your busy life, participating fully in your daily round, but from a center of safety and love.

Experiment with centering breaks throughout the day. Set aside a few minutes every day to visualize a safe place and reexperience feelings of peacefulness. After you have practiced for a few days, ask yourself what you notice. Can you tell what effect such mental techniques are having on you the rest of the time? Do you think this is a good investment of time and energy?

Notes

1. Sherwood Anderson, *Winesburg, Ohio* (New York: Modern Library, 1947).

2. Stephen R. Covey, *The 7 Habits of Highly Effective People* (New York: Simon & Schuster, 1989).

3. Peter Block, *Stewardship* (San Francisco: Berrett-Koehler Publishers, 1993).

4. Gerard Manley Hopkins, "God's Grandeur," in *A Hopkins Reader*, ed. John Peck (Garden City, NY: Image Books, 1966).

5. Shel Silverstein, "Hugo's War," in *Where the Sidewalk Ends* (New York: Harper and Row, 1974).

6. Judith Duerk, *Circle of Stones* (San Diego: Lura Media, 1989).

7. William Shakespeare, *A Midsummer Night's Dream*, Act 3, Scene 1, in *The Complete Illustrated Shakespeare*, ed. Howard Staunton (New York: Gallery Books, 1989).

8. Eda J. Le Shan, *The Conspiracy Against Childhood* (New York: Atheneum, 1967).

9. Epictetus, *The Enchiridion*, trans. Thomas W. Higginson (New York: Liberal Arts Press, 1948).

10. Johann Wolfgang von Goethe, *Faust*, Scene 1, trans. Alice Raphael (New York: Heritage Press, 1959).

11. Louisa May Alcott, *Little Women* (New York: Grosset & Dunlap, 1963).

12. Albert Camus, *The Myth of Sisyphus*, trans. Justin O'Brien (New York: Vintage Books, 1955).

13. Phyllis McGinley, "The Giveaway," in *Times Three* (New York: Viking Press, 1968).

14. William Shakespeare, *Henry IV, Part II*, Act 1, Scene 2, in *The Complete Illustrated Shakespeare*, ed. Howard Staunton (New York: Gallery Books, 1989).

15. Adele Faber and Elaine Mazlish, *How to Talk So Kids Will Listen & Listen So Kids Will Talk* (New York: Avon: 1980).

16. Anne Sexton, "Telephone," in *Anne Sexton, The Complete Poems* (Boston: Houghton Mifflin Company, 1981).

17. William Wordsworth, "To Toussaint L'Ouverture," in *Wordsworth, Selected Poetry* (New York: Modern Library, 1950).

18. *The New Oxford Annotated Bible* (New York: Oxford University Press, 1994).

19. Walt Whitman, "Starting from Paumanok," in *Leaves of Grass* (New York: New American Library, 1954).

20. Character Counts Coalition brochure, a project of the Josephson Institute of Ethics (San Antonio, TX, 1998).

21. James Loehr and Peter McLaughlin, *Mentally Tough: The Principles of Winning at Sports Applied to Winning in Business* (New York: M Evans and Company, 1986).

22. W. H. Auden, "Petition," in *Collected Poetry of W. H. Auden* (New York: Random House, 1934).

23. Allan Luks with Peggy Payne, *The Healing Power of Doing Good* (New York: Fawcett, 1991).

24. Robert Ornstein and David Sobel, *The Healing Brain* (New York: Simon & Schuster, 1987).

25. Oliver Sacks, "Scotoma: Forgetting and Neglect in Science," *Hidden Histories of Science* (New York: New York Review, 1995).

26. Stacy Schiff, "The Runaway Mother," in *The New Yorker*, November 10, 1997.

27. Edward Lear, "The Jumblies," in *Anthology of Children's Literature*, eds. Edna Johnson, Evelyn R. Shields, and Frances Clarke Sayers (Boston: Houghton Mifflin, 1970).

28. Jeremy Taylor, "Sermon 18," in *Jeremy Taylor: A Selection From His Works*, ed. Martin Armstrong (Norwood, PA: Norwood Editions, 1977).

29. Henri Nouwen, *Bread for the Journey* (San Francisco: HarperSanFrancisco, 1997).

30. Adrienne Rich, *Of Woman Born: Motherhood As Experience and Institution* (New York: Norton, 1976).

October

INTRODUCTION TO THE MONTH OF OCTOBER

There are so many ways we can support and encourage our children. There are obvious times of difficulty and disappointment when we try to find words that help explicitly. And there are many other small moments every day when a look, a gesture, or our silence lets our children know that we are with them as they go about the challenging business of growing up.

October 1 ABIDING LOVE

Season of mists and mellow fruitfulness,
Close bosom-friend of the maturing sun . . .[1]

—JOHN KEATS

This is a season of encouragement. The harvest is in, and the leaves that in spring were budding and brilliant green and then in late summer were dry and old have turned into the splendor of a new, if brief, color during "Indian Summer." The holidays have not yet begun, and you still have some time to prepare your garden for winter storms. You and your family have become accustomed to school and the routines of autumn.

In this mellow season we will spend some time thinking about the power of love to fuel the confidence and zest your child will need to face each new day as an adventure of learning and being. Now might be a good time to settle in with a cup of tea and let your thoughts linger over each of your children and the many different ways you love them. How do you express your feelings to each child? Do you flood them with love for their peculiar and endearing originality? Do you find a way to let each of them know the special ways you appreciate them? Can they rely on your love and support they as they venture forth in morning and return to the warmth of home every evening?

We know that life is often complex and difficult. Love is the only antidote we have to the distractions and trials that we face every day. Do you remember what it was like when you were a child, feeling yourself enclosed in the safety net of your parents' love and support? Then you know how valuable that expression was. If you were often looking for love that was rarely if ever expressed, then you also know what you can do now to make your child's life easier. What can you do today to let your child know he is special?

October 2 THE ETERNAL YES

It is not a matter of belonging to a religion or professing one's faith, it is a matter of orientation in life and participation in its mysteries.[2]

—THOMAS MOORE

All of us have a faith journey in life, whether we are believers in a supreme being, an orthodox religion, or nothing formal at all. This journey involves coming to terms with the Universe and our place in it, finding the source of love within all. For some reason, some people hear the Universe saying "yes" more often than others. Perhaps they had parents who said "yes" often and passed this benign and loving view on to them when they were young. A parent who is ready to affirm her child when he asks to do something new or to be someone new has already moved a long way on her own faith journey.

There are many ways to say yes, and not all of them are verbal. You can say yes with hugs and with positive physical contact. You also do it by creating as much fun as you can, even if it stretches your capacities at any given moment. And you do it by listening well to your child and participating in his feelings and ideas.

On the other hand, saying "no," almost by reflex, is a good way to teach your child that the Universe is fearsome or at best indifferent. He can never expect the best and should always be prepared for the worst. There are also many ways to say no, and not all of them are verbal. Physically, you can push your child away when he wants contact or when he needs soothing. Or you can withdraw when he needs to feel the safety net your love offers.

It can be difficult to maintain the idea of a kind and welcoming Universe in the abstract. You may feel buffeted about by impersonal forces, a victim of other people or of unlucky events. In order to nurture your own faith in the positive outcome of events or relationships, you will need to do some important work on yourself. The miracle is that you can improve your own outlook and set the right tone for your child by giving him the very things you want for yourself: hugs, permission to be yourself, being listened to and understood, and opportunities to laugh and experience joy.

Give some thought to how you say "yes!" to your child and to yourself. You can begin to create a more positive universe for your child by thinking carefully about every verbal and physical "no!" you are tempted to say. Sometimes you need to say no, but most times you can craft a response that is affirming, even when it sets appropriate limits.

October 3 GOD IS IN THE DETAILS

I believe a leaf of grass is no less than the journey-work of the stars,
And the pismire is equally perfect, and a grain of sand, and
the egg of the wren . . .[3]

—WALT WHITMAN

As a conscious parent you will want to establish an emotional climate for your children that is unconditionally supportive and loving. And, in addition, you will want to find occasions to let your children know that you love and appreciate them in specific ways. Even those of us who know we are loved in a global kind of way sometimes need to know what it is about what we do and who we are that elicits such positive feelings.

Here are some examples to help you see what we mean: You can say things like, "I noticed that you asked Jeremy if you could help him figure out the bus schedule. He seemed to appreciate that." Or, "I like it when you ask me how my day is when I get home from work." Or, "You cleaned up your room without my asking you to. That makes my life so much easier. Thank you." Or, "You could have gotten frustrated when Mom asked you about band practice for the third time tonight. But you didn't. You stayed cool. *That's* pretty cool." Or, "Your little sister brightens right up when you invite her to stay in your room while you're getting ready to go out. I know it means a lot to her."

We are not suggesting that you try to manipulate your child's behavior through your approval. But we are suggesting that you pay attention to the little things your children do that demonstrate kindness, courtesy, generosity, competence, or the acquisition of a new skill. And then find an excuse to let them know you noticed.

A prayer for today: *I pray for the sharpened power of sight and of understanding. Help me slow down and look at what I have; help me see the evidence of Your handiwork in the smallest details.*

October 4 MORE SPECIFICS

Those who cultivate Power,
Identify with Power,
Those who cultivate failure,
Identify with failure.[4]

—TAO TE CHING

Our perceptions of how the world works directly affect what we do, what we say, and what we feel. If we see the universe as beneficent, then we are likely to interpret events in their most positive light. If we see the universe as punishing and cold, then we act accordingly. If we think of ourselves as good people, we can trust our own feelings about things, but if we think we are inadequate, we worry and wobble.

We can help our children develop a positive sense of themselves as living in a fair-minded and hopeful world by giving them the kind of feedback that supports those perceptions. We can notice when they are making the effort to learn something difficult and when they are showing courage or kindness. We can help them see the potential in themselves when they haven't quite grown into it yet. We can mirror for them the strengths they will have when they mature.

Yes, we see them as they are in all their physical and emotional incompleteness. But we also know that they will grow graceful and whole.

October 5 YOU WILL BE ABLE

Peak performers distinguish themselves from those who merely do well first and foremost by assuming active responsibility for their successes.[5]

—CHARLES A. GARFIELD

Once there was a sixteen-year-old boy who lived in a New York City apartment with his mother and father. He was destined to grow up to be a physician and to become accomplished in many ways. As an adult, he was known for his skill in helping people in challenging situations and his eagerness to embrace challenges. But, as a sixteen-year-old, he wasn't so sure of his abilities.

He remembers one frustrating afternoon when he had spent many hours trying to understand a certain math problem involving a difficult graph. Finally, he threw down his pencil in tears. He couldn't do it! He would never be able to do it! He would forget about going to college and join his father in the factory.

His mother, who was an immigrant with a precarious grasp of English, simply watched him in silence and then walked the few steps from the stove to the kitchen table. She put her hand on his shoulder, and said slowly, "I know you will be able to figure this out." And she went back to her cooking.

The boy picked up his pencil and started in again and, of course, figured out the problem. Later, at different times in his career when someone would ask him where he found the wherewithal to meet a particular challenge, he would say he got it from his mother. He remembered her simple words, and lived by them.

October 6 HOW TO HELP

Margaret, are you grieving
Over Goldengrove unleaving?[6]
—GERARD MANLEY HOPKINS

How do we meet a time of trouble for a child we love? How do we teach useful lessons? All of us are familiar with the story of the father who teaches his son to swim by taking him out into the middle of a lake in a rowboat, throwing him over the side into the water, telling him to swim for it, and rowing just out of reach to watch. We also know about the stereotype stage parent who fights all of her child's battles for her, hovers over her, and browbeats her into superb performances. These represent the extremes of parental involvement: the sink-or-swim parent versus the we-are-really-the-same-person parent.

When it comes to helping a child, one parent's first impulse is to come to the rescue, and the other's is to let the child fend for himself. We have discussed the first parent as a maximizer and the second as a minimizer. But these are unconscious impulses. As a parent with some experience you know that most kinds of effective help involve providing the *needed* support for a child, no more and no less.

But how do you know what is needed? You want to offer support, but you don't want to smother your child. Here are some guidelines for knowing when your help is required:

Your child asks you for help in doing something or in dealing with a problem. Does he want moral support, a hug, empathy during a time of trouble, or is he asking that you share a *part* of the task before him? You can feel good about all these responses. Which you choose depends on what your child wants from you, and how you independently assess his need.

Your child doesn't seem to want your help. Often, all he wants is for you to listen to him with your whole attention. After listening, you may decide that he is capable of going it alone, and he may tell you he doesn't need anything more. You can assure him that you have confidence in him, love him, and are ready to support him if he thinks you can help. Then stand aside and watch from the sidelines, letting him know you are there in case he needs you.

Your child wants you to take over for him, so that he can remove himself from the problem. Sometimes, this is what he says he wants, but you know that it wouldn't really be best. It's a judgment call. Of course, in an extreme case you may need to jump in with both feet, but even then the necessity for such actions is almost always temporary. Generally, your task is to see how the two of you can work together cooperatively. He will learn more from the situation if he is allowed to participate than if you do it all for him. Once you have assured him that you are ready to help, he should probably take some responsibility for implementing the solution you have both decided on.

Can you think of instances in the past when you have been involved with a problem your child has brought to you? What has your role been? Do you give your child general guidelines and then withdraw to let him work things out alone? Or do you define the problem, explain the options, and then implement the solution yourself? Or maybe you take the middle course. Do you think your child feels that you support him adequately with your attention and your experience? What have you learned from these situations, and what do you think your child has learned?

October 7 THAT'S HOW YOU LEARN

For the person on the spiritual path, there is always more to learn.[7]

— RICK FIELDS

How many times have you heard it said that you learn best through your mistakes? The reason we hear this cliché so often is because it's true.

We are certain that you will want your children to know and understand this bit of wisdom, just as you do. The opportunities to teach it are as numerous as the mistakes that you and they make every day. In other words, the opportunities to learn from your mistakes are everywhere all the time.

It's worth a few moments, though, to think about *how* you want to help your children see their gaffes and lapses as educational experiences. In the heat of the moment, this may not be as easy as it sounds. Let's say your four-year-old has just spilled a glass of milk—again. Instead of blaming him for being clumsy or careless, you can point out the "spilling factor" that is under his control, so that he will be reminded of what he needs to be careful about. Something like, "It looks like the carpet isn't level enough to keep your glass from tipping over. Why don't you go get a towel, and we'll clean it up before it soaks in?"

The same principle also works at the other end of the age scale. Let's say your seventeen-year-old has hit the side of the garage while putting the car away for the night. He knows he's blown it, and you can bet that he already feels bad. He doesn't need you to state the obvious. But he may need you to help him understand what the problem is. He may need to approach slower or move the garbage can so he can see better or turn off the radio and focus.

Mistakes in interpersonal relations can feel even more fatal to a young person. But the cliché still applies. You can help your daughter see that blurting out her true feelings about her best friend's appearance can be a scorching lesson about thinking before speaking and about the fine art of discretion. First, she can recover; second, she can apologize; and third, she can learn whatever she needs to know so she won't commit the same error again.

Your kids may not want to hear that learning from one's mistakes is a lifelong process, but if they are at all observant, they will instantly recognize that you yourself are still in school. And probably will be until the end.

October 8 LOVING DETACHMENT

The love, the joy which we can and indeed must take in created things, depends entirely on our detachment.[8] —THOMAS MERTON

In the midst of all the informational details that influence our lives and the lives of our children, it is often difficult to maintain our equilibrium. We seem beset by problems with relationships, illness, finances, and just the day-to-day business of being alive. Somehow we need to cultivate within ourselves an ever-present awareness of hope and a sense of optimism in order to remain balanced.

If we truly live from this positive background—which includes the genuine feeling that we are connected with the universe and with other people, and that this connection holds and nurtures us—then the details of our lives take on meaning and quit being random and threatening. We can be in the world, but not controlled by it. We can be, in some profound sense, detached. We can learn to both love *and* be detached. Can you remain detached from your child at the same time that you are loving her, supporting her, and empathizing with her? That may seem like an impossible question.

Let's take a closer look at what we mean by detachment. We don't mean that you are uninterested in your child or in the outcome of her problems. We don't mean that you are uninvolved. And we don't mean only that you are aware of your separation from her as an individual. What we do mean is that despite all the trials and complexities of life, yours and hers, you are continually aware that what matters is love. Love is the ground that holds us and makes the details of life less critical, less urgent.

It means that instead of jumping into the swim of your child's problems and acting swiftly to correct them, it is often wise to stay quiet and watchful, maintaining a *confident* support. You are, in this mode, confident not only of your child's ability to cope with her problems, but you are also confident in the positive background of life itself. This isn't to say that everything will always turn out the way you and your child want it to. Life will happen to you, and some of it, perhaps a good deal of it, will be problematic. But in a very real way, your acting from confidence will allow you and your child to step back from the immediate difficulty and focus on the long term. Can you practice remaining detached from the immediate and act instead from quiet confidence?

October 9 GIVING LOVE BY SPENDING TIME

He was just not in a hurry to get home, Rufus realized; and, far more important, it was clear that he liked to spend these few minutes with Rufus.[9]

—JAMES AGEE

We have a friend who is a single mother and a CEO of a medium-sized company. She must attend to her job not only at work but often at home in the evenings. Her daughter has just entered elementary school. Although the mother tries to make time for her daughter on the weekends, she has trouble giving her daughter her full attention on weekday evenings. She is conscious of not wanting to park the child in front of the TV so that she can devote herself to work matters, and every time the phone rings she feels torn and guilty. She wants to be more of a companion to her child than time allows.

Perhaps you, too, are having trouble being actually present to your children at home. You want to relax, spend some time in personal rejuvenation, and yet you are aware that this is the very part of the day when you have the time to devote to your child. During time when you and your child are together, you are too distracted to enjoy her company. And she really needs your presence.

Our response to our friend and to anyone with similar concerns is to practice being present where you are. Whenever you are with your children, *be present to them and to the moment*, instead of taking care of them and something else too. This is difficult to do when life asks you to juggle many things at once, but it can lead you into a sense of inner calm that will help you regulate the urgency of daily distractions. When you want to be with your child, "be" with her. Small children have a limited amount of time to be awake with you in the evening, so your personal time or added work time can wait until they have gone to bed. Put everything else aside. Turn off the TV and the ringer on the phone. Your incoming calls can wait.

It may be hard to do this at first. You may have to rearrange your family routines. But when you come home, make a space to be with your children before, during, and just after dinner. Being together may mean that you are both quietly occupying the same space while each of you works on a separate project, or it may mean that you do something fun together: make dinner together, talk about your day and her day, do a puzzle, play a game. Homework can be something you participate in together too, or it can wait until after you have been with each other for a while. Enjoyment is not an act of will, but the time to pay attention to your child certainly is. And your enjoyment of the things you do together will be proportional to the amount of attention you pay to what you are doing. This is saying "I love you" in a way that counts.

October 10 TIME YOU ENJOY TOGETHER

Sometimes I whittle a scrap of wood myself, or I watch Elijah trim the thin hair of customers as old as he is. Some days I just walk around the barbershop.[10]

—MICHAEL J. ROSEN

There is very little in parenting as rewarding as having a shared interest with your child where you spend enjoyable time together. Sometimes you are sharing the interest, and at other times your child is leading or you've stumbled into something interesting together. Whatever it is, you are both involved and happy in what you are doing.

Most of us find ourselves misjudging on occasion and encouraging our kids to get involved in something they aren't interested in or aren't quite ready for. And most of us also make the mistake of focusing on the outcome, wanting the activity done "right," instead of relaxing into the fun of doing it together. That's no fun for the child and frustrating for the parent.

Keep in mind that most children have short attention spans and are still finding out about their own interests. They will want to try a wide variety of activities to see which ones click before you and they make a big investment of time and money. And then be sensitive to the time when interests change. If something you both enjoyed once has lost its magic for you, try something else next time.

Just for fun—and we do mean fun—make a date with your child (with each of your children separately, if you have more than one) to try something that you think he will like and that you know you will. Take a day or a half day together to try it out. Maybe you're attracted to fishing, shooting baskets, hiking, learning to spin wool or knit, or learning to cook something together from a cookbook (especially if you aren't much of a cook yourself). If it turns out to be enjoyable for both of you, you might want to do something like it again. If not, don't be too concerned. Just be ready for the next idea that suggests itself to you. It's not really about becoming an artist or a chef or an expert outdoorsman. It's about having the time together, being in touch, and learning more about each other.

October 11 HOW TO ENCOURAGE INSTEAD OF NAG

. . . in brute reality there is no
Road that is right entirely.[11]
—LOUIS MACNEICE

This is a hard one. All parents at one time or another nag their children when they would rather be teaching or encouraging. Nagging has a negative tone rather than a positive one, and it implies some kind of insistent or persistent demand or complaint.

Part of the art of parenting involves knowing when to suggest or encourage and when to insist. It's the difference between "You might want to call for that appointment" and "I want you to call for that appointment." There are some things you need your children to do, and you want to make those things very clear. "I need you to call when you are going to be late." "You have to do your household chores."

Where it gets tricky is when you want to help your child develop some lifelong healthy habits. Let's say you want your daughter to develop good eating habits. You know that you will need to model those habits yourself, that you will need to serve meals that are generous in fish and vegetables and light on the fried chicken, and that you will have plenty of pita and hummus on hand for snacks. So you make healthy choices available and try to involve her in the adventure of delicious, heart-healthy eating.

Beyond that, how do you encourage? You notice when she makes good choices, you help her make the connection between eating well and feeling and looking good, and you give her some latitude within the limits you set for yourself. For example, we know of one family where the parents are vegetarian, and the rule for their two young daughters is: "When you are home, you will eat as we eat. But when you are visiting at friend's homes, you can eat whatever they eat if you wish."

Whatever behavior you wish to encourage will more likely take root in a climate of positive reinforcement and active participation than in a climate of negative prohibition. Remember to go light on the "shoulds" and hold the criticism.

October 12 GETTING TO KNOW YOU

Dear, dear Erik; perhaps you were after all my only friend. For I have never had one.[12]

—RAINER MARIA RILKE

One of the most useful encouragements you can give your child is support for making friends. Some children seem naturally to fall into the habit of making new friends. They are gregarious and feel positively rewarded for making new acquaintances. They aren't afraid of rejection. If your child fits this description, then be truly thankful. Your task as a parent is made much easier. You merely have to reinforce her natural gifts and begin to include her new friends in your conversation and your home.

But if your child is naturally shy—maybe it's better to say, *when* your child is shy—you can be a real ally in her attempts to make contact with her peers. Here is an opportunity to do some important coaching. After all, even if you yourself are a bit shy, you have learned a great deal about getting to know people. You have had to. Here are some tips to share with your child:

Encourage your child to see the opportunities. At school much of the time spent is outside of class. There is before school when everyone is hanging out, waiting for things to start. There is lunchtime, when there are always some kids who are sitting alone and would like some company. There are after-school activities like sports or scouting or clubs or camps. Not everyone has paired off or joined a clique, and not everyone is comfortably social. There are other shy kids just waiting to be asked to play.

Encourage your child to make the first move. It's often very flattering when someone approaches you in a friendly manner. Making the first move is likely to be rewarded. Many others, even if they seem self-assured, are just as shy as you are. They are looking for someone to break the ice. Remember, if someone isn't interested in you, that is their loss, not yours.

Show your child how to start a conversation. Be ready to help out someone who looks lost or is in need of a helping hand: "Do you want me to help you with that?" Compliment the girl whom you'd like to be friends with on her clothes, or her penmanship, or show an interest in something she said or something she knows how to do, especially if you'd like to learn it. Talk about schoolwork or a movie you have both seen. Invite someone to eat lunch with you later. Or maybe just talk about the weather.

Mostly you will want to let your child know that you are in her corner, that you know she will make friends, and that you care about *her*—not the number of friends she has. Making friends is a combination of being open and taking the initiative, and she can learn to do both.

October 13 I THINK YOU'RE BEAUTIFUL

Imagine liking your own body and taking pleasure in looking at other women's bodies.[13] —JANE R. HIRSCHMANN AND CAROL H. MUNTER

One of the chronic problems of our culture is fat phobia. Young girls, at earlier and earlier ages, are becoming seriously dissatisfied with their bodies. To understand why this is happening is to understand some of the less pleasant realities of our culture. Commercialism commodifies women's bodies, sexism negates our appreciation of the feminine elements of life, and the fit body has become a social marker for high status. These are a few of the broad reasons for this disturbing trend.

What can you do, as a father or mother, to counteract it? First of all, you can discuss such issues with your children as they come up during the course of normal life. Talk to your sons and daughters about sexist attitudes when you see them expressed. Point out the subtle and not-so-subtle examples of fat discrimination when they confront you. Help your children be sophisticated media consumers so they can get a sense of how pervasive is the message that thin equals sexy and sex sells. Through this kind of discussion, you are raising your children's awareness, and by implication, letting them know that such attitudes do not need to be (and have not always been) part of universal human experience.

Second, if you are a mother, you can pay attention to your own attitudes about weight, food, sex, and power. How you feel about your own appearance and your own worth are powerful magnets for your daughter's attitudes about herself. Do you look at yourself in the mirror and convey satisfaction and self-acceptance, or do you look in the mirror and complain about how fat you are? Such seemingly innocuous moments leave an indelible trace in your daughter's self-perception.

Ask yourself about your own eating and exercise habits. Are they healthy? Are they balanced? Knowing that daughters tend to reflect their mothers' neuroses and their mothers' strengths will help you become more conscious of what you are modeling.

Tomorrow, we'll look at how fathers and mothers can interact with daughters in positive ways that counteract poisonous attitudes in the culture.

October 14 I STILL THINK YOU'RE BEAUTIFUL

A violet by a mossy stone
 Half-hidden from the eye![14]
 —WILLIAM WORDSWORTH

One day, your perfectly normal twelve-year-old daughter refuses chocolate ice cream at the dinner table, saying that she is too fat and needs to go on a diet. This common declaration of dissatisfaction seems to come with the age, and it should alert you to the need for a counteroffensive against the prevailing impossible standards of female beauty.

We are talking about a subtle counteroffensive, not an aggressive one. You wouldn't necessarily comment immediately when your daughter says she thinks she's fat. But later, you might ask her about it. Using the techniques of intentional dialogue, look for opportunities to talk about why she thinks she is fat. Has someone called her that? Is she comparing herself to fashion photographs? Is she left out of social situations with her peers?

Whatever she says, you will want to validate her feelings and help her understand why she might feel that way. From your perspective she can gain a larger understanding of how girls and women are made to feel inadequate when they really aren't and how "fat" has become a vicious epithet. After you have understood her feelings and validated them, you can find a way to let her know that you do not see her as inadequate in any way. You accept and love her the way she is, you see the beauty in her, and you believe in the beauty that will reveal itself in the future.

This is an important orientation for both mothers and fathers. Fathers will want to be especially careful to convey acceptance and appreciation of their daughter's physical selves. Fathers and daughters often become wary of each other as the daughter becomes sexual. But there is a way for fathers to stay affectionate with their maturing daughters without conveying either fear of, or attraction to, their daughters' developing sexuality. The father who finds his way onto this path strengthens his daughter's sense of mastery in the world and facilitates her eventual enjoyment of her own sexual nature with another man.

October 15 EACH CHILD

Come away, O human child!
To the waters and the wild
With a faery, hand in hand . . .[15]

—WILLIAM BUTLER YEATS

It goes without saying that each of your children needs encouragement. When one of them needs a little more attention, you usually know it. But in your rush to help the squeaky wheel, don't forget that the child who seems to have it all together needs your attention and support just as much as the child who is obviously struggling. Sometimes you have to overcome your natural inclination to relate to one child more easily than another and make rational decisions about who needs you and in what capacity.

We know of one family, for example, where the father finds it easier to spend time with his two sons than he does with his daughter. He is deeply involved with his sons' sports activities, but knowing how to spend comparable time with his daughter baffles him. As part of family counseling he has come to realize that his desire to be with her is just as strong as his desire to be with his boys, but he's less sure of himself with her and is having trouble getting started.

It is not uncommon for fathers to understand male-oriented activities and feel more comfortable with them. And the same can hold true for mothers. Sometimes a mother doesn't quite know how to participate in her son's activities.

One way out of this dilemma is to follow the child. Let your son and your daughter lead you into their own interests. Keep in mind that these activities don't have to be gender-specific. Think in terms of gender-neutral activities, such as hiking, woodworking, or going to dinner and a movie together. Getting to know your child away from the rest of the family is the key, because the point is to find a way to talk together or simply enjoy each other's presence while your attention is focused on some mutual activity. Your first couple of alone times may seem surprisingly awkward at first, but they will reap big rewards in your daily interactions.

Are you and your partner finding ways to spend time with each of your children alone? Over time, your relationships will be enriched by spirited discussions, and you will discover topics to discuss, shared fun, and in-jokes that only the two of you, parent and child, share. It's not a one-time thing either. It is something to build on.

October 16 CHOOSING FRIENDS

Many times I have loved the people I love too much for either their good or mine, and others I might have loved I missed loving and lost.[16]

—FREDERICK BUECHNER

Whether or not your child takes the wrong road in his choice of friends, it is likely that sooner or later he will come home with playmates that aren't exactly your cup of tea. If you practice conscious parenting early on, you will know how to respond well later should he choose a girlfriend or wife you have reservations about. You will know how to show support for his choices, despite your own reticence. In the meantime, you can influence the choices he makes by helping him learn what to look for in a friend or partner.

Sometimes a child has a hard time knowing who will be a good match for him. It takes a long time for a friendship to develop, and in the beginning your child will not know whether the rocks in the road are passable or not. Your long-term perspective can encourage him not to judge too quickly and comfort him when he gets discouraged.

It can be tempting to choose friends on the basis of looks, popularity, and style. But with your help, your child can learn that alliances built on surface qualities alone are not likely to last. Such people can be important allies and amusing companions, but lasting friendship has to be built on something more.

You can help your child look for deeper qualities like these:

- My friend is kind to other people, even the ones who aren't popular or pretty.
- My friend is usually friendly with me.
- My friend and I share a lot of interests.
- My friend is honest and keeps promises.
- My friend listens to me and is interested in what I have to say.

It would be fun and productive to expand this list. Ask your child what else he values in a true friend. And then you can talk about how important it is for him to give his friends what he hopes to get from them in return.

October 17 HOW HIGH IS THE BAR?

Sometimes they minimize their faults, and at other times they become discouraged by them . . .[17] —SAINT JOHN OF THE CROSS

There are many families in which one of the parents has inherited a child who has been parented for several years by someone else. In a blended family where you and your spouse have married with ready-made families intact, you might find yourself living with a son or daughter who has spent ten or more formative years being guided and influenced by another adult. And it is possible that you might find the quality of that parenting to have been inadequate or contrary to your style and philosophy.

Stepparents (and all parents for that matter) find that one of their constant parenting tasks is to do what they can to foster the self-esteem of their children. If you are a stepparent who comes to the role late, you might be trying to understand why this child feels bad about herself at the same time that you are trying to ameliorate the situation.

Let's say that you are a stepmother with a new daughter who is a perfectionist. She is hard on herself in a hundred ways. How can you encourage her?

Even more important than what you say is how you interact with her. You can surround her with loving acceptance and be steadfast in that intention, even when she tests you by being nasty and unlovable in return. She may judge herself harshly, but you are positive and appreciative of what she does and what she *is*. She may be focusing on performance as a measuring stick for love. But you appreciate the person she is and is striving to be, regardless of today's performance and achievement.

In addition, you can find times to talk to her about her own worth and how you see her. You can indulge in a little philosophizing about the intrinsic value of each human being, independent of the psychic clothing we all adopt to make ourselves look better, sound smarter, and appear more accomplished than we actually feel ourselves to be. You can be a loving reality check for her limitless expectations for herself.

This month, we've talked about learning from mistakes. This is an important concept. Another important idea to impart to our children is a sense of how all life develops, matures, and unfolds. Your daughter needs to hear that she is a work in progress, learning what she needs to know to become the confident woman you know she will become in time.

October 18 ENCOURAGING ALONE TIME

Time, it is well known, sometimes flies like a bird, sometimes crawls like a worm . . .[18]

—IVAN TURGENEV

How well does your child entertain himself? No matter how outgoing she is, there will be times when there are no friends around. Does she know how to spend time alone in her own company? How often do you hear the time-honored refrain, "I don't have anything to do. I'm bored." *You* know that being bored isn't the worst thing that can happen to her, but she isn't so sure. You also know that having nothing to do is an opportunity to learn to amuse yourself or be content with doing nothing.

Doing nothing really is doing something. It's thinking, drifting, daydreaming, experiencing the physical and emotional setting of the moment. It's receiving your own thoughts and being open to the indefinable currents of a particular time and place. Here is how one man recollects such an experience from his boyhood: "As a little boy, I used to enjoy, of a summer's evening, to sit on the top step of the porch and just be there. There was something indescribably good about being there. In the background my grandparents sat, silently, on the porch swing, rarely exchanging a word. I realize now that that something that made this an especially good and memorable experience for me was the currents of love that flowed between those two whose understanding and communion had matured through decades. And these currents reached out to enfold me."[19]

Such moments are sweet and necessary for a full life. Your child can learn that there is more to life than a series of entertainments to be experienced passively. Watching television and playing computer games give the illusion of active involvement, but are often not much more than killing time. They are wonderful when they are chosen as pleasurable punctuation marks in a rich and diverse tapestry of experiences. There are deadly if they consume hour after hour of mindless time.

A small child can occupy herself or himself with crafts and simple activities for an hour at a time. Simple tools are the best, as long as they are age-appropriate: a hammer, a board, and some nails; or watercolors, a wood burning set, finger paints, a kitchen spatula, or a garden trowel. After you have raided the garage and the kitchen, you can scavenge from the closet and put together an old trunk of dress-up clothes. Your child will no doubt want your involvement, at least your encouraging and appreciative responses. An older child may require a more sophisticated survey of his interests and abilities.

Does your child have a hobby? There are many to choose from. It is simple to start collecting something—leaves, pinecones, shells, stamps, bugs, coins. After he gets started, you might want to buy or borrow a book on the kind of collection he is interested in. In addition, here are some other simple suggestions:

- Make up stories or plays using a tape recorder, pencil and paper, or a computer.
- Write a letter to a grandparent or a pen pal.
- Cook dinner for the family.
- Rearrange a bedroom or play space.
- Start a diary.
- Learn to play an instrument or sing.
- Do something for someone else by volunteering.
- Plant some seeds indoors for transplanting outdoors later.

The idea is to encourage activities that lead your child to enjoy his own company as much as he does that of his friends. You can increase his fun and his sense of significance by being available to help and appreciate his efforts. By doing so, you are doing more than helping him with a collection or a project; you are helping him embark on a lifelong program of active and creative involvement in his own life.

October 19 SAYING I LOVE YOU IN TIMES OF TROUBLE

"Lost in desart wild
"Is your little child . . ."[20]
—WILLIAM BLAKE

There may be a time when things go wrong for your child. She (or he) may be involved in an automobile accident. She may be in serious trouble with the law or have been caught doing drugs, or she may be involved with kids you told her were trouble. You may have cautioned her about engaging in risky behavior, and you may understand immediately that she is in some way to blame for the fix she is in.

By way of preparation, let's imagine the kind of scenario you may never have to experience but which is valuable to think about just in case. Imagine a phone call in the night. Your child is on the other end of the line. No one has been hurt seriously, but she and her friends have been in an auto accident. She and the others, including the driver, have been drinking. They were driving your car, which is now totaled. The police are involved. She is at the police station and is calling home for you to come and pick her up.

With any luck this scene or one like it won't happen in your family. But these difficult times *can and do* occur. It is during such emergencies, with all your emotions engaged, that you can be at the mercy of a traumatic situation. How do you react when fear, anger, and a sense of your potential financial loss and liability are directly in conflict with your love for your child and your need to support her?

It is worthwhile to think about how you want to respond *now*, before anything happens. The love and support you show your child in a moment of crisis will be remembered and appreciated as long as she lives. So will rage and rejection. We know one mother, who in the car ride back from the police station, simply reached out and held her fourteen-year-old daughter's hand all the way back home, never saying a word. To this day, that's the most powerful image the daughter carries with her from that terrible night.

October 20 BEST FRIENDS

The presence of friends to one another is very real; this presence is palpably physical, sustaining us in difficult or joyful moments, and yet invisible.[21]

—HENRI J. M. NOUWEN

Even though your child has a best friend, you may find that this doesn't solve her social uncertainties forever. There are still questions and difficulties. Her best friend isn't spending as much time with her as she would like. Her best friend doesn't like her any more. Her best friend has a *new* best friend. Someone else wants to be her best friend. The questions come flying: "What should I do? I like Jamie, but I also like Alyssa. Can't I like both of them? But Jamie thinks I should like her better than Alyssa. And Alyssa doesn't like me as much as she likes Jenny."

Starting with the stage of concern, at about the age of seven, your child will probably become preoccupied with these social intricacies. Discovering a best friend is a first solid attempt to establish a close connection with someone outside the immediate family, or as Anne of Green Gables said, to find a "friend of the bosom." These early attempts are important learning experiences, even when they falter. You have a role to play in encouraging your child to acquire the skills of friendship in ways that keep her options open and help her to develop her own value system.

You can help her learn that friendship doesn't have to be exclusive. There is never a stage in life when one person exclusively satisfies all your needs and desires. No one person has all the interests your child has. One friend may not be interesting all the time. And one friend can't always be available to play with.

You can encourage her to have a range of playmates who may be very different from each other. In that way, she is keeping all her options open, because you never know who might turn out to be interesting. She is also *not* sending the message to others that she is exclusive and that some kids are beneath her. When her special best friend is busy, she will not only have someone else to play with, but she will also begin to realize that there is plenty of friendship to go around. You can be a voice that encourages her to expand her friendships, her interests, and her options.

A prayer for today:

Create in me a clean heart, O God,
and put a new and right spirit within me.
Do not cast me away from your presence,
and do not take your holy spirit from me.
Restore to me the joy of your salvation,
and sustain in me a willing spirit.[22]

—Psalm 51

October 21 SHOWING US THE PAIN

Snail, snail, glister me forward,
Bird, soft-sigh me home.[23]

—THEODORE ROETHKE

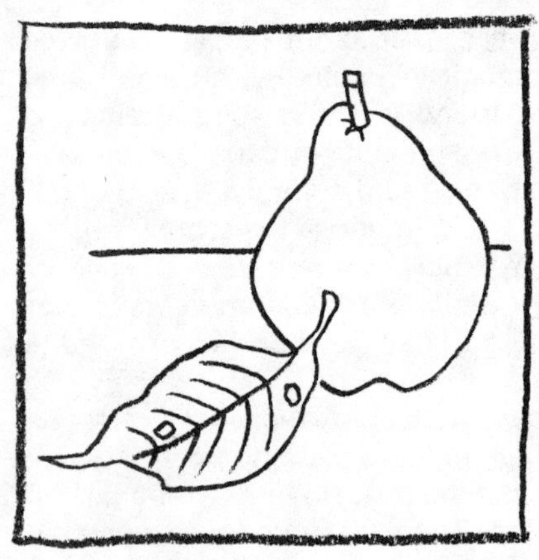

Children of families in crisis need special reassurance. They need the very time and attention from their parents that the crisis situation makes it difficult to give.

We once consulted with a family in which the husband and wife had been married for six months before she was diagnosed with a serious form of cancer. The husband's children were grown and on their own, but the wife had brought a teenage daughter to the marriage. As concern about her mother grew, the daughter became more and more outrageous; so the husband was dealing at the same time with a new marriage, a seriously ill wife, and a difficult teenager he hardly knew. He worried about what would happen if his wife died and he was left to father a resentful, scared, in-your-face fifteen-year-old into her adulthood.

He was worried, and clearly his stepdaughter was worried. When her parents stopped to think about the panic and anger their vulnerable daughter must be feeling, they were able to see more clearly what she needed from them. They stopped branding her a bad kid who was making an extremely difficult situation unbearable and began to see her as the terrified child she really was.

She needed to know that no matter how bad her mother's illness and how much pain they were going through, they were still going to function as her parents. She also needed to know that her stepfather would be there for her, as her father in the future, whatever the future might hold. When her mother and father reinstituted a firm hand and a firm love, things improved. And when the stepfather gathered his courage and talked with her about his own grief and fears, allowing her to share hers, the two of them began to build a strong bond that carried them through the next few months.

Children in the midst of family crisis need to know that their parents (or parent) will continue to function as parents with the welfare of the child as a central concern. They need to know that they can express their fears and their loss without destroying their parents or themselves. And they need the perspective that the pain they are feeling now will change into feelings that are less devastating and more positive. Things change. They will get better.

In other words, they need a strong parental presence that offers consolation in the present and hope for the future.

October 22 BEING DIFFERENT

No one's idea of excellence in conduct is that people should do absolutely nothing but copy one another.[24] —JOHN STUART MILL

Children who are about to plunge into the social world have a powerful fear of being different. As adults we are thankful that everyone is different, or else the world would be a much poorer experience for us. But for children, this concept can be scary, leaving them open to rejection and perhaps even ridicule. As a parent, there is a lot you can do to encourage and appreciate diversity and to see and appreciate the unique qualities of your own children. Your attitudes and ideas will influence them profoundly in this regard.

A first step is really accepting in your heart who your child is, instead of hanging on to some idea of who he ought to be. It must be okay with you that he appears not as big nor as athletic nor as intelligent nor as good at making new friends nor as good-looking as some of his classmates. Conversely, it must be okay with you if he has *more* of these qualities than the kids around him. He may have distinguishing characteristics that are obviously different from the local norm. Your family may be of a different ethnic background or a different religion. He may have a physical handicap.

It may surprise you that his friends are very different. They may have different tastes and even different values. They may come from different economic situations and have families that have more money or less money than your family. These differences will be obvious, and you can look for ways to find them enriching, rather than threatening. If your tone is nonjudgmental, then you are helping enlarge your child's world at the same time as you are keeping the lines of communication open and strong between you. No child wants to share his exploration of the world with an adult companion who is negative and critical.

If you find it necessary to intervene in a situation where a clash of values has important consequences for your child, you can do so in a matter-of-fact way that doesn't run people down for differences in appearance, ethnic background, or social and economic circumstances. You can simply say that his friend's *behavior* is unacceptable, not the fact that he is different in other ways from your child or your family or your group. What a gift it is to help your child stand apart from the crowd in his gracious acceptance of the differences in others.

October 23 ENCOURAGING FROM A DISTANCE

Our two souls therefore, which are one,
Though I must go, endure not yet
A breach, but an expansion,
Like gold to airy thinness beat.[25]

—JOHN DONNE

If you are living with your children every day, then it is easy to find opportunities to give encouragement. But what if you are far away from them or they are not living at home or they are part of another family because of divorce and only live with you part-time? Separation doesn't make your encouragement mean less. When your opportunities are fewer, you have to make them count. You still have to figure out how best to serve your child through your encouragement.

Perhaps the best way to figure out what your children need is to listen to them. If your daughter, let's say, is living with your ex-spouse and is having trouble with her new family, the best way you can help is through the process of intentional dialogue. You can help her clarify her feelings as you mirror, validate, and empathize. Once you understand what she thinks and how she feels, you will know how to lay aside your own agenda and do what you can to encourage her to make her new family arrangements work. As much as you may be tempted to, you won't fantasize with her how about much better it might be if she were living with you.

Strange as it may seem, your emotional distance may enable you to have more credibility with her. Your advice will carry weight because you are more objective about the details. Encouragement doesn't mean adopting her pain as your own, but rather helping her see a little more than the confinements of her pain will allow.

If your child is not living with you, you still have a tremendous role to play in her life. How are you playing that role now, and what can you do to encourage her to explore her world, and enjoy it, whether the circumstances are ideal of not?

October 24 TEACHING CONSCIOUS FRIENDSHIP

However, you're my man, you've seen the world
—The beauty and the wonder and the power . . .[26]

—ROBERT BROWNING

In the same way you model for your child how to be a conscious parent, you can encourage him to be a conscious friend. As you know, being conscious means stepping back from your first reaction to a troublesome situation rather than jumping in with your fears and angers. It means neither walking away from someone in trouble nor intruding on his privacy. It is based on respecting the individuality of others and accepting them as they are because you care, even if your first response to them in a particular situation is somewhat negative. These are the principles that you are learning to act on with your child and with your partner.

When your child has trouble with a friend or when his friend is in trouble, it's natural for him to react in ways he has learned in his relationship with you. If you demonstrate unconscious behavior by overreacting or by walking away, it is easy for him to fall into the same pattern. And when you encourage him to step back, listen, empathize, and give advice only when asked, you also reinforce that behavior in yourself.

Here are some common situations that give you and your child a chance to practice conscious friendship:

Your son's friend is not doing well in school and asks him for help. Encourage your son to talk with you about what he can do to help. Following the principle of neither withdrawing nor smothering, you can discuss why allowing the friend to copy or cheat is not offering good help and neither is telling the friend that it's his problem. Having eliminated these two extremes, your son can generate ideas that support his friend, while allowing him to do the actual work. Your son can offer to help him study or answer specific questions that may be troublesome. You can also let him know that you are available to help them both.

Your child's friend is having a problem but doesn't want to tell your child what it is. This is a good opportunity to teach your child how to offer help and then be at peace about whether his friend accepts it or not. Teach him to offer something specific, to continue to interact in ways that are supportive and understanding, but to refrain from bringing the subject up again. Part of the specific offer of help can include the suggestion that his friend talk to a caring adult, perhaps even to you.

Your child's friend is fighting with another friend and wants to involve your child. Learning to negotiate complex relationships with caring and tact are skills that many adults haven't yet mastered. If you can help your children learn these relationship skills early, you will be doing them a great service. Here are some simple guidelines you can teach your child: First, be a good listener. Second, stay cool and don't get overly involved by taking sides. Third, help your friend see the positive side and do things that will make the situation better.

These guidelines will mean more, of course, if this is the way you yourself operate in your life. If your own philosophy is optimistic about the good in people and their ability to work things out, your children will be inclined to see the world in the same way.

October 25 I WILL BE BACK

The Lord is my light and my salvation; whom shall I fear? The Lord is the strength of my life; of whom shall I be afraid?[27] —PSALM 27

Imagine being a small child, say one, two, or three years old. Your parents are your whole world. When they are with you, you feel safe, and when they are not, you're not so sure. Add to that the realization that the passage of time has very little meaning for such a small child, and you can understand why leaving a very young child with a baby-sitter can be scary the first few times it happens. And yet, we all do it sooner or later, and they do live through it (and so do we).

What can you say and do to make it easier for your youngster? You might try imagining yourself small and scared in your child's place. What you would want to know? First, you would want to know in advance that your parents were leaving you in the care of someone else. You would want time to be prepared. Second, you would feel better if you already knew the person you were going to be left with. A chance to meet the sitter for a visit, while still in the company of the parent, is a very good idea. Third, you would want to know how long your parents would be gone, as far as you could understand it, and what they would be doing while they were away. Fourth, you would want to know that they could be reached if needed. Fifth, you would want to be reassured that they were coming back. . . . If, in addition, you could be distracted by a treat, a game, or an adventure right after they left, that might make the whole thing easier.

The message is really very simple: We love you. You will be fine with the sitter. We will be back.

October 26 DISAPPOINTED IN LOVE

> Lay your sleeping head, my love,
> Human on my faithless arm . . .[28]
>
> —W. H. AUDEN

If your children are lucky, sometime during their teenage years they will fall in love. (It may not feel like luck to you, but it's good for them to get some practice with this most primary of life experiences before they leave home.) It follows then that the chances are very good they will also experience the ending of such relationships.

The kids themselves have an inelegant word for such ruptures. They call it being "dumped." And they either do the dumping or endure being dumped. Although it may seem to you that new alliances are forming and dissolving all the time during the chaotic years from twelve to twenty, each time there is an ending, there is distress. And each time there is something new to learn.

What can you say to a distraught sixteen-year-old who has just been dumped? If you asked her yourself, she would probably tell you that she wants you "to be there" for her. This is another popular phrase that is actually very descriptive. What she means is that she wants you to be available when she needs you, to pay attention to what is happening and to care, to participate with her in the crying and the recovery, and to offer help and advice when needed.

You'll notice that there is something truly passive about your role in this process. There is a quality of waiting on your part that allows room for her to tell you about the situation and how she feels about it, and then to respond with genuine sympathy and with some balance. She doesn't need you to say, "Yeah, I always hated that creep. I knew he wasn't good enough for you. You're better off without him." That is an indictment of her judgment and a negation of her feelings.

But she might need to hear that you know that she will one day feel better, that you believe that she will have everything she wants, and that you are convinced she deserves the best. If you can share similar experiences from your own romantic past, your stories will help her realize what she already knows—that these things happen to everyone and that experiencing both the ecstasy and the sadness help us prepare to live fully and happily in the future.

October 27 THE FIRST DAY

I believe that visions heal. They heal by freeing energy from our inner world, energy that fills us with power.[29] —MICHAEL SAMUELS

Some fourteen-year-olds sail into high school on a high wind without any worry about upcoming challenges. But many others stall for a while in their own uncertainty. What if they can't find their lockers and don't know where to go for class? What if they don't have anyone to eat lunch with? What if nobody likes them? What if their clothes look dorky? What if the schoolwork is too much? What if their skin doesn't clear up?

Even reading this list of worries brings back the anxiety of those times. You might ask yourself what you would have liked your parents to have done for you to make it easier. Some kids want their parents to walk through their schedule with them before class starts. Some want their parents to make a dermatology appointment for them or go with them to the makeup counter at Nordstrom. Others want their parents' assurance that they will work with them on homework assignments. And still others may welcome the suggestion that they host a before-school overnight, so their friends can get together and bond before the fragmentation of the high school experience.

It is also possible that as you think about what your parents could have done to make these times easier for you, you conclude that the answer is "nothing." You may have wanted and needed nothing more than the security of your family carrying on as always. And you may be wise enough now to know that many of the difficulties you encountered were inevitable and could not have been avoided through parental intervention. You now know you not only survived these trials, but you learned from them.

Kids entering high school for the first time need to know what kids need to know at every age: We, your parents, are solid and stable people with a good handle on our own lives; you are a priority for us; we will always be here to listen and help; you will learn much that is valuable in this next phase of your life; we know you are growing up to be a unique and valuable person with a great capacity for fulfillment and happiness. What a message. Come to think of it, we are never too old to draw sustenance from such sentiments.

October 28 FIGHTS WITH FRIENDS

It is perfectly monstrous the way people go about, now-a-days, saying things against one behind one's back that are absolutely and entirely true.[30]

—OSCAR WILDE

Ah, your children's fights. . . In the same way that mammal and human youngsters learn adult skills through play, they seem to learn a lot about relationships through conflict. Some of the common early conflicts take the form of insultingly selfish behavior, domineering behavior, saying nasty things about each other, and violating confidences. Your children will no doubt encounter such affronts and will be guilty of some themselves.

When things do get rough, you can teach your children to talk their feelings out with their friends. It's very important to let them see that strong feelings are normal, that they don't kill you, and that talking about them makes them more manageable.

If your child is guilty of causing trouble, encourage her to own up, admit her mistake, and act first to make things better. You can teach her that admitting her error and making amends adds to her dignity as a person. When she does, she'll get a chance to see the positive effect it has on a person who just a moment a ago was furious, but now is softening toward her.

If your child's friend has played a negative role in this conflict, you can encourage your child to do one of two things: One, ignore the problem, if it isn't a continuing one, and be ready to say something like, "I really got upset, but I don't want a silly thing like this to get in the way of our friendship. Let's forget it and go on." Two, confront the problem, if it is a recurring one, by saying something like, "You really hurt my feelings when you did/said . . . . I want to continue to be friends, so let's talk about what to do from now on."

Even if the friend's behavior is obviously out of line, you can teach your child to look at *her* role in the conflict. Most problems happen because two people were off base somehow. As the conscious adult, you can be a balance for your child in these situations. You see farther than she does, and you have a better sense of what is important and what's not.

October 29 SUPERSTARS GET MORE ATTENTION

I cannot understand why your marks are so low. Both your mother and I are worried about this. We both know that you are not stupid and surely you are not lazy.[31]

—JOHN P. MARQUAND

It's hard for a child who has a superstar brother or sister. Maybe you know firsthand what it is like to feel like the lesser of two siblings. We know a man who is now in middle age who still struggles with having a famous brother, a fellow at a world-renowned research institute whose academic achievements have been bigger than life. The hard part is not that his brother is well-known and highly regarded in his field, but that his mother, who is now a very old woman, talks about his brother's books and travels and international conferences constantly.

If you have experienced this feeling of being "less than" or if you have a sister or brother who has been compared to you in a *less* favorable light, you know the internal struggles such unbending and arbitrary evaluations can create. When you think about it, you know it makes sense—not only on a rational, conscious level, but also on an emotional level—to give equal encouragement and support to each of your children.

As you take a few moments to think about each of your children, loving them in equal measures for their particular graces and gifts and not regretting the lack of anything in any of them, consider how you show your special feeling to each of them. Do you give your encouragement and optimistic support equally to each? Do you assure them by what you say and think and do that, at least at home and within your own sphere of influence, they are whole and fully accepted for who they are? If you can give this kind of encouragement to each child, you are giving them a gift that will carry them through the difficult times they will face in life.

October 30 APPROACHING THE EVE OF ALL SAINTS

That night, a child might understand,
The De'il had business on his hand.[32]

—ROBERT BURNS

Tomorrow is Halloween—a holiday that parents with young children look forward to eagerly, even though they may not understand its origins. All Saints' Day is the feast of all known and unknown saints, observed by the Christian church on November 1. In England the feast was sometimes called All Hallows' Day, giving its name to Halloween (All Hallows' Eve), the preceding day. It was originally a Celtic festival for the dead, celebrated on the last day of the Celtic year, October 31. With the coming of Christianity, elements of the Celtic festival were incorporated into the Christian All Hallows' Eve.

Until recent times in some parts of Europe, it was believed that on this night witches and warlocks flew abroad, and huge bonfires were built to ward off their malevolent spirits. During the nineteenth century these medieval superstitions gradually disappeared and left echoes of their original intent in the rather benign rituals of getting dressed up and playing tricks. In modern times we've dropped the tricks and have come to expect small children and their parents to greet us at the door in beautiful or scary costumes.

Recently, in America, Halloween has been surrounded by all kinds of "urban folklore " in the form of stories about hapless children who are given poisoned candy or apples containing razor blades. Very few of these horrors turn out to be true, but they do add to the sense of danger that pervades the holiday.

Given the mixed origins and modern superstitions about the holiday, many parents look on Halloween with a jaundiced eye.

But no one can take away the absolute delight youngsters (and their parents, vicariously) get from dressing up and ringing doorbells, although it's true that the candy in the outstretched bag can be a problem. Many parents are replacing the neighborhood candy raid with supervised parties that feature games and activities more than sweets. Teenage parties, of course, can be a problem unless they are closely supervised by responsible adults.

But all small children deserve an opportunity to have the fun of dressing up in costume and participating with their friends in something that is safely daring and maybe even a bit "naughty." Halloween is what you and your children make of it. It can be a lot of fun and a good excuse to meet your neighbors and teach your children to be courteous and friendly in a safe environment with strangers. It also gives adults a chance to reconnect with the magic world of small children and to be open and giving in their praise and their treats.

October 31 ALL SHALL BE WELL

Sin is inevitable, but all shall be well, and all shall be well, and all manner of thing shall be well.[33]

—JULIAN OF NORWICH

These are the words of a fourteenth-century mystic, a woman who lived out her vision of connection to God as an anchoress attached to the Church of Saint Julian in the city of Norwich in England. It is difficult for most of us enter into the mystical vision; however, Julian is more accessible than most. And even with her, we may find ourselves reading her words with some skepticism. It is easy for us to think about the difficulties that threaten to grind us down and the uncaring, even hostile nature of the universe. We are assaulted by information that tells us about all the ways that individual lives are difficult and dangerous. The media feed on personal sorrows and misfortunes, since the pleasures and joys of life make tepid news.

We live in a rational age when science seeks to explain the mysteries of life through the accumulation of data and the miracles of technology. Given the state of our world, asserting that "all shall be well" may appear to go against common sense.

As parents and conscious adults, what view of life can we embrace that will allow us to continue in hope except the humble idea that the ends of things are a mystery not available to rational examination? As we grow older, we learn that an exclusive reliance on our own transient desires, emotions, and visions of personal grandeur is not a sufficient answer to life's problems. We know that there is wisdom in the Chinese proverb that it is right to beware of getting what we wish for.

When it comes to the future—and all parents have a stake in that future—we must be hopeful, and we must teach our children to be hopeful. To be anything less is to pretend to know the mind of God—something we will never be able to do—not only to know it, but to expect in some way, like a primitive conjurer, to control the mind of God.

To have faith is to go forward in trust despite the negative experiences we all face. This is what we believe Julian means when she says "all manner of thing shall be well."

Notes

1. John Keats, "To Autumn," in *Introduction to Literature: Poems*, 2nd ed., eds. Lynn Altenbernd and Leslie L. Lewis (New York: Macmillan, 1969).

2. Thomas Moore, *Meditations on the Monk Who Dwells in Daily Life* (New York: HarperCollins Books, 1994).

3. Walt Whitman, *Leaves of Grass* (New York: Doubleday, 1940).

4. Al Huang Chungliang and Jerry Lunch, *Thinking Body, Dancing Mind* (New York: Bantam Books, 1992).

5. Charles A. Garfield with Hal Zina Bennett, *Peak Performance* (New York: Warner Books, 1984).

6. Gerard Manley Hopkins, "Spring and Fall: To a Young Child," in *A Hopkins Reader*, ed. John Peck (Garden City, NY: Image Books, 1966).

7. Rick Fields, *Chop Wood, Carry Water* (Los Angeles: Jeremy P. Tarcher, 1984).

8. Thomas Merton, *The Silent Life* (New York: Farrar, Straus & Giroux, 1957).

9. James Agee, *A Death in the Family* (New York: Bantam Books, 1979).

10. Michael J. Rosen, *Elijah's Angel (*New York: Harcourt Brace, 1992).

11. Louis MacNeice, "Entirely," in *The Collected Poems of Louis MacNeice,* ed. E. R. Dodds (Oxford: Oxford University Press., 1966).

12. Rainer Maria Rilke, *The Notebooks of Malte Laurids Brigge*, trans. M. D. Herter Norton (New York: W.W. Norton, 1964).

13. Jane R. Hirschmann and Carol. H. Munter, *When Women Stop Hating Their Bodies (*New York: Fawcett Columbine, 1995).

14. William Wordsworth, "She Dwelt Among the Untrodden Ways," in *The Complete Poetical Works of William Wordsworth,* Andrew J. George *(*Boston: Houghton Mifflin, 1964).

15. William Butler Yeats, "The Stolen Child," in *Collected Works, vol. 1, The Poems*, ed. Richard J. Finneran (New York: Scribner, 1997).

16. Frederick Buechner, *A Room Called Remember* (San Francisco: HarperSanFrancisco, 1992).

17. Saint John of the Cross, *John of the Cross: Selected Writings,* ed. Kieran Kavanaugh (New York: Paulist Press, 1987).

18. Ivan Turgenev, *Fathers and Sons*, trans. Constance Garnett (New York: Heritage Press, 1941).

19. M. Basil Pennington, *Centering Prayer* (New York: Doubleday/Image Books, 1989).

20. William Blake, "The Little Girl Lost," in *Blake, Complete Writings*, ed. Geoffrey Keynes (London: Oxford University Press, 1969).

21. Henri J. M. Nouwen, *The Genesee Diary* (New York: Doubleday, 1989).

22. *The New Oxford Annotated Bible* (New York: Oxford University Press, 1994).

23. Theodore Roethke, "The Lost Son," in *Collected Poems* (New York: Doubleday, 1966).

24. John Stuart Mill, *On Liberty* (New York: Appleton-Century-Crofts, 1947).

25. John Donne, "A Valediction: Forbidding Mourning," in *Introduction to Literature: Poems*, 2nd ed., eds. Lynn Altenbernd and Leslie L. Lewis (New York: MacMillan, 1969).

26. Robert Browning, "Fra Lippo Lippi," in *Browning, Poetical Works, 1833–1864* (Oxford: Oxford University Press: 1970).

27. *The Holy Bible*, King James Version (Cambridge, Eng.: Cambridge University Press).

28. W. H. Auden, "Lay Your Sleeping Head, My Love," in *Modern Poetry,* ed. Maynard Mack, *et al.* (New York: Prentice-Hall, 1961).

29. Michael Samuels, *Healing with the Mind's Eye* (New York: Summit Books, 1990).

30. Oscar Wilde, *A Woman of No Importance* quoted in *The Portable Oscar Wilde*, eds. Richard Addington and Stanley Weintraub (New York: Viking Penguin, 1981).

31. John P. Marquand, *The Late George Apley* (New York: Washington Square Press, 1970).

32. Robert Burns, "Tam O'Shanter," in *The Literature of England*, eds. George K. Anderson and Karl J. Holzknecht (Chicago: Scott, Foresman, 1953).

33. Julian of Norwich, *A Lesson of Love, The Revelations of Julian of Norwich*, ed. and trans. Fr. John-Julian (New York: Walker and Company, 1988).

November

INTRODUCTION TO THE MONTH OF NOVEMBER

Most positive changes in family life involve a significant commitment of time and resources. But during this month we are focusing on activities you can do with your kids that will fit into odd moments during the day. We are talking about simple games, easy crafts, and a couple of basics from the kitchen. The idea is to look for opportunities to be with your children in ways that are fun and imaginative. If you are finding that a lot of your interaction revolves around logistics, scheduling, and tasks, you might want to reinvigorate your relationship with some of the suggestions found on these pages.

November 1 ALL SAINTS

They were all of them saints of God—and I mean,
God helping, to be one too.[1] —LESBIA SCOTT

On this day that is traditionally dedicated to the memory of Christian saints, you have an opportunity to remember a saint you have known personally. We don't mean someone who has been canonized by the Roman Catholic Church, someone who is a saint with a capital "S." We are talking about someone you have personally known who quietly and steadfastly held within herself or himself a sense of spiritual connection that enabled a life of devotion to the well-being of others—not just a life of service, but an inner life that continually received replenishment and sustenance that kept that service and commitment to others fresh and alive.

Being a living saint is not that easy; it does not come without work. Very few of us have what it takes. But, as parents, we can aspire to some of the same ideals, particularly with regard to an inner spiritual connection. Without the ability to connect to a spiritual center in ourselves that in turn communicates outward to others, we can easily become exhausted from trying to do the right thing.

Our spiritual connection to God, to the universe, and to those around us is something that we should all be aware of and nurture. It helps us step back from our preoccupation with "self," including own fears and inadequacies, to a place where we perceive ourselves to be one part of an interdependent whole. This interdependence is not only a spiritual connection but a practical one that is being explored and described through science and mathematics as well as through ethics and religion. It allows us to look beyond our own problems and keep our strivings in perspective.

Who has the saint been in your life? Was it your mother or grandfather? Is it a close friend who always seems to be able to take time to listen? Is it someone who refuses to whine about his own problems as he cheerfully engages with those of others? Whomever you would nominate for "canonization" models qualities that you can still aspire to. Is it too late for you to become a saint? Who knows, but we can say with assurance that it's never too late to become saintlike.

November 2 THE DAY OF THE DEAD

Because I could not stop for death—
He kindly stopped for me—[2]

—EMILY DICKINSON

Death is a difficult subject in our society. It is a hushed topic, more secret even than sex. We don't realize that people in past ages saw death and dying as a natural part of life. Often our children are more open about taboo subjects than we are, not having learned yet which subjects are to be avoided. They have a way of asking questions that bring us face-to-face with philosophical realities we would rather not confront.

November 2 is a day that in English tradition is called All Souls' Day. It is celebrated, particularly in Roman Catholic countries, as a day on which the dead, especially the dead of your family, are remembered and included as part of the living. In Mexico, for example, it is called *el día de los difuntos,* and it is an opportunity for families to gather at local cemeteries around the graves of their own dead. There they eat a meal and include the dead as part of the family gathering. Far from being somber and depressing, this custom gives people a wonderful sense of the preciousness of life and its continuity through the generations.

Death has real meaning for children and must be faced honestly whenever it occurs. Perhaps your child has already dealt with the death of a pet or grandparent or another relative. If you have already gone through such an experience, you already have a sense of the process that the living go through to integrate the loss. You know how important it is to talk, to feel the grief, to mark the passing in some sort of concrete way, and to honor your own experience as you live on afterward.

These times call for compassion and honesty with your children. You can do them ill service if you treat the loss as if it were not real, pretend that it is not part of everyone's experience, or act as though it doesn't really have to be explained because the subject is too deep and traumatic for children to grasp. Children do not need to have death explained in clinical or philosophical terms, but they need to understand at least this: Death is a part of life. We feel that life has a purpose, and although we can't really know how the details work, death is part of that purpose. It is not something to be feared; it is something we adjust to and accept.

Have you thought about these subjects yourself? If you have coped by avoiding such unpleasantness in the past, you may find yourself short on constructive strategies when you need them in the future. Like sex, death is a subject that will have its way, whether we like it or not. It might make sense to give a little thought to how you understand death and dying and how you want to communicate this understanding to your children as a parent.

November 3 AN INVESTMENT OF TIME

When time no longer separates us, we will have all those whom we love, including all the animals and plants.[3] —DAVID STEINDL-RAST

You have no doubt read by now about the shockingly small number of minutes mothers and fathers spend in direct contact with their children every day, fewer minutes for fathers than for mothers. The exact numbers vary depending on who is doing the counting, but no matter how you count it, we are talking about less than ten minutes a day for fathers and slightly more for mothers.

What would happen if you committed an extra fifteen minutes or so to your children each day? As often as you could, you would want to spend time alone with each child, but spending the time with them together also brings tremendous benefits.

We believe that an extra fifteen minutes of enjoyable time with your children is transforming. You get an opportunity to pass along a wealth of games, stories, skills, and experiences . . . and you build up a surplus of knowledge and good feelings between you that you can draw upon later. Time with you is exposure to your ideas, behavior, and attitudes.

Because we believe that is important, we are focusing this month on simple activities that you and your children can do together that are fun and participatory. Some of them may take less than fifteen minutes, and some can be stretched to longer periods of time. Whether some of them may already be part of your repertoire or not, they can serve to focus your attention on ways you can create a home atmosphere that is safe, exploratory, enjoyable, and enhancing.

A prayer for today: *During my time of silence today, let me remember that there is time enough for the things that I must do. Help me discern the wheat from the chaff and give myself freely to the things that matter.*

November 4 AUTUMN

I speak this poem now with grave and level voice
In praise of autumn of the far-horn-winding fall . . .[4]

—ARCHIBALD MACLEISH

The seasons revolve us slowly through time, gently pulling us through the cycle of the year. Without being aware that things have changed, we wake up one morning and it is dark and cold. We have visions of flannel sheets and cups of hot chocolate.

Finding ways to mark the changing seasons is one of the pleasures of homemaking. Our homes and habits can register the changes that nature decrees. There are hot soups in winter, the forced bulbs on the windowsill in spring, sun tea and homemade jam in summer and . . . what in autumn?

For many people, late autumn calls forth visions of burning leaves, mugs of hot drinks, and fires in the fireplace. What seasonal routines do you observe in your household? What is different about the way your home looks, the way you eat, and what you do?

It is worth spending a little time attending to the sensual possibilities of domestic life. Which of us doesn't respond to the aroma of coffee or baking brownies or the beauty of candlelight? Think for a moment about what memories you want your children to carry with them from their childhood home during the months of autumn.

November 5 ANIMAL SPIRIT

"Go for a vision," Nippawanock said, his wrinkled hands on my shoulders, his starry eyes penetrating my darkness. "It's time. If you are to walk the path of heart, then it is time . . ."[5]

—WHITE DEER OF AUTUMN

Your children may not know how prevalent it is in preindustrialized cultures for individuals to identify strongly with particular animals. Animals are powerful symbols for the strengths and abilities we would like to have, and their spirits are valuable for healing. The oldest cave art we have is rich with the images of animals, but very light on images of the human form. For thousands of years, young people in traditional cultures have adopted animal totems as part of their initiation into adulthood.

You can use this ancient idea with your own children. Ask them to think about an animal they feel attracted to. Encourage them to take their time to see what comes to mind. They don't have to feel that there is only one, right animal, and they don't have to feel they are choosing for life.

Once they have named their animal, ask them to say why they are attracted to it. What qualities does it have that you can see? What qualities does it have that you can not see directly? In what ways would they like to be more like their chosen animal?

If they are interested in going a little further, you can suggest that they close their eyes and imagine the animal in as much detail as they can. They can imagine their muscles moving in the same way as the animal's muscles, their skin feeling the same as the animal's skin. They can see themselves walking or swimming the way their animal does and seeing as she does.

If you like, you can also choose an animal and share your thoughts with your children. Each of you might want to develop a special relationship to your animal by learning more about it and wearing or carrying its image. Your animal can become a symbol for the strength, protection, and health you wish to have.

November 6 LOADS OF DOUGH

Pat-a-cake, pat-a-cake, baker's man,
Bake me a cake as fast as you can;
Pat it and prick it, and mark it with a T,
Put it in the oven for Tommy and me.[6]

—MOTHER GOOSE

Except for baker's yeast, play dough is made up of the same basic ingredients as bread dough. What you do with these ingredients, however, determines whether you get a lump of dough to bake and eat or a lump of dough to push and pull into wonderful shapes and figures.

Many parents of small children already know about the magic of play dough. It's got everything. You can make it at home, it costs practically nothing, your child gets to get her hands gooey as she mixes it up, and it can be used over and over again to make creative creatures that can be baked hard if you want to preserve them.

It's true that you can buy play dough ready-made, but why not give your child the fun of putting it all together under your supervision? Here is the recipe:

- Mix 2 cups of flour in a bowl with 1 cup of salt.
- Into a measuring cup put 2 tablespoons of cooking oil, 3/4 cup of water, and any safe food coloring.
- Pour the liquid mixture into the dry mixture and knead it up with your hands until it becomes soft and doughy.
- Make the dough into any shape you want. If you want to harden it, bake it in the oven, under supervision of a parent, at 250°F for 1 1/2 to 2 hours or let it air dry overnight.
- Paint your creations with poster paints or acrylic paints.

This is the kind of activity that your child can enjoy by herself or with friends, rain or shine, and you will not have to do much of the work yourself. Just be available to appreciate the marvels she creates. You can definitely be part of the game at the same time that you are writing your grocery list, ironing, or fixing dinner. What a perfect tool for the imagination of a small child and the peace of mind of her parent.

November 7 THE MAGIC OF MUSIC

> Hie upon Hielands, and laigh upon Tay,
> Bonnie George Campbell rode out on a day.
> He saddled and bridled and gallant rode he,
> And hame cam his guid horse, but never cam he.[7]
>
> —TRADITIONAL SCOTTISH FOLK SONG

One of the deepest connections we make with each other is through music. Melody is a nonverbal, nonlinear, nonintellectual connection that strikes to the core of our being. We not only connect across time and culture with other people, but we connect more profoundly with ourselves as we explore our own thoughts and feelings through the musical experience.

What music do you share with your child? Is music a part of your bedtime ritual, for example? Can you remember being sung to as a child by your parents? What were some of the songs that your parents shared with you?

Maybe you don't have a beautiful singing voice and only feel comfortable singing in the shower. You have a gift to share with your child nonetheless. Children are not critics; they simply know when love is being poured over them through music, regardless of the quality.

You may have purchased some children's recordings for your child at a very early age. There are many available. And your child may have a favorite that you can sing together. As you repeat songs, you will find ways you can participate together, just as you do with bedtime stories.

How simple and wonderful to have these moments together. You might find, as you begin to share songs, that you are repeating the very songs that made you feel calm and loved as a child. Or you may find some new ones. Because music in public school is fast becoming a luxury, music enrichment is something you can do at home. The world of music has always been a rich one, in great measure because it calls forth participation rather than passive consumption.

You might consider buying a songbook of children's songs or folk songs that you can learn together a few minutes every day. Start with tunes you already know. Do you know any lullabies? How about "All the pretty little horses" or "I gave my love a cherry that had no stone" or "Froggy went a-courtin'"? Do you know "The Foggy, Foggy Dew"? And there are many modern children's songs too, as well as old, familiar hymns. Singing together is not a lost art form, whether at bedtime, over a campfire, around the piano, or with a guitar. It's still there for you and your child to discover together.

November 8 POTATO STAMPS

> Thus wood-block engraving, which made it possible to reproduce accurately the calligraphy and illustrations of texts, became part of ordinary life in the course of the tenth century.[8] —JACQUES GERNET

Small children, boys and girls alike, love to decorate things with stamps. On a mundane level, you may know the small thrill, as well as the convenience, of stamping your envelopes with a signature stamp that places your name and return address on the upper left corner.

In ancient times the Chinese developed the art of stamping wooden blocks with intricately carved characters on official documents. It was a signature, unique to the person who affixed the stamp. It was also the beginning of what later became the basis for movable type and the printing of books. One of the amazing things about this kind of stamp was that it consisted of raised characters carved *backward* on the block.

What if you and your child could create designs that she could stamp on letters or wrapping paper or drawings? You can use the flat surface of a baking potato, cut with a safe knife, as your surface.

Take a potato and cut it in half. Using a felt marking pen draw a design backward on the surface. It could be a letter or your child's initials, or an abstract design—a cross, some diamonds, a Christmas tree, the silhouette of a bird. Now cut around the outline of the design and remove the potato pulp from the outside of the design. This way the design itself will have a flat, raised surface. Now using colored ink, tempera paint, or food coloring in water, dip the potato into the color and press it on any paper surface. Presto! Your child can use it to create his special design on anything from a greeting card to a book to his own stationery.

You will want to participate with your child in this project. You might want to make your own design, and you will certainly want to supervise the cutting. Once the technique has been demonstrated though, your child and her friends can easily spend a rainy or snowy afternoon making themselves happy while being creatively involved.

November 9 THE END OF THE STORY

If you're a pretender, come sit by my fire
For we have some flax-golden tales to spin.[9]

—SHEL SILVERSTEIN

"A long time ago, there was a little boy, just like you, who lived in a deep, dark wood. He lived with his father, his mother, and his baby brother just like you. Only they lived in a simple hut of mud and straw. They dipped their bucket in the nearby creek for water and gathered wood in the forest for the fire that kept them warm and cooked their food. One day the boy was sitting on the bank of the creek fishing. His mother had asked him to bring home a fish for the evening meal. He was sitting there in the sunshine, all quiet, thinking lazy thoughts, when all of a sudden there was a terrific pull on the line, so strong, in fact, that the pole almost jumped out of his hand! But he held on and slowly began to reel in his catch. He could hardly believe his eyes! You would never believe what the boy had on the end of his fishing pole. . . ."

At this point, you can invite your child to finish the story. What had the boy caught? And what happened then?

This is a fun way to engage your child's imagination. You begin a story, and he gets to finish it. Your story doesn't have to be fancy; in fact, it can be made up on the spot. It can be about a relevant situation in your child's life, or it can be fanciful and set in the mystical past. It can feature your child as the hero, along with his friends and the family dog, or it can be about made-up people and places.

Story games like this are great distractions and effective teaching tools. They give you an opportunity to explore themes that are important to your child's understanding of how life works. And you get to loosen the constraints of logic and let your fancy run free.

November 10 THREE WISHES

We would often be sorry if our wishes were gratified.[10] —AESOP

Do you remember the story from the *Arabian Nights* about the fisherman who finds a bottle in the sea and pulls it out of the water and onto the shore? Inside the bottle is a powerful Genie. After a terrific mental struggle, the Genie grants him three wishes and the fisherman goes on to achieve tremendous wealth and success (never mind that through a complex set of problems, he loses everything and has to start over again). Or maybe you remember the story of the peasant who receives three wishes from a magic old woman. First he wishes for a sausage. Then, when his wife scolds him for this frivolous wish, he wishes that the sausage were on her nose. Finally, he uses his last wish to remove the sausage.

You might try playing the wish game with your child: "What if you had three wishes? What would they be?" This is an easy game to play at home or while driving.

His answers might surprise you, especially if you stay uncritical and receptive. Your child may express a wish to win the lottery, for example, and regardless of how you feel about that particular fantasy, you can have some fun talking about what you would do with winnings. However he responds, you've got some fun topics for discussion and creative fantasy together.

You may even be surprised how hard you have to think when your child asks *you* what your three wishes are. This is a good opportunity to express some of your personal values, and as the two of you talk about them, you can point out to your child that there are many different kinds of wishes. The two folk tales above demonstrate that some wishes are better than others and that some lead to nowhere. Beware of what you wish you . . . you might get it.

What do you wish for? If you ask yourself that question periodically, you will have a kind of record of your own developing maturity. All the way from winning the lottery to achieving inner peace.

November 11 MAROONED ON A DESERT ISLAND

Many's the long night I've dreamed of cheese—toasted mostly.[11]

—ROBERT LOUIS STEVENSON

Remember Ben Gunn, the man marooned on Treasure Island? Or Robinson Crusoe, Daniel Defoe's hero who survived shipwreck and who was stranded on an island for twenty-eight years? What would happen if you asked your children to imagine themselves in that situation? You can tell them that all their physical needs are taken care of. They have warm clothes, fire, fresh water, enough food, and good shelter. Now, what three additional things would they want to have with them? They might want a book or more than one. If so, what would it be? They might be quite adamant about keeping company with the family dog. They might list a fishing pole or a hunting rifle or a mirror or a chess set or a star map or a radio. A variation on the question is to invite them to think about what kind of human companionship they would choose, if they could. There are endless possibilities.

But the challenge is to keep the list to three, a very small number. You can ask your children if they would want to be rescued or to try to sail somewhere else or to stay. And why? What problems do they think might come up between two or three people who are isolated together for a long period of time? What challenges would have to be met as your children grew and changed under these circumstances over a period of ten years or so? What strengths can they see themselves developing as a result of having to be so self-sufficient?

As you can see, this kind of game is an entrée into a whole world of interesting questions and problems. And, because it is pure fantasy, you can have some fun discussing the possibilities. The best part of a game like this is that there are no right answers. If you have a child who is shy and unsure of himself, he can extend his self-confidence a bit by imagining himself overcoming the obstacles and flourishing in his independence. But, depending on what he comes up with, there are interesting implications that can be explored. He can enjoy the responsibility for his own safety and enjoyment.

November 12 MOTHER, MAY I?

I knew that the only way to win consistently was to give everybody—from the stars to the number 12 player on the bench—a vital role on the team . . .[12]

—PHIL JACKSON

Before television and computers, kids occupied themselves on long afternoons by playing simple children's games. These games are timeless and can still occupy your children happily today. You may remember Mother, May I? from your own childhood. If you don't, here are is a refresher course. The game involves players and a leader.

- The players line up at one end of the room and the leader stands at the opposite end of the room.
- The leader calls a player by name and commands him or her to come toward him in a specific way. For example, the leader might say, "Jenny, you may take one giant step forward."
- The player must ask, "Mother, may I?" If she forgets, she looses her turn and returns to her original place.

If the player *does* ask, "Mother, may I?" the leader now has three options: He can say, "Yes, you may," in which case Jenny takes one giant step; or, "No, you may not," in which case Jenny stays put; or he may change his command, and Jenny must remember to ask, "Mother, may I?" again. For example, he may say, "No, you may not. You may walk backward for two steps," and Jenny would have to ask, "Mother, may I?" before she moved backward. If she forgets, she goes all the way back to her original place and starts over.

The first player to reach the leader wins.

You can play this game with your children a couple of times, and then they will be on their own.

November 13 YOU'RE A SMOOTHIE

I went down into the orchard of nuts to see the blossoms of the valley, and to see whether the vine had budded, while the pomegranates were in bloom.[13]

—SONG OF SOLOMON 6:11

There are lots of simple things you can teach your children to make from the fruit in the kitchen. Here are the ingredients for a Fruit Smoothie, a delicious and nutritious treat that any child who is old enough to run a blender can make:

1 ripe banana
1/4 cup orange juice
1/4 cup apple juice

To make it, peel and slice the banana and put it in the blender. Add the fruit juices and blend for two minutes. Pour into two glasses and drink.

Here are some variations:

You can add two ice cubes to make the drink frosty.
You can freeze the banana overnight and thaw it for a few minute before you blend it.
You can add 1/2 cup of milk instead of the fruit juices.
You substitute different kinds of juices.
You can add 1/2 cup of flavored yogurt.
You can add 1/2 cup of ice cream.
You can other fruits in addition to the banana, such as apricots, peaches, and berries.

As you prepare meals yourself, you might want to keep an eye out for dishes you can teach your children to make, so that they can have the accomplishment of fixing good food for the family and so that they will be food literate when they are on their own.

November 14 SCRAPBOOKS

Childhood, which is the age which remembers best, is at the same time most forgetful.[14]
—SØREN KIERKEGAARD

One of the great joys of parenthood is watching your child burst with excitement over some new discovery or activity. Her happiness can intject new life into topics that have become old and worn out for you. One of your first impulses is to capture and hold on to this enthusiasm so it can be remembered and reexperienced after the passion has passed.

An old-fashioned scrapbook may be the answer. In a scrapbook you can help your child record and collect things that interest her right now—ancient Egyptian mummies, dogs, horses, Native American customs, rocks, the stars, space exploration, historical periods, movie stars, baseball lore, poetry, holidays, geography, bugs. She can create drawings, copy verses, cut out magazine and newspaper articles, add school papers, take photos, and collect natural objects. You can buy her a large book and a jar of paste or glue and let her go to work.

It doesn't matter whether this interest turns out to be lifelong. Most of them catch fire, burn, and then extinguish themselves before too long. But even when they lose their heat, they have made a contribution to the person your child is becoming. And sometimes, such scrapbooks *are* evidence of the beginning of a serious interest. In either case, this is a good way to spend a quiet afternoon, and at the end, both of you have something that has been created by and for her. Months or even years later, she will look back on this creation and understand a part of herself that she may have forgotten. So will you.

November 15 PEANUT BUTTER

The term "health food nut" has more validity than it may first appear. Nuts are an excellent health food.[15] —ARTEMIS SIMOPOULOS

Turning peanuts into peanut butter! Such a transformation can seem magical to a child. You can show her how to do it in just a minute or two. And then she can show off to her friends when she brings peanut butter sandwiches to school that she made herself.

You will need:

2 cups of unsalted roasted peanuts
1 tablespoon vegetable oil
Salt to taste

Pour the peanuts and the oil into the bowl of your food processor. Turn it on and process for two to three minutes. When the mixture is smooth, it is done. Turn off the processor and taste. Does it need salt? If so, you can add a little and process again until it's thoroughly mixed.

After your child has made the peanut butter, she can invite the rest of the family to a "tasting." You can have all kinds of other possible accompaniments on hand. What are some of the wild combinations your children can come up with? Peanut butter and pickles, peanut butter and bananas, peanut butter and ketchup, peanut butter and mustard, peanut butter and brown sugar, peanut butter and potato chips, peanut butter and coconut, peanut butter and chocolate. Have some fun with this idea. Your few moments of effort will yield great dividends.

November 16 GRANDMOTHER'S TRUNK

. . . people have a tendency to change "odd" or unfamiliar figures into conventional or familiar ones.[16] —ROBERT ORNSTEIN AND PAUL EHRLICH

Here's the situation: You are on a long car trip. The kids are in the back seat, and you and your spouse are in the front. You've run through the cookies and the oranges. And you've already exhausted the possibilities of looking for out-of-state license plates.

Grandmother's Trunk is a memory game you can play to revive your spirits and keep the peace. It works like this:

- You start out by saying, "My grandmother is going on a long trip, and I am helping her pack. I am packing grandmother's trunk and I am taking . . . [and then name something that starts with the letter *A*]."
- The next person to take a turn says, "I am packing grandmother's trunk, and I am taking . . . [the item beginning with *A* that you named] and . . . [an item beginning with *B* that he or she names]."
- The third person to take a turn says, "I am packing grandmother's trunk, and I am taking . . . [the *A* item, the *B* item], and . . . [he or she names an item beginning with the letter *C*]." You keep taking turns over and over again until someone gets stuck and can't remember the items in order.

Here is an example. First person, "I am packing grandmother's trunk and taking an apple." Second person says, "I am packing grandmother's trunk and taking an apple and a Boy Scout." Third person says, "I am packing grandmother's trunk and taking an apple, a Boy Scout, and a Cadillac."

The object is to see how many items on the growing list each person can remember. The real object, of course, is to have fun and pass the time pleasantly together.

November 17 THE NEVER-ENDING STORY

At that time, the earth was young and pliable, and monsters often roamed at will. Human beings were lifted into the sky, and sky beings came to earth.[17] —JEAN GUARD MONROE AND RAY A. WILLIAMSON

On November 9 we talked about telling a story that your child gets to finish. This kind of imaginative play is so important we want to give you some additional ideas for variations you might try.

You can play this story game with more than one child so that after the scene is set, each child gets to add something to it until it's time for a natural ending. You get a chance to see the story twist and turn in all sorts of directions when different people contribute different parts. And it's fun to see each child's personality and interests reflected in his or her imaginings.

You can play the game and let your child set the scene first. He gets to conjure an imaginary world that captures his interest and then see how other people embellish it.

You can play the game so that you tell a story that mirrors a situation you know your child is currently involved in. The advantage to this is that you can explore together different possibilities for its resolution. "Once upon a time there was a very smart and strong boy who carried his lunch to school every day in a special lunch box. One day, a bigger boy came along and took his lunch from him. The boy was mad and a little bit scared. He didn't think it was right that his lunch got stolen, but he was afraid that if he made a fuss the bigger boy might push him down on the playground. What did he do?"

We have talked throughout the year about the importance of reading to your children. It is important also to take whatever opportunities you can to tell stories verbally, to play imagination games, and to help create a magical world for your children that is full of positive characters who do good, who overcome odds, and are rewarded.

November 18 A JOYFUL NOISE

Just as my fingers on these keys
Make music, so the self-same sounds
On my spirit make a music, too.[18]

—WALLACE STEVENS

There is more light, and more humanity, in a home that is filled with music. Exposing your children to music of all sorts is a gift to them. Playing the CDs you love, talking to them about your passion for the blues or gospel or classical or country is planting the seeds of musical passion in your children's hearts.

And giving them the chance to participate in music-making gives them a taste of the creative potential that is in them, as it is in all of us. Music making can be a serious effort in the form of music lessons, or it can be much more informal and spontaneous than that.

You can start by playing patty-cake with your one-year-old and become more sophisticated from there. Little kids love to beat out rhythms with whatever implements are at hand: wooden spoons on saucepans, two sticks of wood, two spoons, two feet stomping the floor—all of them work just fine. Your eight-year-old can make his own eerie sounds by wetting his index finger and slowly rubbing it around the rim of a glass. A crystal glass makes a clear, ringing sound like a bell.

If you have a piano, you have a treasure. Simple folk songs can be picked out with one finger and sung by you and the children together. They can learn that no one should be barred from song by the quality of his or her singing voice. More important than the tonal quality is the spirit of the effort.

All of you can sing on car trips. You can whistle. You can sing rounds. Remember "Row, Row, Row Your Boat," and "White Coral Bells." They are simple enough to make any four people sound good.

Go ahead! Clap your hands, stomp your feet, exercise your voice, open your ears, and fill your home with the sounds of adults and children making a joyful noise that fills up the house, spills out into the street, and surges down the whole block into the neighborhood.

November 19 TODAY'S NEWS

Arthur Koestler has put it poignantly, "Statistics don't bleed; it is the detail which counts. We are unable to embrace the total process with our awareness; we can only focus on little lumps of reality."[19]

—V. W. BERNARD, P. OTTENBERG, AND F. REDL

Your children can learn a lot by having the opportunity to discuss the news of the day with you. It's not just a chance to learn some facts about what is happening in the world; it's also the chance to discuss the social, moral, and ethical implications of decisions that newsmakers and ordinary people make every day.

You have to be a little careful with this idea. We are not suggesting that you become polemical and preachy. The goal is not to make your children see things the way you see them. If you get too hot under the collar about the economy or crime or foreign affairs, your family is going to want to run and hide.

You have to keep it simple. World affairs are complex. For example, it is unfortunate that most adults have no idea what's going on in Bosnia. Since that's the case, we probably cannot expect our children to have it all sorted out. But international news *is* a great opportunity to learn some basics. You might at least find out where Bosnia can be found on the map of Europe. It's true that we are becoming a global village, but that does not mean that all cultures are located in the United States. Having a world globe within reach of the dinner table provides an excuse for pointing out that India is part of Asia and not in the Near East.

Human interest stories give children a chance to try out various ideas about how they would act in certain situations. And, if you screen the subjects, it allows them to see that people sometimes take action on behalf of their values and act heroically and recover from hard times. It's true that the media slant reality, but if you are there interpreting, it's possible to attain a somewhat balanced view of what is going on in the world.

The screening you do is important, of course. While encouraging your children to read anything and everything they want, you will not want the news subjects you introduce for general discussion to be filled with murder and mayhem. If *they* want to talk about the murder and mayhem, that's different. Then you can share with them your understanding of how such things can happen and how life's tragedies fit into the bigger picture.

November 20 TONGUE TWISTERS

Betty Botter bought some butter,
But, she said, the butter's bitter;
If I put it in my batter
It will make the batter bitter . . .[20]

—ANONYMOUS

Remember tongue twisters? Stumbling over them again and again is a great way to pass the time on a long drive or at any other time when boredom threatens. Saying them, even quickly in a moment of idle time, can serve to distract your children from something serious or inject a bit of humor into a conversation that needs to be lightened up. Why are tongue twisters so much fun? Besides the magic of sifting similar silly sounds safely, they tend to equalize parents and children. Parents go down in flames just as often as kids, and it's funny when they do.

Tongue twisters can be a competition: How many times can you say *this* without messing up? Here are a few examples:

A rich wristwatch is the Swiss wristwatch?
Red leather, yellow leather.
Double bubble gum bubbles double.

You can make a game of the alphabet:

A—Alfred ails after afternoon algebra.
B—Bobby bales, but boats bottom.
C—Candy coats Caroline's crumbly cake.
D—Diving doesn't daunt Don, does it?
. . . and so on.

Like any game you play with your child, your role is to avoid being too competitive yourself. The point is, let's get silly and have fun together. Humor is one of the strongest links we have with our children.

November 21 STRETCHING

Chronically tense, chronically short muscles don't work as they should.[21]

—RUNNER'S WORLD

If you asked *us* what we would like to do if we had an extra fifteen minutes, back rubs and yoga-type stretching would be near the top of the list. And the same might be true for your children, once they are introduced to these practices. In just a few minutes you can rub your son's shoulders where it hurts from playing basketball or give your daughter a back and shoulder rub to ease her headache. Or offer these gifts to your children for no particular reason . . . just because. We know a wise parent who tells his children that they don't have to have a sore back to get a back rub.

You can also get down on the floor with your kids and lead them through some gentle stretching exercises. You can put on some relaxing music and run through the moves that will stretch—gently—aching neck muscles, shoulder and back muscles, arms, wrists, thighs, calves, and ankles. If you aren't sure how to do this kind of stretching, this is a good time to learn something that will benefit your health also. A trip to any grocery store or newsstand will yield a wide variety of fitness, sports, or women's magazines that will have articles on the subject.

Spending a few minutes with your children this way puts you into positive and welcome physical contact with your children, and it teaches them to pay attention to the signals they receive from their bodies. They can learn that they can do something positive to care for themselves when they are tired, sore, or injured. They can help themselves feel better when they need to or want to.

Research has shown that people of all ages benefit from this kind of body care. The next time you want to interact with your child for a few minutes, ask her if you can give her a back rub. Maybe when she gets older, she'll return the favor.

November 22 WHERE DO I COME FROM?

> Ikkyu was a real man who lived nearly 600 years ago. He was so famous for the "impossible" things he did that he has become a folk hero.[22]
>
> —I. G. EDMONDS

Children have a keen interest in who their ancestors are. If you know where you come from, you'll know something important about who you are. Educating your child about what part of the world his people came from and how is ancestors lived will help instill a sense of pride in his identity.

If you have heirlooms or keepsakes that have been passed down in your family, you can teach your children to value them for what they are in themselves and for what they represent. A pewter cream-and-sugar set from your great-grandparents undoubtedly gives more depth to the experience of afternoon tea than one you just purchased. A menorah from your family in Poland is an invaluable reminder of your family's history.

Photographs make family history even more vivid. They add flesh and bones to the characters in your stories of the past. Uncle Bertrand may be only a name to your children until they can see that he had a big mustache and looked like a wrestler.

Take the time to educate your children about their roots. Tell them what you know about the challenges their forebears faced in the past. Help them learn about the nationalities that mix in their blood. America may increasingly be a homogeneous culture, but awareness of the differences lends color and flavor to our conception of who we are.

November 23 GROWING THINGS

I will go out to sow the seed,
In the name of Him who gave it growth . . .[23]

—CELTIC PRAYER

Every child can enjoy growing and tending plants. In the summer, if you have a garden, your child can have a small plot for experimenting with vegetable and flower seeds. Although it's sometimes hard to sustain the process over the course of a summer—including weeding and watering and harvesting—it can be a wonderful lesson in how just a little bit of work every day yields real carrots and beans and strawberries everybody can eat.

But what about November when most areas of the country have lost those sunny growing days? You don't have to wait till spring comes around again to have some of the same kind of experience. Since Thanksgiving is just around the corner, why not create a simple experiment indoors with a sweet potato?

Here's how to do it. Take a wide-mouth canning jar and fill it halfway or a little higher with water. Now find a sweet potato or a yam that fits within the mouth of the jar. Wash the potato, and poke toothpicks around the middle. Set the potato in the jar with the toothpicks resting on the rim and one end of the potato well within the water. Set it in a window where there is light. Within a few weeks roots will begin to sprout from the bottom of the potato, and green leaves will begin to grow from the part above the water level. Soon you will have a leafy, green windowsill plant that will continue to grow for a long time. Continue to fill or refill the water in the jar as long as you want to keep things growing.

It's true that this plant will not yield food for the table, but it will become a green reminder of the bounty of nature throughout the dark days of the winter. Like gardening in general, a little care reaps great rewards and object lessons. And there is no weeding or watering to hamper the delight.

November 24 WE GATHER TOGETHER

When we bless the fruits of the harvest, let us at least realize that blessed fruits need to be shared. Otherwise, the blessing turns into a curse.[24]

—HENRI J. M. NOUWEN

Ironically, it is often most difficult for people to feel thankful when things are going well and there are no great crises or difficulties to overcome. At those times it is easy to accept our comfort and contentment as a given and focus most of our attention on what we think is still missing. To enter into the spirit of thankfulness, we must pause and give the matter at least a moment's thought.

Imagine the first Thanksgiving. On the edge of the wilderness a small group of Europeans sat huddled at the end of a time of trial. To the west stretched a vast unknown forest that lay unbroken for fifteen hundred miles, but which the earliest colonists thought was without earthly limit. Within that space, they knew, lay fearsome dangers. They had been befriended, through divine Providence it seemed to them, by the native tribe closest to them. Through great effort and some luck, they had wrested a small harvest from the rocky, New England soil near the seacoast. They had no idea what trials lay ahead, but they knew it would most certainly contain times of conflict, disease and, hunger. On this one day, they paused to celebrate the bounty of the land and a temporary peace of mind that they could attribute only to God's grace.

Later, during the American Civil War, a terrible period that we now romanticize and glamorize, President Lincoln proclaimed a national Day of Thanksgiving. It extended this local New England celebration countrywide in the darkest period our nation has ever faced. Today, we gather together around the table on Thanksgiving Day and wonder if there is more to celebrating than eating a turkey dinner, watching football games, and preparing for the biggest shopping day of the year.

If there is to be more, it will come from your decision to pay homage to the blessings in your life, to live for one day in the spirit of thanksgiving. What will your Thanksgiving celebration be like? Will you be able, even in the midst of confusion and plenty, to concentrate on the things that give your life shape and meaning? Surely your children are among your blessings. What other blessings do you experience, and how can you and your children pause and reflect on the richness of this your one and only life?

Perhaps the best prayer we could make on this day would be, "May we be truly thankful now."

A prayer for today: *May this day be filled with my recognition of the blessings that have been given to me by the Giver of Gifts. May my every word and my every movement reflect my thankfulness for the bounty I enjoy.*

November 25 DANCING

They had been dancing and singing for six days and nights already. From across the river valley; the songs drifted into our last waking moments, into our dreams.[25]

—LUCI TAPAHONSO

Have you ever seen little kids dance? It's as though they enter into the music with their whole bodies. Everything moves and with great abandon. Moving to music is one of the most natural and basic instincts we have.

The next time you have five or ten minutes free from other obligations, put on some music and start moving. Invite your children to hold your hands and move along with you. It doesn't matter whether you are performing the steps to a recognizable waltz or tango. Just let your yourself go and have a good time. Your kids will love seeing you carried away in one of your less dignified moods.

We guarantee that when the song is over, you and your kids will feel more energetic, happier, and less burdened than when you started. The blood is pumping and the music beckons. And they may even keep quiet about how you look when you get down and boogie!

November 26 THE MEMORY OF WORDS

And still of a winter's night, they say, when the wind is in the trees,
When the moon is a ghostly galleon tossed upon cloudy seas . . .[26]

—ALFRED NOYES

Reciting poetry is an old-fashioned skill, one that used to be mandatory for every school child. You may remember your parents or grandparents narrating old poems from memory and the joy this brought both to them and to their listeners. Spoken verse is vital and alive in a way that the printed word is not. Not a bad reward for the effort of memorization.

There is magic in the words of old poems, whether they are nursery rhymes that don't make too much rational sense or a good story poem with its alliterations and assonances. Even if the words don't always seem understandable, your child will absorb the magic, if you work with him to help him memorize and recite. Consider this *Mother Goose* rhyme:

Pussy cat, pussy cat,
 Where have you been?
I've been to London
 To look at the Queen.
Pussy cat, pussy cat,
 What did you there?
I frightened a little mouse
 Under her chair.

Or this one:

Bobby Shaftoe's gone to sea,
Silver buckles at his knee;
He'll come back and marry me,
Bonny Bobby Shaftoe.

In ancient times, before reading and writing, oral tradition was an art that passed along the wisdom and the lessons of the culture to the next generation. Even though storytelling and recitation are less evident today, our appreciation for it is still with us. We respond to the magic of spoken poetry. And we see vital variations of it today in children's games and in inner-city musical forms like rap.

You can make a wonderful game of poetry by becoming poetry conscious yourself. We are not talking about Nobel Prize–winning poetry either. Ditties, lines from songs, a verse or two from the poems of your childhood, even doggerel—all add humor and depth to your child's life. What lines do you have in memory already? There are probably many you have not thought of for years. In a few minutes you can teach them to your children. And who says you can't learn more?

November 27 CARDS

"Sir," saith the Verser, "I am but an ignorant man at cards, and I see you have them at your fingers' end. I will play with you at a game wherein can be no deceit; . . ."[27]

—ROBERT GREENE

Playing cards, whether innocent or not, is a time-honored tradition that goes way back. Cards are extraordinarily versatile. You can use them to build miniature houses and castles on the one hand, or in the same amount of time it takes to construct a tiny turret, you can gamble away your family and fortune. Like so many simple things in life, it depends on what you do with them. In games like cribbage, you can even teach your young children to count and add numbers as well as plot strategy. Focus on the fun, though, rather than the educational opportunities, and you can't go wrong.

Here are two simple games that you can play in a few minutes or for an extended period, as you wish.

The first is Snap. This is usually a game for two players, but more can play if you use two decks. Deal out all the cards evenly to the players, with the cards facedown. The players count "one-two-three" together, and on "three," they quickly snap a card faceup in the center of the table or playing area. If the numbers or faces of the cards don't match, they continue to lay cards faceup until there is a match. The first player to call "Snap" after a match takes the pile. If both players call "Snap" at the same time, neither player takes the cards. If one player calls "Snap" by mistake, he has to give a card to each player. The player who winds up with all the cards is the winner.

The second game is Slap-Jack. It's similar to Snap, but not as complicated. Players take turns turning their top cards over and quickly laying them on a pile in the center of the table. As soon as a jack turns up on the pile, all the players try to slap their hand on it. The player whose hand is actually over the jack takes the whole pile. If a player runs out of cards, he sits and waits for a jack to turn up, then tries to slap it to get back into the game. The one with all the cards at the end wins the game.

These simple games can be used to teach young children patience, cooperation, and the benefits of winning and losing gracefully. One way to look at it is that your children have a chance to see how you operate under the strictures of competition.

November 28 AN EXTRA FIFTEEN MINUTES FOR YOU

Even when we're feeling happy, we don't usually give in to our joy in public places by letting out a whoop.[28] —LEWIS G. MAHARAM, M.D.

Many of the activities we have suggested this month are good for you, as well as good for your children. Surely you benefit when you do things that allow you to laugh, use your creative imagination, and take care of your body. But today, we are going to help you turn your attention to yourself alone, as a person, not a parent.

Just for fun, adjust your schedule so that you have an extra fifteen minutes to spend in some solitary pursuit that is a treat for you. You will notice that taking care of yourself is a theme throughout these pages, because it's hard to be a giving parent when the well is dry and because many hyper-responsible people have a hard time giving themselves even a fraction of the attention they lavish on others.

Today, give yourself that treat. It may be that what you covet is a nap or a slightly earlier bedtime. Possibly, you relish a quick look through your favorite magazine. (It's amazing how many mothers look forward to dentist appointments so they can sit and read *People* magazine undisturbed.)

It may be that a chocolate sundae would feed your soul. Or a walk at lunchtime. Possible, a quick turn at a hardware store is just the ticket. How about the perfect cappuccino? Or rereading your favorite poem?

We would have no trouble coming up with a hundred treat ideas. But the point is to get you thinking about yourself and what you would enjoy. Whether it's silence or clamor you crave, indulge yourself as often as you can in the simple pleasures. Such indulgence is good for you and good for your kids, because you will be ready to turn your attention to them, refreshed and relaxed.

November 29 HANGMAN, HANGMAN

Hangman slack the rope, slack it for a while.
I think I see my sister coming,
Traveling many a mile,
Oh, traveling many a mile . . .[29]

—TRADITIONAL BALLAD

Spelling is an essential skill that can be taught early, and turning the learning process into a game is a painless way to teach basic skills. You can play Hangman any time you are waiting, as you so often do, for something to begin—at a restaurant while waiting for your order, at the doctor's office, or when you are expecting friends to arrive, for example.

All you need is a piece of paper (even a napkin will do) and a pencil or pen. Someone, usually a parent to begin with, is the Hangman. She thinks of a word and writes down on the paper a dash for each letter in the word. Each player takes a turn and guesses a letter that might be in the word. If it is a correct guess, the Hangman writes it down in its proper place in the sequence of dashes. But if the letter is not part of the word, the Hangman draws the first part of her drawing of a figure hanging from a gallows. A completed drawing would contain a gallows (an inverted *L*), a rope, a head, a body, legs, and arms. With each person's turn, either a letter is added to the word or a new part of the drawing appears. The person who guesses the word correctly gets to think of a new word and be the Hangman for the next round. And so on.

This is an old game that continues to give lots of pleasure. There are no consequences for not doing things exactly right. You can make up your own rules and conventions. Why not enjoy each other's company for a few minutes playing this simple word game?

November 30 SMALL MOMENTS

. . . where time to come has tensed
Itself, enciphering a script so fine
Only the hourglass can magnify it.[30]

—HOWARD NEMEROV

The texture of family life is composed from a rich tapestry of small moments, as well as from memorable events. We show who we are by the things we enjoy. We express something fundamental every time we take time out from our busy schedules to play a game with our children or to point out the beauty of the light reflected on the water.

Such small moments are saying something important about how to live. They let our children know that joy is free and available to everyone and that we live in a beautiful world, if we have eyes to see it.

Our children learn that they are important to us, important enough to claim our attention even when their presence is inconvenient. And they learn firsthand about the endless fascination that any two people can have when they are present to each other and open to the moment.

We are not proposing big, expensive, time-consuming changes. We are advocating an increased responsiveness to the opportunities of the small moments. Time is a gift, our children are a gift, and life itself is a gift. All we are called upon to do is to use them wisely, and our plates will overflow.

Notes

1. Lesbia Scott, "I Sing a Song of the Saints of God," in *The Hymnal of the Protestant Episcopal Church* (New York: The Church Pension Fund, 1940).

2. Emily Dickinson, "712," in *Major Writers of America*, ed. Perry Miller, *et. al.* (New York: Harcourt, Brace, & World, 1962).

3. Fritjof Capra and David Steindl-Rast with Thomas Matus, *Belonging to the Universe: Explorations of the Frontiers of Science and Spirituality* (San Francisco: HarperSanFrancisco, 1991).

4. *Reading Modern Poetry,* eds. Paul Engle and Warren Carrier (Glenview, IL: Scott, Foresman, 1955).

5. John Gattuso, ed. *A Circle of Nations: Voices and Visions of American Indians* (Hillsboro, OR: Beyond Words Publishers, 1993).

6. "Mother Goose Nursery Rhymes," no. 1, *Anthology of Children's Literature,* eds. Edna Johnson, Evelyn R. Shields and Frances Clarke Sayers (Boston: Houghton Mifflin Company, 1970).

7. "Bonnie George Campbell," in *Fireside Book of Folk Songs*, ed. Margaret Bradford Boni (New York: Simon & Schuster, 1947).

8. Jacques Gernet, *A History of Chinese Civilization*, trans. J. R. Foster (Cambridge: Cambridge University Press, 1972).

9. Shel Silverstein, *Where the Sidewalk Ends* (New York: Harper and Row, 1974).

10. Aesop, "The Old Man and Death," in *Aesop's Fables* (New York: Grosset & Dunlap, 1947).

11. Robert Louis Stevenson, *Treasure Island* (New York: Grosset & Dunlap, 1963).

12. Phil Jackson, with Hugh Delehanty, *Sacred Hoops* (New York: Hyperion, 1995).

13. *The Holy Bible*, King James Version (Cambridge, Eng.: Cambridge University Press).

14. Søren Kierkegaard, "Either/Or," in *A Kierkegaard Anthology*, ed. Robert Bretall (Princeton, NJ: Princeton University Press, 1946).

15. Artemis Simopoulos and Jo Robinson, *The Omega Plan* (New York: HarperCollins, 1998).

16. Robert Ornstein and Paul Ehrlich, *New World New Mind* (New York: Simon and Schuster, 1989).

17. Jean Guard Monroe and Ray A. Williamson, *They Dance in the Sky* (Boston: Houghton Mifflin Company, 1987).

18. Wallace Stevens, "Peter Quince at the Clavier," in *Harmonium* (New York: Knopf, 1931).

19. V. W. Bernard, P. Ottenberg, and F. Redl, "Dehumanization," quoted in Alfie Kohn, *The Brighter Side of Human Nature* (New York: HarperCollins, 1990).

20. *Anthology of Children's Literature,* eds. Edna Johnson, Evelyn R. Shields, and Frances Clarke Sayers (Boston: Houghton Mifflin, 1970).

21. The Editors of *Runner's World, New Exercises for Runners,* (Mountain View, CA: World Publications, 1978).

22. I. G. Edmonds, *The Possible Impossibles of Ikkyu the Wise* (Toronto: George J. McLeod Publishers, 1971).

23. "The Consecration of the Seed," in *The Celtic Vision, Selections from the Carmina Gadelica*, ed. Esther de Waal (Petersham, MA: St. Bede's Publications, 1988).

24. Henri J. M. Nouwen, *The Genesee Diary* (New York: Doubleday, 1989), p. 187.

25. Luci Tapahonso, "The Kay River Rushes Westward," in *A Circle of Nations,* ed. John Gattuso (Hillsboro, OR: Beyond Words Publishing, 1993).

26. Alfred Noyes, "The Highwayman," in *One Hundred and One Favorite Poems,* ed. Roy J. Cook (Chicago: Reilly and Lee, 1958).

27. Robert Greene, "The Art of Cony Catching," in *The Literature of England,* eds. George K. Anderson and Karl J. Holzknecht (Chicago: Scott, Foresman, 1953).

28. Lewis G. Maharam, *The Exercise High* (New York: Fawcett Columbine, 1992).

29. "Hangman," in *The Telynor Songbook,* eds. John and Anna Peekstok (Seattle, WA: John and Anna Peekstok, 1991).

30. Howard Nemerov, "Runes," in *Reading Modern Poetry: A Critical Anthology,* eds. Paul Engle and Warren Carrier (Glenview, IL: Scott, Foresman, 1968).

December

INTRODUCTION TO THE MONTH OF DECEMBER

These meditations are intended to help you live your life during the holiday season with a sense of calmness and joy. We bring you back time and again to your feelings, your desires, and your values. We remind you to honor your own pacing and to take care of yourself as you give generously to others. Because the month is dominated by one theme—Christmas—and because you may want to use these pages to plan the month, they can be read all at one sitting, if you like, as a continuous stream of thoughts and reflections.

December 1 THE BEGINNING

The room was suddenly rich and the great bay-window was
Spawning snow and pink roses against it
Soundlessly collateral and incompatible . . .[1]

—LOUIS MACNEICE

December is a month of incredible richness and contrast. Indoors there is the opulence of seasonal store windows; outdoors there are the somber colors of the natural landscape (unless, of course, you happen upon the unusual occurrence of a pink rose against the snow, as in the poem above). There is great cold fighting our efforts to keep warm. There is the tug and pull of conviviality vying with our natural tendency toward inward-turning reflection.

Out of these riches, each of us will fashion a holiday season. December will contain both our public celebrations and our private meditations. We will experience both our public face and our private face, as we thread our way through the obligations and the pleasures of the month.

This month we talk a lot about Christmas. We know that not all of our readers celebrate this holiday. We know that our nation is increasingly blessed with an intermingling of faiths and beliefs from all parts of the world. But because many of our comments refer to the effects of the secular, commercialized culture on individual and family experience, we believe the issues we raise will be valuable for Christmas celebrants and non-Christmas celebrants alike.

Our purpose is to help you see that you already have inside you what you need to invest your December days with meaning and joy. And you have the capacity to choose options that reflect in many beautiful ways your own preferences, beliefs, and desires.

A prayer for today: *I enter a time of quiet, as I will often throughout this month, and focus my thoughts on my children. I hold each of them tenderly in the center of my mind and surround them with my sustaining love.*

December 2 COMMON THREADS

Search we must. Each man must set out to cross his bridge. The important thing is to begin.[2] —SHELDON B. KOPP

There are some common threads in our reflections about the holiday season this month. One is the importance of talking with the people close to you about how you feel, how they feel, and what you want to plan for. Christmas is generally more satisfying if it is a participatory democracy, rather than an expression of only one person's ideas and hard work.

We will talk quite a bit about connecting what you think is important to what you actually do. In other words, Christmas is generally more satisfying if it is an expression of your values. A discrepancy between your values and your actions causes you to become bored or resentful of how you are celebrating.

Most people want and need for Christmas to be simpler, easier, and less expensive. There are exceptions, of course. But Christmas is generally more satisfying if each event, each gift, and each person can be savored and appreciated with a calm spirit. You have more freedom than you think. The commercial celebration rushes in to fill a vacuum. If you spend even a few minutes thinking about what is important to you and how you want to plan your season, you will have filled the vacuum with your own essence. There will be no room for things you find irritating or empty.

It is contrary to common practice to conceptualize this month as a month for reflection and meditation. But that is what we are suggesting. No matter how busy you are, you can make a commitment to become more aware of what you see, think, and feel. You can slow down long enough to notice what fills you with life and what saps your energy and good feeling.

Your life belongs to you. This month belongs to you.

December 3 POPULAR OPINION

Torches here, Jeannette, Isabella!
Torches here to His cradle run![3]
—TRADITIONAL FRENCH CAROL

It is often said, and most of us believe, that what makes the holidays special is children. If you look back on your favorite Christmas or Hanukkah celebrations, the chances are that the happiest memories you have are those of yourself as a child. Now that you are a parent, your own remembered experiences of excitement and wonder probably serve as a guide for the kind of celebrations you want to create for your children while they are young.

You may also come to the season with a strong legacy of inherited traditions from your own family that you want to repeat. Especially if you are a woman, you may not be able to envision a celebration that doesn't reflect the customs and activities that are cherished by you and familiar through long years of repetition. It can be a rude awakening to realize that your husband also has his own family traditions and that your children, too, might have ideas of their own. If they are ignored, you run the risk of knocking yourself out for a celebration that turns men and children into passive consumers instead of enthusiastic participants.

In order to avoid the possibility of your ending up on Christmas Day overworked and underappreciated, you will want to do some planning and thinking right now, at the beginning of the month. The most important thing you can do is schedule a time soon when your entire family can gather to talk about how they want the season to unfold. If you are a blended family, with members scattered in different places, you can at least talk together on the phone.

Your goal is to make Christmas alive and vital. In order to do that, your plans need to reflect the desires and preferences of everyone, with each person having a role and a stake in the outcome. That way you will not have to bear the entire responsibility for setting the stage and making things work, nor will you shoulder by yourself the entire burden of meeting everyone's emotional needs and making sure they are happy.

Here are some questions that will ensure that you get input from everybody. Even young children can add their two cents:

- What did you like best about last year or any Christmas/Hanukkah in the past?
- If you were in charge, what would our celebration be like this year?
- If you were to pick your three favorite activities during the season—not including opening presents—what would they be?

You may be surprised at what you learn. For example, if you are feeling that a particular activity is worn out, don't be surprised if other people are bored or irritated with it also. On the other hand, little things you hardly noticed may figure prominently in someone else's pleasure. This is a time of discovery, and whatever it is you learn, the information will help make this season a time of fun and satisfaction for everybody.

December 4 MAKING A CELEBRATION CALENDAR

Some say that ever 'gainst that season comes
Wherein our Savior's birth is celebrated . . .[4]

—WILLIAM SHAKESPEARE

The long and gracious season stretches out before you. And if you want to take full advantage of the time, you can help it unfold in a well-paced and organized way by doing some planning now. The easiest way to do this is to make a big seasonal calendar where you will use both pictures and words to show what is going to happen when.

You can buy a large calendar with space for writing each day or, better yet, create a simple calendar out of drawing paper that you and your children can decorate with simple drawings of trees, candles, stars, and other motifs for designating specific activities. You can start by filling in those activities that are already scheduled. If you know that choir rehearsal is on Wednesdays throughout December, you can put them down first. If you know that you are leaving for Minnesota on the seventeenth, you can add your travel dates next. Then, using what you learned from your family discussion, you can add other activities on other days. This visual representation of your season will allow you to see when there is a blank spot or (more likely) when things are getting a little too crowded. It also gives your kids a chance to see that their requests are so important that they are scheduled into the calendar.

If you celebrate Christmas, then you will set aside time for getting the tree and decorating it. In some parts of the country where it is very cold, getting the tree and decorating it may occur on separate days. You can alert everyone when tree day is by drawing a big tree on the calendar in the appropriate space. You may want to draw a picture of Saint Nicholas for Saint Nicholas' Day, on December 6, or a crown of candles on Saint Lucy's Day, which is celebrated, especially in Scandinavian countries, on December 13. If you are celebrating Hanukkah, you can draw a menorah with different candles lighted on different days or a dreidel to symbolize the different days of the festival. If Grandma is flying in for the holiday, you can draw an airplane for that day.

Other more individual events can also be put on the calendar. For example, you might want to set aside time for a family reading of *A Child's Christmas in Wales,* by Dylan Thomas, *A Christmas Carol,* by Charles Dickens, or the Christmas story from the Bible. You may also want to schedule a favorite family video or a long anticipated football game. Planning in this way will allow you to see the shape and velocity of the season and make adjustments that take into account your children's capacity for busyness, your own obligations, and your ideas about what is important during the season.

An often neglected but equally important time is the period after Christmas is over, when everyone feels at loose ends. You might want to schedule days to look forward to during this time also. You can set aside a day for the family to gather at the end of the holiday time and take down the decorations. You can give some thought to how you want to welcome the New Year. You might want to mark January 6 for the Feast of Epiphany in order to celebrate the ending of the season.

Christmas is more than a big bang of gift opening. It's a time of year for expressing your deepest values and enjoying your family in special ways. Such a simple action as making a celebration calendar can help you create such a relaxed and joyous season.

December 5 WHAT CHILDREN REALLY NEED AT CHRISTMAS

My babe so beautiful! it thrills my heart
With tender gladness, thus to look at thee,
And think that thou shalt learn far other lore,
And in far other scenes![5]

—SAMUEL TAYLOR COLERIDGE

Now that you have a good idea of *what* you will be doing during the month of December to help your family have a wonderful holiday season, we will be spending most of the rest of the month working out *how* these events and activities can be experienced so that the season will be meaningful, valuable, and fun.

If you asked your children right now what they think they need most to have a meaningful holiday, the chances are they would come up with a list of presents. That's how they have been coached to think by our consumer-oriented culture. If pressed, they undoubtedly could name some important values, such as having fun and loving each other, but these are harder to talk about and harder to detect in the typical American celebration. Presents are the easy way out. They are also, unfortunately, an easy way out for some parents too.

In their book *Unplug the Christmas Machine,* Jo Robinson and Jean Staeheli talk about what children really want and *need* at this time of year:

Children need relaxed and loving time with the family. Ironically, this is exactly what they usually get less of. Ask any child whether he would rather have distracted, exhausted, and irritable parents or parents who are responsive, happy, and well-rested, and you will see the point. Most kids won't care if there are six different kinds of cookies if their mothers are too busy to enjoy the goodies with them. Children want their parents to be present and accounted for as the presents are wrapped and Christmas dinner is eaten.

Children need realistic expectations about gifts. Parents often feel helpless about managing their children's desire for gifts, but in truth, they are not helpless. If you have firm ideas about what is enough, you can let your kids know whether they will open twenty different presents on Christmas Day or untie the ribbon on three. A few quality—not necessarily costly—presents will end up being more satisfying anyway. If your child is voicing a desire for something that you cannot afford or that you do not consider age-appropriate or that may not fall within your value structure, let him know not to expect it and why. You can help him experience the pleasure of giving as well as receiving by talking about what he may want to give to others.

Children need to have an evenly paced holiday season. We have already discussed the "big bang" holiday. It can lead to serious overstimulation followed by depression. If Christmas is nothing more than a frantic buildup to present opening on Christmas Day, your child could end up asking, "Is that all there is?" And you may end up feeling resentful: "After all I did for you, and you don't even appreciate it." Make an effort to spread the fun out over December and early January. You might try giving small presents at various times during the season rather than saving them all for a "potlatch" on one day. Christmas Day can still be a time for one or two very important gifts. If you are celebrating Hanukkah instead of Christmas, you already understand how well this holiday lends itself to gradual gift giving.

Children love and need strong family traditions. How do you define a tradition? Sometimes we get confused and mix up habits and traditions. Just because you did something last year doesn't mean that you need to repeat it this year. Some ideas get worn out or outgrown. We should caution you, however, that children can be very conservative. They often want the sense of continuity that comes from repeating things *exactly* from year to year. As you plan this year, think about those activities that inspire beauty, express important values, or invite spiritual associations. These are most likely meaningful traditions that you will want to keep from year to year.

If you follow these guidelines, you will be better able to avoid clutter, excess, and burnout, the three greatest enemies of a quality family celebration.

December 6 MORE ABOUT GIFTS

> Had I the heavens' embroidered cloths . . .
> I would spread the cloths under your feet.[6]
>
> —WILLIAM BUTLER YEATS

By now you are living in the belly of our country's commercial Christmas push. Ads are everywhere, making real the economists' contention that the U.S. economy is dependent on Christmas spending for its health and vigor. Many retail businesses rely on Christmas for over fifty percent of their yearly profits.

Where does that leave your children? The answer is that they become the targets of the some of the most sophisticated thinking and creative technology our society has to offer. Advertisers know they can stimulate children's desire for products, and they know that children can get their parents to buy them what they want.

If you aren't already doing so, we suggest that you sit down and watch TV with your kids this month. You will be amazed at the quality and quantity of the ads, and you will understand how young children have trouble distinguishing the ads from the programming. In many cartoon shows, there is little to separate them from each other.

If your child is very young, she may not understand the purpose of advertising. You owe it to her to watch some television with her and help her learn when an ad is on the screen. This will give you a chance to explain that the purpose of the ad is to make her want this toy or game, even if she has no particular interest in it.

There is hope. And that hope is you. No matter how much pressure there is from outside forces, your influence is greater. You can keep in mind our previous discussion of what your child really needs at this season of the year. She needs to be a participant in the celebration. She needs to have parents who are not so busy. She needs to have strong family traditions. And, most particularly, she needs to have an idea about the place of gifts and gift giving.

The best way to counteract the commercialization of Christmas is to plan a celebration that is interactive, and that expresses your own values and family history. You will not only have more fun, be more relaxed, and save money; you will spare your child the emptiness of overconsumption.

December 7 THE CHRISTMAS BUDGET

We have got a little purse
Of stretching leather skin;
We want a little of your money
To line it well within.[7]

—TRADITIONAL ENGLISH CAROL

Whether we like it or not, Christmas costs money. There is no doubt that a conventional Christmas is expensive, and unfortunately, many people end up spending more than they can afford. Merchandisers and advertisers count on it. Credit card companies plan on it.

Many men view their ability to provide a sumptuous Christmas as an indicator of their ability to provide for their families in general. Ironically, because women do most of the actual buying, men may not have an accurate idea of how much Christmas actually costs. There are the obvious costs of gifts and travel, but there are many hidden costs as well. How much does a spool of gold ribbon cost or postage for mailed gifts or hazelnuts for the stuffing or new candles throughout the house? How about new towels for the guest bathroom, extra dinners out, and housecleaning before the big party?

If you don't want a nasty surprise in March when the credit card bills start arriving, you and your partner ought to sit down together and take a clear-eyed look at what your season is going to cost. You now have some idea of how your celebration is shaping up, so this is a good time to do some realistic budgeting. Here are some areas to consider:

Christmas cards—Do you want to send cards this year, and if so, to how many people? What will it cost to buy and mail the cards?

Gifts—Who is on your gift list? How much can you afford to spend overall, and how do you want to allocate this amount? What other gifts do you know you will have to buy? How big a contingency fund for small gifts should you plan?

Food—In addition to your normal food budget, what additional expenses for entertaining and special meals should you plan? What will you need to budget for liquor and soft drinks? What about snacks and hors d'oeuvres?

Houseguests—Will you be entertaining overnight guests? What extra expenses do you anticipate as a result?

Travel—Will you be traveling or will you be paying for anyone else's travel?

Decorations—Before you succumb to that beautiful string of lights that just caught your eye in aisle four, think ahead of time about whether you actually need anything new. And if you are planning to make your decorations, don't forget to figure the cost of materials.

Without some budget planning, many families can spend months recovering financially from the excesses of the season. You don't want arguments over money to cloud your celebration. For the sake of your family's peace and financial health, take some time now with your partner to discuss your priorities for spending.

December 8 WHAT ROLE DO YOU PLAY?

Because men often have less decision-making power at Christmas than their wives, they sometimes feel as if they are playing a walk-on part in someone else's dramatic production.[8]

— JO ROBINSON AND JEAN COPPOCK STAEHELI

Because Christmas is such a traditional holiday, men and women often fall into traditional roles, even when they are liberated from such stereotypic behavior the rest of the time. You and your spouse may have developed a workable division of labor the other eleven months of the year, but at Christmastime you may find yourselves slipping back into the patterns of previous generations.

For starters, there simply is much more work to be done during this month than you are used to. On top of that, normal routines are disrupted. Because children are out of school during much of the season, extra child care has to be managed. You may be invited, uncharacteristically, to several parties, or you may be planning to give a party. You may have out-of-town guests. And then there are all the traditional Christmas tasks to be done like baking cookies, shopping for gifts, decorating the tree, and preparing special holiday meals.

In generations past, these tasks have not been split equally down the middle, wives doing half and husbands doing half. How many men do you know who bake Christmas cookies? This isn't to say that men are slackers and women are saints. The reality is that it is often difficult for women to give up the control necessary to share tasks democratically. And since much of the work is domestic in nature, men haven't had the opportunity and/or the desire to become interested in it. Having said that, we must acknowledge that there are exceptions.

If you and your spouse would like to become an exception to this traditional imbalance in the Christmas workload, this is a good time to talk honestly about it. When the desire for change is in the air, both men and women need to do some soul-searching. Women can ask themselves whether they really need to be in charge of everything. Would it be okay if some things got done somehow but not according to their standards? Men can ask themselves what they can take on in the interest of a more relaxed, more participatory celebration? And both of them can ask themselves whether any particular activity adds something of value to their enjoyment of the season or whether the activity simply uses up resources without a positive return.

December 9 A WOMAN'S WORK

It takes a woman all powdered and pink
To joyously clean out the drain in the sink.[9]

—JERRY HERMAN

This song wasn't written about Christmas, but in a humorous way it points to an underlying reality of the season. Beginning in late October, magazines and newspapers as well as TV talk shows are full of helpful hints about how to make this holiday special and more than special: perfect. There are recipes for cakes and cookies; there are designs for homemade gingerbread houses; there are instructions for making angels and place mats and little girls' dresses and gifts for your neighbors and . . . so on.

A woman can feel like a bad mother and a bad homemaker if she isn't measuring up to the visions of holiday perfection she sees in the women's magazines. Never mind that she is also holding down a job and being a wife and mother at the same time. At Christmas she feels a strong pull toward the tradition of female domesticity that pays homage a long line of women in her family.

Women today have to make choices about where to put their energy. Many don't have full days at home to devote to beautifying their homes, although they may want to. They must do what is important, get help where they can, and let the rest go.

You can give yourself permission to create a peaceful, simple celebration, knowing that the *feelings* that underlie the celebration are ultimately more important than how it looks. Homemade cookies can be fun if you let your children do the decorating. The cookies won't be beautiful, but they will be special. Homemade presents are also special, but they require an amazing amount of work. If you follow your heart and do whatever you decide to do in the spirit of love, you will not go wrong.

December 10 PARTICIPATION IN FAITH

The Sea of Faith
Was once, too, at the full, and round earth's shore
Lay like folds of a bright girdle furl'd.[10]

—MATTHEW ARNOLD

One of the most wonderful aspects of the season is the opportunity you have to be in touch with your faith tradition. Regardless of your particular religious or spiritual practice, there are times when you can feel the Infinite flowing into the ordinary realities of daily existence. There are moments when the deep mystery of life touches your heart and your surroundings. Even small children can feel this wonder, and when they do, you can see it in their faces.

It is true that Christmas has always had both religious and secular elements in it. Pagan solstice festivals and many old folk traditions are interwoven into the Christian fabric. Throughout history, there have been groups who have viewed Christmas as antireligious and dangerous. The Puritans, for example, forbade the celebration of Christmas, because they saw it as a completely pagan festival. If they were scandalized then, they would be especially shocked by the form it has taken on today.

But you don't have to succumb to the pressures of a commercial celebration. You have the ability and the vision to celebrate in ways that have meaning to you. You can put on blinders and avoid or ignore media messages to buy, buy, buy! You can focus your time and attention on aspects of the season that touch you. You can use these weeks to turn inward and anticipate once more our experience of the miraculous. You can start becoming the person you are called to be. And you can openly share these sensibilities with your children. This month can be a time of hope and confidence that we are held within a wider bond of love that enfolds us, our families, humanity, and all the natural world. Your challenge is to decide how you want to do this.

A prayer for today: *Make me today like a little child, full of wonder and expectation. Brush my tired, jaded self with the refreshing breath of joy. Help me feel the miracle of life as it really is, not as I have boxed it in.*

December 11 CELEBRATING YOUR VALUES

The willingness to feel vulnerable—to open your heart—is essential to real intimacy.[11]

—DEAN ORNISH, M.D.

Without realizing it, we ask Christmas to "solve" problems in many parts of our lives. We want it to be the antidote to lives that are too busy and too superficial. We ask it to carry quite a load. It's a time for strengthening the family, for getting in touch with friends, for being a host, for eating rich foods, for being involved in church or synagogue—even if we don't do this most of the year—and perhaps for extending ourselves to others. It is the only extended period of family togetherness that most families experience during the year, so there is a lot of pressure on us to "get it right." Whew! That's only a partial list, and that's a lot.

Maybe it's time to stop and ask some basic questions. Let's start at the beginning. Do you know what you are celebrating? What values will you bring to the season? Here are some areas for consideration:

Having a good time. You get to take some time out from work, and you want to relax and be with your family. You may want to attend parties and see friends and extended family. You get to give and receive gifts. Maybe you eat and drink more than usual.

Decorating your home environment. You can, for a few days at least, re-create your surroundings with ornaments, greenery, and lights. Your living room is transformed by the polish and sparkle of Christmas themes.

Helping those less fortunate. The opportunities are certainly there to help other people who need warm clothing, hot meals, or presents under the tree. Your concern for your fellow man can be expressed in the form of a check, your labor, and/or your goods.

Reconnecting with the people you care about. The pull toward extended family, old friends, and your immediate family is strong this time of year. All of us, no matter what our living situation, carry around visions of warmth and good cheer that have been formed through thousands of exposures to such images. Children's book illustrations, Christmas specials, TV ads, Normal Rockwell paintings—all inspire in us a desire to love and be loved.

Celebrating the birth of Christ. For some people this is a private matter; for others it means increased participation at church, and for some it means encouraging public discussion. Every Christian must decide how to make his or her religious convictions part of the December scene.

As you reflect on each of these areas of involvement, what do you value most and least? How do you live out your values during the season? How do you want to make them manifest for your children?

December 12 HIS AND HERS

Most men aren't overly upset about Christmas, but at the same time they don't find the deep enjoyment they're looking for. . . . On a scale of 1 to 10, most would probably give Christmas a 5.[12]

—JO ROBINSON AND JEAN COPPOCK STAEHELI

You like to get the tree two weeks before Christmas. He likes to put it up just before the big day. You like to open the presents on Christmas Day. He has always opened them on Christmas Eve. You like to entertain. He wants to sit quietly in front of the fire.

When two separate people join to create a single set of traditions, they enter into a period when things aren't quite worked out yet. It feels bumpy. Both of you may find yourselves thinking, "This isn't the way *my family* does it. This doesn't feel right."

Often such subterranean conflicts are resolved in favor of a wife's customs. In fact, many women have never talked to their husbands about their childhood observances and don't know how Christmas was done in their husbands' homes. They just naturally assume leadership of the newly created family unit when it comes to such domestic decisions. This may work out fine. But, for some men, not being able to live out the traditions they are familiar with creates distance between them and the celebration. They find themselves losing interest.

The safest course is to talk together about what has meaning to you both. It is okay if you discover that you have different ideas about how to celebrate. However, when these differences extend beyond minor matters and into a difference in values, then you certainly need to stop and talk.

You will want to search for ways you can do a little bit of what is important to him and a little bit of what is important to her. This may mean doing an activity alone when only one of you is drawn to it. In this way Christmas is a metaphor for life: you want a nice balance that preserves your uniqueness while expressing the harmony of the whole.

December 13

WHAT YOU LEARNED ABOUT VALUES AS A CHILD

> . . . I can never remember whether it snowed for six days and six nights when I was twelve or whether it snowed for twelve days and twelve nights when I was six.[13]
>
> —DYLAN THOMAS

One of the unique qualities of Christmas is that the celebration we are experiencing now contains echoes of all the ones we have experienced in the past. Each year adds its own richness to our long line of December mornings. Our found memories help shape the celebration we are trying to create for our children now as parents. You may love picking out gifts because you received something you cherished when you were small. You may be sensitive to the role of grandparents because you remember a grandfather who made you feel special. You may remember with delight the carols your family sang around the tree or the magic of a midnight service at church. Even the unpleasant or uncomfortable memories serve a purpose. They can remind you not to fan the fires of family discord or not to be too busy to spend relaxed time with your kids.

Can you put into words the lessons of your own past, both good and bad? Think about your favorite Christmas. What were your parents like? How did they both show you their love? Did your family extend hospitality to friends and neighbors or perhaps to the less fortunate in the community? Was there a sharing of the Christmas story? Do you still retain some of your childhood faith?

What are the blessings your childhood Christmas has bestowed on you? As you review your experiences and the values you derived from them, imagine telling your child a story about your favorite Christmas. What would it include, and what would your children learn about you and how you want to keep Christmas this year?

December 14 MAKING CHANGES

Galileo shook the earth by turning his newly invented telescope upon the cosmos and reporting that the moon is a planet with mountains and valleys, not the perfect sphere required by older science and theology.[14]

—STEPHEN JAY GOULD

We have suggested that Christmas can be a time for reflection as well as activity. You will learn so much about yourself and the people around you if you are a good observer as you go through the season. It may take courage for you to be honest with yourself about what you don't like, but registering your true feelings is the first step toward making things better.

If you make note of your feelings, you have information to work with about what and how to make changes. We are not suggesting that you necessarily voice disappointment and disagreement every time you feel it. We *are* suggesting that you go through this year with a heightened awareness of what you are doing.

It may be difficult for you to suggest changes this year that involve other people. You may be able to slow yourself down or change your attitude, because these actions are private and under your control. But if you notice big things that affect others around you and that you would like to change in the future, you can make note of them and bring them up well ahead of time next year.

If you and your spouse agree to a change that involves parents and in-laws, for example, the best time to bring it up is early in the fall. You can initiate such a conversation by sharing your own observations and feelings; then outline the change you are considering. You can then say you'd be happy to hear the other person's thoughts on the matter and conclude by suggesting that you will think about it. There is enough time to decide for sure.

The key is to be true to yourself and sensitive to the reality that change is disruptive. People need to be approached softly and given plenty of time to absorb what you are saying. Of course you are not going to blame anyone or anything or be defensive. Even so, pioneering a different kind of Christmas can require a surprising amount of tact and self-confidence.

December 15 SINGLE PARENTS AT CHRISTMAS

I arise today
with the powers of heaven,
the sun in brightness,
the moon in splendour,
the flashing of fire,
the swift stroke of lightning
the rushing of storm-wind,
the deepness of ocean,
the firmness of earth,
the hardness of bed-rock.[15]
—ATTRIBUTED TO ST. PATRICK

At this time of year, nontraditional families have to search to find equal representation for their varied family structures. It seems that the whole culture is fixed on Mom and Dad with their Biological Two Children, even though that family configuration is in the minority. There seems to be a conspiracy, of sorts, to ignore those parents and children who don't fit the mold.

Sometimes single-parent families who do just fine the rest of year start feeling that something is missing in December. Parents can be alert to these feelings in themselves and watch for signs of sadness in their children. No matter what form it takes, you can send a loud-and-clear message that We Are A Family; We Are Whole. Of course, the problem is particularly difficult for families with parents who have recently separated. Support groups have not yet been built up, and the recent memory of family togetherness is fresh, especially to children. If your single parenthood is recent, your loneliness and the loneliness of your ex-spouse may seem overwhelming.

One way to counteract this is to include other single parents with children in your celebration. If you don't know any yet, search out families like yours through your child's school, through your church, or through friends of friends. The chances are that there are several other single adults or single parents with children who would be delighted to join you for parts of their celebrations. You can plan to attend events together, and you can include them with other friends and extended family at events in your home. It will be especially helpful if your children have other kids around whom they already know, so it might make sense to have a slumber party or two during their vacation time.

As with so much of life, your attitude makes all the difference between enjoyment or depression. Whether you intend to or not, you will transmit your feelings to your children and they will end up living in the climate you have created.

If you are not a single parent, ask yourself whether you know a nontraditional family that would enjoy an invitation to take part in your celebration. This kind of hospitality will bring richness to you and your family as well as to your guests.

December 16 ISOLATED PARENTS

London was but a foretaste of this nomadic civilization which is altering human nature so profoundly, and throws upon personal relations a stress greater than they have ever borne before.[16]

—E. M. FORSTER

It could be that you will find yourself without your children on Christmas Day. You may be a member of the Armed Forces, or you may be divorced. If this is the case, planning what you will do in advance will help you counteract any feelings of isolation and loneliness. We have great sympathy for those parents who find themselves in this place. There is no escaping the difficulty of the situation, but there are some important things to remember about being a conscious parent in these times as well as in better times.

Don't let your preoccupation with your loneliness spill out into your relationship with your children. You don't have to be falsely cheerful, but it is a good idea not to play for sympathy. Your children will be only too ready to take on your pain. Don't confuse them; love them. Your task is to diffuse sympathy rather than ask for it.

Don't let your bitterness or sense of competition spill over into your interactions with your children. You don't have to overcompensate by spending more money or by treating them to more events. And talking in a disparaging way about their other parent isn't helpful. And it isn't healthy. You don't want to force your children to choose sides.

Don't let the limited amount of time you have to spend with your children lead you into excesses of affection or involvement. As much as possible, allow your children to see you for who you are: a parent who loves them, who is concerned for their welfare, and who is there to provide <u>safety</u>, <u>support</u>, and <u>structure</u> for their lives. An even disposition and predictably warm interaction will allow your relationship with your children to grow stronger and healthier over time. Don't try to accomplish too much in a short period.

Be patient with your children. They are probably under as much stress as you are, and they are not as well equipped by experience to deal with it. As much as possible, practice stepping back and calming yourself when you are tempted to react to a negative situation. Not only will this be healthy for you, but it will help your children relax into the relationship faster and more successfully.

If you are fortunate enough not to be an isolated parent, please take the preceding discussion to heart so that you can be empathic with those who are. This is a season of forgiveness, healing, and good cheer, and opportunities to exercise them are everywhere.

December 17 FAMILY CONFLICT

Every human being is gloriously constituted, but what ruins so many is, among other things, also this wretched tittle-tattle between man and man about that which should be suffered and matured in silence.[17]

—SØREN KIERKEGAARD

Christmas is a time for families to gather together and celebrate. And, by implication, it's also a time when people who may have little in common except long-standing resentments or indifference are thrown together for the purpose of renewing old bonds.

The atmosphere at such times is heavy with hope, disappointment, and resignation. Add to that the situational tensions inherent in the celebration itself—tiredness, anxiety over someone else's behavior, pressure for things to be perfect—and you've got yourself quite a volatile mix. You undoubtedly know what we mean. Grandpa drinks too much, and everyone is waiting for the results with trepidation. Uncle Ralph is chronically depressed and makes everyone feel down. Aunt Jane talks too much and never listens to anyone else; she makes everyone nervous. You yourself are a hostess who is trying to make things happen for everyone else, and part of the dinner is ruined by being left too long in the oven. If only everyone would just be their real selves—only better.

At such times, it's a good idea to stop for a minute and get some perspective. Remember your values and your understanding of what's really important under the surface of things. And remind yourself that the greatest gift you can give anyone (including yourself) is the gift of acceptance. If you take upon yourself the responsibility for each person's joy and fulfillment and resent others when things don't go well, you are being symbiotic. What you can take responsibility for is your own behavior and your attentiveness to others. Interact with them in joy and love. You have done what you can do to set things up. The rest is subject to the complex forces of time, place, and personality, which you cannot possible fully understand, much less control. There is peace in that realization.

If you anticipate that the family reunion is going to be difficult for you, you can mentally rehearse ahead of time. Think about each person and mentally review their irritating behaviors and their strengths. If you are pretty sure that the behaviors that are difficult for you are the ones you are going to see, then make peace with it now. This is a lot easier than trying to cope in the heat of the moment.

December 18 BECOMING A PEACEMAKER

The good of eye be thine,
The good of liking be thine,
The good of my heart's desire.[18]

—CELTIC PRAYER

Too often parents see themselves as peacekeepers rather than as peacemakers, especially if they are maximizers and feel inclined to pursue others out of their own sense of insecurity. Peacekeeping often has the flavor of dampening things down, keeping a lid on conflict.

Often a peacekeeper is after the illusion of peace, wanting to escape the situation without any disturbance. This function certainly has its place at family celebrations. There is no point in pursuing deep conflicts over the roast turkey on Christmas Eve. Rodney King made a powerful point when he asked, "Can't we all just get along?"

But a peace*maker* takes upon himself or herself a different task. A peacemaker consciously and proactively seeks to bring peace to a situation where there is conflict. Almost always this involves behind-the-scenes work, rather than on-the-spot improvisation. He refuses to become a part of the problem, and he also sincerely takes an interest in understanding opposing points of view. He holds each person in love and seeks to empathize with them.

Probably you recognize the underlying principles of intentional dialogue at work in peacemaking. That is, a peacemaker seeks to use the spirit of intentional dialogue to mirror, validate, and empathize with each person he encounters.

You may not be able to perform acts of peacemaking in the heat of the moment. A family celebration is not an easy time during which to solve large problems that have been festering for a long time. But it is possible to begin the process by acting from your internal directive for healing.

Before the bulk of the holiday gatherings are upon you, take some time to hold in your mind each of your family members in love. If you know about existing family conflicts, think about how each participant in the conflict might express her grievance. Mirror that in your mind, give validity to it, and see if you can empathize, no matter how difficult that seems. Even as you are preparing for your part in the family drama, you can be preparing yourself to help resolve conflict.

This is more than an exercise in self-control. You aren't acting from negative motivations, but from positive ones. You are responding to others out of a sincere desire to create loving interactions that will eventually—maybe not this year—bear fruit. But whether your efforts have practical, successful outcomes or not, it is what you are called to do. However things work out, it will be worth the effort. Have faith.

December 19 GIVING MEANING TO CELEBRATION

How, when the aged are reverently, passionately waiting
For the miraculous birth, there always must be
Children who did not specially want it to happen, skating
On a pond at the edge of the wood.[19]

—W. H. AUDEN

You want to invest this holiday season with meaning, and by now you probably have some ideas about how you want to go about it. But let's face it. You have a limited amount of energy, and can't be "up" for everything that comes along. In order to find meaning, you need to simplify the number of events that you support heart and soul.

Simplifying is also a good idea for your children. They, too, are being asked to involve themselves in a wide range of activities, all of them designed to rouse them and get them excited. Some of these activities are valuable ways to add depth and enjoyment to the season, and some are not.

The commercial Christmas offers many choices. They range from Christmas concerts and school plays to "traditional" programs on TV and seasonal events at shopping malls. It's wise to keep your planning and your values in mind as you sift through these possibilities. Do you and your children really need to watch every Christmas special? Do you really have to expose your children to all the opportunities they will have to meet Santa? Is Rudolph the Red-Nosed Reindeer a meaningful part of your celebration? What makes sense? Which of these offerings is a distraction that ends up diminishing your family's ability to respond to the season in the way you value?

When sorting through the possibilities, you can ask whether you yourself get anything out of this activity. Does it bring a smile to your face? Does it resonate with your sense of religious values? Does it teach you something? Does it add to your appreciation of beauty? If not, your children can probably do without it too.

December 20 QUIET TIMES

> Her [Julian of Norwich] breathtakingly serene trust in the visions, for instance—in her own <u>experience</u>, that is, as opposed to what she had been taught as a Christian—seemed to me deeply consistent with the great value contemporary feminism sees in claiming one's own experience.[20]
>
> —CAROL LEE FLINDERS

It is important to know our own minds, to integrate our own experience, and rely on our own sense of how things are. But we can't possibly operate out of this strength if we never take the time to get to know ourselves.

We know a father who decided he would take time out to read one poem a day during the month of December. Every night, he would delve into his anthology of English poetry and choose a poem at random. His rationale was that he wanted to counterbalance the extra hubbub with some quiet reflection. We also know a woman who made a commitment to continue her exercise program undisturbed right through the month. Her friends laughed, but she was able to stick to it.

There is no reason to abandon good food, exercise, and sleep habits just because it's Christmas. In fact, it may be more important to take care of ourselves in December when life is stressful, than during the lazy days of summer. If you can find an extra half hour today and tomorrow, you can spend it in a way that will nourish your body and feed your soul. Good music, meditation, a warm bath will help you greet Christmas Day with happy expectation.

December 21 THE SEASON OF EXCESS

While Gabriel and Miss Daly exchanged plates of goose and plates of ham and spiced beef Lily went from guest to guest with a dish of floury potatoes wrapped in a white napkin.[21] —JAMES JOYCE

As an outgrowth of our pagan past Christmas and New Year's are times of excess. It made sense for our ancestors to hold feasts in the dead of winter when things are at their darkest and coldest. By spreading cheer, burning fires brightly, and consuming great quantities of food and drink, they were not only "whistling in the dark," but also giving themselves the sense that sunlight, warmth, the spring planting, and the greening of the year were just around the corner.

It is perhaps with this same longing for light and warmth that we gather together at this season. We, too, want to feel warmed and comforted. But we live today in a time of relative plenty. Many of us have the ability to eat and drink whatever we want when we want. Not that there is *no* hunger and need, but if you are reading this book, the chances are that you do not go to bed hungry at night. You have the option of indulging your desire to feast throughout the year. Does it really make sense for Christmas to become a festival of overabundance? Perhaps it's helpful to think about the difference between "treating" yourself and overindulging.

This year you might give yourself the treat of slowing down to savor the small moments and the quiet times. Each beautiful ornament, every smile on your baby's face, contains everything you are frantically seeking by going off in a thousand different directions.

December 22 CANNED ATMOSPHERE

How pure, how beautiful, how fine
Do teeth on television shine![22]

—PHYLLIS McGINLEY

You slip a CD of Christmas songs into your player and listen to some lovely carols. You light the candles and prepare a lovely family dinner. You leave the family Bible open to the Gospel of Luke, chapter 2. The tree is shining, and a fire is burning on the hearth. You pour yourself some eggnog. Your halls are beautifully decked with holly and mistletoe. . . . But where are your children?. . . And then you hear the TV . . . They are sitting in front of a droning television set, while you are waiting expectantly in front of a glowing fire.

During the rest of the year, you may sometimes be grateful for times when they are so dedicated to *Friends*, *90210*, or MTV. But this evening, you would like the family to be together enjoying the beautiful surroundings and each other's company. If this is important to you, then it's important to tell your family how you feel. It may be that they are used to having free rein with the TV, and your request to turn it off seems out of character.

In this as in other matters, it is a good idea to tell people directly how you feel and what you want. You could say something like, "I have planned for us to have a family evening tonight. We've worked hard decorating the tree, and everything looks so beautiful. Could you please plan for us to have an hour or so together so we can enjoy it?"

Our partners and our children are not mind readers. You need to let them know what is important to you ahead of time. If you want less TV, talk to your family in advance about which programs they can watch and when you want it turned off.

December 23 MODELING CHARITY AND ACTS OF MERCY

Therefore, Christian men, be sure,
Wealth or rank possessing,
Ye who now will bless the poor,
Shall yourselves find blessing.[23]
—TRADITIONAL ENGLISH CAROL

At its heart and soul Christmas is a tradition of generosity, charity, and goodwill to others, whether they be family, friends, or strangers. How do you best perpetuate this tradition and teach it to your children? The answer is very much in keeping with the way you teach all important values to them: You do it by modeling them yourself.

Your children can see the pleasure you get from giving gifts and the spirit of appreciation with which you receive them. You make your family and friends feel good. They know that when you give them a present, you are expressing your love to them, not magnifying your own ego or attempting to control their interests and actions. Involve your children in the giving process. Let them help you decide on what presents you are giving to their siblings, to your spouse, and to other family members. Spend some time helping them decide, if they are comfortable with your help, what they will give to the people on their list.

And in a broader sense, try to involve your children in expressions of love and concern to others. You can do this in innumerable ways. For example, a simple way is to go out of your way to give greetings to strangers at Christmas in the name of the season. You can help your children draw lots to see for whom they will perform some chore or special act of kindness: it can be as simple as doing the dishes or taking out the garbage or as complex as making a homemade present. You can collect gifts and food for a family in need. You can do the same for a charitable organization.

Whatever you decide to do, allow your children to participate as an act of their love for others, not as a heavy duty. Make it fun, a family project. It doesn't have to take a lot of time or money, but it will give your children the gift of your generosity of spirit, which is the best gift of all.

December 24 O HOLY NIGHT

Angel: Rise, gentle herdsmen, for now is he born
That shall take back from the Fiend what Adam had lost . . .[24]

—MEDIEVAL MYSTERY PLAY

How many traditions have grown up from the Christmas story! Each culture in Western Europe picks up slightly different details, leaving some things out and adding others. If you have a crèche scene in your home, you can see some of these traditions at work. Such a scene places all the events surrounding the story in one time and place, including the Three Kings and their camels, which, for example, as told in the Gospel of Matthew, would have happened sometime after the birth. Did the Kings have camels? Were they kings? Were there three of them? Were their names Gaspar, Melchior, and Balthazar? The gospel certainly doesn't say. These and other embellishments grew up around the central story much later.

The gospel writers, who were themselves artists and theologians, created a picture that contains elements they found to be necessary and helpful for the immediate understanding of this momentous event. They knew that the important thing was the mystery of the birth itself.

We, as inheritors of a Western European delight in "fact" rather than Truth, are sometimes fixated on the details in a way that makes them more important than the birth itself. We are much more comfortable with the evidence of video camera and sound equipment than we are with the poetry of oral tradition.

As you think about the events of this evening, whether you read the Christmas story in Luke's gospel or not, take a moment to remember how the miracle of God touched the world of ordinary men and women. However you describe the details to your children and regardless of whether you have an orthodox belief, this is the heart of the story. The details add beauty and make the story more meaningful. The human heart has very little trouble with ambiguity, despite what the human head tells it.

December 25 OH HAPPY DAY!

There's a star in the East on Christmas morn,
Rise up, shepherd and follow . . .[25]

—TRADITIONAL SPIRITUAL

Throughout the Christian world, especially in North America, people are gathered together in one spirit. As well as participating in the central story of the birth, we share a rich collective memory Christmases Past. We wax nostalgic about Old World Christmases and about our own past celebrations. Like Ebenezer Scrooge, we relearn meaning by journeying back through our own history until we gain a fuller understanding of who we are now.

At last you have come to the time and place your family has been looking forward to. On this day you will progress from expectation to completion. Let's hope you attain the peaceful and loving conclusion you want and expect.

This is a time to reflect on the blessings that have been given to you and your family. Yes, there have been hassles. There may have been confusion and conflict. But you can put them aside now in a spirit of pure enjoyment. You have done everything you needed to do.

Now to the Lord sing praises,
All you within this place,
And with true love and brotherhood
Each other now embrace;
This holy tide of Christmas
Doth bring redeeming grace.
O tidings of comfort and joy.

December 26 THE DAY AFTER

We climb to the light in spirals,
And look, between us we have come all the way,
And it never ends[26]

—DAVID WAGONER

Many people have to go right back to work the day after Christmas; those fortunate ones who don't can make some choices about how to spend the twenty-sixth of December. If you are traveling or are visiting or entertaining visitors, your day may already be outlined for you. But it may happen that you are free to enjoy another vacation day.

When you have children at home, particularly if they are young, you would be wise to schedule a treat or two into the day. You can let your children know that something special will be happening in the middle of the afternoon or right after breakfast. The surprise doesn't have to be elaborate. It can be something as simple as taking a walk in the park or reading a story or playing a game or making brownies. What you are looking for is something to give shape to the day.

The big buildup to Christmas and the letdown afterward can feel to a young child as if he has just walked off a cliff. Christmas is over, and he's just fallen into a big hole. A little bit of planning can avert such a semicatastrophe.

You might want to plan a taking-down-the-tree ritual. Decorating it probably has ritualistic elements to it; there is no reason that taking it down shouldn't also be ritualized. Perhaps at the end, you can all celebrate with a cup of hot chocolate or a special food treat. You can save one of your seasonal confections especially for when you are putting the decorations away for next year. The ongoing idea is to make Christmas a *season* and not just a day.

December 27 SHARING STORIES

"It is dolphin weather," thought the mermaid. "It is for chasing whales and telling tales and exploring far beneath the sea."[27]

—JANE YOLEN

One of the important functions Christmas plays in our lives is as a thread of continuity. We can mark significant changes in our lives by remembering what the holidays were like in years past. Christmas makes our memories sharp as we reexperience ourselves at the age of five or eight or thirteen. Christmas brings it all back.

When your children are young, they will be receptive to creating memories of Christmas, just as you did when you were a child. They are eager to hear about your mom and dad and the presents you gave and the traditions you had.

Telling them about such moments enriches their lives. Now they have their own experiences as well as some of yours. What stories do they have from past Christmases to add to their stock of memories? What stories will they want to tell about this Christmas just passing? If you spend a little bit of time with your children today talking about what was funny and what they will remember about this year, you will have started an oral tradition that may wind its way down into the next generation and enrich the lives of your grandchildren. See if they remember their stories from this year when you are planning next year's celebration.

December 28 TIME ALONE TOGETHER

Their hearts have not grown old;
Passion or conquest, wander where they will,
Attend upon them still.[28]

—WILLIAM BUTLER YEATS

When was the last time you and your spouse had two or three hours together undisturbed? Sure, you've had logistics consultations and shared happy experiences, but you may be feeling the lack of some relaxed, happy alone time together.

Is it possible for the two of you to schedule an evening out so you can focus on each other and have a conversation that doesn't revolve around your children or your parents? Imagine yourself in a beautiful environment that you didn't clean and decorate, enjoying delicious food that you didn't cook or coordinate, talking with your beloved about any subject that takes your fancy.

If going out doesn't work for you, then give some thought to how you might enjoy an evening at home. How can you refresh yourselves with the pleasure of each other's company and remind yourselves what lies at the heart of the family life you are so carefully building. Your *relationship* is the heart and soul of your family.

If you are without a partner at this moment, then take these suggestions and apply them to some other adult relationship that nourishes you. This is a time for you to get back in touch with yourself as an adult person and to experience the deep satisfactions of friendship.

December 29 NEXT YEAR

Allow yourself to be.[29] —THICH NHAT HANH

We have already talked about being an observer at your own celebration this year so that you can use the information to create an even more satisfying holiday next year. This would be a good time to sit down and collect your thoughts.

You might want to write yourself a memo about your observations. It might seem unlikely that you would forget how deeply you're feeling about things now, but twelve months from now, you will have mellowed. Time has a way of rounding the corners and softening the edges.

You can simply start writing. Whatever is most pressing will come tumbling out without a lot of help from you. Let your thoughts flow. You aren't planning on showing this masterpiece to anyone, so invite your internalized critic to sit this one out, and let your words tumble across the page freely.

If you would like some help to get started, here are some questions that might be useful:

- Did you like the way your activities were paced throughout the season?
- Do you think this was well paced for your children?

- Were you comfortable with the amount of money you spent?
- Were you happy with the gift-giving part of your celebration?
- Are there changes you would like to consider making with regard to the amount and kind of socializing you did?
- What did you do that added meaning and depth?
- What did you do that was superfluous or irritating?
- What worked well between you and your partner?
- What was a source of irritation or conflict between you?
- If you were in charge next year, how would your family celebrate?

Now that you have an honest appraisal, you can take your time deciding what you want to share with others, and how.

December 30 LOOKING BACK

Your children are not your children.
They are the sons and daughters of Life's longing for itself.[30]

—KAHLIL GIBRAN

You are one day away from completing this book of meditations. If you began reading on the first day of January, you have spent 364 days immersing yourself in the ideas and the reflections of conscious parenting. That's just a few minutes every day, but repeated over the course of a year, those minutes add up. A year is long enough to begin to change the course of your parenting, and to discover streams of thought and feeling in yourself that you were unaware of this time last year.

What did you learn?

We have invited you along on a journey that has been focused inward. Almost every day, we have suggested that you pause long enough to register your own feelings, recall memories, examine the way you see yourself as a parent, or begin to understand your child in a new way. We have wanted to help you become the author of your own life by seeing the themes that hold you together and define your presence in this world.

But the journey has also been focused outward on your interactions. We have wanted to help you see how you influence and shape in a profound way the people around you. What you say and what you do matter tremendously to your children and your partner.

The most important suggestion we have made all year, we are making now, as we invite you to reflect on your progress as a conscious parent. Ask yourself how your life has deepened as a result of the attention you have paid to yourself and your own inner life. Ask yourself how your relationships have improved as a result of your awareness that you can choose to re-create yourself as a strong and loving person when you interact with your children. No one is absolutely bound by early scripts. There exists in all of us the potential for re-creation and renewal into people who love freely, let go lovingly, and stay connected to each other no matter what.

December 31 LOOKING AHEAD

Would you know your Lord's meaning in this?
Learn it well.
Love was his meaning.[31]

—JULIAN OF NORWICH

The years turn in continuous circles as they spin us onward through our lives. In reality, time is seamless, but it is convenient for us to pretend otherwise. So we invent stopping points along the continuum that allow us to mark one period from another. New Year's is one of those stopping points. At this moment, we are on the cusp between the old and the new. The old year is at our back, and we stand face-forward toward our own uncreated future.

Yesterday, we asked, What did you learn? Today, we are asking, What do you want? Two questions we can glance over quickly, but two questions that are, in fact, profound. What would happen if you sincerely asked yourself what you wanted and you paid attention to your answer as though it were a matter of life and death. What do you want? What would happen if you knew that you had the power to make it happen . . . dared to live as though your life mattered?

We send to you, through these pages, our prayers for you and your family. And we send you our absolute belief in your power to become the parent you want to be.

A prayer for today: *I am humbled today by the grace that is given to us to change, by the power we find within our selves to do the impossible, and by the love that makes it possible. I pray that I may continue to be worthy of such grace and power and love.*

Notes

1. Louis MacNeice, "Snow," in *The Collected Poems of Louis MacNeice,* ed. E. R. Dodds (London: Oxford University Press and Faber and Faber, 1966).

2. Sheldon B. Kopp, *If You Meet the Buddha on the Road, Kill Him* (New York: Bantam Books, 1982).

3. "Jeannette, Isabella," in *Fireside Book of Folksongs*, ed. Margaret Bradford Boni (New York: Simon & Schuster, 1947).

4. William Shakespeare, *Hamlet,* Act 1, Scene 1, in *The Complete Illustrated Shakespeare*, ed. Howard Staunton (New York: Gallery Books, 1989).

5. Samuel Taylor Coleridge, "Frost at Midnight," in *Introduction to Literature: Poems*, 2nd ed., ed. Lynn Altenbernd and Leslie L. Lewis (New York: Macmillan, 1969).

6. W. B. Yeats, "He wishes for the Cloths of Heaven," in *Collected Works, vol. I, The Poems*, ed. Richard J. Finneran (New York: Scribner, 1997).

7. "Wassail Song," in *Fireside Book of Folksongs*, ed. Margaret Bradford Boni (New York: Simon & Schuster, 1947).

8. Jo Robinson and Jean Coppock Staeheli, *Unplug the Christmas Machine* (New York: Quill–William Morrow, 1982).

9. Jerry Herman, *Hello Dolly*, Act 1, Scene 2 (New York: E. H. Morris, 1964).

10. Matthew Arnold, "Dover Beach," in *Poetry and Criticism of Matthew Arnold*, ed. A. Dwight Culler (Boston: Houghton Mifflin, 1961).

11. Dean Ornish, *Love and Survival* (New York: HarperCollins, 1998).

12. Jo Robinson and Jean Coppock Staeheli, *Unplug the Christmas Machine* (New York: Quill–William Morrow, 1982).

13. Dylan Thomas, *A Child's Christmas in Wales* (New York: New Directions Books, 1995).

14. Stephen Jay Gould, "The Sharp-Eyed Lynx Outfoxed by Nature," in *Natural History Magazine,* May 1998.

15. *Saint Benedict's Prayer Book* (York, Eng.: Ampleforth Abbey Press, 1994).

16. E. M. Forster, *Howard's End* (New York: Vintage Books, 1921).

17. Søren Kierkegaard, "Postscript," in *A Kierkegaard Anthology*, ed. Robert Bretall (Princeton, NJ: Princeton University Press, 1946).

18. "Good Wish," in *The Celtic Vision, Selections from the Carmina Gadelica*, ed. Esther de Waal (Petersham, MA: St. Bede's Publications, 1988).

19. W. H. Auden, "Musée Des Beaux Arts," in *Modern Poetry*, ed. Maynard Mack, *et al.* (New York: Prentice-Hall, 1961).

20. Carol Lee Flinders, *At The Root of this Longing* (San Francisco: HarperSanFrancisco, 1998).

21. James Joyce, "The Dead," in *Dubliners* (New York: Viking Press, 1958).

22. Phyllis McGinley, "Reflections Dental," in *Times Three* (New York: Viking Press, 1968).

23. "Good King Wenceslas," in *Fireside Book of Folksongs*, ed. Margaret Bradford Boni (New York: Simon & Schuster, 1947).

24. *The Second Shepherd's Play*, Scene 7, in *Medieval and Renaissance Poets,* ed. W. H. Auden and Norman Holmes Pearson, trans. M. Staeheli (New York: Viking Press, 1961).

25. "Rise up, Shepherd an' Foller," in *Fireside Book of Folksongs*, ed. Margaret Bradford Boni (New York: Simon & Schuster, 1947).

26. David Wagoner, "A Guide to Dungeness Spit," in *Collected Poems* (Bloomington, IN: Indiana University Press, 1976).

27. Jane Yolen, *The Mermaid's Three Wisdoms* (New York: Philomel Books, 1978).

28. W. B. Yeats, "The Wild Swans at Coole," in *Collected Poems by William Butler Yeats* (New York: Macmillan, 1919).

29. Thich Nhat Hanh, *The Long Road Turns to Joy (*Berkeley, CA: Parallax Press, 1996).

30. Kahlil Gibran, *A Treasury of Kahlil Gibran,* ed. Martin L. Wolf, trans. Anthony Rizcallah Ferris (New York: Citadel Press, 1951).

31. Julian of Norwich, "All Shall Be Well," in *Daily Readings from Julian of Norwich,* abridged and arranged by Sheila Upjohn (Harrisburg, PA: Morehouse Publishing, 1992).

GLOSSARY OF IMAGO TERMS

The following terms and definitions are useful in understanding parenting within the context of Imago Relationship Theory and are used throughout this book. The definitions are taken from Giving the Love that Heals *(Harville Hendrix and Helen Hunt, Pocket Books, 1997).*

Attachment Stage

Birth through eighteen months of age. For the child, connection to her parents is crucial for survival, so she comes equipped with capacities that will help her maintain the attachment. She is born with the ability to use her senses—she can see, hear, smell, and respond to touch—even, if at times, she seems to do so from a distance. This is the time when parents do almost all the work to take care of the baby's physical needs and strengthen the connection between them, although the baby is helping more than they know through the subtle signals of responsiveness she is sending. Even at this young age the baby is a social creature, constantly interacting with her world.

Behavior Change Request

The behavior change request is often used in conjunction with intentional dialogue. Begin with an intentional dialogue—following all three steps. After the expression of empathy, the receiver asks the sender to name three specific behavior changes that the receiver might make, any one of which will render the frustration obsolete. The sender should be encouraged to make them specific and time-limited. The receiver mirrors the three requests back, picks only one, and states exactly what she will do. After the exchange, it is important to make physical contact, with a hug or handshake, in order to reinforce the restoration of connection.

Boundaries

There are two kinds of boundaries: First, there are the boundaries that parents and children set together that allow for safety and structure. Obviously, throughout all the stages of growth, there may be some physical dangers that must be considered. The goal is to keep the child safe while not being overprotective.

Second, there are the personal boundaries that exist between individual people. Personal boundaries protect personal safety, and in a less obvious but equally important way, they maintain the integrity of personal space, the right to privacy, and a personal sense of identity. If a child doesn't learn what appropriate boundaries are in his relationship with his parents, he won't know where they are in his other relationships. Obviously, physical and sexual abuse are extreme transgressions of personal boundaries. Less obvious are intrusions into privacy, shaming, manipulation, sarcasm, and demeaning words and actions on the part of parents. Treating the child as though he were an adult confidant or adult companion is also a violation of appropriate boundaries.

Competence Stage

Four through seven years of age. The child's impulse is to discover her power in relation to other people and in relation to the objects in her expanding world. She wants to see what her newfound self can achieve. She relishes the process of discovery and is not afraid to try something new. She loves to learn. Competition makes the child feel qualified, and winning is a primary goal. She will also continually test to see what belongs to her, activating a drive for possessiveness. The biggest prize is the parent of the opposite sex, and the biggest obstacle to attaining the prize is the parent of the same sex. And so begins the classic struggle that most of us recognize and which Freud called the œdipal conflict.

Concern Stage

Seven through twelve years of age. In this stage of growth the child's perceptions undergo a fundamental shift. He has been appropriately egocentric, concerned with *his* world, *his* ideas, and *his* feelings. He has been developing a sense of self within the context of his own family, learning to be a fully functional individual in relation to his parents and his siblings. Now he begins the task of reorienting himself in the social context of the outside world, the world of his peers. The child begins to have room in his world for other people besides himself and his parents. His arms stretch wider than they did before, as he hugs more of the world to him.

Connection

We are born connected, the circumstances of our birth being a reflection of the mechanics of the universe. We know that we are different one from another, but we are also able to see what connects us as we become more sensitive to the processes that include us in the same system. We recognize the energy flow *between* different forms of life and also the interaction that includes them all.

The most important job of the parent is to maintain connection to the child. Through this connection the child learns about her connection to other people and to the rest of the cosmos. Her relationship to her parents helps her expand her connection in an ever-widening circle of relationships through all the developmental stages of attachment, exploration, identification, concern, and intimacy.

Conscious Parenting

The conscious parent meets the needs of his child by providing safety, support, and structure for the child as she moves through each developmental stage. He is intentional in his interactions with his child, rather than reactive. And this intentionality can be seen in his use of intentional dialogue in conversations, especially when the conversations are difficult. He has tools for dealing with his child's frustrations, anger, and regressions that turn these potentially disruptive emotional responses into occasions for strengthening the child's wholeness and maintaining her connection to her parents, her immediate environment, and the larger world. And he has ways of promoting laughter, creative expression, spiritual depth, and moral character in his child, as the child's life begins to express the unique and innate being with which she was born.

Denied Self

When the child perceives a trait of his to be negative, he will deny it. Often these "negative" traits are really manifestations of the child's drive to survive and are, in and of themselves, neither negative nor positive. The child may be experiencing a legitimate developmental impulse that the parent, because of her own wounding, has trouble dealing with. The trait gets labeled as negative by a critical parent and, therefore, becomes assimilated as negative by the child because of the parent's reaction.

Disowned Self

In this form of repression, the child doesn't just hide or act. She disowns the existence of certain traits or characteristics in herself, even when they are obvious to others. Ironically, these parts of the self are disowned as *not me*, even though *other people may see them as positive*. Perhaps the most common example is sexuality. Many children feel that sexual impulses are unacceptable. Through interaction with parents and other adults, they come to see the sexual part of themselves as naughty, ugly, unmentionable, and even dangerous.

Empathizing; to Empathize

Empathizing is the process of recognizing the feelings of another person while he or she is expressing a point of view or telling a story. There are two levels of empathy. On the first level we reflect and imagine the feelings another person is expressing. On a deeper level we experience emotionally—actually feel—what he is experiencing. Such empathic experiences are healing and transforming in themselves to the participants, *independent of what is being communicated.* During these moments, both participants transcend their separateness and experience a genuine meeting of minds and hearts.

Exploration Stage

Eighteen months through three years of age. The exploratory impulse of the child at this stage begins the process of differentiation, the first step toward becoming a *self*, distinct from his parents. During this time it is important for the young child to experience aloneness (which is different from loneliness) and noninterference from the parent. The child requires a kind of *positive solitude*. This is a prerequisite for exploration and creativity. In one of the paradoxes of childhood, he can experience the aloneness he requires only in the context of a secure relationship with the parent. If the parent is available when needed, the young child is able to predict future availability and can therefore be alone in comfort.

Fragmented Self

A child who is wounded by symbiotic parenting will feel under attack. His impulse to act for survival directs him to get rid of whatever behavior unleashed the fury of the all-powerful parent. He will put up defenses around the parts his parents don't approve of and begin to protect his soft, vulnerable inner self with a tough, impenetrable outer self. In unconscious interactions, the child feels that his survival is threatened, and will respond by unconsciously hating the part of himself the parent has injured. This action serves the very real purpose of keeping him safe, but at a terrible cost. Below the surface the core self splits into four different "selves" as a defense against the wounding that results from symbiotic parenting. These are the *presentational self,* the *lost self,* the *disowned self,* and the *denied self.*

Growth Point

Growth points are those places of conflict or discomfort a parent experiences with her child that indicate that she needs to do some healing of her own incompleteness. Parents know they have touched a sore spot in themselves when they find themselves overreacting or underreacting to something their child says or does. Emotionally intense reactions that occur repeatedly and that seem excessive to the parent, the child, or another adult are indications of a potential growth point for the parent.

Identity Stage

Three through four years of age. At this stage the child's question is, Who am I? He is embarking on the journey of becoming his own person distinct from his parents, a separate self he can count on forever. What is becoming clear to him is "I am not you; I am me." By now, his experiences have enabled him to develop the ability to store the image of his parents in his mind. He no longer needs them to be available in order to feel secure about his survival. They are with him even when they are not physically present, and this knowledge gives him the confidence he needs to venture out into the world with a new purpose. He can copy behaviors, imitate the voices of real and fictional characters, and identify with animals as he discovers how it feels to be tough sometimes and vulnerable sometimes. He measures himself against all important figures in his life in order to find the right combination of characteristics that give expression to his innate sense of his own unique identity. He is ready to develop an authentic self.

Imago Relationship Theory

We think of Imago Relationship Theory as the science of patterns in marriage and parenting. Like all good and true patterns, those in Imago Relationship Theory explain "what is," suggest what causes deviations, and proposes what can be done about them. Important patterns can be discerned as parents go about the daily business of raising their children. Imago understands human behavior in families to be subject to two universal laws: The first is that *within entities, general patterns get passed on*. The second is that *things change*. Things tend to stay the same, *and* they can change. Sometimes these changes can happen within a generation. But many of the changes are so slow that our human time frame doesn't allow us to chart their evolution.

These two great processes are examples of how patterns in the universe are reflected in us and in all of life. And they are fundamental to Imago Theory. We can say that parents pass on to their children all kinds of patterns that they, in turn, will pass on to *their* children in an unbroken line, unless something is done on purpose to disrupt the family legacy.* This is true for marriage, and it is particularly true for parenting. *The most accurate predictor of how you will parent is how you were parented.* Human beings have a very strong preference for the familiar. Unless we consciously think to do otherwise, we will do "what comes naturally" and repeat what we are used to, the way things have *always* been done. In order to do something different, we need to become self-conscious about our functioning and take definite steps to replace the familiar with new and better patterns.

---

*The influence of one generation on another and the passing of family patterns and problems from parents to children is an ancient insight. Its sources include the Bible as well as modern family systems theory which has charted the direct line of intergenerational conflict.

Intentional Dialogue

Intentional dialogue is a formal communication process that can be used between parenting partners or between parent and child whenever an understanding must be reached regarding an area of conflict, particularly conflict resulting from unconscious behavior. It is a way of reestablishing a conscious connection in order to resolve a problem so that the needs of both parties can be explained, understood, taken into account to form a cooperative solution. Within the context of intentional dialogue, three different processes are evident: *mirroring, validating, and empathizing.*

Intimacy Stage

Twelve to eighteen years of age. This is the final passage before adulthood. The adolescent child has come a long way. He is maturing sexually and is feeling drawn to the dance of romantic partners. The stage of intimacy can be broken into three distinct phases, covering the big difference between a thirteen-year-old and an eighteen-year-old. The first stage, early adolescence, includes the onset of puberty, when a physical growth spurt initiates developmental changes. About twelve to eighteen months after puberty begins, mid-adolescence arrives, and with it comes a preoccupation with the opposite sex that throws the established order out of balance. Well-established peer groupings and intimate friendships are tipped upside down. It takes a while before these new and old elements rebalance themselves in preparation for the third phase. But before the second phase is over, a tension between revolt and conformity begins to build which often manifests itself as revolt from parental and societal dictates and conformity to peer group standards, depending upon how parents handle their part of the relationship.

Lost Self

In this form of repression, the child seems to lose sight of one or all four functions of the self: thinking, feeling, movement, and sensing can partially disappear from the child's awareness and from view of parents and others. The parent still sees parts of her child, but the parts that are not supported become fugitive, even to the child himself. These parts are different from the "presentational" self that the child shows to the world and to himself. The lost self simply seems to be missing. There are many figures of speech to describe this hidden psychological process. We can say the lost self has camouflaged itself and forgotten itself, thereby escaping from view in order not to encourage parental rejection. Continued disapproval from a parent not only forces the child's real self underground but creates a sense of loss that the child may recognize only later in life.

Maximizing; Maximizer

The maximizer parent is so full of unmet needs that he smothers his child with affection as a way of vicariously meeting his own needs. He is full of feelings and fears, often sharing them with his child in the form of warnings about the dangers of the world. When he is frustrated at his child, he will explode with anger or rage and then collapse with remorse and apology. He invades every part of his child's life, giving advice she hasn't asked for. Having little sense of self, he takes direction from others about how to raise his children, keeping himself and his children dependent. Since his boundaries are lax, he does not know how to protect his space from his children or how to honor their space in turn. He presents himself as a sacrificial person who meets others' needs before his own, but those who benefit from his generosity end up feeling guilty after he repeatedly points out what he has done for them. The child of a maximizer parent grows up without being able to clearly separate from his parent and become an independent adult.

Minimizing; Minimizer

The minimizer parent has little time for her children. She's not warm and seems to be incapable of empathy. Whatever feelings she has she keeps to herself, and she is impatient with the needs of her child. She shares little of her thoughts or experiences with her children, and she doesn't ask about theirs. Her boundaries are rigid, and she substitutes rules for interaction. Having had no support as a child, she tends to take direction only from herself and offers little direction to her children. When she is crowded, she may react impulsively, handing out punishment or making demands. When she is involved with her children, it is usually to engage them in competition or to talk to them on an intellectual or abstract level. She does not know how to share her feelings and become intimate. Her children do not feel close to her. They often fear her, and they learn very early not to bother her.

Mirroring; to Mirror

Mirroring is the process of accurately reflecting back the content of a message. Repeating back the content accurately is called *flat mirroring.* A person who gives back a little more is doing *convex mirroring.* A person who gives back less, by zeroing in on one point that interests him and ignoring the rest, is doing *concave mirroring.* Repeating another person's words back to him is one form of mirroring. But the most common form of mirroring is paraphrasing. We may be good guessers, and we may be right most of the time, but unless we mirror and check whether we've got it right, the danger exists that we will misunderstand. It can also be tempting during the process of mirroring to interpret before we fully understand. Besides ensuring accuracy, a parent's mirroring lets a child know that her parent is willing to put aside his own thoughts and feelings for the moment in order to understand her point of view.

New Brain

The capacity to engage in most of what we consider to be "rational" thought processes are functions of the more sophisticated new brain, the cerebral cortex. It is this segment that controls the cognitive functions of conscious thought—the finer distinctions between you and me, between then and now; observing, planning, organizing, responding, and the creation of new ideas. This is the part of your mind that you think of as being "you." Becoming conscious requires overriding the gut-level, me-centered survival instincts of the old brain.

Old Brain

What we refer to as the old brain consists of two parts: the inner layer of the brain stem, which controls automatic biological functions, such as the circulation of blood, breathing, sleeping, the contraction of muscles, and the limbic system, which controls emotions. Our old brain, even when we are not wounded severely, has trouble distinguishing between what *has* happened to *me* and what is happening to my children who are *not me*. It has trouble distinguishing between what happened *then* and what is happening *now*.

Presentational Self

If the child's real self is not acceptable to his parents, then he will create a presentational self that runs interference for him. Often this presentational self is socially acceptable, charming, outwardly successful, and positive: a source of parental pride. Sometimes, however, the presentational self is tough, uncooperative, and a source of parental embarrassment. In either case the child may sense the artificiality in the beginning; but if the persona works for him, this awareness will gradually diminish, and he will actually believe that he is the character he has adopted.

Safety

One of the requirements of conscious parenting. The conscious parent is aware that children have safety requirements that must be met, whether it is convenient to meet them or not, and that these requirements change over the course of a child's development. A child who has confidence in her own physical and emotional safety when she *needs* to feel safe is likely to grow into a curious and adventuresome child.

Stages of Growth

Children mature in stages. A new developmental stage is really an entire collection of changes, preceded by an initial period of disequilibrium that is often upsetting to both the child and the parent. The shift to another developmental stage can be dramatic. Each stage is characterized by an impulse which is an expression of the child's desire for connection and her impulse to experience that connection in the real world.

Structure

One of the requirements of conscious parenting. In addition to boundaries that encourage safety, structure helps a child to establish an ethical and moral framework and to develop behavior patterns that express this framework. It also requires that parents set an example for children that they want them to emulate.

Support

One of the requirements of conscious parenting. Support includes encouraging a child's self-expression according to her needs. A child will require different kinds of parental support at different times based on her stage of development, but the primary ways a parent supports a child are by maintaining her self-esteem and allowing her to experience the joy of being alive.

Symbiosis

Symbiosis is present when a parent acts as though his child necessarily feels and thinks as he himself does, with no recognition of or respect for the otherness of the child. A parent who is symbiotic with his children is unsure about where he ends and they begin. He gets frustrated and angry when they don't read his mind and act accordingly. Symbiosis is an expression of incomplete development on his part. He had children before he finished his own growing up. Problems such as blaming, distancing, inconsistent responses, and emotional incest can result from symbiosis.

A parent who had a symbiotic relationship with his own parents will exert pressure on others to be more like him by threatening, devaluing, or criticizing their experience, unless his does some healing. In his unconscious insistence that other people share his subjective states, his thoughts, and his feelings, he will become more like his symbiotic parent until he functions with the same code of behavior. He will treat others in the same way he has been treated and follow the same maxim: *We are one, and I am the one.*

Unconscious; Unconscious Parenting

This term refers to the beliefs we hold, the actions we take, and the behaviors and feelings we experience that are "out of awareness" and therefore out of our control. The parent acts from his perceptions of what the child is doing but with *no understanding of how the child feels* or why he is doing what he is doing. The unconscious parent operates symbiotically out of her own view of how the world works and what she thinks is best. In this sense the child becomes an object in the subjective drama created by the parent instead of being encountered as another, separate, sacred person. The parent is not being intentional, even when she is well-intentioned. It is the incomplete, unacknowledged, fearful, and shamed part of the parent that speaks and passes the legacy on to her children. Because unconscious parenting is reactive, parents don't realize that they are often overreacting to their child's normal behavior.

Validating; to Validate

Validating is the process of indicating to another person that what he or she says is making sense. You are setting aside your own frame of reference and appreciating the logic, the reality, and the worth of another within his own frame of reference. Your words send the message to your child that her way of looking at things is valid. To validate her experience *does not* mean that you necessarily agree with her or that her thoughts and feelings reflect your own. It means that you surrender your place at the center of and source of "truth" and allow space for *her* interpretation of reality.

Wounding

When a child experiences a parent who develops a symbiotic pattern that does not see and respect her for the person she is, a part of her is wounded. This is what we mean by *wounding: stunting a child's impulse toward wholeness in order to make him more acceptable to his parent.* The parent, of course, does not intend to stunt the impulse. But he does intend to regulate or control behavior. It is important to understand that wounding can be in the form of giving a child too much, as well as not giving enough. A child who is overprotected is as wounded as one who is underprotected. A "spoiled" child has not been given the boundaries and limits he needs in order to thrive.